Economists

Economists

PHOTOGRAPHS BY MARIANA COOK

EDITED WITH AN INTRODUCTION BY
ROBERT M. SOLOW

Yale UNIVERSITY PRESS
New Haven and London

Yale University Press books may be purchased in quantity for educational, business, or promotional use. For information, please e-mail sales.press@yale.edu (U.S. office) or sales@yaleup.co.uk (U.K. office).

Designed by Debbie Berne
Set in Arno Pro and TT Norms

Printed in Italy.

Library of Congress Control Number: 2019940802
ISBN 978-0-300-24997-2 (hardcover : alk. paper)

A catalogue record for this book is available from the British Library.

This paper meets the requirements of ANSI/NISO Z39.48-1992 (Permanence of Paper).

10 9 8 7 6 5 4 3 2 1

CONTENTS

Introduction

ROBERT M. SOLOW

THE FAMOUS SOCIOLOGIST ROBERT K. MERTON, whose son's portrait appears on page 118 of this volume, wrote a delightful little book on serendipity. He would have been amused by the serendipitous origin of this project. A few summers ago, close friends invited me to a dinner party at their house in Chilmark on the island of Martha's Vineyard. At the table I was (serendipitously) seated next to Mariana Cook, whom I had never met although she and her husband also have a summer house in Chilmark. In the normal course of conversation I learned that she is a distinguished portrait photographer, and had recently published a book of portraits of contemporary mathematicians. "Oh," said I, casually, "Why don't you do one of economists?" Lesson: there is no such thing as a casual remark. The idle thought became a reality, and I found myself involved in many ways.

Naturally I had to ask myself: Was making a book of portraits of academic economists a useful or reasonable or even a sane thing to do? I came to the conclusion that it was, and I want to explain why. For a long time it had bothered me, as a teacher of economics, that most Americans—even those who, a long time ago, had wandered through an economics course—had no clear idea of what economics is and what economists do. That is not really surprising. The only contact most of us have with economics and economists is through sound bites on television, radio, or in a newspaper. These snippets are usually about what the stock market has done or might do, or perhaps about next quarter's gross domestic product. But only a tiny fraction of academic economists spend their professional time thinking about the stock market or forecasting GDP. So I suspect that the general image of what economists do and what economics is about is way off-base.

Eventually we thought of a way to make a small dent in that problem, and also to make this collection of portraits more thought-provoking. We posed a question to each of the economists included here, and asked him or her to write a very short—no more than one page—answer to it in plain English. The questions were specially tailored to the research interests of each individual. Now the reader can look at a face and at the opposite page and think: this is the kind of issue this particular person works on and worries about and tries to understand, and here is a small sample of what he or she believes. It is the beginning of understanding; something graspable and, we hope, enlightening.

It is, however, definitely not everything. Here you see a question and there you see an answer. But the hours and days—sometimes the lifetime—of work that have gone into producing that particular answer from that particular person are not visible. There is not space on the page, and the process is not easily described. Something has to be said about that process, because that is how the people in the portraits spend their time. Normally, a working, teaching economist is trying to measure and understand some particular aspect of the real economy, some causal mechanism that makes it behave one way rather than another. It may be a very large-scale aspect: What determines the fraction of all the income produced in the economy that gets paid out in wages and salaries? Or it may be a relatively small-scale, but still significant, aspect: How do the provisions of health insurance contracts affect the volume of use of the health-care system?

In either case, the economist usually starts with some simplified theoretical picture of the way the real economy works, what is usually called a "model": a model of wage determination in industry or a model of health-care decisions by consumers and doctors. The model is probably inherited from earlier work in the field, but our economist—the person in the portrait—may also have some new ideas to try out. But what does it mean to "try out" a new idea, or an old one for that matter? And what does it mean to succeed?

Here I need to make a short digression. The economist's model, or simplified causal story about the world, is usually formulated these days in mathematical terms, as a few equations or inequalities. This was not always so; when I was a beginner, there were bitter arguments about the use of mathematics in economics. But that dispute is now settled. The most recent issue of the leading scholarly journal has just arrived in the mail. It is unusually slim; there are only six articles, and every one of them formulates its underlying story in the form of an equation or equations. (One of them is essentially all equations. The other five include appeals to empirical data, and I will come back to that.) This way of doing things is entirely natural. Most of economics is about quantities of goods and services, and their prices: in the first example above, hours or years of labor of various kinds and their respective wage rates, and in the second example amounts of various medical services and their costs or prices. These prices and quantities are inherently numerical; it would be an act of idiocy not to use the intellectual tools that have evolved over centuries to deal with numbers. Formulating a model mathematically adds precision, but it does not add truthfulness. A model can be no better than the underlying ideas about the world that it presupposes.

So the economist's model consists of a few equations, usually fairly simple ones. Each of these equations (or inequalities) says that some concepts with suggestive names (like wage rates or employment or the dollar-euro exchange rate) are related in a certain way. As the names indicate, each of these concepts is supposed to correspond to something in the real economy that can be observed and measured; otherwise we are wasting our time. The question is whether these things in the real world turn out to be related in approximately the way the model says they should be. Believe me: this is much more complicated than it sounds.

Trying out (or testing) a model involves seeing whether the relevant observables behave in roughly the way the model says they should behave. Does this observable zig when the model says that the concept with the same name should zig? Does that one zag when the model says it should zag? Does the model "fit the data?" Of course the correspondence is never perfect, or even nearly perfect, and that is where the trouble begins. Why do those errors occur, and are they tolerable? One obvious reason is that the model is not an exact representation of reality, and was not intended to be one, any more than a road map good enough to drive by is intended to be an exact reproduction of the road.

A second, related, reason is that the observables often do not quite match the theoretical concept with the same name; the concept was defined to make analytical sense in the economist's way of thinking while the observable was produced for some different purpose like regulation or taxation or accounting.

But these sources of error pale in comparison to a third. The economist is studying some mechanism, some piece of the economy. That piece of the economy is embedded in the broader economy and inevitably gets pushed around by forces (called "shocks" or "disturbances") emanating from the part of the economy that is not under study here and now. When this observable zigs, how are we to know if it is zigging because the model says it should, or because it is responding to some unidentified "external" shock? Or if it zags instead, is that because the model is all wrong or because the model, though correct, is in this instance overwhelmed by a shock coming from outside the model? (It would be simplistic to shrug and say that the model should just be enlarged to internalize those shocks. The same problem would arise in the larger model, and no one can construct a detailed model of everything.) This difficulty has given rise to an enormous literature and perpetual controversy.

The device that many sciences have developed to get around this obstacle is the controlled experiment. If a laboratory scientist can truly isolate the little piece of nature being studied, he or she can be pretty confident that the relations among observables are not being pushed around by outside, irrelevant forces. Then, if observed behavior does not match what theory requires, either there is a measurement error or the theory is wrong. Economics does not offer much scope for laboratory experiments. It offers a little, and there are economists who do interesting laboratory experiments; but they cover only a tiny fraction of the ground, for financial and other reasons. Instead there is a continual search for "natural" experiments: situations in which history seems to have imposed a single dominating cause whose effects can be measured and compared with theory. For a well-known example, see David Card's reference to the flow of Marielitos from Cuba into the Miami labor market on page 36.

For the most part, however, the economists whose faces you see here spend their days, and occasionally their nights, trying to puzzle out a clear theoretical story about part of the economy, a story not so complex that it is impossible to understand and not so simple that it is impossible to believe. And they are forever checking to see if the implications of that story—that model—are compatible with the known or knowable facts. They try to purify direct observations of the influence of "external disturbances" irrelevant to the question they are trying to answer, using either statistical methods or native cleverness. They know that whatever they do will be challenged by some bright young student looking for a thesis topic. No one likes to be wrong. So, when you read in these pages a scholar's short answer to a large question, you should understand that this is not an off-the-cuff response, a mere personal opinion. It is an attempt to distill a considered view that emerges from a long history, by many economists, of a back-and-forth, between data and model, model and data and, one hopes, a little common sense.

Readers will notice the enormous variety of questions—not remotely limited to GDP and the stock market—that has stimulated the research of these economists and their predecessors. They approach these varied questions, mostly, using a common mental apparatus learned from classrooms, textbooks, and the literature. This apparatus generally features self-interested goal-seeking behavior, a combination of greed and rationality. Not always, of course: see Kahneman (page 88) and Thaler (page 172) for warnings. Economists are much criticized for this appeal to greed and rationality in their models; the criticism is often phrased in terms of the ridiculousness of the mythical *homo economicus*. I think this criticism is not so much wrong as misdirected. Economics does not have to assume that people are naturally greedy and rational in all their actions. They are not. A man or woman or a couple that treated their children as mere assets to be bought, sold, or deployed simply to make money efficiently for the parents would be universally regarded as not only weird but despicable. But if the same couple buys, sells, and deploys their land, their capital assets, or their skills so as to run a business efficiently and profitably, they are just behaving conventionally. Capitalist societies (and not only capitalist societies) define certain activities as a legitimate field for greed and rationality (or may sometimes legislate against them). Read what Dasgupta (page 42) and Sen (page 150) have to say. The economists represented here are generally sophisticated in the way they interpret human motivation.

The American Economic Association, the main learned society in the profession, currently has about twenty thousand members, not all of whom work in universities, of course. The faces of only ninety of them appear in these pages. All of them are, or once were, academics. How did these ninety come to be included? Are they in any way typical of the profession?

They are certainly not a random sample of academic economists or of any well-defined segment of the profession. The truth is more slapdash. From the beginning of this project it was clear that I would have to suggest subjects for Mariana Cook to photograph and would have to introduce her to them when she first requested an appointment. So this is primarily a (very incomplete!) unsystematic list of eminent, mostly well-established scholars whom I know, like, respect, and admire. It is therefore undoubtedly a biased list: geographically, methodologically, ideologically, and in ways that now escape me. (Gender bias is not among them, however: there are seventeen women here, whereas I have read that only about one in eight full professors of economics in the US is female. Why that number is so small is worth talking about.) They teach mainly in elite university economics departments, or occasionally in business schools. MIT is overrepresented, but that is simply a matter of local pride; it is where I spent my life as a teacher.

Now about ideology: everyone knows that there are reliably "conservative" and reliably "liberal" economists who are usually quoted (in sound bites) on opposite sides of hot-button issues. The liberals are undoubtedly overrepresented in these pages, because I am one of them. That is not very interesting. What should be interesting is the role of ideology in the everyday work of doing economic research. I have already tried to sketch what most economists do: they start with a plausible model, a simplified picture, part inherited, part original, of some large or small aspect of the real economy, and then mess with whatever observables they can find, to see whether the model adequately describes what actually happens. Naturally they are hoping that it does (though sometimes they are trying to refute rather than to confirm it). Where does ideology enter into the equation?

My (educated) guess is implicit in what I have already said about the process. The big difficulty is that the relevant observables are always, always, being influenced by economic and other forces that are not and cannot be fully accounted for in the model. Much of the work goes into trying to allow for those forces, so that one can see if the model is doing its job or not. There is rarely, if ever, a straightforward, mechanical way to do this. Ingenuity matters. There is always more than one defensible way to skin this particular cat. Here is where it may be possible for the researcher's bias to tip the scales, perhaps unconsciously, in the direction of the desired outcome. (I am reminded of the way, long ago, that my friends and I would try to tip the pinball machine imperceptibly, to move the ball in the right direction without setting off the TILT alarm.) I realize that this is a vague description but to go further would descend into impenetrable technicality.

Does the process of economic research have a built-in defense mechanism to announce TILT when some ideological or other bias seems to be creeping in? Yes, and it seems to work fairly well though of course not perfectly. The first line of defense is peer review. Any research results submitted for publication in a respectable scholarly journal are supposed to be read and critically reviewed by at least two anonymous experts in the field. These "referees" usually have an intellectual stake in the research area, so they are motivated to weed out sloppy or slippery work.

There is a second, at least equally important, defense mechanism. University economics departments are teeming with smart, energetic graduate students and junior faculty who are forever scanning working papers and the published literature in their specialties. For them to demonstrate an error or a weakness or a bias in some previously authoritative work can be a ticket to a job, a promotion, or simply a reputation as a sharp cookie in the field. It is not easy to get away with slippery practice. Of course coteries can sometimes form and sustain themselves, especially with the help of high authority. Some of my friends did seem to be able to influence the pinball machine while evading the TILT sign. But they never seemed to get rich at it.

John Maynard Keynes wrote that economists are not the guardians of civilization, but they are the guardians of the possibility of civilization. Even that seems a little grandiose to me. But economic mechanisms and economic policies are important, and so economists are in their way important. We hope that this book of images and texts will tell readers something interesting about economists and their ideas.

Note: Kenneth Arrow and Anthony Atkinson were photographed before the question-and-essay formula had been worked out. Sadly, both these great economists died before the gap could be filled. We did have the transcript of Mariana Cook's conversation with Atkinson during the portrait session and a piece that Arrow wrote for *Fruitful Economics* (Palgrave Macmillan, 2015). As a makeshift, I tried to extract a coherent essay from each, and then invented a question to which it might conceivably be an answer.

Economists

Daron Acemoglu

"Does the theory of directed technological change offer advice about an efficient policy aimed at achieving clean energy?"

GLOBAL CLIMATE CHANGE is one of the most formidable challenges facing humanity, and a gradual transition to cleaner sources of energy appears as the only viable long-term solution. Most economic analyses and commentators view such a transition as a costly process, because it would involve reductions in energy consumption, and may even translate into lower long-run growth. The same considerations make the leading economic models recommend gradual increases in carbon taxes (so as to delay the contraction in output that would result from sharp tax hikes), while fully realizing that these taxes would have to rise over time.

These analyses ignore the endogenous and directed nature of technological change, however. There are many different technological paths that are often highly substitutable (meaning that they have the potential to achieve similar outcomes), and businesses, workers, and policy determine which of these paths society pursues. More specifically, the rates at which different technologies develop depend on current production, research, and policy choices, and by directing investment and research towards certain technologies, we can change the balance of future technologies. In the environmental context, all of this means that by increasing research and investment in clean technology areas, such as solar, wind, geothermal, and biotechnology, we can close the gap between the costs of fossil fuel-based energy production and these alternatives, and even ultimately make clean energy cheaper than conventional energy. Put differently, society may secure a successful transition to clean technology.

Incorporating these insights from directed technological change fundamentally alters how we should view and design environmental policy. Specifically, in the presence of directed technological change, optimal environmental policy should no longer be gradual but much more aggressive in the short run. The reason is that the longer we delay decisive policy, the greater will be the gap between conventional energy and alternative cleaner technologies, and it would then be more costly to close this gap. Conversely, while the standard policy approaches recommend a path of carbon taxes that will increase over time, this is no longer the case in the presence of directed technological change. Early decisive action can help close the gap between conventional and clean energy, and once this gap is closed or lessened, there is no longer a need for such aggressive interventions.

It is not just the timing but also the form of policy that changes when directed technology is factored in. Instead of relying on just a carbon tax, optimal environmental policy should make use of both carbon taxes and research subsidies for clean energy. The latter policy tool directly spurs additional research in clean technology, helping to close the gap between these nascent technologies and conventional energy. Without such research subsidies, the requisite levels of carbon tax to redirect technological change towards cleaner energy might end up being prohibitively high. Clean research subsidies achieve this more directly and more cheaply.

Directed technological change doesn't just change the timing and form of optimal policy, but provides a more optimistic outlook about the future. If a successful transition to clean, alternative energy sources can be engineered using carbon taxes and clean research subsidies, we can reduce carbon emissions and limit global climate change without sacrificing long-run economic growth (or, at the very least, without sacrificing too much of it).

DARON ACEMOGLU is Professor at the Massachusetts Institute of Technology. He received the John Bates Clark Medal in 2005.

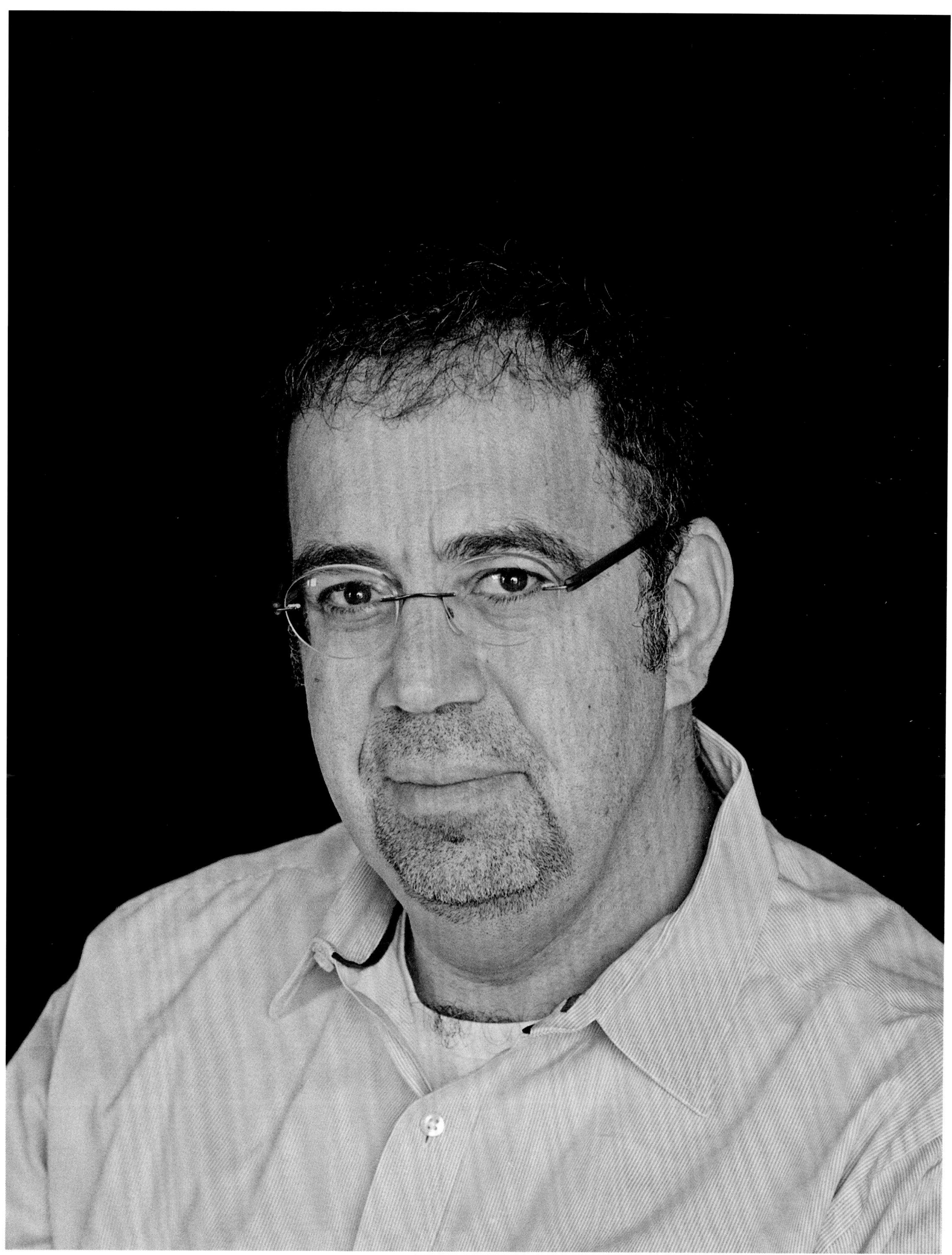

Anat Admati

"You have been a persistent critic of the way finance is currently regulated. What are the main changes you would make?"

THE FINANCIAL SYSTEM is meant to help people, businesses, and governments transact, fund, invest, and manage risks. This system, however, is rife with conflicts of interests and asymmetries of information and control. Deceitful and reckless practices, if uncontrolled by market forces and effective rules, can cause great harm. Yet, the harm from deception and excessive endangerment in finance is often invisible and the culprits and enablers of this harm remain unaccountable.

Persistent scandals and cycles of booms, busts, and crises illustrate the problems. The symbiotic relations between governments and financial firms are key to understanding the root cause of preventable harm. Politicians often view the financial sector as a source of funding and tolerate excessive risk and harmful conduct. Few are willing and able to challenge this unhealthy system.

Because the issues are abstract and confusing to the public, false and misleading narratives suggesting that this financial system is as good as possible, and that different rules would require us to sacrifice the benefits of the system, have impacted the policy debate. Such narratives claim that scandals and crises are unpreventable and shift the blame to "a few bad apples" or to unforeseeable "shock." These false narratives help maintain blindness to the issues and absolve those in charge from responsibility for their failures or from the need to change processes or policies.

Comparing finance and aviation illustrates the issues. Despite its enormous complexity, commercial aviation is remarkably safe. Thousands of flights take off, fly across jurisdictions and land in crowded airports. The interests of those involved in controlling aviation safety, from manufacturers to airlines and regulators, are largely aligned with the public interest in safety. Importantly, when safety is compromised in aviation, it is almost always possible to find the responsible individuals and hold them accountable, and policy often changes. By contrast, those who control the financial system in the private and public sectors often stand to benefit personally even as they endanger and harm others, and they rarely suffer significant negative consequences. The harm either remains undetected or, even if it becomes known, it is difficult or impossible to connect it to specific individuals or policies and to create proper accountability to bring about change.

Had the political will existed to improve the financial system, the most beneficial steps would be to significantly reduce the dangerous and inefficient reliance on debt funding and increase the transparency of the system so it is harder to hide risk, indebtedness, and misconduct. The current regulations of indebtedness are poorly designed, inadequate, and ineffective. They are based on flawed analyses of the relevant costs and benefits and rely on manipulatable information. Changes to counterproductive parts of tax and bankruptcy codes that perversely exacerbate the conflict of interest between the financial sector and the rest of society would also help.

Better monitoring of the financial system is essential, akin to the systems that enable safe aviation. Tracking financial commitments and exposures to risk through the interconnected and opaque financial system is technologically possible, but it requires better international collaboration. To combat deception, fraud, or other harmful practices and to detect the evasion of rules, governments can actively lower the cost to individuals who report wrongdoings. More resources for investigating such claims can prevent reckless practices from persisting and continuing to cause harm.

Positive change can only come from the collective action of many and requires that more people understand what is wrong and demand better. Everyone should become a savvier consumer of the financial system, and a better-informed and active citizen. Educating the public requires economists and others to become aware of the problems themselves and explore, rather than ignore, the nexus of corporate governance and the forces of political economy that are at the heart of problems beyond the financial system. It takes a village to prevent the abuse of power and especially to hold policymakers accountable to the public.

ANAT ADMATI is Professor at the Stanford Graduate School of Business.

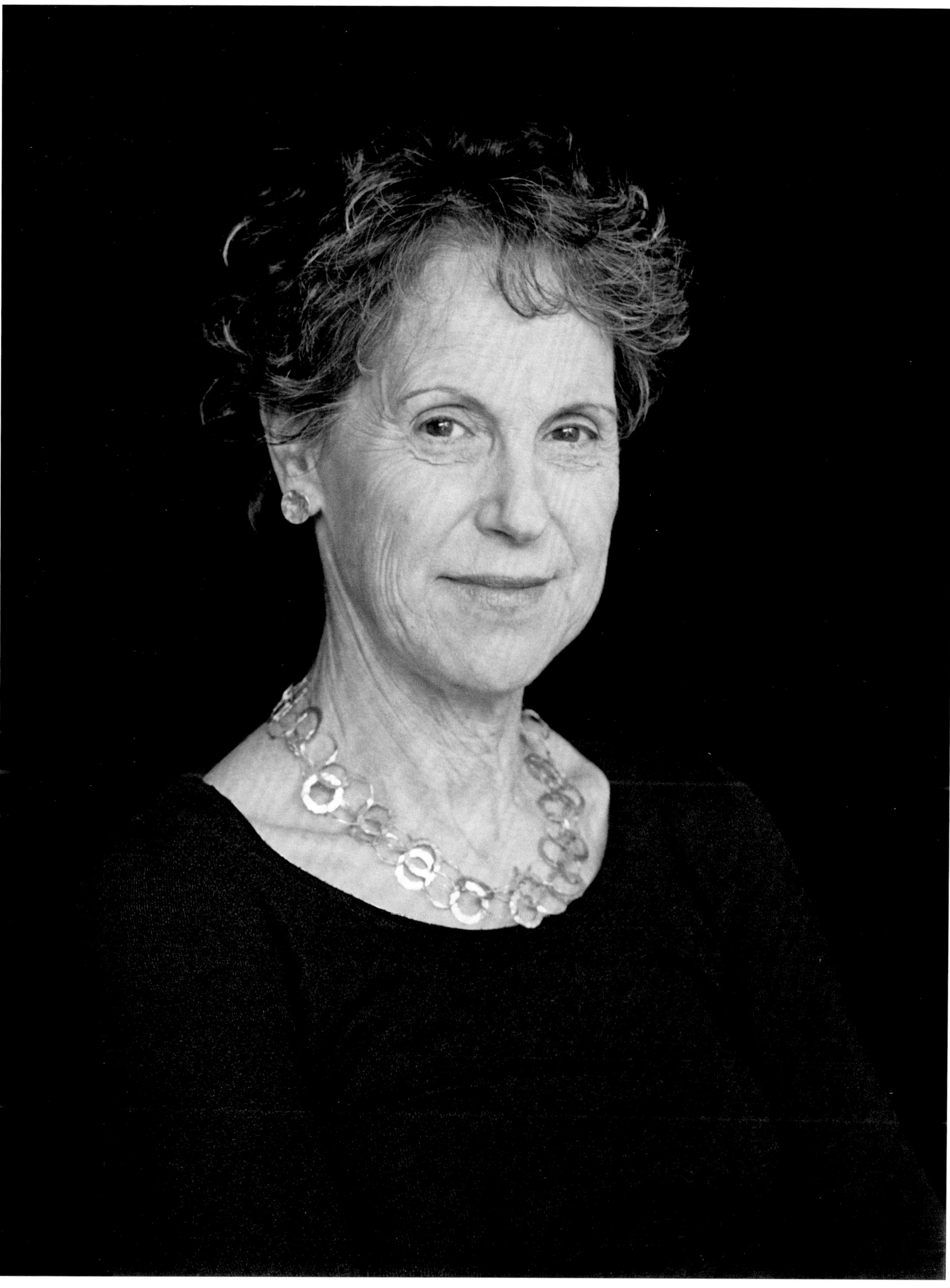

George Akerlof

"Do you think online retailing favors knowledgeable consumers or rent-seeking sellers?"

ACCORDING TO STANDARD economics, competitive markets are benign in the following sense: in equilibrium, no person's welfare can be improved without making someone else worse off. That proposition will be true under the usual assumption in economics: that people know what they want. But is that how people invariably think? How they invariably behave? On the contrary, people make many decisions that are bad for them. They gamble; smoke; take drugs; overconsume sugar, salt, and fat; drink too much alcohol; overspend; vote for the wrong person; take overhyped medicine; are gulled into bad investments; become addicted to computer games. The list goes on. And, as I explain in my book *Phishing for Phools* (co-authored by Robert Shiller), if there is a profit to be made from a "phoolish" buyer, the seller will be there: according to standard economic theory, in competitive markets all opportunities for profit are taken up.

This brings us back to the question: In general, does the normal consumer gain because the internet makes online search easier? Initial research suggested that the answer was ambiguous: several studies found that online prices and offline prices, such as for books, were not all that different. But then Jeffrey Brown and Austan Goolsbee said that these studies were asking the wrong question. Instead, the studies should have asked whether the internet resulted in increased competition and thus reduced prices generally, both online and offline. They examined the market for term life insurance at the time of the introduction of internet websites with pricing. They found that at this time, from 1995 to 1997, the average price of such insurance declined by 8 to 15 percent—presumably as a result of the use of the internet.

Apps like OpenTable present another possibility. It allows diners to make reservations free of charge. That seems like a good deal to the diner, who also gets the convenience of one-stop shopping. If Molly's does not have a free table at 6:30 on Friday night, the same website will show that Mike's has a table that's free. OpenTable should also be a good deal for the restaurants, as long as its charges are sufficiently low. But economic theory tells us that, on the contrary, OpenTable might be charging too much. Each restaurateur (Molly, for example) might rightly worry that if she fails to fork over that fee, her empty table may be filled at some other restaurant (like Mike's) instead. OpenTable can then charge the hold-up costs to Molly and Mike and all those other restaurateurs, which are then absorbed either by the customers through higher prices, or by the restaurants, with lower profits. Luckily, OpenTable's charges are probably not that high. The $1.00 fee per booking is offset by reduced costs to the restaurant in fielding the reservations. And, even with its fixed fee to Molly of $200 per month, OpenTable is probably a worthwhile convenience, or, at the worst, only a mild rip-off.

But that does not mean there are not serious online rip-offs. Consider the phish for phools by an online "payday lender," which was based in Overland Park, Kansas. Its modus operandi was to clearly present the amount of interest payment on the loan. What remained hidden (or, at least, very obscure) were exorbitant finance charges, as the loans were typically renewed again and again with large renewal fees. More than 4.5 million (presumably needy) people were suckered in; they took out billions of dollars in loans. The owner of the firm, Scott Tucker, was sentenced to two hundred months in prison. This was a true phish for phools, and indicative of the continued need for consumer protection for online business transactions.

GEORGE AKERLOF is University Professor at the Georgetown University McCourt School of Public Policy and Professor Emeritus at the University of California, Berkeley. He received the Nobel Prize for Economics in 2001.

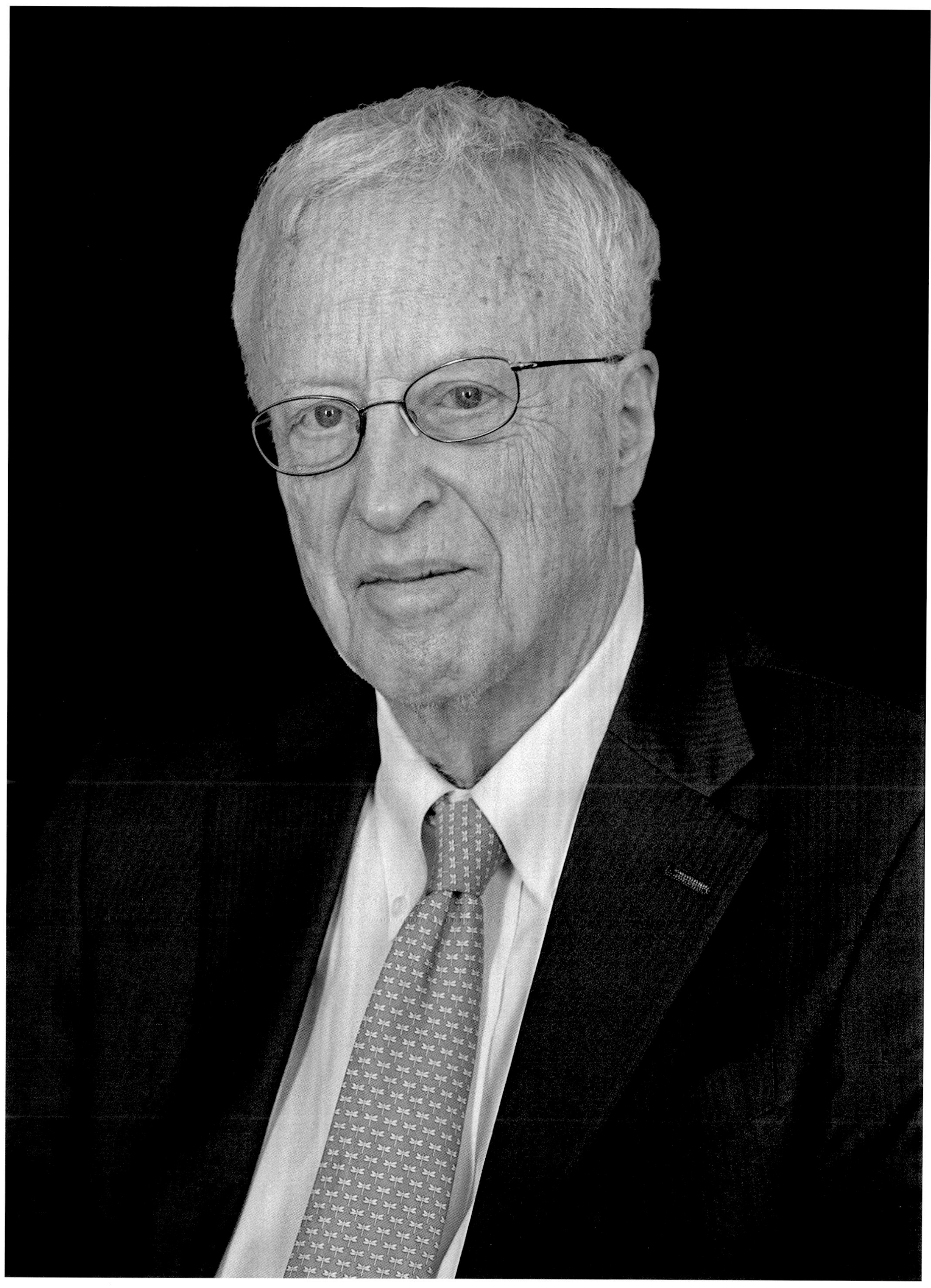

Isaiah Andrews

"Why are predictions for the effect of macroeconomic policy so unreliable?"

PREDICTING THE EFFECT of macroeconomic policy is difficult in part because we cannot run experiments. Policymakers implement fiscal stimulus or change interest rates in response to changes in the economy. When we observe both policy and economic conditions evolving over time it is difficult to know whether changes in policy drive changes in the economy or the other way around.

To address this challenge, we can isolate historical policy changes we think were determined by factors unrelated to the health of the economy and examine subsequent economic outcomes. Such incidents are relatively rare, however, and are by nature nonrepresentative. As a result, this approach uses relatively little of the available data and may produce estimates which differ substantially from the effect of economic policy in more normal times.

As an alternative, we can estimate the effect of policy by fitting a model to the data. If the model predicts that policy changes induce different patterns of effects than we would expect from the natural evolution of the economy, viewing the data through the lens of the model may allow us to separate cause and effect. Unfortunately, many modern macroeconomic models do not lend themselves to this purpose. Even if we assume these models are correct, the available data do not allow us to form precise predictions for the effect of policy. Hence, in many cases our models provide us with limited leverage to disentangle cause and effect.

Since models are at best approximations of reality, estimating the effect of policy by how it fits a model further exposes us to the risk of modeling mistakes. Using a model helps us predict the effect of policy only insofar as the model captures the relationship between the patterns in the data and the policy of interest. In practice, macroeconomic models fit some aspects of the data poorly, and it is often unclear what these modeling errors imply for the models' predictions. Hence, even in cases where our models deliver precise predictions, it is unclear how much we should trust them.

Macroeconomic prediction is difficult even apart from questions of causality. Data-driven prediction methods necessarily assume that patterns observed in the past are informative about what to expect in the future. The economy changes over time, however, and patterns need not persist. This limits the amount of data available for analysis, and macroeconomists must think carefully about how far back in history to look. This adds data scarcity to the list of challenges facing macroeconomic analysts, though recent methods using regional and individual data to address macroeconomic questions increase the range of usable data.

Given the difficulty of the problem, our predictions for the effects of macroeconomic policy would be imperfect even if we made the best possible use of the available data. That said, there remains considerable scope for improvement.

ISAIAH ANDREWS is Professor at Harvard University.

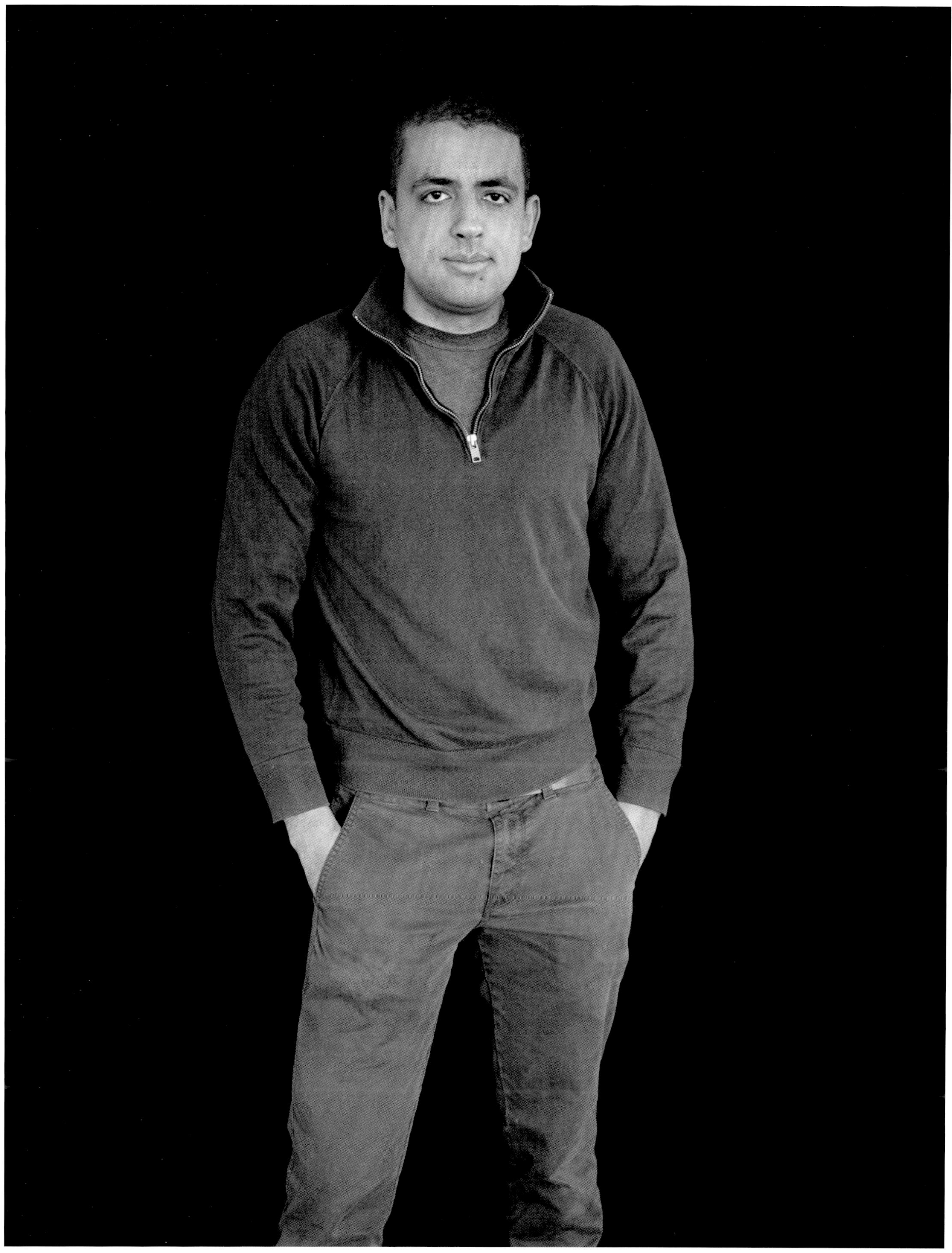

Kenneth J. Arrow

"How could we go about creating an overall measure of 'how well' an economy is doing?"

A WELFARE STATEMENT is a statement about values and about the variables to which values are assigned. The variables are the commodities being measured. The values are inferred from behavior. The standard economic analysis assumes these commodities are purchased on a competitive market, so that (marginal) values are proportional to prices.

Many commodities, however, entering into welfare are not well represented on markets. There are (at least) two broad types of such commodities: externalities (or, more specifically, public goods) and future goods.

Let us consider externalities, which can be both obvious and subtle. What have been called "fugitive resources," water and air, flow from place to place, and clearly property rights cannot be assigned to a drop of water or to molecules of nitrogen and oxygen. Water is valuable, especially in areas depending on irrigation, like my home state of California. As a result, a very complex set of laws provides property rights, which, for the most part, create strong incentives for inefficiency. For example, a farmer or other owner must use the water assigned or lose rights to it, a strong incentive to use it for low-value activities to preserve the rights for the future. Air is not scarce. However, both air and water can be bearers of noxious substances; indeed, the most classic textbook example of an externality is air pollution.

These externalities should, of course, be included in any measure of welfare. But now we have the problem of finding a price for the externality when there is no observed price in the market. The practical solution is to find some point of contact with some market. An outstanding example is the "value of statistical life" (VSL) introduced by Richard Thaler and Sherwin Rosen. They noted that industries have differing risks of accidental death and that, controlling for other variables, wages increase with the increasing probability of accidental death. Indeed, the value of health has turned out to be a very significant modifier of welfare comparisons whether across nations or over time.

The question of future goods is intimately related to the now widespread interest in sustainability. In income terms, it corresponds to saving on one side of the ledger and investment on the other. The most brazen failure in current national income accounting is the omission of depreciation of natural resources, even from net national product. The failure to account for depreciation in gross national product is also an obvious fallacy. The only defense is statistical; depreciation cannot be measured accurately, essentially because the markets for used capital goods are so lacking.

Some attention has been devoted recently to looking at sustainability in wealth terms. We must value future as well as present consumption and include all the future externalities, such as health. When we look to the future, concepts that seem identical when looked at within a single period become differentiated when considering development over time, such as the concept of capital stock. The concept was originally designed to cover land and reproducible capital (buildings and machines). It has three characteristics: (1) it is productive, that is, increasing the amount of capital increases the production of goods, including health; (2) it constitutes a store of value to the owner, available for purchasing present and future consumption; and (3) it is alienable. The capital concept has been fruitfully extended, most notably to human capital and to health. However, it must be noted that these extensions are by no means without difficulty. Human capital satisfies conditions (1) and (2) but not condition (3). Human capital is indissolubly linked to a particular person. Health capital (i.e., discounted value of future years of life) satisfies only condition (2) and can be used only for future health, not for other kinds of consumption.

These considerations are all part of a movement toward the measurement of an inclusive definition of wealth, a concept of economic potential that is a dynamic analogue of national income.

NOTE: This is an edited excerpt from Laurent, Éloi, and Jacques Le Cacheux. *Fruitful Economics: Papers in Honour of and by Jean-Paul Fitoussi*. (Palgrave Macmillan, 2015).

KENNETH ARROW (1921–2017) was Professor at Stanford University. He received the John Bates Clark Medal in 1957 and the Nobel Prize for Economics in 1972.

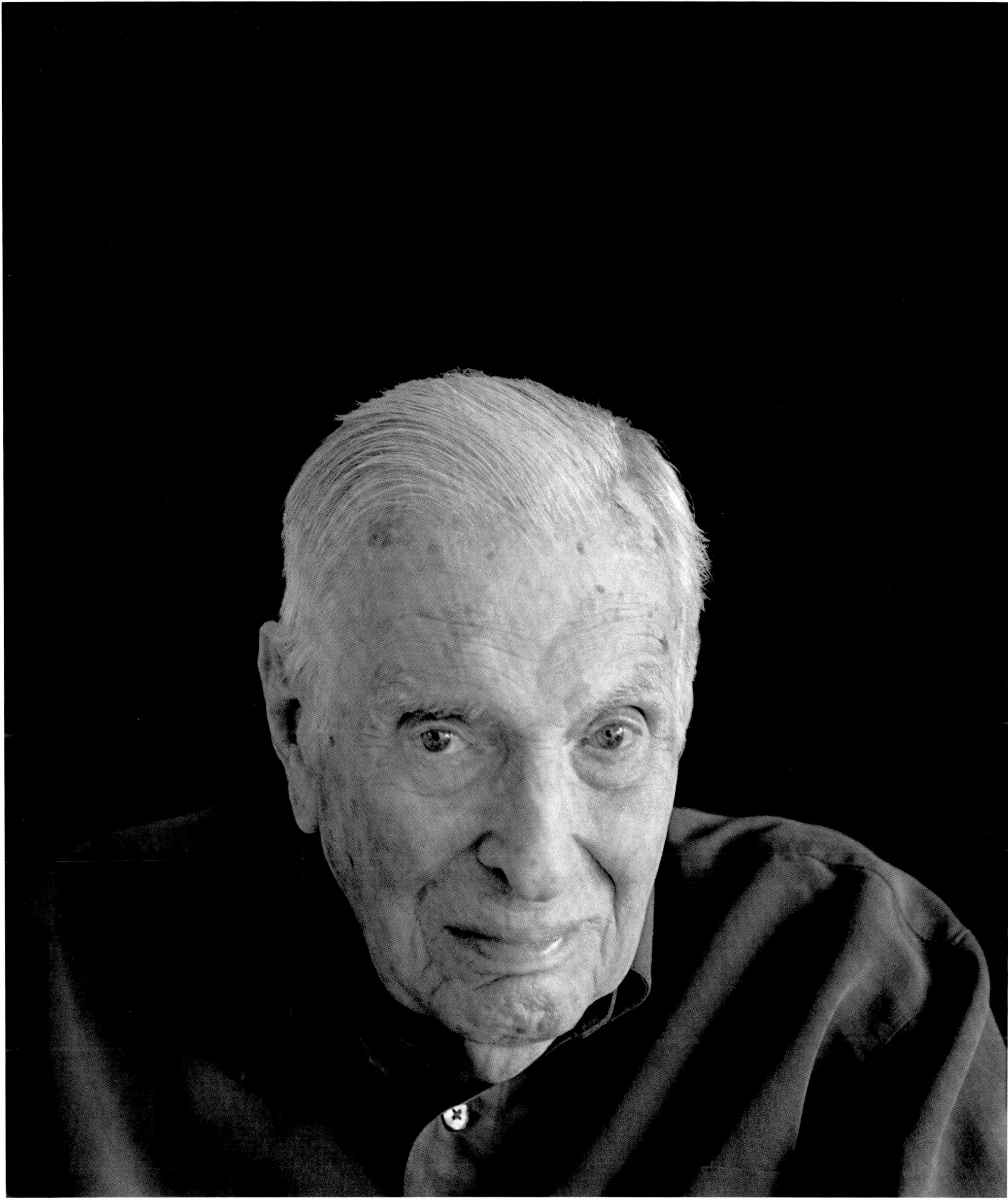

Orley Ashenfelter

"Do you think the recent productivity slowdown in the US has anything to do with exhaustion of returns to education? What's the latest on the rate of return to schooling?"

SOMETHING HAS GONE wrong in the world of economics and productivity. When I was a graduate student it was common to construct macroeconomic models of wage or price determination (I did it myself!) by assuming that real wage growth (that is, the growth in wages measured in purchasing power) equaled productivity growth (that is, the growth in output per hour worked). This relationship could be used in many ways. Since real wage growth is just the growth in nominal wages minus the growth in prices (inflation), one could equally well say that inflation was equal to the growth in nominal wages minus productivity growth. Assuming productivity growth was exogenous, a theory of nominal wage determination was thus a theory of inflation too.

Moreover, when real wage growth and productivity growth are equal, the share of labor income (and capital income) in the value of total output (that is, national income) is a constant over time.

It is hard to abandon old assumptions that have worked so well empirically for so long, but slowly economists have begun to adjust. However, simultaneous with the breakdown of old empirical relations has come new disquiet over the overall pace of productivity growth, which, by the standards of the immediate postwar period, has been 1 to 3 percentage points lower than in the past. With wages growing more slowly than productivity growth, this has meant that labor's share of national income has declined, and that what there is to share has been growing slowly too.

It should come as no surprise that this state of affairs has led to disquiet among working-class people. The wealthy are doing just fine, especially those who receive their income from capital. At the same time, ordinary workers, whose parents could once count on regular real wage growth, have stagnant wage growth.

What are the causes of these changes? As for overall productivity growth, a leading candidate for explaining slower growth is some form of hypothesis about the nature of technical change. As more than one commentator has noted, the 20th century gave us the airplane and the automobile, while the 21st gave us social media. Although the comparison is meant to be humorous, these innovations have one thing in common: they all disrupted other established industries. In the case of airplanes and autos, it was other modes of transit that were disrupted. In the case of social media, where earnings come almost entirely from advertising, it was other advertising-driven industries (especially newspapers and magazines) that were disrupted. It is perhaps not surprising that the former innovations are associated with the greater productivity growth.

A second, but less often discussed, source of concern is the role of education and its effect on productivity. It is now well established that higher education levels lead to higher wages for individual workers. And although other causes for this relationship cannot be entirely ruled out, the evidence strongly suggests that education is causally connected to higher wages and productivity. However, there is no evidence to suggest that the education level of the US population has stagnated. Although growth in schooling levels has not been as fast as in other developing countries, there are many areas in which to be optimistic. For example, the National Center for Educational Statistics reports that the "status dropout rate" (the percentage of 16- to 24-year-olds who are not in school and have no high school degree) has dropped steadily over the last two decades, from 10.9 percent in 2000 to 5.9 percent in 2015. Educational attainment at higher levels has increased as well.

In recent years I have begun to think that there is another underestimated factor involved in changes in the US economy: the decline of competition in product and labor markets. Increased profit margins may come from the failure of competition in either product or labor markets. Both increased monopoly and increased monopsony result in lower shares for labor in national income. The last few decades have seen a decrease in competition in many product markets through massive mergers, which at one time were thought to be either benign or efficiency enhancing. The evidence available shows the opposite. Likewise, the widespread use of no-poaching agreements in localized labor markets, coupled with the observed decrease in labor mobility and the virtual demise of trade unions, suggests that there may be widespread failures of competition in labor markets too. Economists have been reluctant to change their views about the extent of competition in product and labor markets, but perhaps this will change too.

ORLEY ASHENFELTER is Professor at Princeton University.

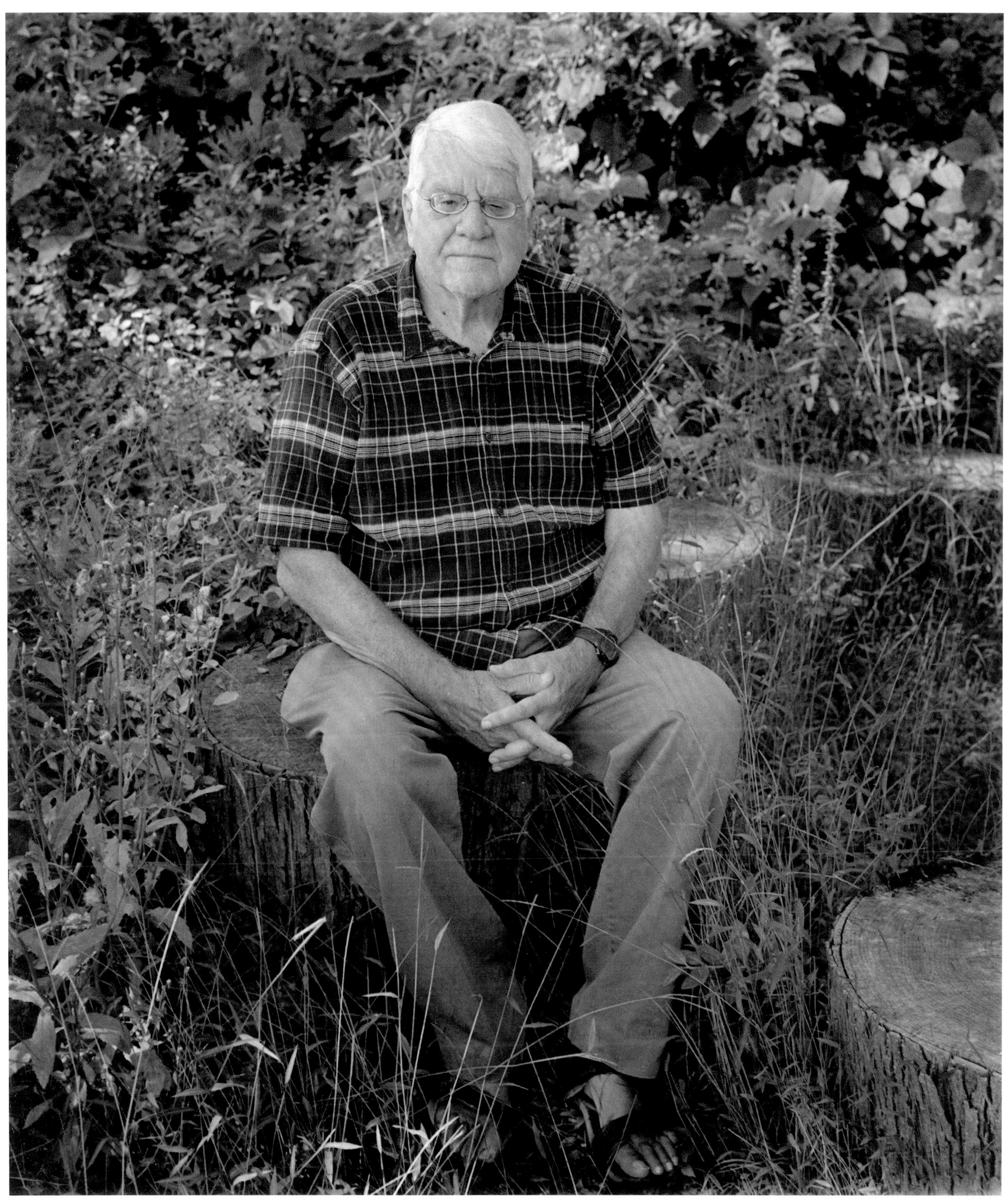

Susan Athey

"How do the new marketplaces and intermediaries affect the economy and welfare?"

ONE OF THE first successful e-commerce companies in the 1990s was eBay, a marketplace for goods. In the early 2010s, a new set of marketplaces emerged, including companies like Uber, Lyft, Airbnb, and Rover.com, providing transportation, room rentals, and dog sitting. In the 2016 presidential election, digital intermediaries like Facebook played a crucial role in how consumers received news. What are the effects of these marketplaces and intermediaries on the economy?

Marketplaces solve several problems. One is search, discovery, and matching: the marketplaces help consumers find sellers that have what the consumers want. They also solve the short-term relationship problem: consumers and sellers who don't expect to interact again have no incentive to fulfill their promises, but when they interact repeatedly with a platform, the platform can enforce good behavior and support reputation through mechanisms like reviews. The platform further takes care of payment, often holding funds in escrow until the transaction is confirmed as completed, and sets rules that govern disputes. The marketplace incentivizes good behavior in other ways; sellers who respond quickly to inquiries, ship quickly, and have good reputations may be ranked higher in the set of results displayed to users in response to a query. The marketplace makes other "market design" decisions such has how payment is structured, who pays, who is allowed to participate, and how new entrants are treated.

Marketplaces often allow consumers a much wider and more customized set of alternatives, from rides in a few minutes at their location, to vacation homes that offer desired amenities, to replacement parts for discontinued consumer products. They offer sellers a way to allocate resources to higher-value uses—ranging from used clothing crowding a closet, to time that could be available for short bursts of work between classes or while children are at school. Some individuals have made a career of "gig economy" work. Economists have recently starting building evidence that the flexibility of gig economy work is particularly valuable to workers. Marketplaces frequently displace older systems of middlemen that solved trust and reputation problems; for example, limousine dispatch services that advertised to consumers and helped book jobs for drivers seeking airport rides. Modern marketplaces often forge a direct relationship with individual workers. The marketplaces often result in a fairly large expansion of economic activity; low-density cities and suburbs historically had a handful of taxis and long waits.

Marketplaces change the incentives for providing quality. Performance and reputation are measured at the level of the individual provider of goods and services, potentially providing both digital monitoring as well as much stronger incentives for quality relative to alternatives where reputation is measured at the level of a fleet of drivers or an entire taxi company and where customers complain to the company. In many cases, competing at the level of an individual service provider or product leads to higher quality, but not all. For example, in the case of news, readers used to select a newspaper based on its reputation; but in the online world, articles compete for clicks on Facebook or news aggregators based on their headlines and snippets, creating perverse incentives for "clickbait" rather than quality reporting.

Marketplaces can also have negative effects as industries transition; a taxi driver who took out a mortgage to buy a taxi medallion bears a loss if that medallion is no longer valuable. The equilibrium price of rides may go down as supply expands, reducing the hourly wage of incumbent transportation providers (but providing large gains for consumers and increasing consumption of paid transportation). Overall, the welfare effects must be evaluated on a case-by-case basis.

SUSAN ATHEY is Professor at Stanford Graduate School of Business. She received the John Bates Clark Medal in 2007.

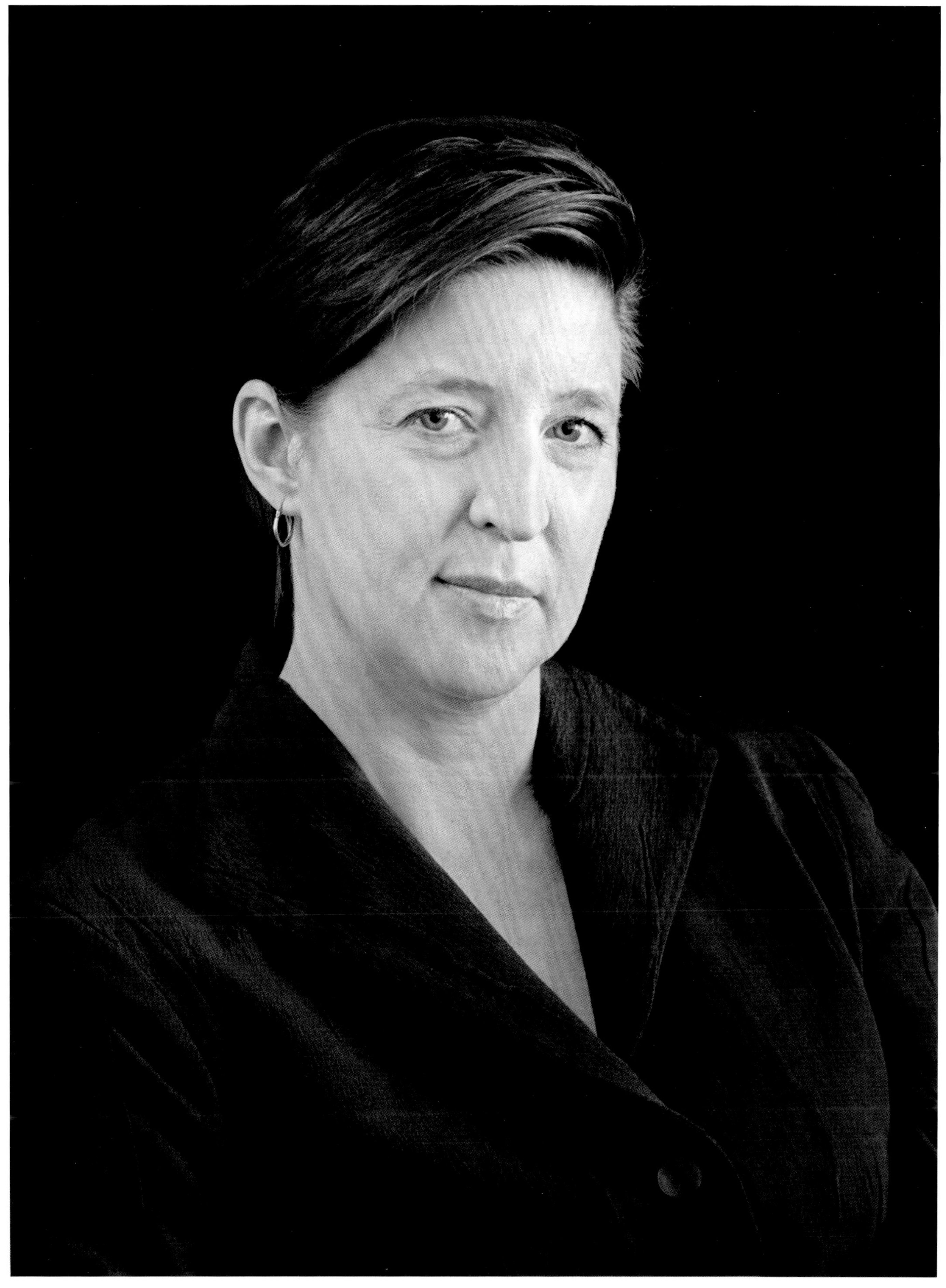

Anthony B. Atkinson

"Does economic policy have to adapt, more or less reactively, to 'outside forces'?"

THE ECONOMY USED to serve the wider society, but these days it seems as though the roles are reversed and society serves the bidding of the economy. Economics, in my view, should not just be about understanding markets, but also about what the consequences of those markets are for people.

My path to economics was not straightforward as such. Early on, I worked at a hospital as a male nurse in a depressed area of Hamburg, Germany, which piqued my interest in social science. Although I began as a student of mathematics at Cambridge, I switched to social science after the first year and then became interested in economics and how it relates to economic and social policy. The first book I wrote, called *Poverty in Britain and the Reform of Social Security,* caused quite a stir. The war on poverty had already started in the United States. It gave birth to important programs such as Medicaid, Head Start, school breakfast programs, etc., which sought to contend with the poverty that pervaded in the United States in spite of its wealth. The legislation that was passed in the United States under President Johnson had a significant impact on poverty levels, and I argued that Britain had a similar problem, particularly with child poverty, and that it could likewise be tackled by following the United States' example.

While inequality is not currently on the rise in Britain, in the United States it has been following a path that resembles a *V* shape—it began slowly decreasing in the United States from the 1950s to 1970s, only to increase more and more rapidly from the 1980s onward. Most economists claim that this rapid increase in inequality can be attributed to globalization and technological change—and with it usually comes, sotto voce, as it were, the underlying subtext that this increase in inequality is something we cannot do anything about: globalization is something which keeps happening, just as technology keeps evolving, and neither can be halted.

The assumption, however, that the trajectories of both globalization and technology cannot be altered is simply wrong—both of these things are subject to human control. All sorts of factors, such as trade negotiations, affect globalization. Similarly, technological innovation is not a given. Take driverless cars, for example: auto manufacturers have admitted that the demand for driverless cars was created by the auto manufacturers themselves and not the consumers. The technology for driverless cars is in fact being developed for the profitability of the American automobile industry and not to satisfy any major consumer demand. In Europe we are investing large sums of money into driverless cars; in actuality, it is the European Union that is using governmental funding to spur this technological push. Which is to say that technological innovation, and all innovation for that matter, is ultimately a deliberate choice.

If not for the investment in driverless cars, we could instead be investing in chefless kitchens—a technology that could aid the elderly, who are primarily prevented from living independently in their own homes for a more extended period of time because they cannot cook. My mother was a good example. She would put her saucepan on, go off, and come back three hours later wondering why her kitchen was on fire. Chefless kitchens would allow people independence, and it would generate jobs because these individuals would still need support from caretakers. Few chefs would be displaced because restaurants would still be in demand. Why did they invest money in driverless cars rather than chefless kitchens? It is because the manufacturers made a deliberate decision to do so.

Unemployment is another issue that skirts these same assumptions. Globalization, technological innovation, and unemployment are all presented as though they are immutable, when in fact they are not. Rich societies have a choice–they can either continue down the current path of encouraging a low-wage and low-productivity economy for the sake of very high profits, or they can embrace the path set forth by countries such as Denmark, Norway, Sweden, and France, which all boast high-wage economies with higher productivity, and yet are not markedly less profitable.

We, as a society, should have more of a say in how we invest in technological innovations so that it isn't a profit-driven choice on the part of the companies creating the technology. We, as economists, should insist that economics be the servant of society, not its master.

ANTHONY ATKINSON (1944–2017) was Professor at the London School of Economics and Fellow of Nuffield College, Oxford.

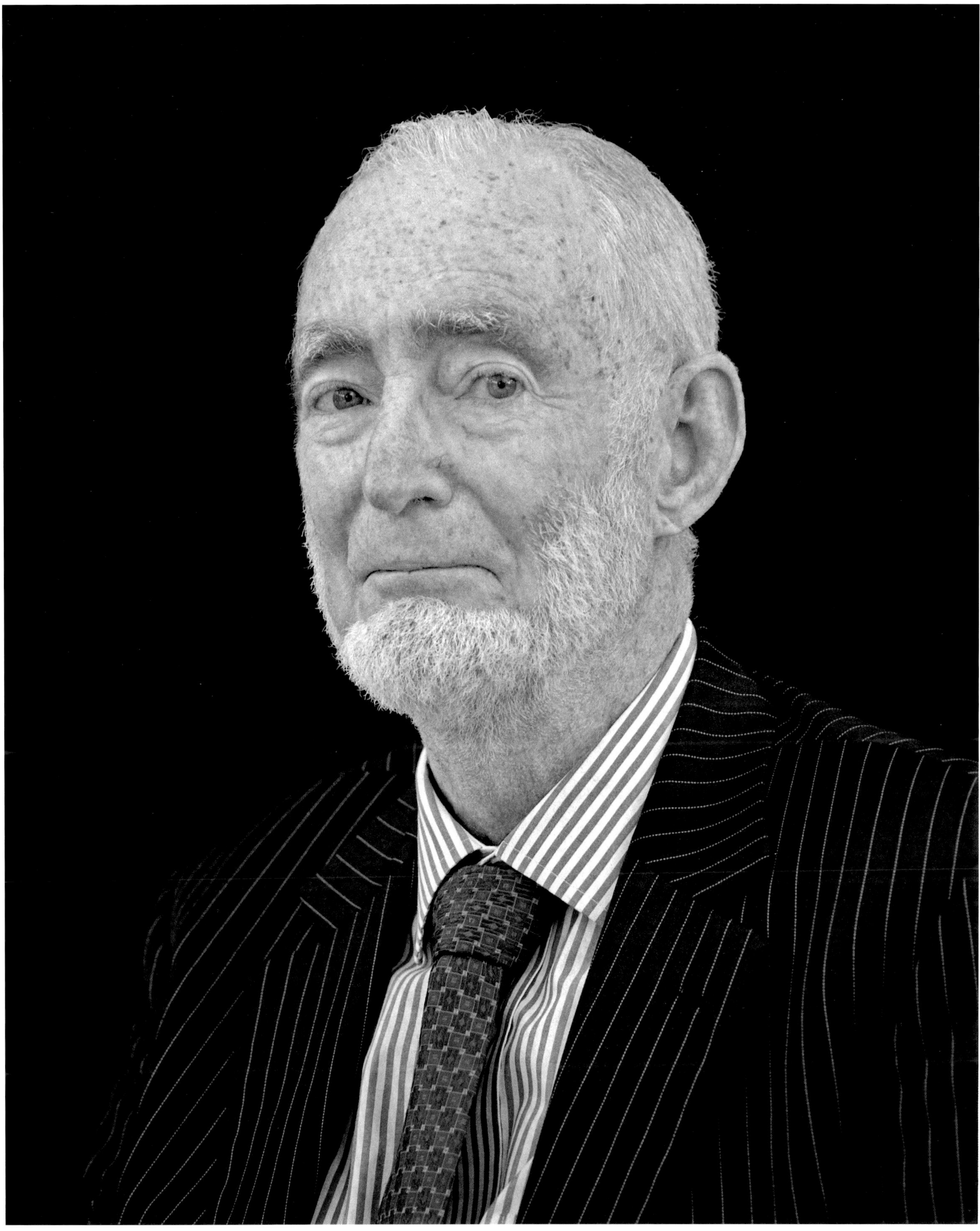

Abhijit Banerjee

"What do you think rich countries could do, and actually might do, that would contribute most to the improvement of living conditions in poor countries?"

THE FACT THAT aid is mostly irrelevant today does not mean that it *has to be* that way. Fifty years ago, the developing countries were much poorer, and it is possible that aid had a much bigger impact. I vaguely remember the drought years in the late 1960s in India, when we were fed "Food for Peace" wheat from the United States and people were saying there would be a major famine without it. I am not at all saying that all of this aid was good—but it was probably more consequential, which makes it definitely worth trying to understand what, if anything, it did right. There is still aid (and important private charities that look very much like aid), and we need to try and make sure it is better used, rather than dismissing the whole project.

I mentioned the almost-famine in the India in the late 1960s. This was, however, the very last time. There is still lots of hunger in India, but not because there is not enough food to buy. What saved India was a remarkable success of aid. CGIAR (the Consultative Group for International Agricultural Research), a consortium of research centers created and funded by the Rockefeller Foundation, the World Bank, and the United Nations, among others, is dedicated to the development and testing of new staple crops that dramatically improved the food security in Asia.

Something similar happened in 2003 with the launch of the United States President's Emergency Plan For AIDS Relief or PEPFAR. While attributions of causality are always fraught, there is good evidence to believe that it saved the lives of many millions of HIV-infected people in sub-Saharan Africa and prevented the birth of a million or more HIV-infected babies. In this case the drugs were already there, but the countries most affected by the disease had neither the money to buy the drugs nor a system to deliver them effectively. PEPFAR made all of that happen.

There is other good news. Between 2010 and 2015, the number of malaria deaths in Africa fell by 31 percent according to the WHO. A substantial part of that has been attributed to the use of insecticide-treated bed nets for children. The science of these bed nets was known for some years: what changed was the fact that countries were now distributing them for free and therefore they were being used more. This was the culmination of an ideologically inflected battle where one side was adamantly opposed to free distribution on the grounds that if people get it for free they will not use them. Rigorous evidence generated by our colleagues in the Abdul Latif Jameel Poverty Action Lab showed that these fears were unfounded and helped clear the way for the recent explosion in use.

These success stories have several features in common. They were trying to solve a very specific problem. There was some science and/or social science to develop along the way: How to combine the virtues of various strains of wheat? How does one identify and work with the HIV-infected population where the health system on the ground is thin? Does "free" mean "worthless"? And there was a focus on rigorously testing out various approaches and a willingness to learn from evidence.

This is not how much of foreign assistance is conducted. The usual aid program starts from a broad objective (better governance or transportation or education) that often reflects the preferences of the donor. The donors also come, all too often, with their own views on what the right strategy ought to be, not necessarily based on any clear evidence. When combined with (legitimate) sensitivities about the autonomy of the recipient government, it generates an elaborate *pas de deux* where all conversations are in code, hard questions are avoided, and evidence finishes last. No wonder the outcomes are not always what they are intended to be.

But it does not have to be this way. The great value of aid is precisely that it does not face the kind of political constraints that national governments live with. Aid donors can choose their target as narrowly as they want, without feeling the compulsion to be evenhanded. And they can try things that have a high risk of failure and if need be, openly admit failure, without risking the same amount of censure by the voters and therefore serve as a conduit for new ideas that national governments can learn from and adapt/adopt. By doing so, donors can enormously leverage their limited funds and, I hope, eventually set off a virtuous cycle where governments start delivering more and more and that will encourage voters to hold governments to higher and higher standards, so that aid finally delivers what it has long promised.

ABHIJIT BANERJEE is Professor at the Massachusetts Institute of Technology.

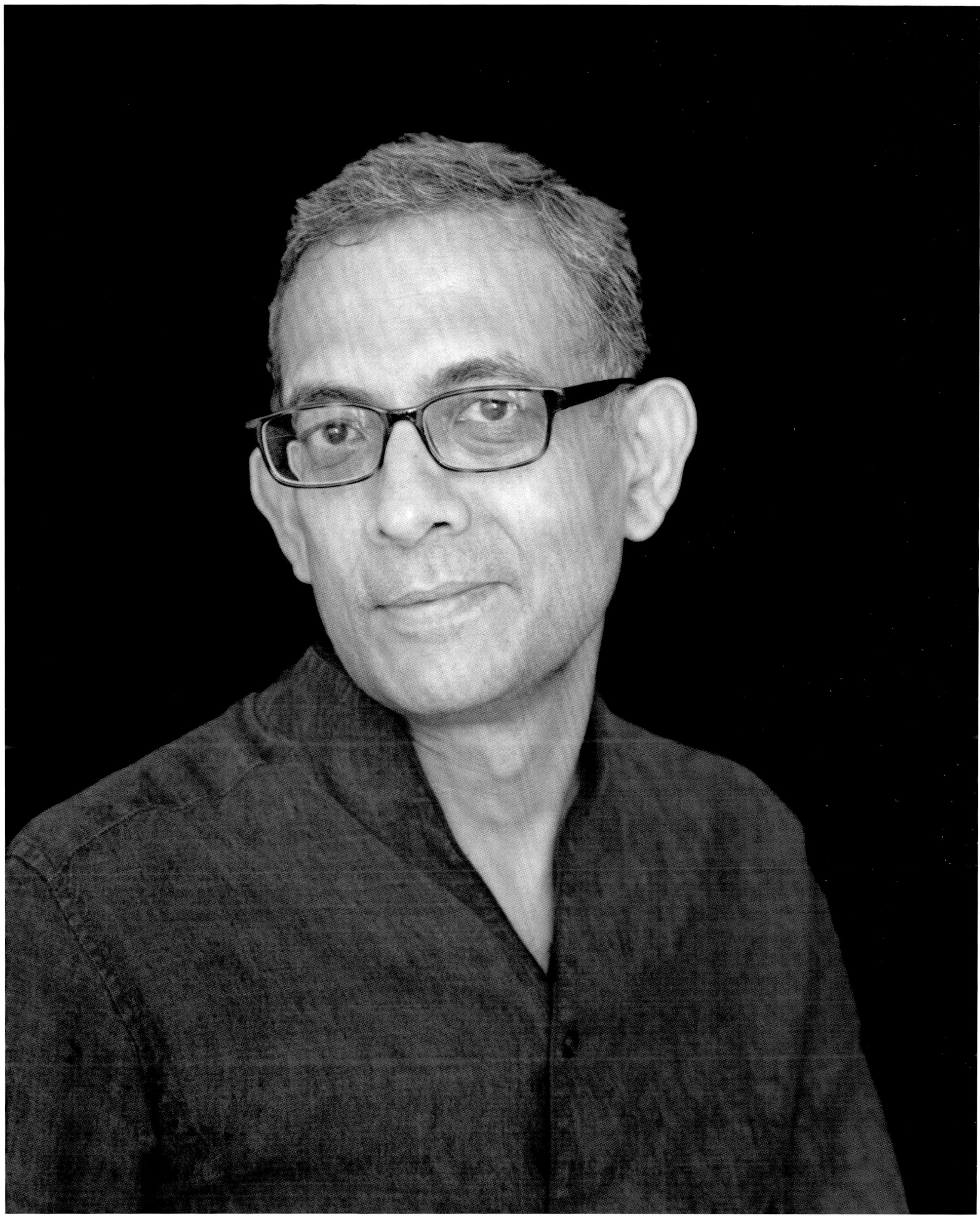

Ben Bernanke

"Should the Fed keep its balance sheet large?"

THE FEDERAL OPEN Market Committee's (FOMC) publicly announced strategy is to allow its balance sheet to shrink "naturally," by phasing out reinvestment of the proceeds of maturing securities. The ultimate size of the balance sheet is still being debated but would be well less than its peak. I believe, however, there is a strong argument for keeping the balance sheet close to its current size in the long run.

Firstly, a large Fed balance sheet could be a tool for enhancing financial stability. There is a strong demand from the private sector for safe, liquid, short-term securities. Rather than leaving it entirely to the private market to supply such assets, which incentivizes risky behavior, the Fed could provide safe short-term assets, in the form of bank reserves and especially through an expanded reverse repurchase program (RRP) that would be open to a wide range of counterparties. In order to do so, however, the Fed would have to keep its balance sheet near its current size and continue (or expand) its RRP program.

A second argument is that a larger balance sheet could improve the transmission of monetary policy. Monetary policy can only have its desired economic effects if changes in the federal funds rate are reflected in broader financial conditions. The Fed could better ensure that its interest rate decisions are transmitted to money markets and financial markets by maintaining a sizable RRP program, through which nonbank institutions can deposit directly with the Fed and earn the RRP interest rate. With the RRP program providing a direct link between the short-term policy rate and the securities markets, the Fed could rely less on the indirect transmission of monetary policy through the banking system.

A third possible motivation for the Fed to keep a large balance sheet in the long run relates to its potential role in financial crises. During a panic, depositors and other providers of short-term funding run on financial institutions, which can lead liquidity-short institutions to dump assets at any price (the "fire sales" problem). By serving as a lender of last resort (i.e., by standing ready to lend cash against good assets), central banks can replace missing liquidity, avoid the fire sale dynamic, and calm the panic. However, financial institutions have to be willing to borrow, which they may be reluctant to do if they fear this will identify them as particularly weak financially; this inhibition to borrowing is known as "stigma." The Fed had to work hard to overcome stigma during the financial crisis of 2007–2009. In striking contrast, European firms routinely engaged with the central bank in normal times, which meant that during the crisis they appeared able to use their reserves or adjust their level of central bank borrowings without signaling sharp changes in their financial conditions, thus mitigating stigma. If the Fed can encourage firms to borrow during noncrisis periods, its larger balance sheet coming into a crisis would improve its vital function as a lender of last resort.

As always, there are tradeoffs: in providing more backstop liquidity to the financial system, central banks may reduce the private sector's incentives to manage its own liquidity effectively (the moral hazard problem). The legal environment in the US is also more restrictive than in Europe, in that the European Central Bank can lend routinely to nonbank financial institutions but the Fed cannot. Still, there's a good case to be made that maintaining significant baseline levels of bank reserves and bank borrowings from the Fed would reduce stigma and thus enhance the Fed's ability to respond effectively to a panic.

The appropriate size and composition of the Fed's balance sheet inevitably depends on a range of complex decisions about the management of monetary policy and the role of the central bank in preventing and responding to financial crises. We've learned a lot about both areas since the crisis, and some important arguments have emerged for keeping the balance sheet larger than in the past. Maybe this is one of those cases where you can't go home again.

BEN BERNANKE is Distinguished Fellow at the Brookings Institution. He was Chair of the Federal Reserve from 2006–2014 and Chair of the Council of Economic Advisors from 2005–2006.

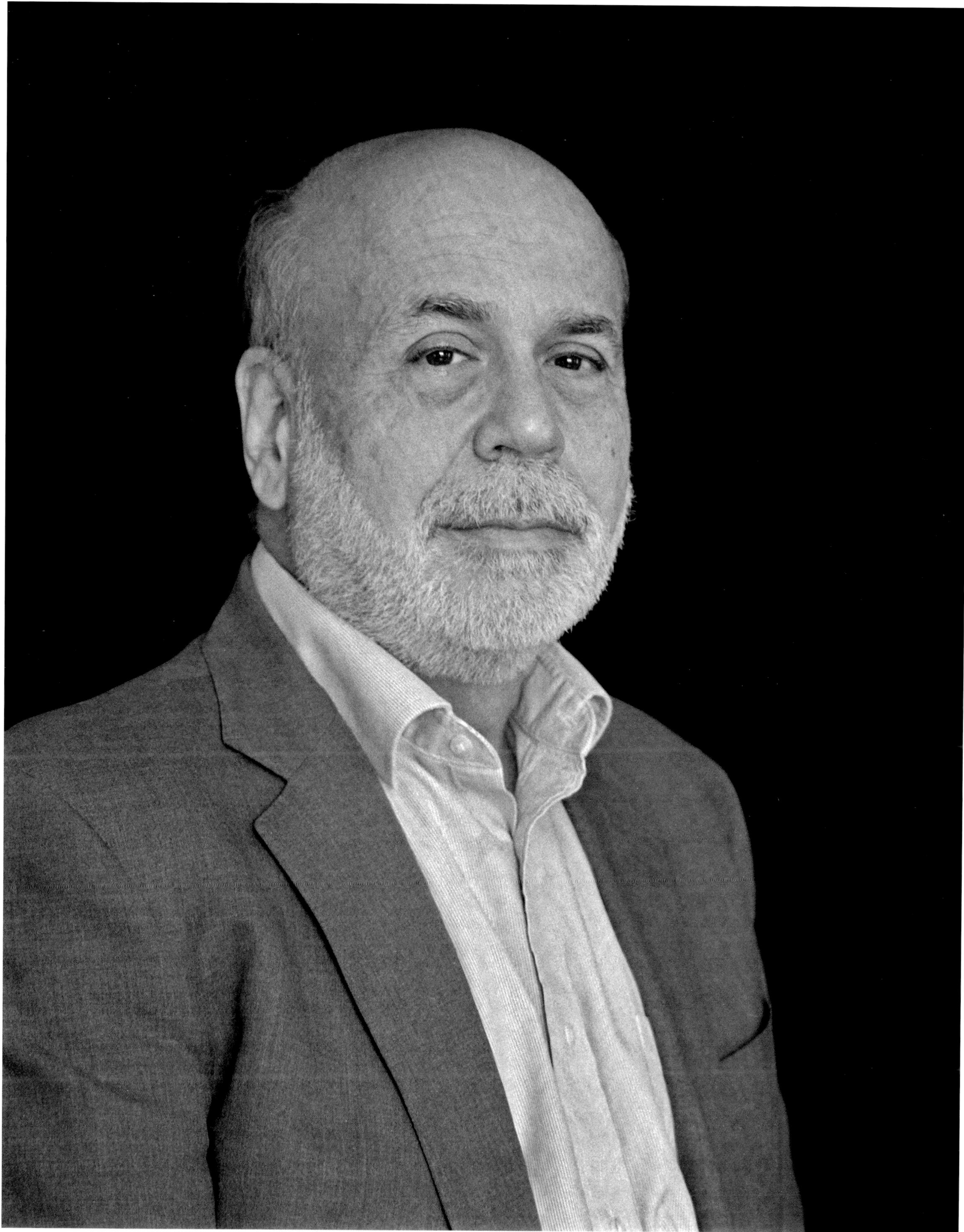

Marianne Bertrand

"You have written about the glass ceiling. What is the gender situation in academic economics?"

THE COMMITTEE ON the Status of Women in the Economics Profession (CSWEP), a standing committee of the American Economic Association (AEA) charged with promoting the careers and monitoring the progress of female economists, has been surveying some 250 departments annually since 1993. A few key facts emerge from the data CSWEP has been collecting over time. First, while the share of new PhDs awarded to women increased from 1993 to the early 2000s (from 28 percent in 1993 to 35 percent in 2003), there has been no improvement since; in fact, the share of new PhDs awarded to women in 2016 was only 32 percent, lower than in 2003. Second, within the tenure-track, the higher the rank, the lower the share of women. In 2016, about 28 percent of assistant professors were women, compared to 26 percent of associate professors and 13 percent of full professors. CSWEP also highlights another trend that does not bode well for the future representation of women in academic economics: the fraction of women with baccalaureates who major in economics has been decreasing over time. Overall, the progress of women (and other minorities) appears to have stalled in economics and is lagging behind other academic disciplines.

The factors responsible for this situation are not well understood.

When it comes to what I would call the "pipeline" problem (i.e., too few women considering majoring in economics in college), I believe the profession could do a better job in marketing itself to women. Undergraduates may not fully appreciate the broad range of research questions that economists tackle. For many college students, economics might be perceived as the study of interest rates, stock prices, inflation, GDP growth, quantitative macro-modeling exercises, etc. These are, of course, important topics that are central to many economists' research agendas. But economics is so much more than that! Many of us are invested in using the rich tools of economics to understand deep social problems such as income inequality, lack of intergenerational mobility, discrimination, poverty, climate change, etc. I strongly believe that we could raise the appeal of our profession among young women by better communicating who we are and what we do.

Some have also argued that academic economics is too often characterized by a confrontational and hostile work culture, which extends to seminars and conferences. To the extent that more women than men dislike such an uncivil culture, this may deter them from entering the profession or induce them to exit at a higher rate than men. Furthermore, some have argued that the economics profession has not done enough to address the conscious and unconscious biases that may have come in the way of women's success in academic economics. I am personally not sure how important these factors are in practice. I, of course, know women who have given up on economics because they disliked the work environment; I also know women who have been victims of bias and, worse, harassment. What I do not know is just how pervasive these issues are in the profession. But I certainly believe that they deserve serious consideration. And some recent work suggests that there might indeed be some systemic issues. For example, a recent study made a splash by showing that female economists receive less credit than male economists for coauthored work. In this regard, I am happy to see that the AEA has recently shown a renewed commitment to invest human and financial resources in better understanding the professional climate in economics for women and other underrepresented groups, as well as a commitment to support the development and adoption of best practices to foster equal opportunity and fair treatment across departments, divisions, and schools throughout the US.

MARIANNE BERTRAND is Professor at the University of Chicago Booth School of Business.

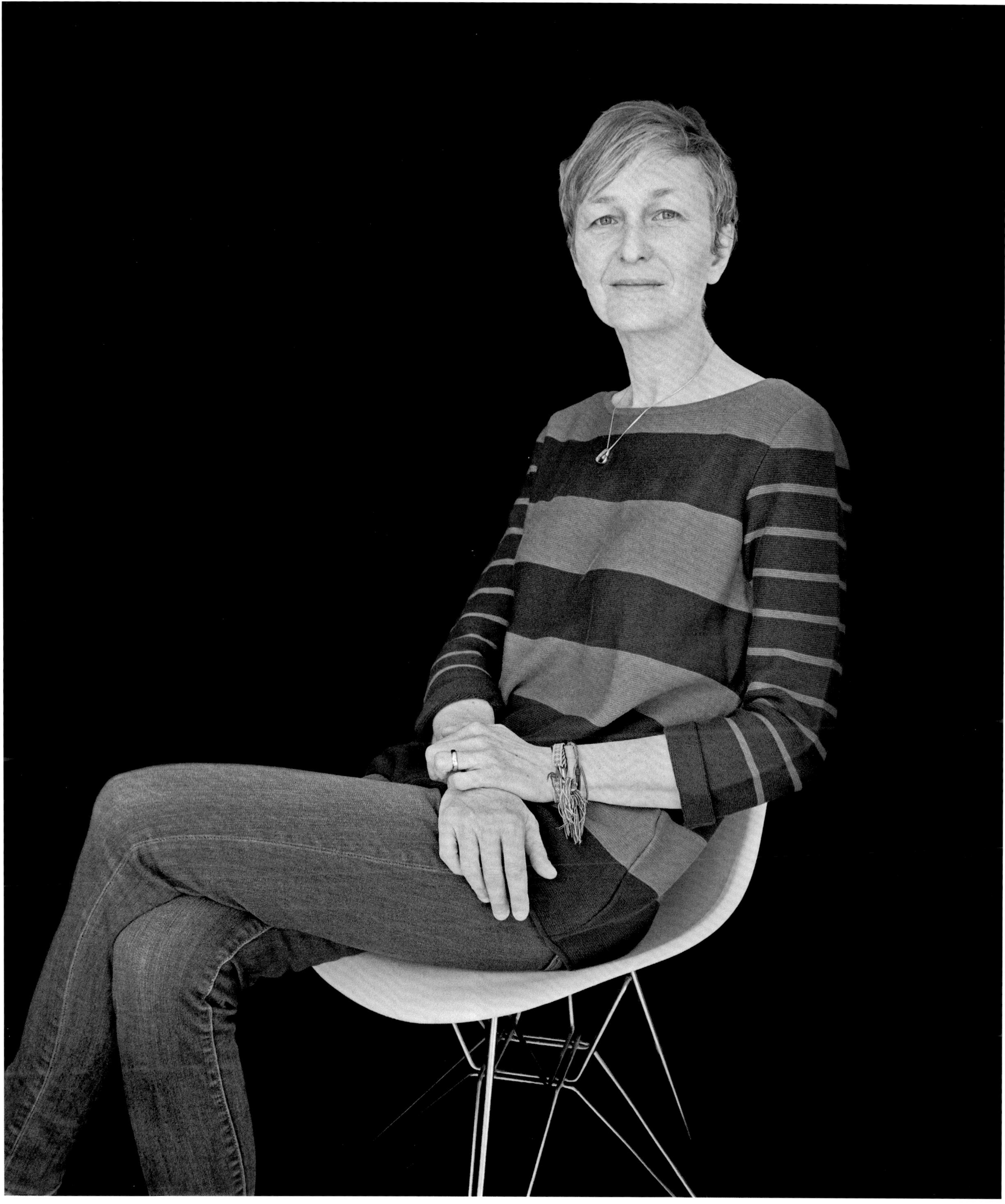

Jagdish Bhagwati

"If you could design an immigration policy for the US, what would it be? Could it ever be politically acceptable?"

THE CURRENT DEBATES regarding immigration policy owe to the fact that, while cross-border flows of humanity were generally free in the 19th century, they have been subjected to restrictions since the 20th century. These restrictions apply to both migrants seeking economic opportunity and to refugees fleeing war, pestilence, and discrimination.

While the refugee flows at the Southern border have recently emerged as a major policy problem, the debate in the United States has instead been focused on three policy questions raised by economic migrants: 1) How many economic immigrants should be admitted; 2) Who should get the resulting quotas; and 3) Since restrictions can be avoided, how should one deal with illegal immigration?

While some anti-immigration lobbyists think that the United States' share of legal immigrants in relation to its total population is too high (and it is currently at an all-time high of 13.7 percent in 2017), this fails to account for the fact that the economy is now diversified and the need for unskilled labor services such as cleaning and hospital staff has risen dramatically. The ability of large numbers of American women to enter the labor force has also been facilitated by the immigration of relatively unskilled women who mind the children and the household when the female employers are at work.

But pro-labor lobbies have also argued that the entry of immigrant workers lowers American workers' wages. Two arguments are advanced, but they are wrong, in my view. First, if immigrants will not do a job at a low wage, the employer will have to hire American workers at higher wages. However, this presumes that the employer can pay the higher wage. If not, the job will simply disappear. Also, the employer may shift to automation. Second, it is feared that more labor, with the given capital and technology, will lower wages. But, studies in Israel and the US have shown that increased labor supply may be absorbed without lowering wages simply by expanding labor-intensive production relative to other output.

Regarding the allocation of the quotas, there is greater consensus today that the United States' family-unification based system should shift instead to one based on either auctions or on the Canadian-style points system, with President Trump rejecting the current system as one of "chain migration" which pays no attention to US needs. But both have problems.

Those favoring auctions argue that it will result in having immigrants who are productive for the US as more productivity will mean they can bid higher. But that argument fails to convince: President Marcos and the Duvaliers can bid very high! The alternative is the Canadian-style points system whereby potential immigrants with skills will be given higher priority. It is asserted that this will bring people with skills into the US, which will help the US. Today, however, the economy changes rapidly and skill requirements cannot be easily forecast.

The problems that mainly dominate the public debate, however, relate to illegal immigrants. Americans have a right brain, left brain problem here. We are a nation of immigrants, so we extend our embrace to the illegal immigrants. On the other hand, these are illegal immigrants, who have flouted our laws, so we disapprove of them for that reason.

Humanity requires, however, that we bring the estimated stock of over 10 million illegal immigrants out of the shadows. Many Democrats in particular (who have their self-interested eyes on getting votes from this constituency) talk about giving them a path to citizenship. But we know that a green card is enough to guarantee one almost all rights that a citizen enjoys. So, we ought to work on the less contentious path to a green card.

As for the inflow of new illegal immigrants, presidents on both sides of the political divide have stressed the need for greater border security. We should supplement it, however, with foreign aid, which would help Mexican prosperity, and thereby reduce the incentive to come across the Rio Grande.

JAGDISH BHAGWATI is Professor at Columbia University.

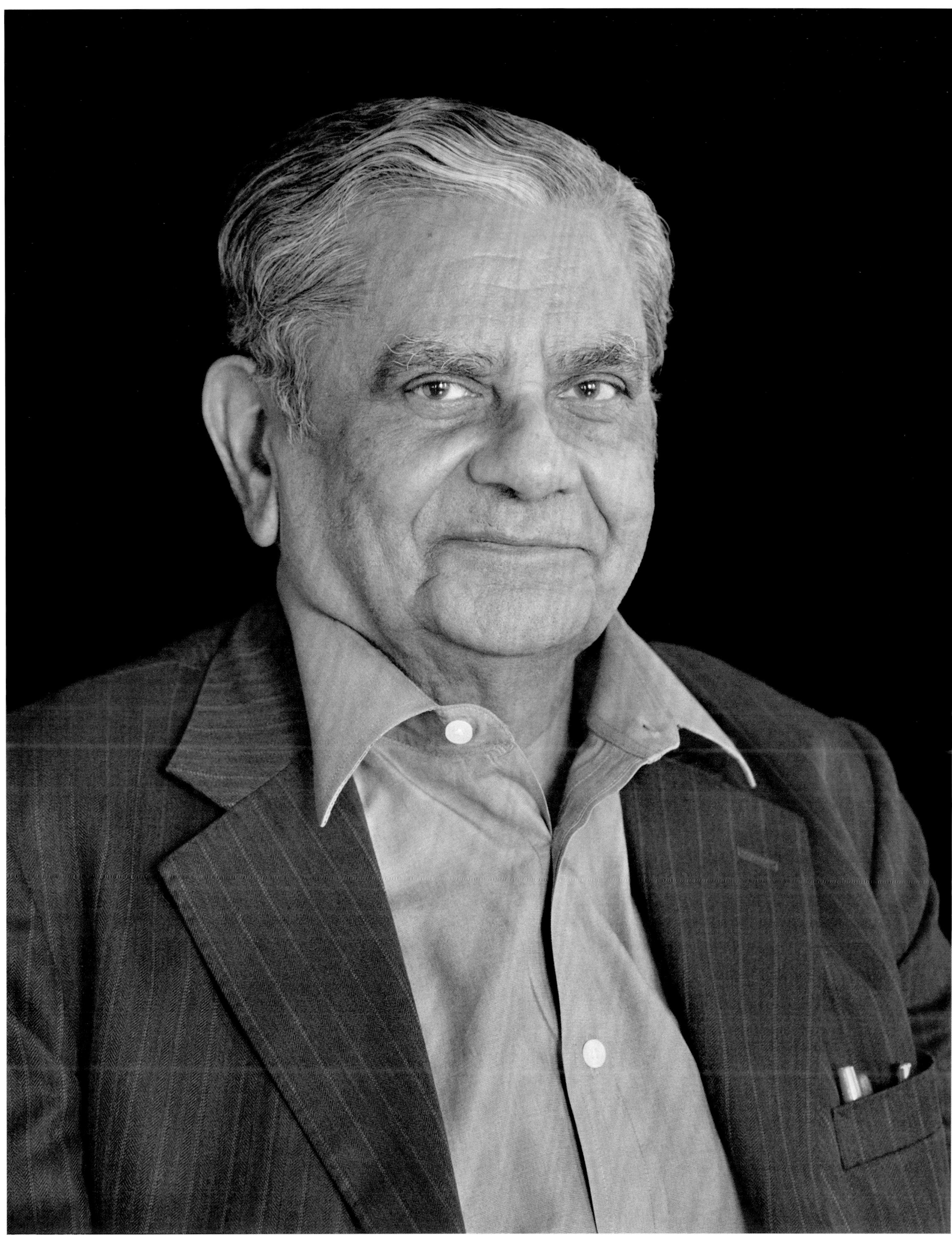

Olivier Blanchard

"Do you think it is possible to achieve reasonable coordination of fiscal and monetary policy without compromising the independence of the central bank?"

START FROM THE beginning: There is wide agreement that the market economy can suffer from large, inefficient, fluctuations; that unemployment can increase far above the level needed for efficient reallocation; or instead, that the economy may overheat, leading to inflation pressure.

There is also wide agreement that governments have and should use the two main tools at their disposal—fiscal policy and monetary policy—to reduce these fluctuations.

Put simply, fiscal policy can be used to affect demand directly through public spending, or indirectly, through the effects of changes in taxes on private spending. Monetary policy, on the other hand, can affect private spending through changes in interest rates.

Why use one or the other? In some cases, one may work better than the other. Both also have side effects that one must consider. For example, an expansionary monetary policy, by leading to lower interest rates, leads investors to look abroad for more attractive investments, and may trigger a decrease in the exchange rate. Fiscal policy, by increasing demand, may require a tightening of monetary policy, and lead to an increase in the exchange rate.

Often, what is needed is a combination of the two. For example, if the budget deficit is too large to start with, the right combination may be a fiscal contraction, with its adverse effects on demand offset through a more expansionary monetary policy.

In an idealized world, one could give overall responsibility to a benevolent policymaker, who would choose the right combination. Or it could be given to two, still benevolent, policymakers, one in charge of fiscal policy and one in charge of monetary policy. They would work out the optimal package.

In the real world, policymakers are not that benevolent. Indeed, in democracies, their time in power, and thus their relevant time horizon, is short and often leads them to favor the present over the future; for example, they tend to decrease taxes and run large deficits, even if this leads to higher debt and higher taxes later, or to finance deficits through money creation, even though this leads to high inflation later.

Through constitutions and laws, countries typically put in place constraints to limit such dangers. Arrangements vary, but, nowadays, they typically take the following form: fiscal policy remains the domain of the executive and legislative branches, subject to some limits on debt and deficits. Perhaps the best current example of such limits is the set of "Maastricht criteria" for deficits and debt, which eurozone members must respect. The domain of monetary policy is given instead to an independent central bank, which is free to use whatever tools at its disposal to achieve its government-given targets.

Why the asymmetry? It is due to the fact that fiscal policy has many dimensions beyond just the size of the deficit. Changes in taxes, transfers, or public spending all have potentially large distributional implications, and it is rightly felt that these should be debated and voted on by elected officials. Monetary policy, on the other hand, is seen as more distributionally neutral. Changes in the interest rate, the traditional instrument of central banks, are seen as mostly affecting activity, largely benefitting all, rich and poor. Thus, the argument goes, giving the central bank its independence eliminates the risk of political interference, at little risk to democracy.

Is this arrangement the right one? Largely, but not entirely so. History abundantly shows that, absent central bank independence, political interference can lead to pressure on the central bank and lead to high inflation or even hyperinflation. But the argument that central bank policy is distributionally neutral is not quite right. Low interest rates lead to high asset prices, which primarily benefit those with high wealth. Also, some of the new tools used by central banks clearly have distributional effects. The increase in required down payments for new mortgages, a measure used by many central banks to limit increases in housing prices, makes it harder for first-time buyers to become homeowners. For such decisions, the right arrangement cannot purely be central bank independence, but should be a responsibility shared by both the government and the central bank.

To go back to the initial question: Does central bank independence, whether total or partial, make it harder to coordinate between fiscal and monetary policy? I do not see any strong reason to think so. If democracy works—i.e., the fiscal authorities have the right objective function or are forced to do so through additional restraints on debt and deficits, and the central bank is independent and competent—then I see no reason to be worried about the policy outcome. If democracy fails, if the restraints do not work, or if the central bank is incompetent, then there are plenty of reasons to worry, but the origin of the problem is far worse than anything discussed above.

OLIVIER BLANCHARD is Senior Fellow at the Peterson Institute for International Economics, Professor Emeritus at MIT, and was Chief Economist at the International Monetary Fund from 2008–2015.

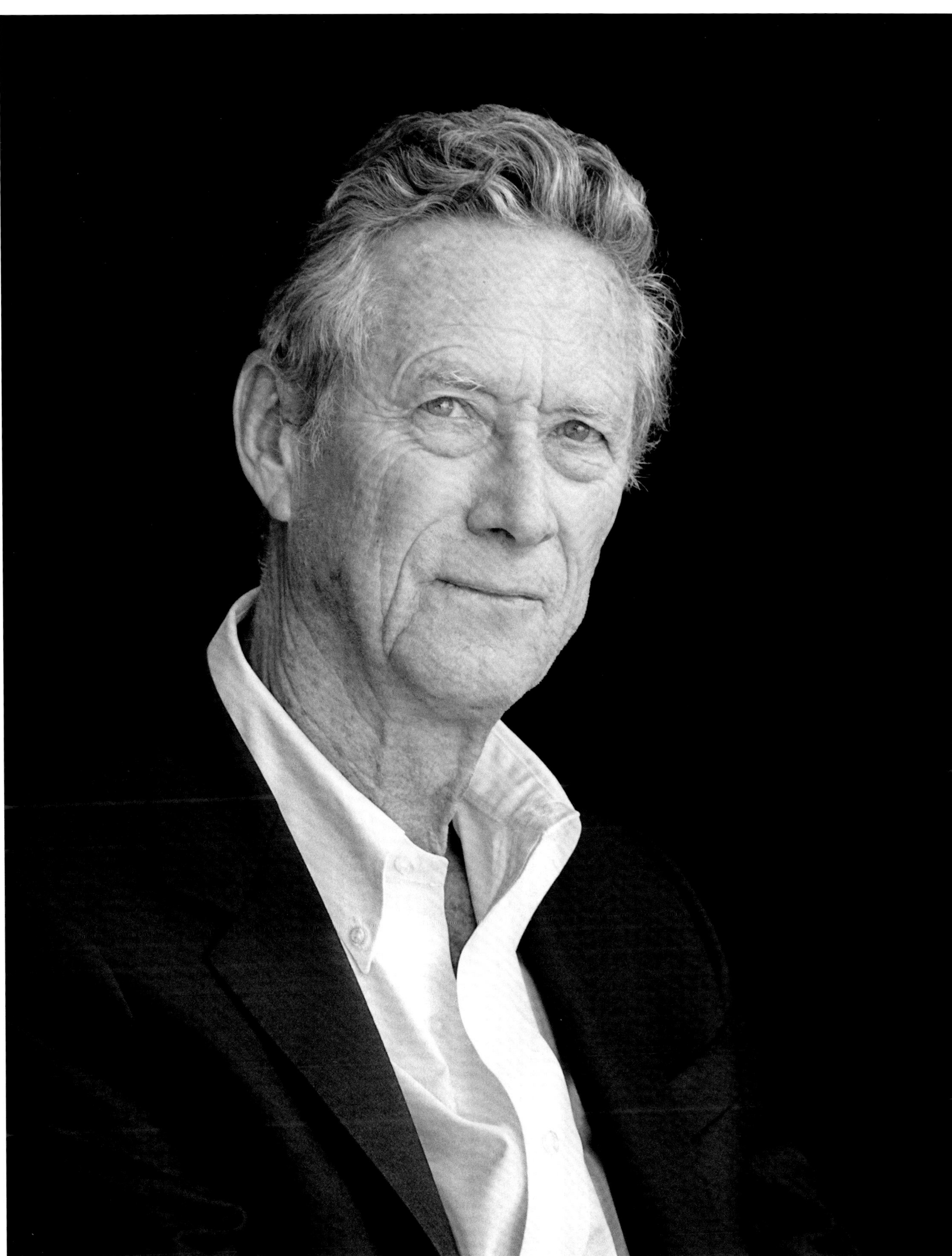

Alan Blinder

"Do you think that the financial system has become so large that it entails more risk and more cost than it adds to economic efficiency?"

AT SOME LEVEL, the answer must be yes. The financial systems of the US, the UK, and several other countries are now so large that no one can tell any longer which is the "dog" and which is the "tail." But I think we do know that the real economy *should* "wag" the financial markets more than the other way around. The financial system should be about enhancing economic efficiency (e.g., in the allocation of capital), not about creating rents for the people who work there. It does a lot of the latter.

That said, I don't think its large *size* is the essence of the problem. It is related, for sure; but the real problems stem from high *leverage,* excessive *complexity,* and (often, but not always,) lax *supervision.*

As is well known even to beginning students, leverage is wonderful on the upside: it magnifies gains. But as is just as well known, but sometimes forgotten, leverage is dangerous on the downside, where it magnifies losses. And in the financial context, sharp declines in asset values can—and in crises *do*—have further ill effects, such as when large losses leave Firm A bankrupt, and therefore unable to pay back Firms B, C, and D; or when concerns about possible failures of counterparties cause the credit system to seize up, damaging credit flows not just inside the financial sector but also to nonfinancial borrowers; or when such fears result in runs, whether on banks or on nonbank financial intermediaries. The case of Lehman Brothers in September 2008 was, of course, the mega-example; but things like that happen on a smaller scale in almost all financial crises. A highly leveraged financial system is an inherently risky system, and the risks that it poses can threaten the entire macroeconomy.

Complexity presents somewhat different, though related, hazards. For starters, extreme complexity leaves unwary buyers vulnerable to frauds or, as I like to call them, *near-frauds*—meaning shady or deceptive sales practices that do not cross the line into illegality. Economists learned in 2008 that such unscrupulous behavior can scale up to the extent that it damages the macroeconomy. Even if there are no shady sales practices, buyers of financial assets who don't understand the bundle of risks they are acquiring may be prone to panic when something goes wrong—or is even rumored to go wrong. Finally, perhaps prosaically, but directly germane to the efficiency question, complexity impedes the ability of prospective buyers to comparison-shop for the best deals. Over-the-counter derivatives prior to the crisis were a prominent case in point.

These dangers can be mitigated—but never eliminated—by better regulation or, perhaps more accurately, by better supervision. ("Regulation" refers to setting rules; "supervision" means looking over banks' shoulders to make sure they follow the rules and operate safely, soundly, and honestly.) The leverage and complexity problems are always present, though they wax and wane in intensity. A thorough and vigilant supervisory regime can keep those risks manageable. But when regulators grow inattentive, whether lulled into complacency by a run of good years or pushed there by their political masters, the time bomb starts ticking. Here, it is important to point out, the wise old adage, "personnel is policy," applies with special force. The laws and regulations that govern finance may be fine, but if regulators don't enforce them, they won't provide effective safeguards against risky or dishonest behavior. The run-up to the 2008–2009 crisis is a bone-chilling case in point.

In principle, even a huge financial system can be regulated and supervised to make sure it yields net benefits to society, not net costs. *In practice,* however, a financial system that is large relative to its underlying economy probably got that way through excessive leverage (which, by definition, means a lot of debt instruments), innovations that lured savers and borrowers into "sexy" new instruments they may not have understood, and a permissive regulatory regime. That's the unholy trinity that needs to be avoided.

ALAN BLINDER is Professor at Princeton University and was Vice Chair of the Federal Reserve from 1994–1996.

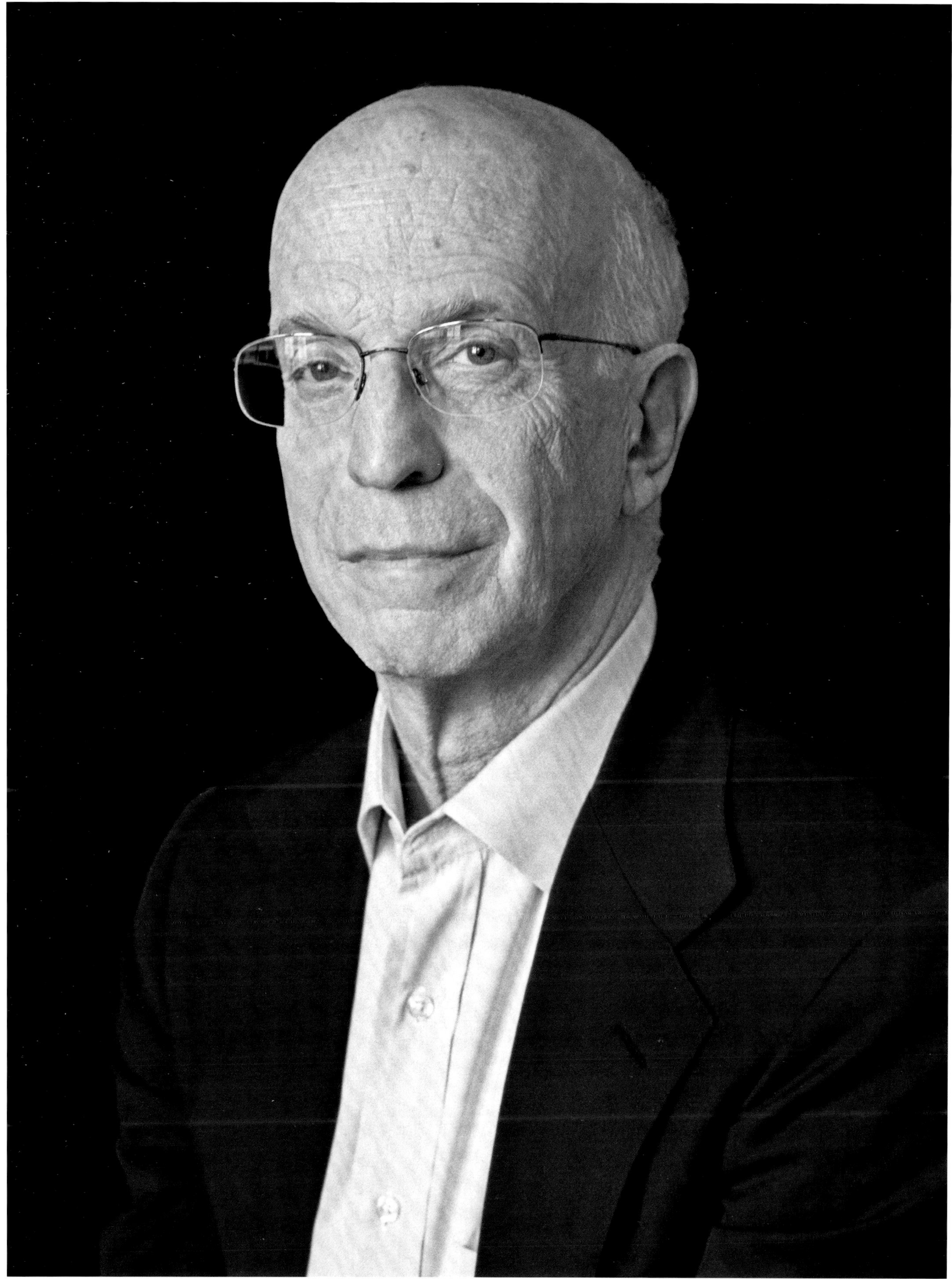

David Card

"How does immigration affect native opportunities?"

IT SEEMS OBVIOUS that when there are more people available to work, increased competition for jobs will lower wages. This is the idea behind Thomas Malthus's thesis that unfettered population growth leads to human misery. And yet, average wages are invariably *higher* in bigger cities than in smaller cities and towns. And many countries try to promote population growth through baby bonuses and tax incentives. The neoclassical economists of the 19th century resolved the Malthusian curse by postulating that if a nation could expand the stock of capital (machinery, buildings, infrastructure, etc.), then the number of jobs could keep pace with population without lowering average wages per worker.

Despite the widespread acceptance of this basic idea, the effects of an immigration-induced population inflow are still controversial. At issue are two main points: First, how long does it take for investment to catch up with population growth? Second, what if the immigrants are concentrated in lower skill groups, as they tend to be in the United States, posing greater competition for natives at the bottom of the job ladder? The simplest kinds of evidence—comparing average wages across cities with more or less immigrants, or looking at periods of faster and slower immigration—shows little relationship between immigration and average outcomes for lower-skilled natives. But there is a problem with this evidence. People are drawn to places with more opportunities. Perhaps the negative effects of immigration are masked by underlying differences in local (or national) conditions that attract or repel both immigrants and natives.

One way to strengthen the evidence is to look at episodes when large numbers of immigrants were induced to move into a particular labor market by forces outside that market. From May to September of 1980 some 125,000 Cubans were transported on a flotilla of small boats from the Port of Mariel to Miami. About one-half of the Marielitos stayed in Miami, resulting in a big jump in Miami's working-age population, and an even larger boost in the supply of less-skilled workers. Surprisingly, however, the inflow did not seem to hurt native workers in the city. Comparisons of wages and unemployment rates between Miami and other similar cities do not show any indication that lower-skilled natives were hurt by the arrival of the Marielitos. Subsequent studies of other similar episodes—including the massive emigration of Jews from the former Soviet Union to Israel in the early 1990s—have confirmed the lessons from the Mariel Boatlift and suggested that modern labor markets can adapt to inflows of immigrants with few negative spillovers on natives.

A closely related approach builds on the fact that immigrants tend to follow earlier family members and friends to the same places. For example, in the 1990s many new immigrants from the Philippines were drawn to historical naval-base cities (like Honolulu and Norfolk, Virginia) following the steps of previous generations of Filipino men who served in the US Navy. This distinct enclave pattern means that when a foreign country is experiencing economic or political difficulties some US cities can expect a surge of immigrants, while others will be largely unaffected. Such forces were at play in the 1990s when Mexico experienced a decade of slow growth: US cities in California and Texas with strong historical ties to Mexico gained many new immigrants. Studies using this idea to isolate "supply-driven" inflows of labor again show very small or negligible effects on native workers. Instead, many natives are pushed up the job ladder to positions requiring abilities that immigrants lack, like language skills.

DAVID CARD is Professor at the University of California, Berkeley. He received the John Bates Clark Medal in 1995.

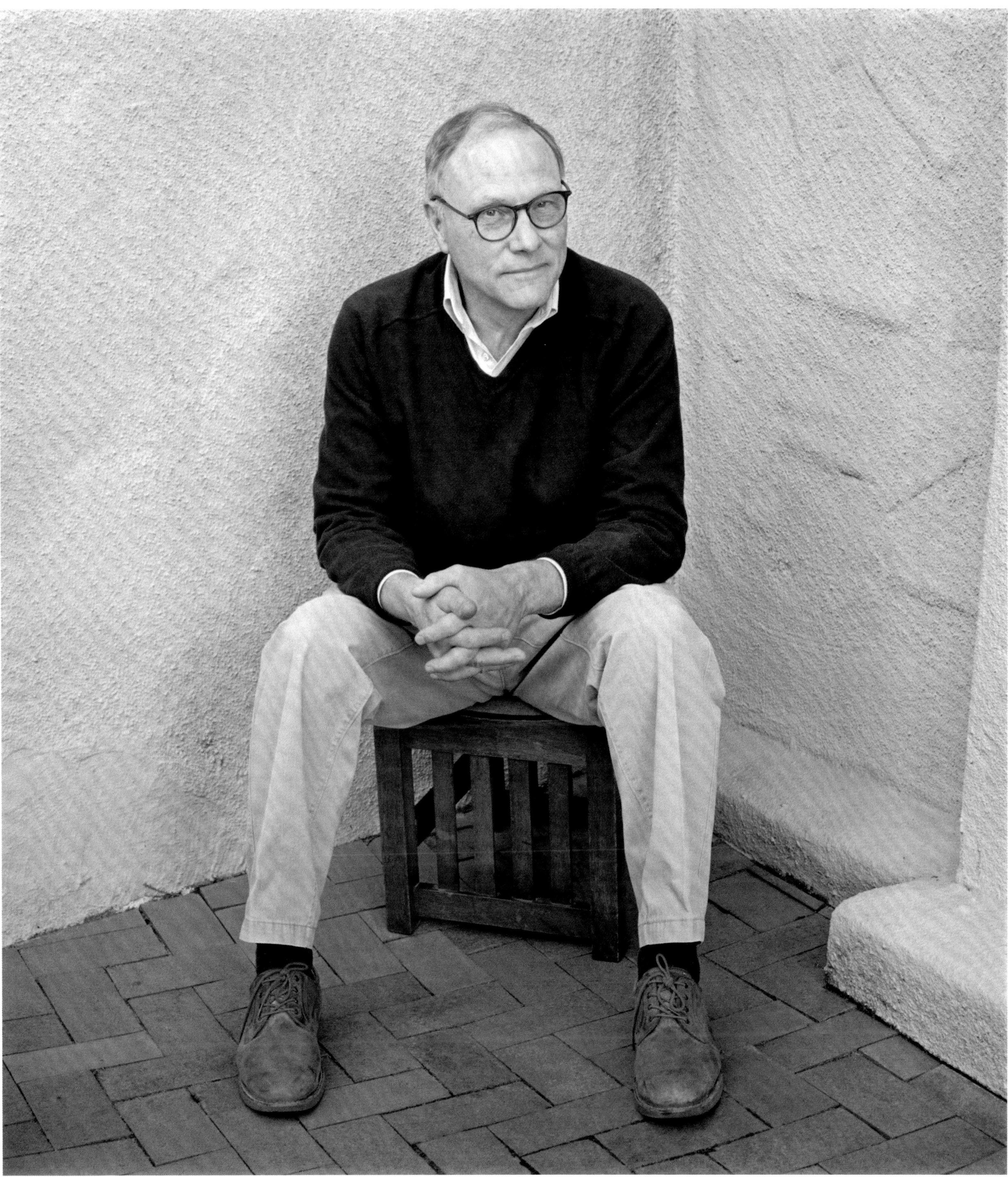

Anne Case

"You have identified the prevalence of 'illnesses of despair' in the American middle class. Can it be said when that began? Is it identified with developments in the economy?"

THERE HAS BEEN a slow but steady year-on-year increase in "deaths of despair" (suicides, drug overdoses, and alcohol-related liver mortality) among whites with less than a four-year college degree since at least the early 1990s. Before that time, not all states recorded education on death certificates, which stops us from being able to give this (predominantly working-class) crisis a precise start date. But our ability to follow the crisis back even to 1990 can tell us a great deal. Deaths of despair were rising years before the FDA approved the sale of new, highly addictive, prescription painkillers. While the arrival of legal, heavy-duty opioids in the late 1990s almost certainly made this a perfect storm, alcohol and suicide mortality were quietly killing middle-aged whites at ever-faster rates before then. We can also document that the financial crisis of 2007 and the Great Recession, which walloped the US in 2008 and 2009, had no noticeable effects on the rate of increase in deaths of despair.

That's not to say that economic conditions aren't an underlying cause, perhaps *the* underlying cause, here—only that contemporaneous economic conditions don't appear to be a driver. To understand why working-class men and women started killing themselves, either slowly with drugs and alcohol, or quickly with guns, I think we need to look at changes in the US labor market that began in the early 1970s. Median real wages for men in the labor force have not risen since 1972. The wages and benefits for a "typical" American worker (one working in production, or in a non-supervisory role) not only stopped keeping pace with productivity growth at that time, but flatlined altogether. Men and women entering the labor market beyond that point, who had been raised on the expectation that a high school degree and a strong work ethic could deliver a middle-class life, found that they were sorely mistaken.

This has had profound effects on American society. Marriage rates for whites without a college degree started falling: women didn't want to marry men who lacked good economic prospects. White working-class men and women started living together in ever-higher numbers, and increasingly had children outside of marriage. Unlike Europe, where cohabitation is quite common, and relatively stable, cohabitation in the US is quite fragile. People leave their options open, in case someone with a brighter economic future comes along. Over this period, younger people also began moving away from the Catholic or mainline Protestant churches of their parents and grandparents. They are less likely to affiliate with a church; those that do are more likely to identify with an evangelical church that emphasizes one's personal relationship with God and personal moral choices.

Our current working hypothesis is that all of this upheaval, taken together, has left many lives unmoored. Work life, home life, and more traditional church communities no longer provide the support they once did. Lack of a secure job, a secure marriage, and social connection have left working-class people more vulnerable to anxiety and depression, which in turn leaves them open to self-medication through drugs and alcohol, and to suicide.

In my own research, I am back in the weeds, sorting through data and causes, trying to document the role played by economic forces. To date, we've used education as a marker. It appears on death certificates (income and occupation do not), and it appears to divide whites into two Americas—those with a BA, who continue to fare well economically and who can expect to live healthier, longer lives than their parents did; and those without a BA, who face a hostile labor market with inadequate support. But I don't think that sending everyone to college for a BA is a sound policy response. If we do indeed find that the cancer is in the labor market, the cure is likely to lie there as well.

ANNE CASE is Professor Emeritus at Princeton University.

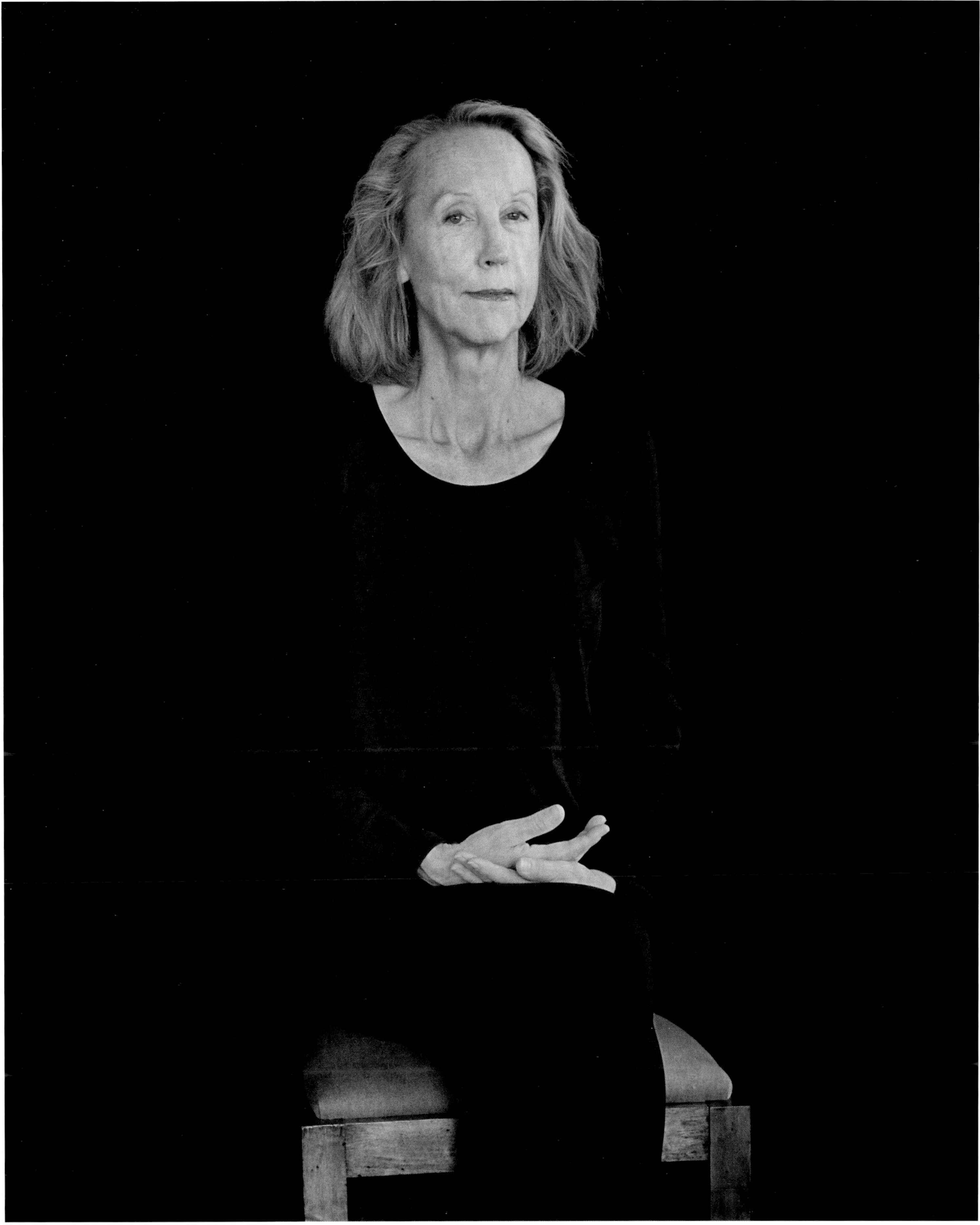

Raj Chetty

"You have recently done research on the relation between income and life expectancy, the effects of better neighborhoods on children, intergenerational income mobility in the US, and the effects of teacher quality on students' lives. How do you find or select research topics?"

I SEEK TO ask questions that speak to key issues that matter to the general public, like "How can we achieve a better future for our kids?" Many of these questions have been studied by social scientists for years, so I look for places to step in where my team of research collaborators and I can make a distinctive contribution by bringing new ideas and data to bear on the issue. This often involves a careful comparison of what people discuss in the "real world" and how that differs from what existing theories in economics or sociology predict or assume.

One way we seek to have an impact is simply by illuminating a new trend or empirical regularity, such as documenting the steep decline in children's chances of achieving the American Dream of upward mobility or showing how kids' chances of success vary across the country. Another way we seek to contribute is by casting light on policy debates. For instance, some of our recent work presents evidence that test-score based value-added measures can be informative predictors of teachers' quality, a result that has shaped legal and policy debates across the nation.

Throughout all our research, regardless of the particular topic, we strive to maintain the highest standards of scientific integrity and accuracy. Much of our analysis draws upon "big data"—large databases typically obtained from administrative sources—that allow us to obtain particularly precise answers to complex questions. We never publish a study where we feel our analysis has not yielded clear progress on a question. Since the questions we seek to address are important to many people, we want them to have confidence that our analysis and data provide a solid scientific foundation for making policy decisions that improve their lives.

RAJ CHETTY is Professor at Harvard University. He received the John Bates Clark Medal in 2013.

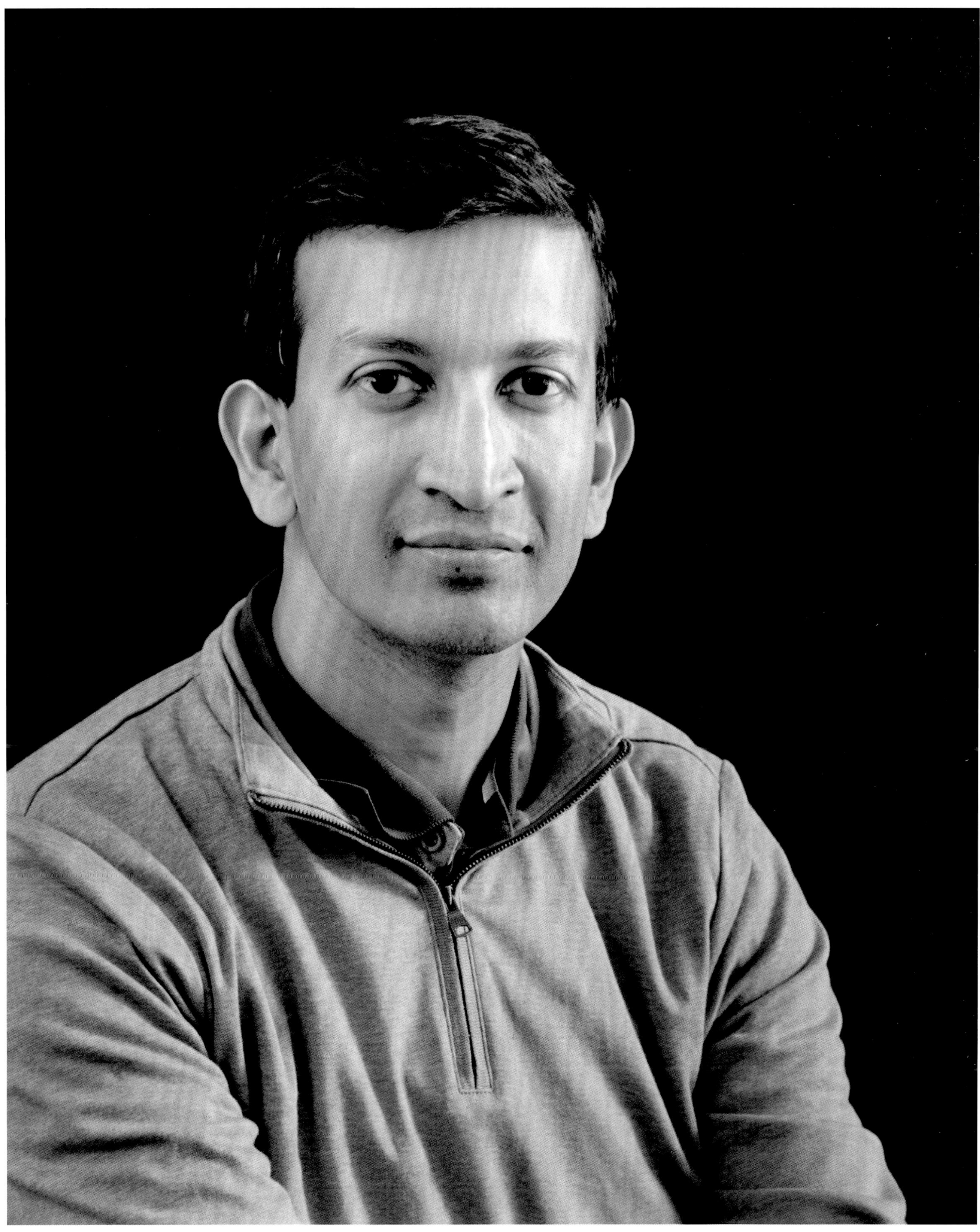

Partha Dasgupta

"What would a world population policy that respected democracy look like?"

CHILDREN ARE VALUABLE to us not only because of the innate desire we have to bear and rear them, but also because they represent the fulfilment of tradition and religious dictates, and are the clearest avenue open to self-transcendence. So we say our children are priceless. But couples considering parenthood not only look into their own desires and needs and the economic constraints they face, they also consider the effect of an addition on all family members; and they consider the kind of life that would be on offer to the potential child. These considerations are in the couple's private domain; indeed, I know of no other human activity that feels so private. Which is why it is not at all obvious that democratic societies would wish to entertain population policies.

There is, however, another class of considerations that thoughtful couples will want to think through. They will want to consider the potential effects of their newborn on others outside of their family, including people who will appear in the future. I have in mind here in particular the environmental consequences of new births (habitat destruction), most especially perhaps the all-too-easily missed global environmental consequences (biological extinctions). Those consequences are not mediated by the price system nor (typically) by social norms of conduct; which suggests there is a clash of rights between prospective parents and others, including future people. And that tells us that procreation should not be seen as an entirely private matter. It also isn't a private matter because parental motivations are shaped by the social milieu. We look at others' behaviour when choosing what to do, and we know that others look at the choices we make when they decide what to do. No doubt we each are negligible on the societal stage, but the effects we each impose on others when summed across all of us is not negligible.

I am talking here of "externalities," which are the unaccounted consequences of our actions for others, including future people. The presence of externalities explains why and how it can be that people are settled on a pattern of reproductive behavior they all would prefer to alter but cannot because no couple has the necessary motivation to change their behavior unilaterally. And that tells us even democratic societies need to discuss population policies.

In recent years there has been a focus on yet another feature of reproductive activity. Demographers have pointed to the inequalities in power between the genders, most especially in the poor world. So the inner workings of households in poor countries have come under scrutiny in studies of population and development. The United Nations' declaration of 1994 on the primacy of women's reproductive rights was in part built on that recognition, but in large part it was formulated in response to coercive measures then in place in certain countries. However, the line joining women's reproductive rights, their expressed desire for children, and their need for family planning assistance is not simple.

So, when there is talk of population policies we hear alarm bells, ringing "coercion." But over sixty years of research on externalities has uncovered a vast range of policies that can address these issues while avoiding command and control. The UN's Population Division estimates that more than 130 million married women in the developing world have an unmet need for family planning. And yet family planning organizations are mostly at the bottom in terms of both funding and prestige in national governments and international aid agencies. Facing up to environmental externalities is an indirect way of framing population policies in the poor world and consumption policies in the rich world. A direct way to address the high fertility rates that continue to prevail in sub-Saharan Africa (five live births per woman over her reproductive life) is to enhance family planning programs financially, and to include entire communities in their design and implementation. That's a cry in the direction of democratic action.

PARTHA DASGUPTA is Professor Emeritus at the University of Cambridge.

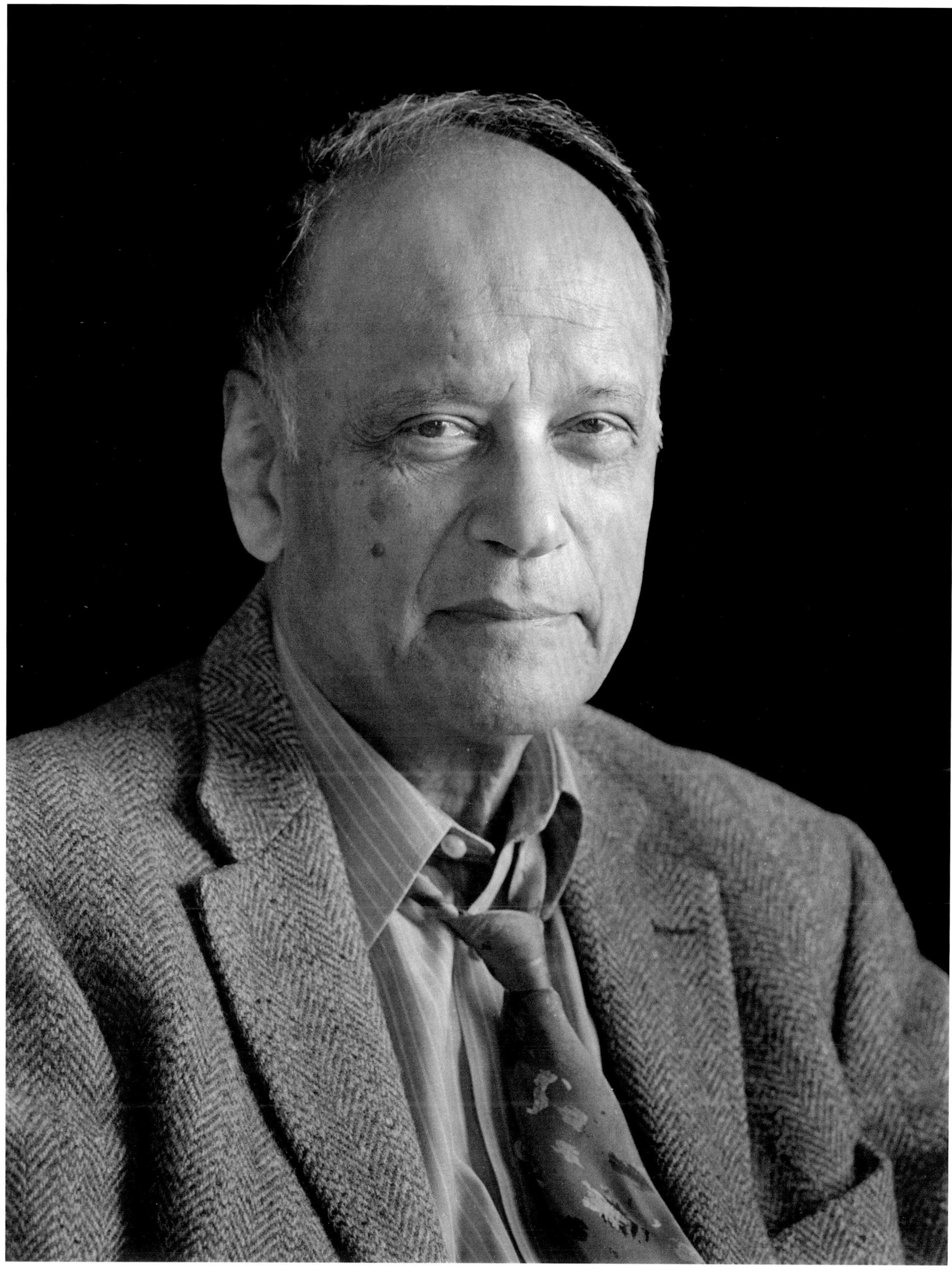

Angus Deaton

"Do you think that providing more income (and job) security to families would necessarily come at the cost of slower economic growth? Would it be worth the cost?"

THE HALF-CENTURY OF stagnation in median real wages is not only an economic threat to America, but also a political one. Modern American capitalism is failing a large segment of the population, particularly those who do not have a university degree. It cannot continue to do so without generating legitimate challenges, some of which, like right-wing populism, will only make matters worse. In the meantime, many people are suffering. The long-term decline in real wages for those without a university education is contributing to the destruction of a once thriving working-class life. Among the symptoms, we see declining marriage rates, declining rates of labor force participation, increasing rates of out-of-wedlock childbearing, greater social isolation, and increasing levels of pain. Worst of all are rising rates of death from drug overdoses, suicides, and alcoholism.

If we do not find a way of returning to a healthy labor market for working- and middle-class Americans, slower economic growth will be just one, but perhaps not the worst, of the difficulties that we will face.

I have come to believe that the best way to think about this is *not* through an explicit policy of redistribution, even if such were more politically palatable than is currently the case. The lack of support for redistribution is not merely confined to the wealthy who would have to pay for it; many working-class people want good jobs, not income support. And while many of the wealthy oppose redistribution on narrowly selfish grounds, there are broader concerns about the effects of high taxes on incentives, particularly for innovation. Using the fiscal system to redistribute should not be our first choice to solve the problem of stagnating wages.

There is another way that is likely to be more effective, and might even garner wide political support, which is to note that although the implacable and unstoppable forces of globalization and technical change affect stagnant wages, they are also deeply influenced by policy. We control policy, but that is where it seems that we have been shooting ourselves in the foot.

I have several policies in mind. One is to do something about our disgracefully expensive and ineffective health-care system. Not only is it contributing to death and distress through gross over-prescription of addictive painkillers, but much of its escalating cost is borne in the form of lower wages. American health care costs a trillion dollars a year more than it ought to. A public option, Medicare for all, single payer, or one of the several systems that work in other rich countries would remove one of the forces that is reducing wages. Our system today, with few cost controls, allows doctors, hospitals, device manufacturers, and pharmaceutical companies to enrich themselves by predating on working-class Americans.

The share of labor in national income is falling, some of it explained by increasing monopolistic and monopsonistic practices by employers. Workers are forced to sign noncompete clauses—even in fast-food jobs. Workers and consumers are forced to resolve their disputes with firms through arbitration, decisions that go, in a large fraction of cases, in favor of the firms. Some economists have implicated monopoly in slow investment and innovation. If so, tackling this will not only benefit the real wages of workers, but *increase* the rate of economic growth.

We have constructed a welfare system that often includes work requirements, as in the Earned Income Tax Credit, and requiring work for Medicaid is a proposal that is frequently aired. Work is good, but such arrangements also put downward pressure on wages.

There has been no increase in the federal minimum wage since 2009.

Capitalism is capable of working for everyone if it is properly regulated, and properly subject to an effective democracy. If we stop it becoming a vehicle for redistributing upwards, from poor to rich, we can restore working-class and middle-class life, and have healthy economic growth besides.

ANGUS DEATON is Professor Emeritus at Princeton University. He received the Nobel Prize for Economics in 2015.

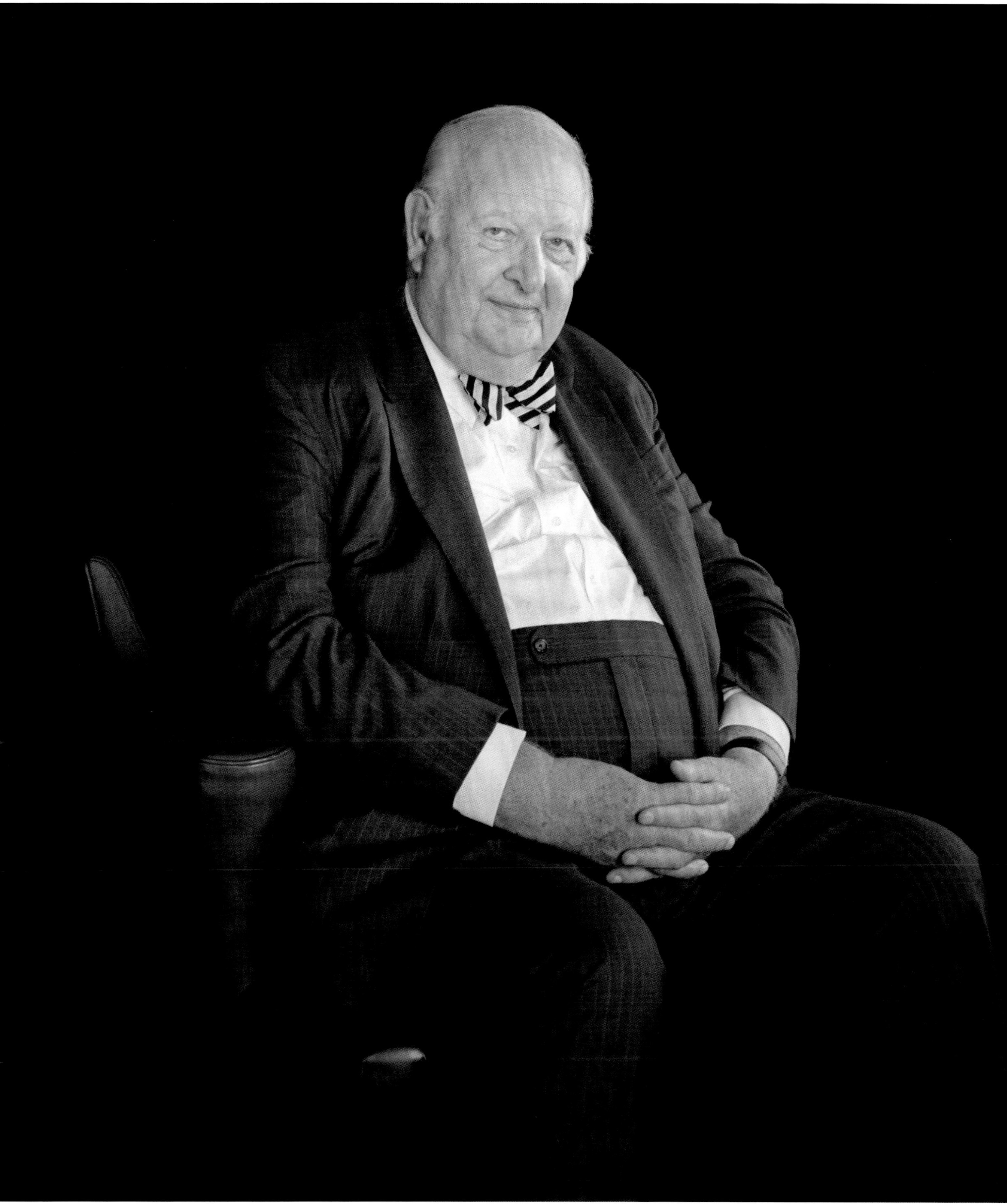

Padma Desai

"You were a leading student of the Soviet economy. What do you think of the current Russian economy? Would different transition policies have led to a better outcome?"

ON BECOMING GENERAL secretary of the Communist Party of the Soviet Union (CPSU) in March 1985, Mikhail Gorbachev sought to address the twin problems afflicting the Soviet Union: a declining economy and the centralized political authority of the CPSU. *Perestroika* aimed at liberalizing economic reforms that would loosen the straitjacket within which the Soviet economy operated; *glasnost* was to introduce electoral politics that would undermine the stifling monopoly of the CPSU.

Both sets of reforms, however, were halting and piecemeal. Gorbachev and his advisers feared that liberalizing prices would lead to price increases, given a situation of repressed demand, and that would provoke popular unrest. As for political reform, Gorbachev was a prisoner of his conviction that Communism could be given a human face, that it did not have to be abandoned.

By contrast, Yeltsin had no illusions and was bent on wrecking the Soviet economic system, which he regarded as incapable of providing better living standards to the people. The reformers he collected around him were, in Yeltsin's colorful description, his "kamikaze crew." They set out to do away with the long-standing inflexible Russian economy and authoritarian political arrangements that had undermined the economy's performance to date. So, while this was a slow, uphill task, Yeltsin did introduce the transformative changes that would ultimately take Russia into a new era.

But there were unanticipated problems. The decision to privatize state-owned assets led to the creation of the oligarchs and their dominance in Russian economics and politics. The public viewed privatization as a transfer of valuable assets to favored oligarchs for a pittance. The freeing of prices, in a situation of repressed demand, also fed popular unrest and backlash. The growing chaos and anxiety following the progressive dismantling of the old Soviet regime was exacerbated by the fact that little was done to replace the existing "welfare state" with new institutions that could provide a safety net.

So, while Yeltsin bonded with the United States, Russia was collapsing into chaos, needing external assistance to cope with the new situation. As a wit remarked, Yeltsin had unwittingly turned a superpower into a super-beggar. When he resigned in a surprise move in December 1999, his approval rating had fallen below 5 percent.

Enter Vladimir Putin, Yeltsin's handpicked successor, a former KGB operative and an active judo master. Yeltsin remarked that he approved of Putin because he was not a "maximalist," meaning presumably that the wide-ranging economic reforms introduced by the "kamikaze crew" had been disruptive. Putin would therefore bring order into the chaotic situation. But what Yeltsin had not bargained for was that Putin was, one might say, a maximalist anti-reformer on the political front.

On the economic front, Russia's energy sector, the principal source of foreign exchange earnings, was subjected to Kremlin monitoring. Foreign companies were bullied into becoming minority partners with Gazprom, Russia's natural gas monopoly. The accumulated foreign exchange reserves also helped Putin moderate the impact of the 2008 worldwide financial crisis on Russia.

On the political front, Putin's early moves were marked by measures aimed at consolidating his power: he abolished gubernatorial elections by the public, restricted the electronic media, modified parliamentary election rules, and curtailed the activities of foreign NGOs. He believed that Russia needed a strong state, which meant that his authority should not be challenged by others in his government. His geopolitical moves such as seizing Crimea from Ukraine in 2014 and annexing it to Russia via a fake referendum raised his approval rating among Russians to 87 percent even as the economy continued performing unevenly. The post-Crimea annexation sanctions imposed by the West have contributed further to his acceptance among Russians and guaranteed him a presidential re-election in 2018.

Clearly, the reformation of the Russian economy and state through *perestroika* and *glasnost*, begun by Gorbachev and advanced yet further by Yeltsin, has now been halted, even reversed in some ways, by Putin. We have seen Russia go from progress to regress. Could a different, more favorable, scenario have developed? It is hard to tell.

But one may speculate that the Western powers could have played to reassure, rather than challenge, Russia on several fronts. Did G-8 have to be restructured into G-7 to exclude Russia? Was the NATO expansion close to the Russian border, pronounced as a provocation by many distinguished diplomats and experts on Russia, really necessary? Maybe; maybe not.

PADMA DESAI is Professor at Columbia University.

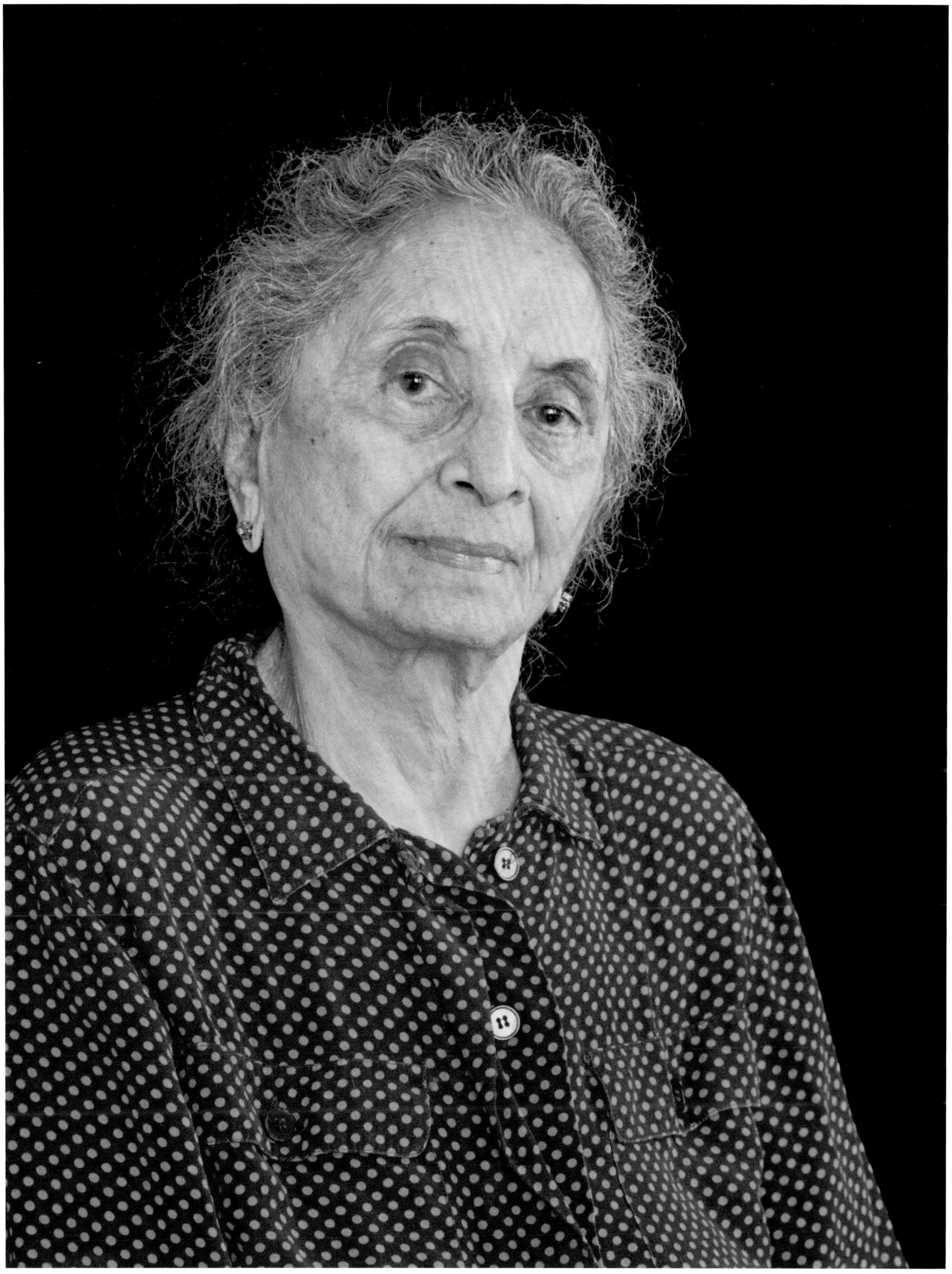

Peter Diamond

"What needs to be done to get and preserve a healthy Social Security system?"

ACCORDING TO THE 2017 central projection of the finances of Social Security, without new legislation, the Social Security Trust Fund will be exhausted in 2034, resulting in a 23 percent benefit cut for every beneficiary, with larger cuts in the future. It is reasonable to expect Congress will take some action to avert this outcome. But it is hard to predict what will come from Congress. Waiting for unpredictable legislation is an unhealthy position for us to be in currently, and the eventual legislation may give us an unhealthy outcome.

As a start to projecting possible congressional actions, consider the reform plans that have been put forward by the two ranking members of the House Social Security subcommittee. The Republican plan includes no revenue increases and so continues an ongoing pattern of benefit cuts to address both the currently projected shortfall and the further effects of continued aging. The Democratic plan includes enough tax increases to cover the currently projected shortfall and also to increase benefits.

A healthy Social Security system needs to be large enough to address the retirement and disability needs of the sizable fraction of the working force that is heavily reliant on the system. This reliance reflects the widespread presence of low savings and the large cost of saving for retirement when done on an individual basis by a small saver.

And, a healthy system needs to adapt to the changes that are bound to come as earning opportunities change and as the aging of the population continues. Changes in technology and further global interactions are going to affect retirement concerns. Good Social Security adaptation needs a wider degree of automatic changes than at present, an approach that has been legislated increasingly in other advanced countries. And good adaptation needs political cooperation across party lines to design automatic adjustments and to address issues not adequately addressed by the automatic adjustments. Again, there are examples in other countries of sustained cooperation across party lines to adapt national pensions.

We need to get away from the pattern of having Social Security actions only when they are desperately needed. And we need to get away from the wide disagreement between the parties about Social Security, a disagreement sustained by the shielding of congressional attitudes toward Social Security from much public scrutiny. Indeed, the press releases accompanying the two plans mentioned above were full of euphemisms. On the Republican side, benefit cuts were referred to as "modernizing," "updating," "keeping up with changes," and "targeting benefits." And on the Democratic side, tax increases were referred to as "ensuring Social Security remains strong."

To push political cooperation, addressing Social Security's current imbalance and long-run needs should become a central part of election cycles, at least until we have a healthy system. Benefit cuts and tax increases are understandably politically unpopular, but some combination of them is necessary for preserving this popular program. The popularity of Social Security will affect political cooperation more strongly when cooperation matters for election and re-election. We are likely to use a commission to design a plan for Congress to consider. Such a commission should be instructed to determine the mix of overall benefit cuts and overall tax increases. Candidates for Congress and the White House should be pressed to say what mix they favor. Voters need to respond to the answers, or to a lack of an answer. Maybe then, we can get to a healthy Social Security system with a healthy future.

PETER DIAMOND is Professor Emeritus at the Massachusetts Institute of Technology. He received the Nobel Prize for Economics in 2010.

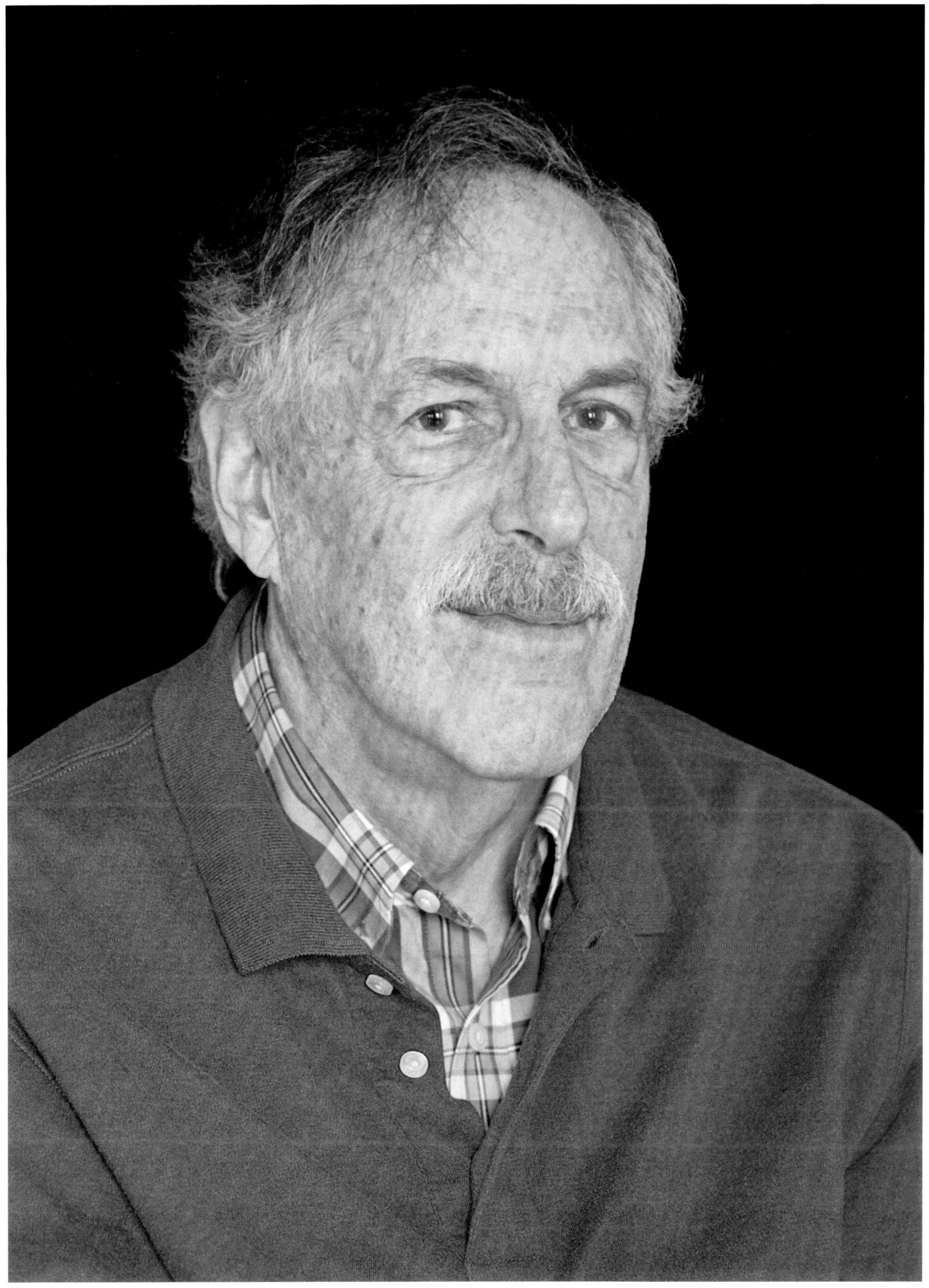

Avinash Dixit

"Can you think of institutional changes that might reduce the amount of public and private corruption?"

IN SOME SOCIETIES corruption is the way of life. If everyone is complicit in taking or giving bribes, or deriving other private benefits from one's official position, no one feels any guilt or shame about it. Even if laws exist on the books, no one will report corruption to a law enforcement agent; anyway, these agents can themselves be bribed. In other societies corruption is widely regarded as evil. Corrupt acts are likely to be reported or detected quickly and punished. The corrupt also feel guilt and shame; these are often better deterrents than formal sanctions. Thus a whole culture can be either corrupt or clean. In technical jargon, the society plays a "game" of strategic interaction with two equilibria, one corrupt and the other clean. To eliminate corruption, reforms must change the culture and flip the equilibrium.

If a society starts near the corrupt equilibrium, every member has strong temptation to be corrupt also; reforms must push against this force. But once enough people are persuaded to be clean, the rest start to find it in their own interests to be clean also. This virtuous cycle gathers its own momentum. In the initial difficult phase of resistance, reformers must marshal and sustain multiple efforts, enlist support from the top and build coalitions from the bottom. They must run education and publicity campaigns, use traditional and social media and civil society groups, promote norms of good behavior, and deploy selective sanctions. Most importantly, they must anticipate and defeat opposition from beneficiaries of the corrupt system, who will try to discredit reforms and malign reformers using all the power and devices at their disposal.

For the same reason, we cannot leave it to governments to enact and enforce tough anti-corruption laws—politicians and bureaucrats are the main beneficiaries of corruption. Very rarely does a purely top-down solution work; Singapore under Lee Kuan Yew may be a rare example. Some support from a powerful person or group at the top is important, but in most instances bottom-up social movements play at least as important a role. Reforms in Hong Kong started when Governor MacLehose empowered an independent anti-corruption agency, but it then built a broad social coalition to conduct public relations and teach ethics and values to primary schoolchildren. Both these countries benefited from their largely free and open economic systems—less rent at the disposal of politicians and bureaucrats leaves correspondingly less scope for corruption.

In medieval Italian city-states, elites active in civic affairs developed a sophisticated system of hiring an outsider as city manager (*podestà*) whose contract had complex incentives and penalties. This was a top-down imposition. In modern Italy, a campaign led by youth with minimal support from the top has made significant headway in reducing the Sicilian mafia's extortion scheme known as the *pizzo*.

Mid-nineteenth-century United States was rife with corruption. This decreased slowly over several decades, through a combination of factors: the progressive movement, political entrepreneurs like the two Roosevelts, some rent-reducing deregulation, investigative journalism, better-educated population, disbursing welfare benefits federally using objective criteria instead of local clientelism, and so on.

In some European countries, a war or other crisis destroyed established corrupt power structures and started processes leading to reforms. One would not deliberately create a crisis hoping for such results, but if one happens, the opportunity should be seized.

Private firms also suffer corruption—embezzlement, kickbacks to purchasing managers, etc. Top management can control this optimally for the firm's profit, trading off costs and benefits. In technical jargon, this is just the firm's internal "principal-agent problem."

What, then, should be done? A top-down or bottom-up solution? Formal laws or social norms? Ex ante deterrence or ex post punishment? My answer is: do anything and everything. Experiment, see what works in your context, and build on it. Be patient; don't expect quick or complete success. Above all, don't wait for some "best" solution to emerge. Waiting for 100 percent success only guarantees getting 0 percent.

AVINASH DIXIT is Professor Emeritus at Princeton University.

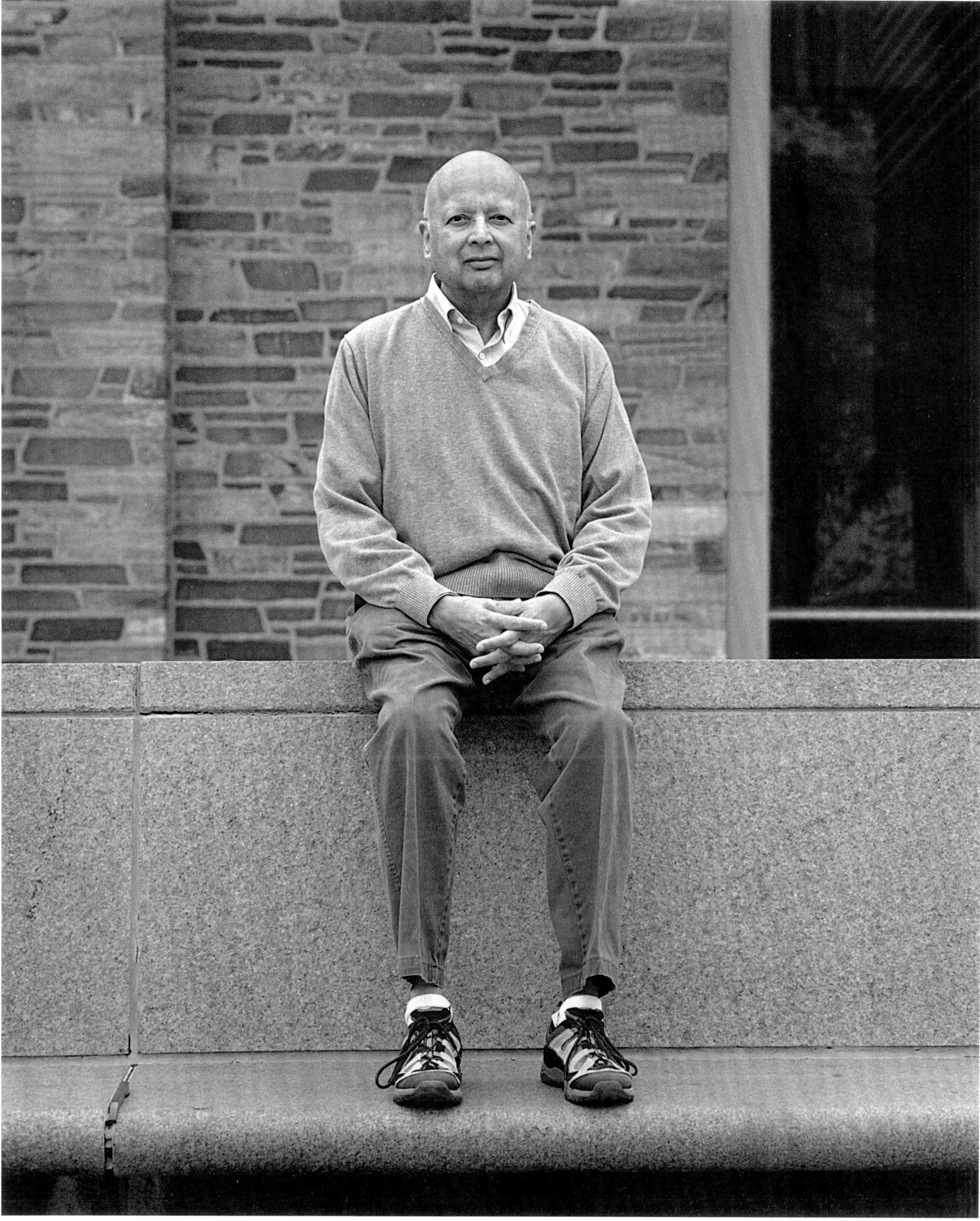

Dave Donaldson

"Are regional free trade agreements a good substitute for open trade in general?"

THE BASIC APPEAL of free trade is seductive. When two consenting adults want to engage in mutually beneficial exchange we tend to think that it would be good policy, even for a policymaker that cares more about one of the adults than the other, to simply get out of the way and let them do what they want. So why should it be any different when we talk about two *groups* of adults—that is, about countries? If people in one country don't want to trade with people in another country, they won't; if they do, they will, and we should let them do so.

Things get more complicated, however, when there are three countries. And unfortunately we can't think about regional trade agreements (RTAs) without embracing trilateral realities because an RTA is a partial, or preferential, trade agreement among a subset of the countries in the world. NAFTA, or its potential successor, USMCA, is a good example: for most products, US tariffs are lower on goods coming from NAFTA members (Canada and Mexico) than from non-NAFTA countries (such as China).

How is preferential free trade different from truly multilateral free trade? There are two complications. The first is the bystander effect. In general, we should expect that when two countries lower trade barriers between them (as the US and Mexico did under NAFTA) then left-out bystander countries (like China) will be harmed. The underlying economics of this is not that different from the playgrounds of my youth: When a new kid, Paul, turns up and Pete chooses to divert some of his scarce play time to Paul instead of me, who could blame me for wanting to take my ball and go home? This complication is plausibly important, but also fundamentally inevitable in a market economy. When video killed the radio star we relished the fact that consumers could now trade with better entertainment trading partners, even at the expense of the radio-star bystander. Three-member trading patterns are always going to harm a bystander—and such is life, both in childhood and adulthood.

The second complication is subtler—but, thankfully, this one doesn't seem to be particularly relevant in the real world. The usual argument is that trade agreements involve changes to taxes on trade (import tariffs), and hence also to the revenue that those taxes generate. When a country offers lower taxes to one country (say, Mexico) than it does to another country (China) there is the risk that it will end up foregoing tax revenue in order to help its consumers buy from the wrong supplier. In principle, this doesn't sound like a good idea for the RTA-joining country. But in realistic, modern scenarios this perverse outcome rarely occurs. This is partly because modern trade agreements are usually more about enhancing trade through the reduction in administrative and regulatory burdens, rather than by reducing tariffs, and so the reduction in such burdens is just a good idea in its own right (to paraphrase Joan Robinson, it makes no sense to drop rocks into our harbors just because other countries might have rocky coastlines). In addition, an undeniable feature of modern trade patterns is the importance of proximity—all else equal, two countries tend to halve their volume of trade for every doubling of the distance between them. In such a world, a country's neighbors are both the ones that a country should be trading with, and the ones it will usually sign a preferential—*regional*—trade agreement with. So the risk that a country ends up using taxes to pay consumers to make mistakes probably doesn't arise very often in practice.

All in all, I am optimistic about the role that RTAs play in advancing the cause of global free trade. Life would be simpler without the complex "spaghetti bowl" of such bilateral connections, in Jagdish Bhagwati's memorable image, but just like kids on the playground, consenting adults can probably handle the complexity.

DAVE DONALDSON is Professor at the Massachusetts Institute of Technology. He received the John Bates Clark Medal in 2017.

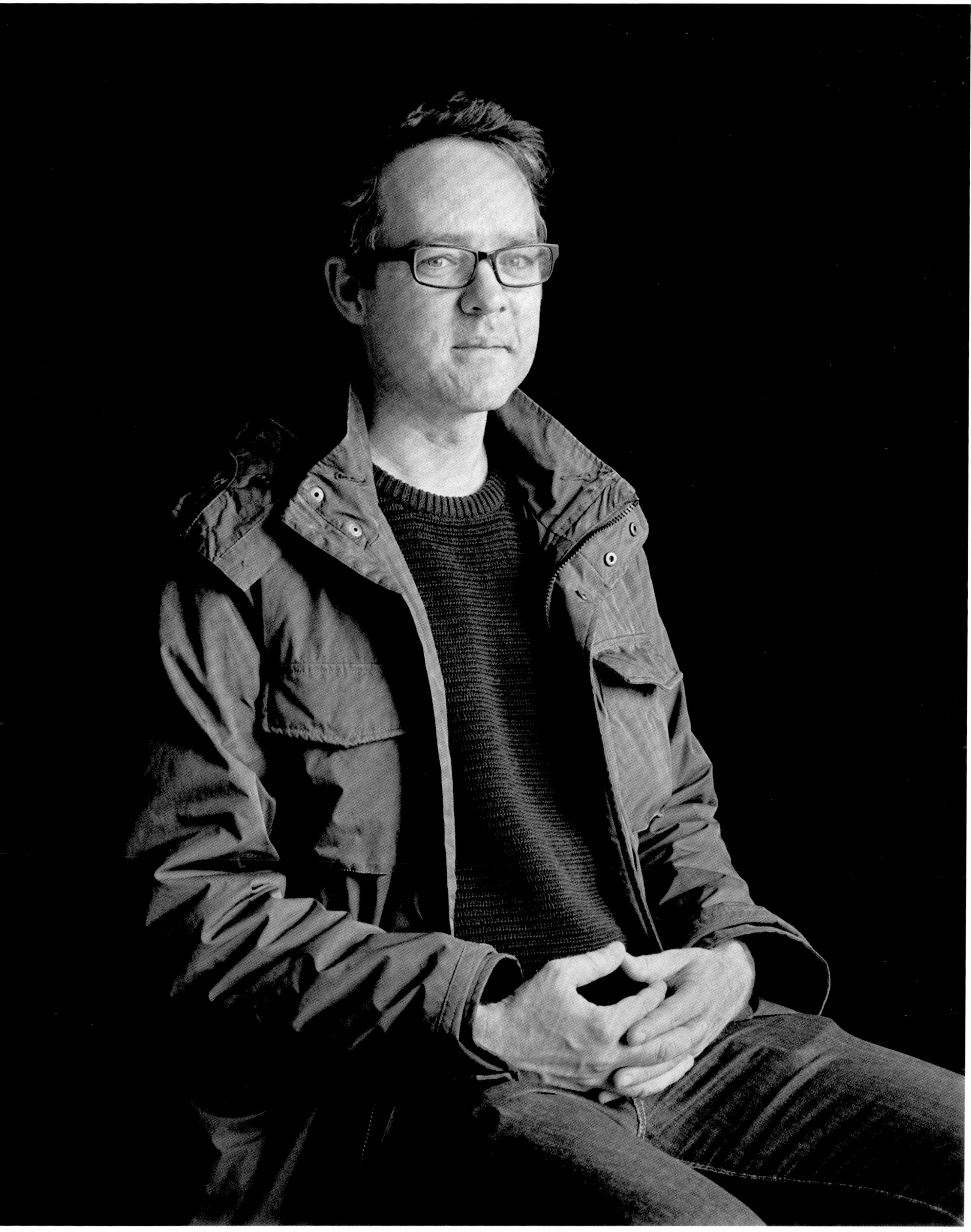

Mario Draghi

"If you could make one change in the way macroeconomic policy is made in the eurozone, what would it be?"

THE EUROZONE IS a group of countries that have decided to share a single currency, and therefore no longer have their own exchange rate or monetary policy. In this sense, being a member state of the eurozone is analogous to being a region in a large country. In all such monetary unions, successful macroeconomic stabilization depends on two factors.

The first is structural policies: the efficiency and integration of the financial sector, and the flexibility of product and labor markets. This determines how well changes in the common exchange rate and monetary policy feed through to the different parts of the union. It also helps countries adjust to shocks and share risks through market-based mechanisms.

Structural reforms in the financial sector and the real economy therefore create the first layer of adjustment in any well-functioning monetary union. In the past this has been lacking in the eurozone and justifies the ongoing drive for more convergence in this area, not least through completing a banking union.

That said, it is clear that structural policies are not sufficient. There is no monetary union where the common exchange rate and monetary policy is optimal for all regions at all points of the cycle. And market-based adjustment is slow moving and cannot cater to large shocks. This means other policy tools are needed for regional slumps, notably fiscal policy.

So the second factor for successful macroeconomic stabilization is how well fiscal policy is organized between the regions and the center. Broadly speaking, there are two models for allocating fiscal responsibilities that can prove effective.

The first is to have a large federal budget that complements the automatic stabilizers at the regional level and provides discretionary stimulus in difficult times. This is what we see in the US. Such a budget rests, however, on the presence of an ambitious political union that makes fiscal transfers democratically legitimate, which is not the case in the eurozone.

Thus the second model is to have decentralized fiscal policies mediated through large regional budgets, as we have in Europe. This can provide significant automatic stabilization so long as fiscal sustainability is maintained. But that depends on credible fiscal rules.

Ideally, such rules should work in both directions—they should be able to induce tightening and easing when needed—and they should facilitate coordination across countries in order to produce the right aggregate fiscal stance for the union as a whole. The eurozone's fiscal rules, however, have not so far conformed to this ideal.

This is in part a question of implementation: the rules have often not been applied consistently or transparently, and they have frequently been broken. But it is also a question of design.

The rules now function in only one direction—to contain deficits and debt levels—and there is no democratically agreed mechanism to force member states to coordinate their policies in line with the needs of the wider area. The result has been recurring pro-cyclicality in national budgets, and insufficient consideration of the aggregate fiscal stance.

These shortcomings have come at a cost: they constrained fiscal policy during the crisis and put the burden of stabilization almost entirely on monetary policy. That made the recession longer and more painful than it needed to be. And this is why addressing how fiscal policies are organized is, in my view, the priority for macroeconomic policy in the eurozone today.

What we need is a coordination mechanism that is politically accountable and accepted by our different democracies, that works for both individual countries and the union as whole, and that can produce appropriate national fiscal policies through booms and busts. This could be complemented by a euro area fiscal capacity of adequate size and design.

Such a mechanism could be designed in a way where all eurozone member states participate in the decision-making of a single institution and produce a common position based on the aggregate view. It could be led by a new eurozone finance minister with a truly eurozone perspective and the authority to enact it.

MARIO DRAGHI was President of the European Central Bank from 2011–2019 and Governor of the Bank of Italy from 2005–2011.

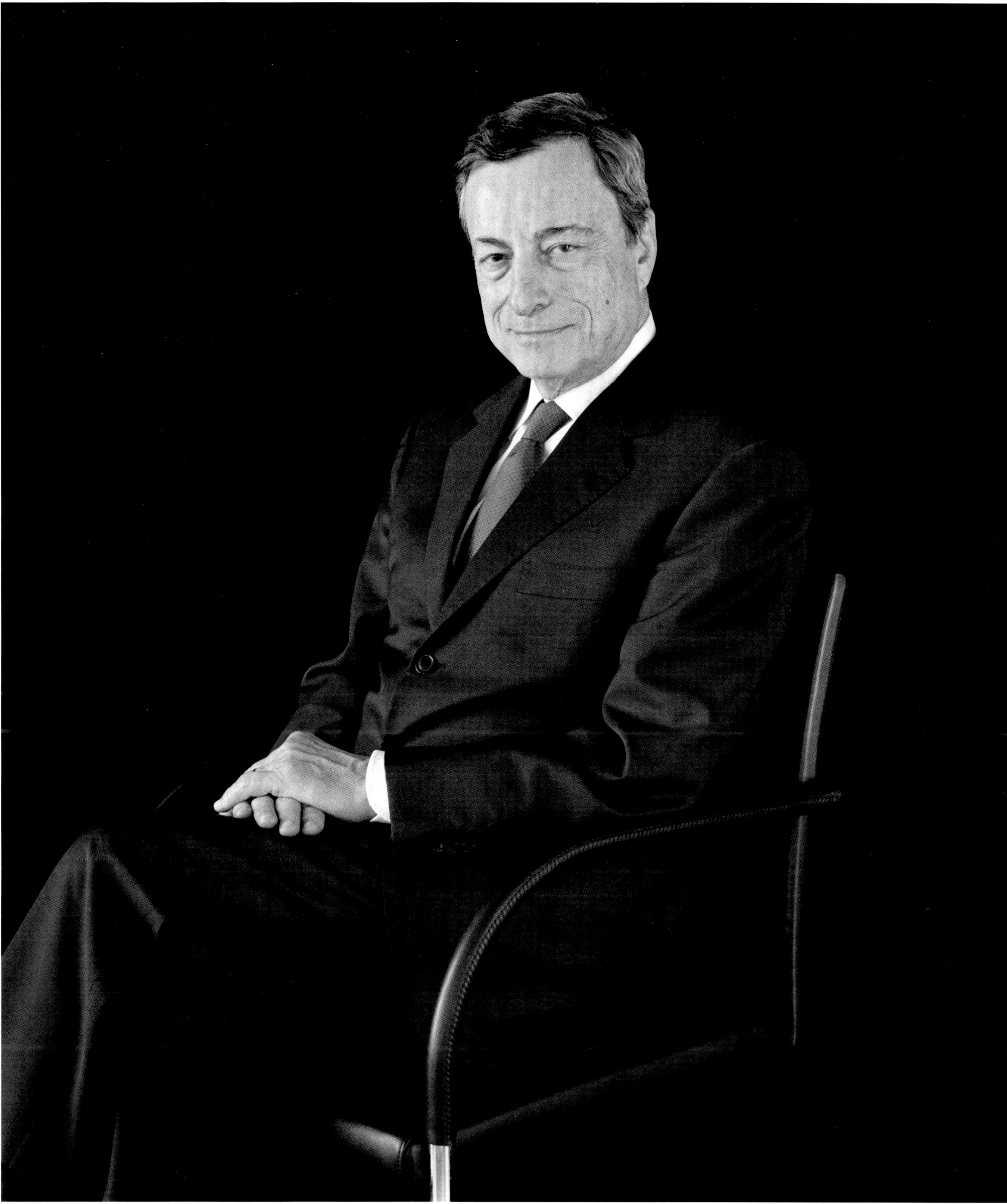

Esther Duflo

"What do you think rich countries could do, and actually might do, that would contribute most to the improvement of living conditions in poor countries?"

POVERTY IS FALLING, falling fast. The number of very poor people by the World Bank's definition was halved between 1990 and today. Most children are now in school and the risk of dying in childbirth is about half of what it was in 1990. But this has little or nothing to do with aid. The decline in poverty, for one, is driven in a large part by India and China, two countries that received almost no aid. Poverty went down because these countries grew fast, but also because they took steps to help their less well-off, and paid for it out of their own pockets.

Nevertheless, debating the role of aid in promoting or hindering development—"ruining development with easy money" is a phrase that one often hears—remains a popular pastime in the drawing rooms of the developed world. It matters little that in most poor countries aid is a very small part of the story. In 2015, the average inhabitant of a developing country received just 25 dollars of overseas development assistance. In the same year, the average inhabitant of a European country received 44 dollars in aid, which is just a little bit more than what the average African got (43 dollars, or 2.36 percent of income per capita). Moreover, a lot of what gets counted as aid is strategic or military assistance, and is in no way intended towards improving the average Joe's (or José or Jyoti's) life. Africa's biggest aid recipient for many years has been Egypt, which is one of the richer countries on the continent (though still very poor). This was its payback for signing the Camp David Agreement with Israel—a lot of it goes towards keeping Egypt's military establishment from getting into more mischief. And a lot of aid is like that, which is something that the opponents of aid often use to beat up on the whole idea, but that is either just confused (we don't have to call bribes "aid") or disingenuous. The truth is that there is too little aid to make much of a difference, one way or the other.

Perhaps instead of agonizing so much about their somewhat overblown generosity, citizens of rich countries should worry more about all the things rich countries do that directly hurt the poor. Climate change for one threatens poor countries much more than rich ones. Poor people in poor countries are more likely to die on hot days, and even if they don't, they are less productive at work, learn less at school, and live less pleasant lives. Anti-immigration policies, like the rather draconian ones popular these days, are another example. All the evidence suggests that relaxing immigration policies would not open the floodgates as many people fear—it turns out that most people seem to like it where they are—and would have very limited impact on wages. What it would do is offer opportunities to a relatively small number of highly energetic workers from the developing world to support their families better, and in the process, make the host countries more productive. The same holds true for trade policies. The European Union, for example, could stop using safety rules as a thinly disguised trade barrier. Opening their borders to goods coming from poor countries by actually honoring the WTO rules that they claim to abide by would help some of the world's poorest people, such as farmers in Africa, Asia, and the Caribbean.

Unfortunately, in the current climate it does not look like any of this is about to happen. In the meantime we might as well stop worrying about what rich countries can and cannot do for the poor and focus on what poor countries can do, and might actually do, to improve living conditions for themselves.

ESTHER DUFLO is Professor at the Massachusetts Institute of Technology. She received the John Bates Clark Medal in 2010.

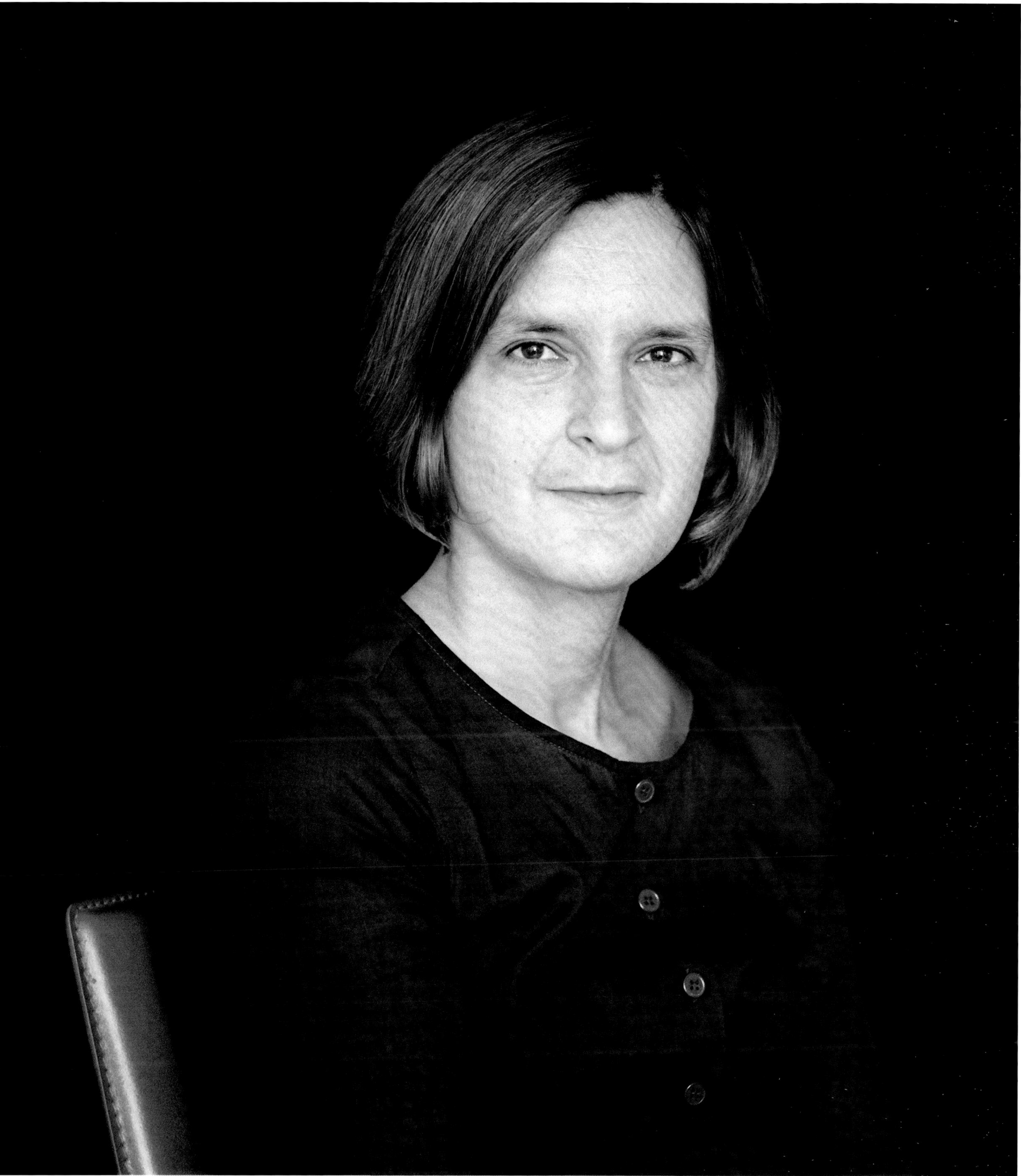

Robert Engle

"Do you think the current episode of stock market volatility has a particular message, or is it part of a larger pattern?"

I BELIEVE IT is human nature to think that the current volatility in financial markets is especially severe. I hear my students and audiences remark on high market volatility even in the midst of the long periods when volatility measures are very low. Fortunately, we can use quantitative measures to observe the swings of volatility from high peaks to low valleys and back.

Market watchers have been observing the extraordinarily low measures of volatility of many financial assets for almost a decade following the financial crisis of 2008. Is this a new regime and is it a result of government regulation and stabilization? In February 2018 we learned once again that when volatility is low it will eventually rise. After all, volatility reflects the new information that becomes available about the value of assets such as stocks, and this information flow fluctuates. In February of that year we learned that the Federal Reserve was determined to raise interest rates and the market would have to adjust. Later, the President threatened trade wars that would hurt many US companies. The volatility was a natural response to this new information. Similar shocks followed the British Brexit vote, the US withdrawal from the Trans-Pacific Partnership, the great financial crisis, and the European sovereign debt crisis. As a volatility observer, I can see how news impacts all of the countries in the world, much as a doctor looks at an EEG. This is a fascinating way to follow and interpret economic news.

There is, however, an interesting new development that has stimulated much discussion. Because volatility has become a traded asset, there is a possibility that trading has a direct effect on the volatility beyond the news itself. The most widely followed volatility measure is the VIX, and there are now highly liquid futures traded on the VIX. These futures are used as assets for exchange-traded funds (ETFs) and exchange-traded notes (ETNs) on volatility. A very popular ETN was XIV, which was an inverse exchange-traded note on short-term VIX futures. This made money as volatility fell and even when it was constant. However, it was always clear that if volatility were to rise, XIV could fall dramatically and, since an ETN cannot become negative, it could go to zero. An ETN is a debt contract and can therefore be called by the issuer. On February 5, 2018, XIV's value essentially dropped to zero and it was called by Credit Suisse, which terminated the ETN. I remember the expression: "Selling volatility is a profitable short career!" Did trading cause the volatility? I don't think so, but it may have made the rise more rapid than it would have been otherwise.

In spite of new technologies, stratospheric levels of asset prices, and changes in political and regulatory regimes, the rise and fall of volatility around a stable level remains one of the most extraordinary features of financial markets.

ROBERT ENGLE is Professor at the New York University Stern School of Business. He received the Nobel Prize for Economics in 2003.

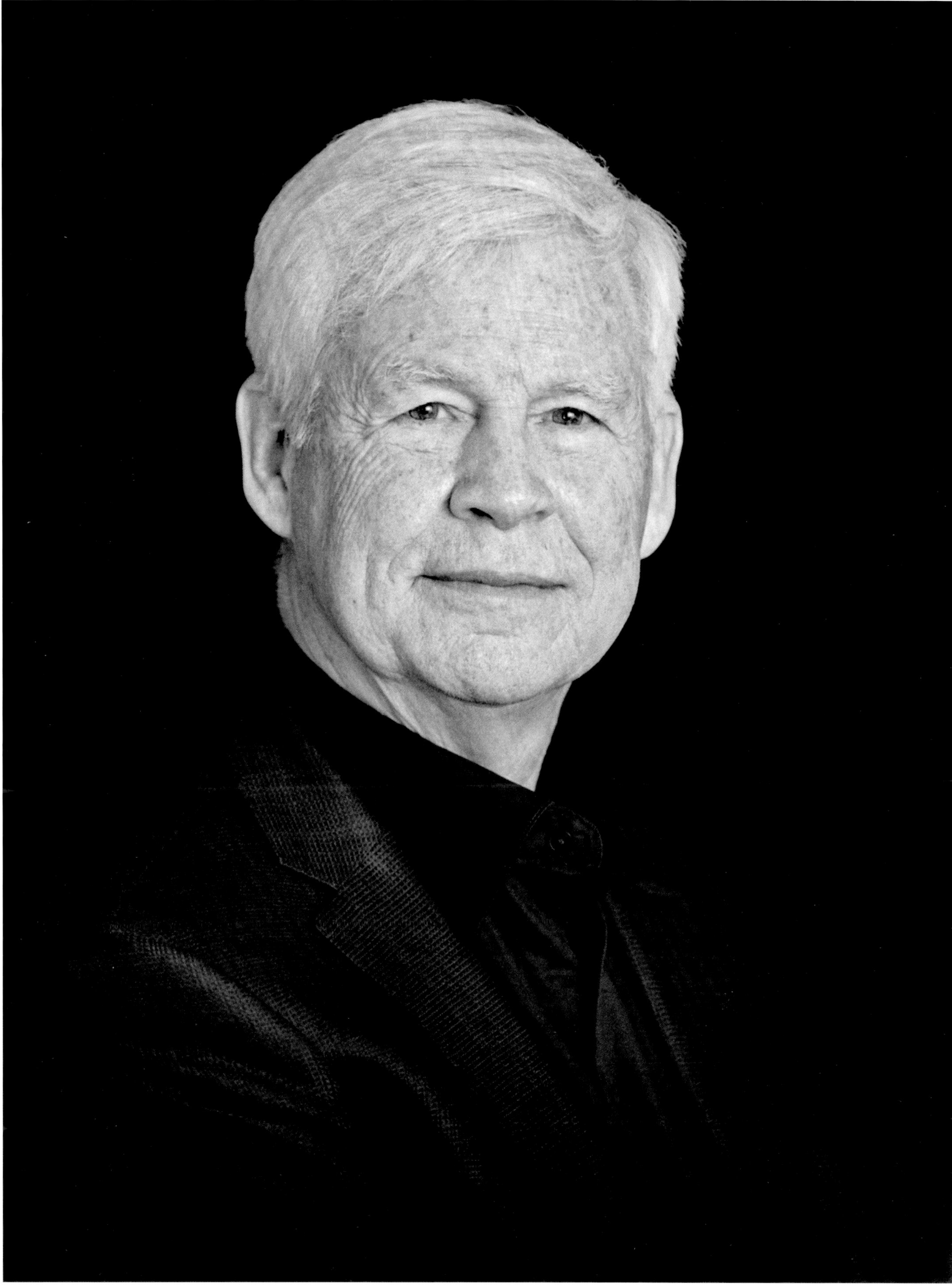

Emmanuel Farhi

"Is there a shortage of safe assets in world financial markets?"

ECONOMIC ACTORS NEED stores of value. Households save for retirement, for a rainy day, or to transmit wealth to their offspring. Corporations need to hold cash. Financial institutions need collateral. Central banks and sovereign wealth funds need to hold foreign assets. These stores of value come in many forms: cash, bank deposits, US government Treasury bills, and also corporate bonds, stocks, repurchase agreements, derivatives, or real assets such as real estate, land, gold, and others.

All stores of value are not created equal. They differ in their degree of liquidity and in their safety. These differences are reflected in their expected rates of return. The rate of return on the safest and most liquid assets is the interest rate. The rates of return on riskier and less liquid alternatives are higher because of risk and liquidity premia.

The past four decades have seen the materialization of a growing shortage of safe assets with demand outstripping supply. The telltale sign of this trend is that safe assets have been getting more expensive, as indicated by the 6 percent secular decline in US interest rates.

In comparison to their safe counterparts, riskier assets have become more expensive, since their rates of return have not declined nearly as much. For example, the average rate of return on capital in the US economy has remained remarkably stable throughout the period, even after excluding plausible estimates of monopoly profits. Similarly, most estimates indicate that the expected rate of return on US equities did not decline as much as interest rates, especially since the early 2000s. According to this view, stock market valuations are high because interest rates are so low, way into the future, and despite high-risk premia. It suggests that diagnoses of bubbles or over-valuations based on historical comparisons with higher-interest rate eras should be interpreted with caution. All in all, declining interest rates and a growing risk premium are the signature of an intensifying safe asset shortage.

There is a global market for safe assets, where global demand meets global supply. Together with the intensification of the global shortage of safe assets, important national and regional disparities have materialized. For example, the US is the main global supplier of safe assets. Its international liabilities are to a large extent debt security denominated in dollars, while its international assets are riskier and less liquid investments largely denominated in foreign currencies. The US is therefore acting as a "world banker" by performing risk and liquidity transformation on a global scale.

This situation is not without historical precedent. During the Bretton Woods era, the US was the main supplier of reserves assets. At that time, Robert Triffin exposed the fundamental instability of the US-centric Bretton Woods system and predicted its ultimate demise. He explained that the US was facing an insurmountable dilemma between satisfying the increasing demand for safe dollar assets and maintaining their safety. He prophesized that the US would stretch its position and expose itself to a confidence crisis that would force a devaluation of the dollar. Indeed, time proved Triffin right, and a full-blown run on the dollar brought the Bretton Woods system to its end in 1973.

It is tempting to dismiss this episode as a historical curiosity associated with the peculiarities of the gold-exchange standard with no current relevance. This dismissal is unwarranted because of a fundamental similarity between the earlier explicit commitment to a fixed dollar parity to gold, and today's implicit promise of stability and safety of the dollar in times of global crisis. In both cases, the edifice is built on confidence.

The current global safe asset shortage can be diagnosed as a new Triffin dilemma. In its new incarnation in a world of large private capital flows and exploding volumes of increasingly sophisticated financial transactions, it applies not just to the official sector, but also to the broader financial system. It is difficult to say for sure how long the global safe asset shortage will persist as a structural trend beyond its predictable cyclical fluctuations. As long as it does, it will keep acting as a powerful destabilizing force to global financial stability.

EMMANUEL FARHI is Professor at Harvard University.

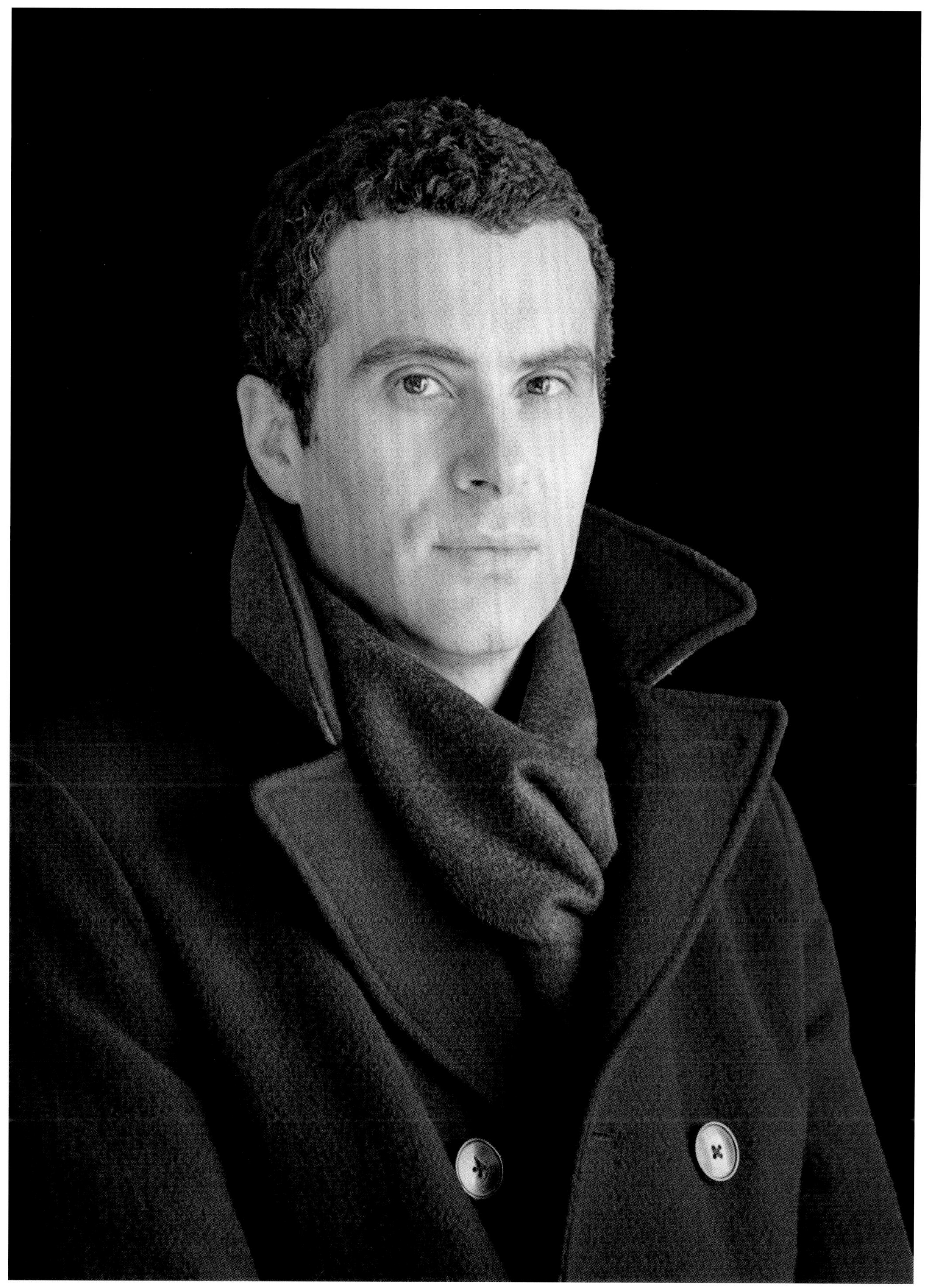

Martin Feldstein

"You started your long career by working on health care. What do you think is called for now?"

ALTHOUGH I NO longer do research on the economics of health care, I believe the two fundamental policy problems remain the same as they were fifty years ago when I was doing such research: providing access to affordable care and limiting the rise of health-care costs. The key to dealing with both problems is the design of appropriate health insurance.

Health care is different from other forms of household spending because of the risk of large and unpredictable medical bills. Individuals cannot know when they will be hit by a health problem that requires a large expenditure. That is why we have insurance to pay for health care but do not have insurance to pay for food or clothing.

Appropriate insurance should allow individuals to obtain needed care and should prevent the financial hardship that would result from health costs that are large relative to the household's income. Insurance should therefore focus on the risk of large expenditures.

Unfortunately, too much of current health insurance is designed to pay for small, recurring health expenses with little out-of-pocket cost to the patient at the time of care. When health expenses are paid by insurance, individuals will naturally want more care and more expensive care. Such comprehensive "first dollar" insurance coverage therefore pushes up the total cost of care, encouraging more tests and procedures and driving up the cost of each day of hospital care.

Well-designed health insurance policies would have large deductibles and copayments while limiting the maximum out-of-pocket cost to a reasonable fraction of each household's income. This principle should apply to the government programs of Medicare and Medicaid as well as to private health insurance.

The government health programs are the fastest growing part of the federal government budget. Members of Congress vote to provide comprehensive first dollar insurance so that voters will then recognize what their elected representatives have done for them.

The Medicare drug benefit is a good example of the way politics drives badly designed government health insurance. When the Medicare program was expanded to cover prescription drugs, economists advised that insurance should pay for prescription costs only after the individual had incurred a significant out-of-pocket cost for drugs, but should also protect individuals from very expensive drug costs. Members of Congress rejected this advice because it would have meant that most Medicare beneficiaries would not receive any benefit from the new program. The political compromise was to create what is known as the "donut hole": individuals receive Medicare drug insurance on small outlays (for which they really don't need insurance); that insurance stops at a certain level and then resumes once outlays exceed a new higher level. This strange compromise allowed Congress to give drug benefits to most Medicare beneficiaries, and then to save money by not insuring expenses in the uninsured gap (the "donut hole") while protecting individuals from the hardship that might result from very large drug bills.

Most individuals who do not have government health insurance obtain their insurance through plans paid in whole or in part by employers. Their demand for expensive first dollar coverage with small deductibles and low coinsurance is driven by the tax rule that makes employer payments for health insurance an untaxed fringe benefit. Individuals and employers recognize that paying \$10,000 for an employee's health insurance policy does not create any tax liability while the same \$10,000 in wages would typically lead to a combined income tax and payroll tax liability of about \$4,000. Exclusion of employer payments for health insurance from taxable income and from the payroll tax base reduces tax revenue by \$250 billion a year.

Changing the tax law to eliminate the current incentive for excessive first dollar insurance would refocus health insurance to protect individuals against very expensive illnesses that could otherwise prevent access to needed care or cause financial hardship. This change in the nature of private insurance might cause the political process to change the nature of Medicare and Medicaid to increase deductibles and coinsurance in line with private policies. These changes in the structure of private and public insurance would reduce the market pressures that cause the rapid rise of health-care costs.

So this is what I believe is called for now. Unfortunately, I am not optimistic that these changes will occur anytime soon.

MARTIN FELDSTEIN is Professor at Harvard University and President Emeritus of the National Bureau of Economic Research. He received the John Bates Clark Medal in 1977 and was Chair of the Council of Economic Advisors from 1982–1984.

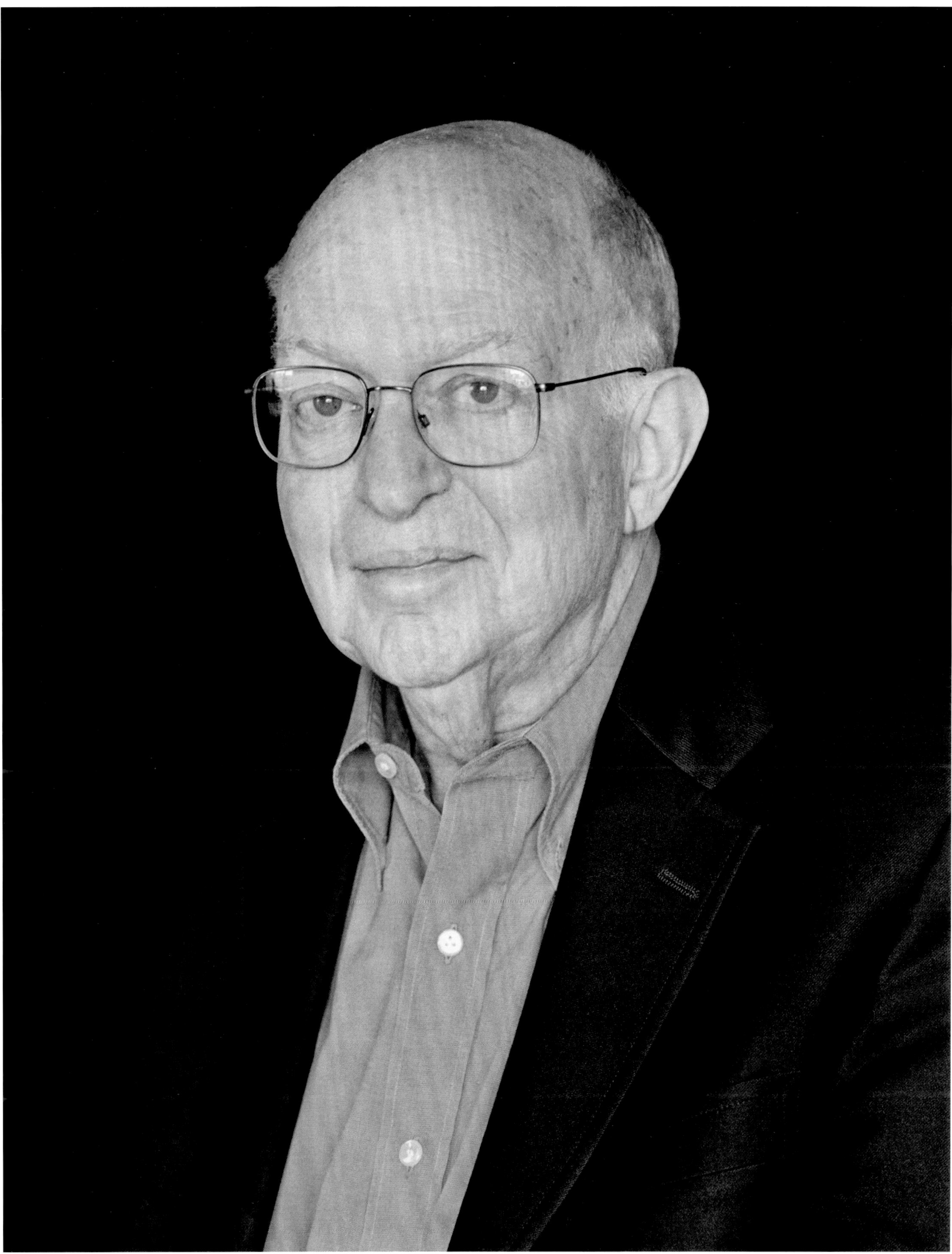

Amy Finkelstein

"What does the opioid crisis tell us about the United States' health-care system?"

THE OPIOID EPIDEMIC is considered the most severe drug crisis in United States history. Deaths from opioids have risen dramatically over the last two decades. In 2015, ninety Americans died daily from opioid overdose—more than ten times the rate of cocaine-related deaths at the height of the 1980s crack epidemic and more than double the current homicide rate.

A distinguishing feature of the opioid epidemic is the prominent role played by *legal* drugs: the Center for Disease Control (CDC) has estimated that about two-fifths of opioid deaths involved a prescription opioid, such as oxycodone or hydrocodone. Rising rates of opioid deaths have tended to closely track increases in rates of legal opioid prescriptions.

The opioid epidemic is also a distinctly US phenomenon. The US consumes nearly all (over 95 percent) of hydrocodone worldwide, and over 80 percent of oxycodone. The US accounts for about one-quarter of all opioid overdose deaths worldwide, despite having about 4 percent of the world's population.

As a distinctly American phenomenon with a direct link to the health-care sector via legal prescriptions, it is only natural to ask a health economist what we can learn from the opioid crisis about the US health-care system. And as an academic health economist, it is only natural for me to reply: it's a bit of a puzzle . . . but then go on to speculate about what I suspect are two likely contributing factors.

First, the role that pharmaceutical companies play in the US is very different from most other countries. Purdue Pharmaceuticals—one of the leading producers of prescription opioids in the US—actively promoted and marketed the efficacy and alleged safety of opioids for treating chronic pain to the academic medical community, physicians, and patients in the US.

It is natural for drug companies to focus on the US market: prescription drug prices—and hence profits—are substantially higher in the US than in other countries. Restrictions on pharmaceutical companies' marketing activities are also considerably more lax in the United States; for example, only one other country besides the US (New Zealand) allows direct to consumer advertising (DTCA) which enables pharmaceutical companies to directly promote their prescription products to potential patients via popular media. The pharmaceutical industry has tried unsuccessfully to overturn bans against DTCA in Canada and the EU.

Second, the United States has historically been more reluctant than other Organization for Economic Cooperation and Development (OECD) countries to limit physician autonomy. This has made it harder to curtail, let alone reverse, the opioid crisis once it began. It is now clear that the risks of prescribing opioids for chronic non-cancer pain are far higher than was understood in the 1990s when pain became the "fifth vital sign." A natural policy would be to limit physicians' ability to issue such prescriptions. Yet CDC guidelines recommending that physicians start patients with lower dosages have been met with pushback from the American Medical Association. By contrast, curtailment of physician autonomy is much more common in the rest of the OECD, where governments often decide what treatments are eligible for reimbursement for which patients.

Having now used up the proverbial two hands of the economist, let me close by noting that in the last few years there have been signs of the opioid crisis starting to spread to other countries, with opioid deaths on the rise in, for example, Canada and the UK. I have long conjectured that high pharmaceutical prices in the US encourage the development of new drugs that eventually spread to other countries, so that the US is in effect subsidizing technological advances in medicine for the rest of the world. Indeed, many new medical practices are first adopted in the US and then gradually spread across the OECD. Unfortunately, it appears that this pattern may also hold for opioid use.

AMY FINKELSTEIN is Professor at the Massachusetts Institute of Technology. She received the John Bates Clark Medal in 2012.

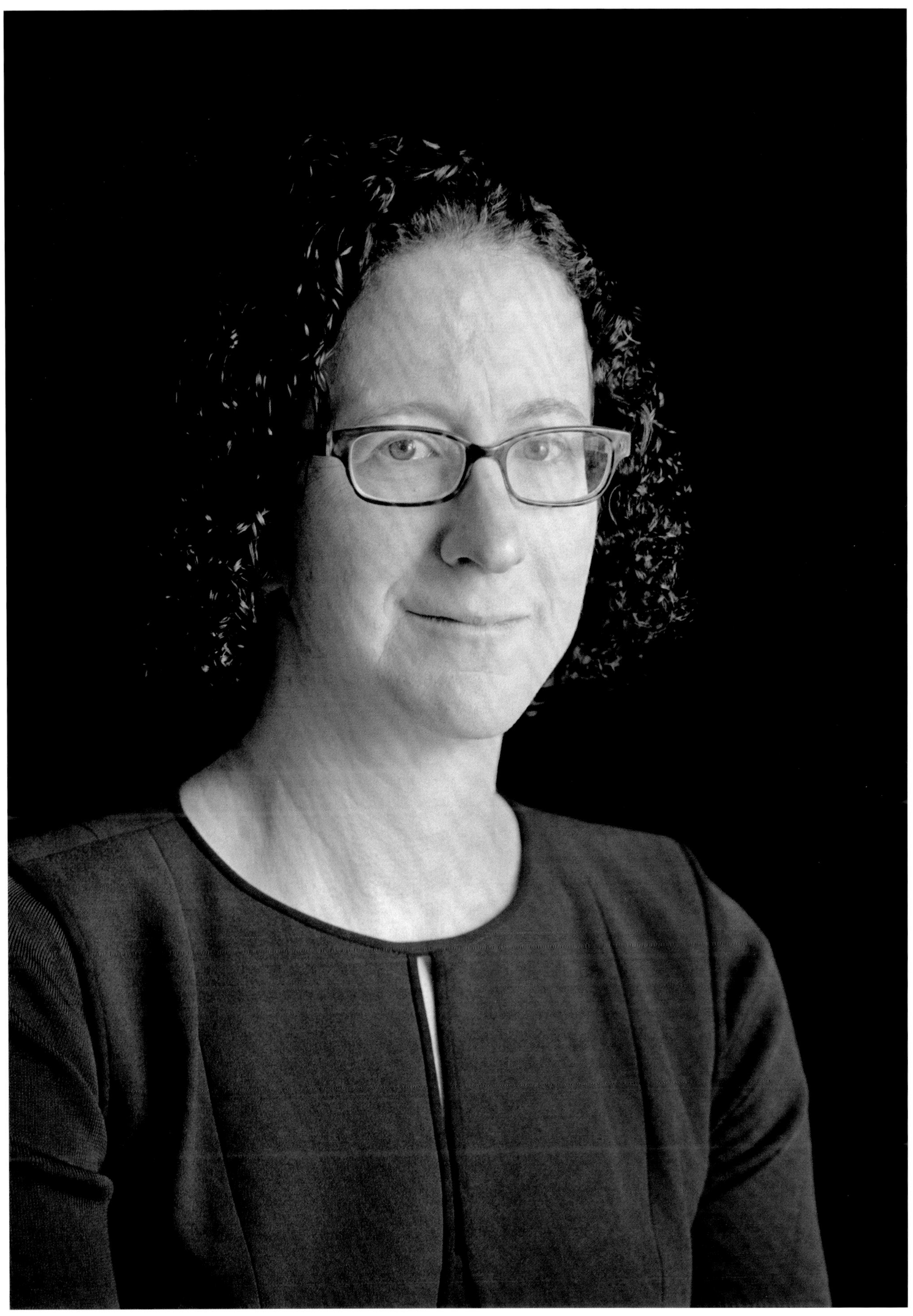

Stanley Fischer

"Do you think it would be a good idea to raise the near-universal target rate of inflation to something higher than 2 percent a year?"

EVERY YEAR SINCE 2012, the Fed has stated that its target inflation rate is 2 percent. This is also the target rate in many economically advanced economies. Two percent has generally gained credibility, both as each country's long-run inflation target, and as the annual inflation rate expected ten years from now. This is no small achievement; indeed it could be a credible definition of monetary stability. Nonetheless, several leading economists, among them my friend and coauthor, Olivier Blanchard, have suggested that the target inflation rate be raised to 4 percent.

The approach to monetary policy that includes a defined target inflation rate specified for or by the central bank became accepted mostly during the 1990s and the first decade of this century. The 2 percent target rate was based on an analysis of the costs and benefits of inflation. That research showed that despite some benefits of low positive inflation, higher inflation is a source of inefficiency, and that inflation should be kept low, close to 2 percent.

The link between the inflation target and the real economy comes from the fundamental distinction between the *nominal* and the *real* interest rate. The *nominal interest rate* is the rate of interest expressed in dollar terms: if the interest rate is 3 percent, a borrower has to pay back 3 percent more per annum in dollars than she was lent. The *real interest rate* is the percentage amount that has to be repaid, measured in terms of its purchasing power, its *real value*.

The difference between the nominal and the real interest rate is the inflation rate: the real interest rate (r^*) is equal to the nominal interest rate minus the inflation rate. For example, if the nominal interest rate is 3 percent, and the inflation rate is 2 percent, the *real* interest rate is 1 percent. The real interest rate is positive in this case. But if the inflation rate is 5 percent, and the nominal interest rate is 3 percent, the person receiving the 3 percent interest is *losing* 2 percent in real terms. The real interest rate in this case is *minus* 2 percent.

At any one time, there is a real interest rate that is consistent with the full employment of labor. Indeed, r^* may be negative; that is, it may take a negative real interest rate to generate sufficient aggregate demand to ensure full employment. If r^* is negative, say at $-x$ percent, then for the nominal interest rate to be positive, the inflation target has to be at least x.

The argument for a higher inflation target starts from the existing 2 percent target. But it also takes into account the fact that real interest rates were negative during the Global Financial Crisis (GFC), and that—as argued by proponents of the secular stagnation hypothesis, such as Larry Summers—they could be even lower in future.

Several countries with fiscally responsible reputations, among them Switzerland and Sweden, set short-term nominal rates at negative values during the GFC but did not change their target inflation rates. However, central banks are often wary of negative nominal interest rates, whether out of fear of being regarded as irresponsible or merely strange. Thus, the central bank would likely not implement a real interest rate below −2 percent.

The argument for a higher inflation target is that in the event of a recession, with r^* below −2 percent, a central bank with an inflation target of 2 percent and a refusal to implement a negative nominal interest rate, cannot cut the interest rate to a level that would be at or below −2 percent; this limits the incentives that it can provide in the form of a very low interest rate to encourage investment and thus aggregate demand. But if the target inflation rate were 4 percent, the central bank could lend money at a real rate equal to or below r^*, and thus provide an interest rate incentive that would encourage economic activity. Inflation, however, is not neutral, and higher inflation typically reduces the efficiency of the market economy.

We would need to compare the performance of economies operating at an average inflation rate of 2 percent and 4 percent, respectively, to ascertain which inflation target is better. To do so, we also need to attribute a cost—perhaps a prestige or credibility cost—to the frequency with which the nominal interest rate becomes negative. It will be negative more frequently with a 2 percent rather than a 4 percent inflation rate.

It will require more research to determine whether it is preferable for an economy to operate with a 2 percent or 4 percent inflation rate. But because the costs of higher inflation are highly nonlinear, and because some economies have learned to live with negative nominal interest rates, my money is on 2 percent rather than a higher inflation target.

STANLEY FISCHER was Vice Chair of the Federal Reserve from 2014–2017, Governor of the Bank of Israel from 2005–2013, and First Deputy Managing Director of the IMF from 1994–2001.

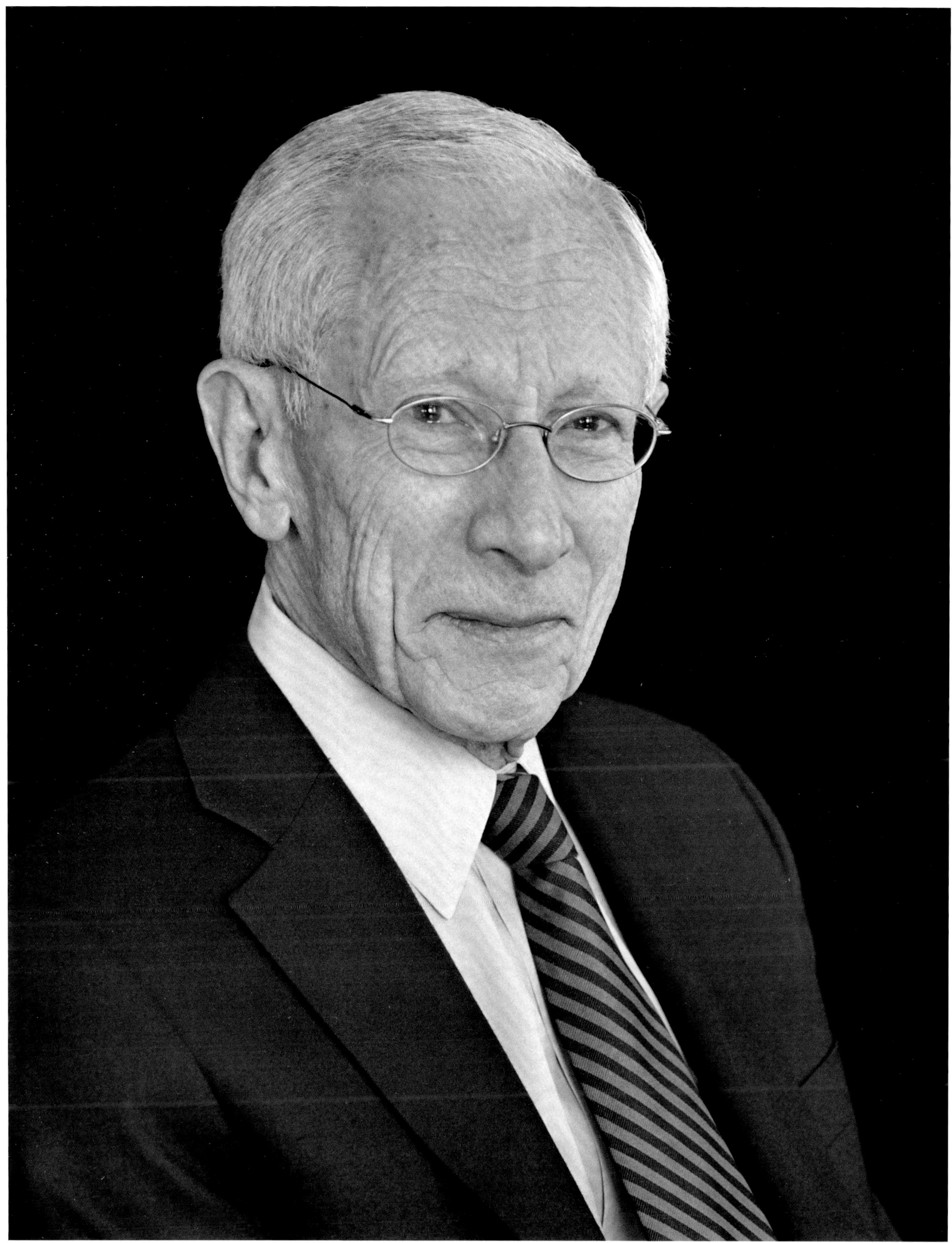

Claudia Goldin

"How has the employment life cycle of women been changing? And what do you think has been driving this change?"

WOMEN'S INCREASED INVOLVEMENT in the economy as paid workers has been the most important change in labor markets during the past century or more. The significance is not just for the United States, but for just about anywhere in the world. I say, "just about," because in the most undeveloped parts of the globe most people work, often in agriculture, at small family businesses, or in their homes.

The real gains to women's employment arise when markets expand and people are hired by others to work away from their homes and farms and for considerably higher wages. The benefits also appear when the women who work are older, married, and with children because they are the biggest share of society. Young, single women almost always work. Just how much has employment increased for women in a country like the US, and why did it increase when it did?

Just 5 percent of married women worked for pay outside their homes around 1900. Most would not be employed as long as they remained married. Fast forward more than a hundred years to today when almost all women are employed at some time during their married lives, and about 75 percent are employed when they are around 35 years old. We are considerably richer now than we were in 1900 (about nine to ten times on a per capita basis, and that doesn't include increased lifespans). The value of the additional income from a working wife would have been considerable in 1900. But married women's employment, outside agriculture, was very low. Why weren't women working then and what accounts for the expansion of their employment?

There are some obvious explanations. The home is like a small factory. Much needs to be done, and the division of labor operates there just as it does in actual factories. As labor-saving devices (think washing machines, microwave ovens), together with electricity, running water, and sanitary systems spread, women were freed from domestic labor. The fertility rate matters as well, and as it fell, women have spent less time pregnant, nursing, and caring for the young ones. Fine and good. But this explanation goes just so far. It needs more.

The parts that are lacking are what economists call the "income" and the "substitution" effects. As general levels of income rise, because of technological changes throughout the economy, two effects occur. The first is that the value of time, as measured by the wage per hour, rises for all on average. With higher wages, the incentive is to work more hours and do less of other things. However, the increase in income has an opposing effect, particularly on women. With higher levels of income, husbands would want to shield their wives from hard, dirty, and dangerous work. Most jobs, until some time in the early 20th century, would have been viewed in that manner.

But with modern economic growth, employment shifted from the shop floor to the office, from farmers to professionals, from mines to desks. The returns to education rose. A working wife no longer made a statement about the ability of her husband to provide for her. Work is not just a way to earn a living, but is also a part of an individual's identity and companionship. Increased income has far less of a negative impact on women's work; an increase in her wages has more of a positive effect. The "income effect" declines and the "substitution effect" rises.

Women's labor force participation is, therefore, U-shaped over the course of economic development. In its earliest stages, everyone works at home and on the farm, as they do today in the less developed parts of the world. As markets expand, agriculture and small family businesses shrink. Men work in manufacturing firms and women remain in their homes. In consequence, women's employment, appropriately measured, declines. But as development proceeds, more "nice" jobs emerge in the white-collar sectors, "brain work" is valued more than "brawn work," and women's employment responds positively to the increase in real wages in the market economy. Their education increases and their employment increases.

There is much more to the grand story, including the role of social norms and public policies regarding family leave and childcare. But a good outline of the broad sweep of history of women's employment is to begin with a *U*.

CLAUDIA GOLDIN is Professor at Harvard University.

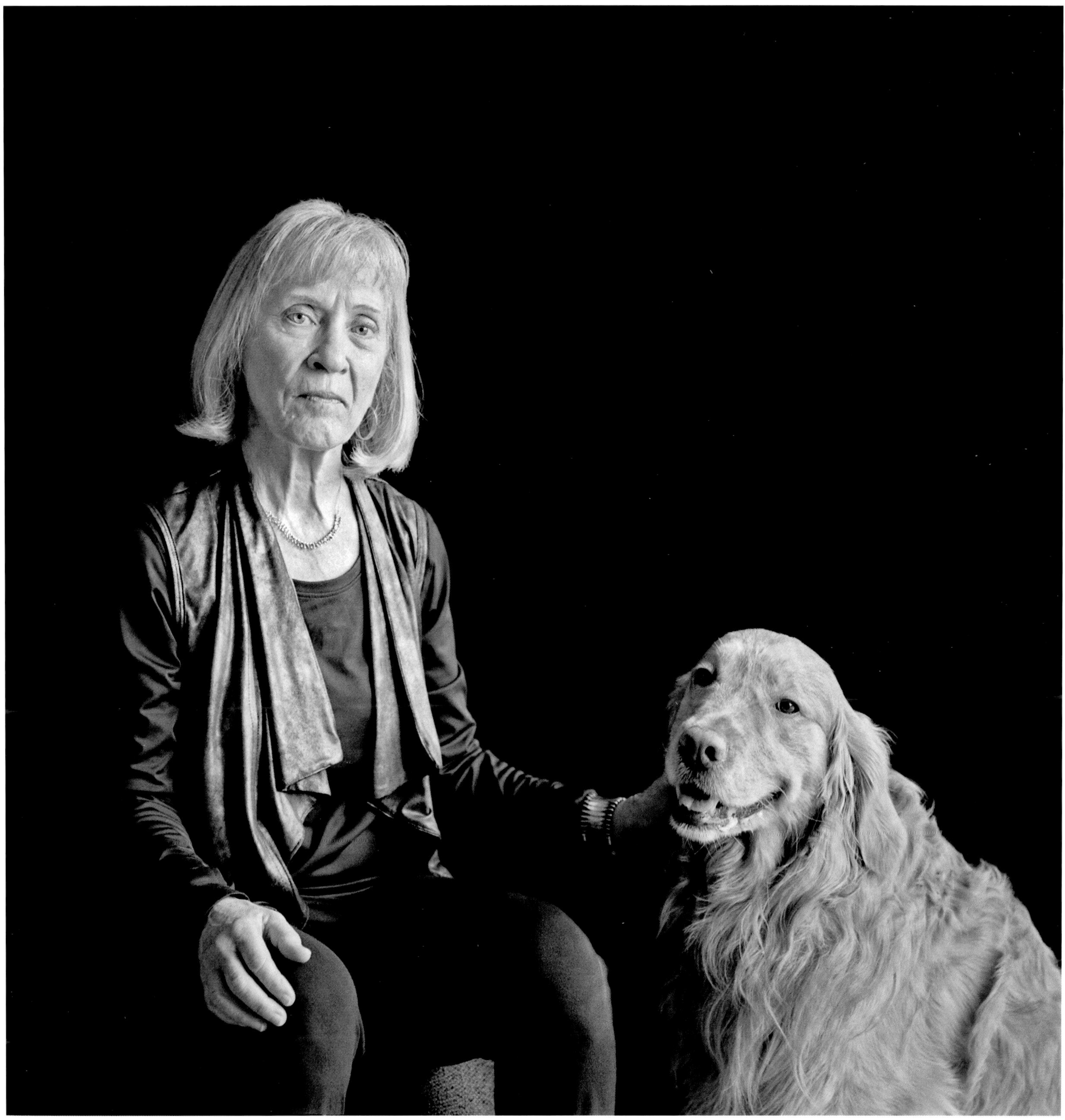

Austan Goolsbee

"Would a reduction in the corporate tax rate induce a large increase in business capital investment?"

IT'S A CLASSIC question of public finance and often fought out in the political arena, too. I think the answer for a large, domestically dominant economy like the United States is "probably not a large one, no."

At first glance, raising after-tax profits from capital seems like it should lead businesses to want more capital, so investment should rise.

Yet, investment did not boom in the US in recent decades, even as corporate profits reached their all-time high as a share of GDP and corporate taxes paid hit their all-time low; and more detailed microeconomic research has tended to find relatively small effects of prices (of which taxes are one component) on the amount of investment. Some have gone so far as to say that investment mostly just follows demand or whether companies can get credit and that marginal incentives are irrelevant. Others, not willing to go that far, observe that many complications in the real world can explain why corporate rates may have modest impacts.

First, the sum total of past investments (termed by the economists as the "capital stock") is large compared to the amount that companies will invest this year. So cutting the corporate tax rate, which benefits all of those investments, will mostly give a big windfall to the investments that companies already made rather than incentives for new purchases. On strictly bang-for-the-buck terms, most economists recognize that it's better to give incentives for new investment rather than to cut the corporate rate on everything, and that can explain why corporate rate cuts don't matter so much.

Second, many complications in the tax code reduce the impact of corporate rates on investment. Take one well-documented example: if a company finances its investment out of debt and the interest on the debt is fully deductible, the corporate rate becomes largely irrelevant. Indeed, if the tax code subsidizes investment AND allows full deductions of interest payments, it can easily create a negative tax rate on capital investment (in which case, cutting corporate rates would actually have a reverse impact).

Third, the majority of business income in the US goes to companies that do not have to pay corporate income taxes at all because they aren't traditional corporations, such as partnerships, LLCs, S corps, and legal forms of organizations that the law calls "pass-throughs," where the owners treat corporate income as personal income and avoid corporate taxation entirely. These types of companies have grown so pervasive that they now account for more than 50 percent of business income. Investment doesn't increase much from cutting rates that companies don't pay.

Finally, policymakers have mostly proven rather terrible at timing rate cuts to encourage investment. They try to do so when investment is low but by the time their actions come online, conditions have often changed. If policymakers end up cutting corporate taxes at times when investment is already high and capital goods makers have capacity constraints, the tax cuts may end up more inflationary than investment generating.

The overall answer to the question is probably different for small open economies where capital is more sensitive to rates (which itself probably explains why corporate rates in these small economies tend to be much lower). As larger economies become more internationally oriented and as multinationals grow in importance, the one kind of capital decision where corporate rates could have a large impact is where companies locate their profits and label where their activity is located. Multinationals have developed deep expertise at shifting their profits into tax havens and their expenses into high tax places (where they can be deducted) or at moving their headquarters or intellectual property in order to qualify for lower rates. Cutting corporate tax rates could have a large impact on that sort of behavior but is probably not what normally comes to mind as the investment response to corporate rates.

AUSTAN GOOLSBEE is Professor at the University of Chicago Booth School of Business. He was Chair of the Council of Economic Advisers from 2010–2011.

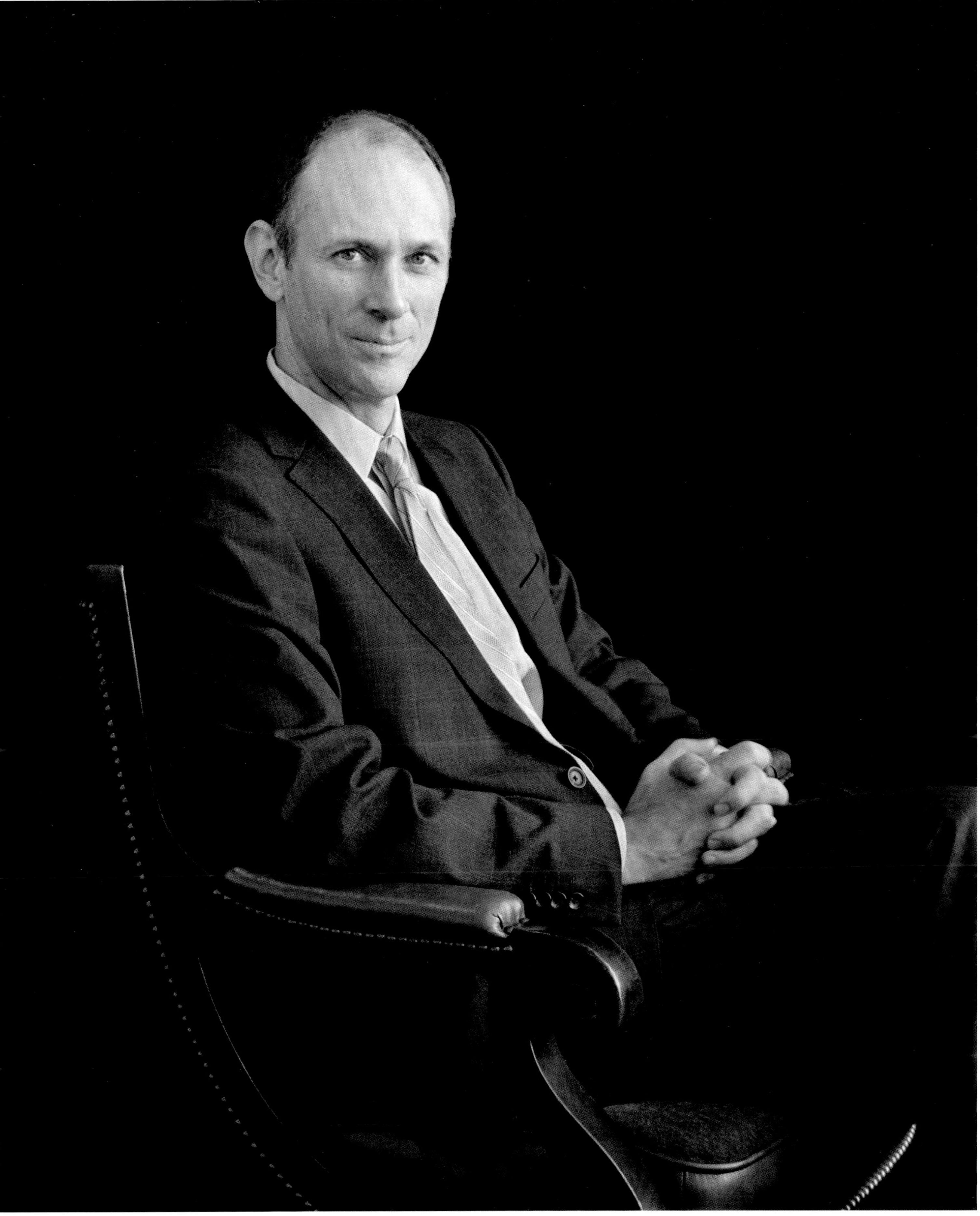

Gita Gopinath

"What does your research say about the role of the US dollar in international trade? How does this change our understanding of how exchange rate fluctuations impact inflation and global trade?"

WE DOCUMENT THAT a large share of world trade is invoiced in dollars even when the US is on neither side of the trade transaction. Specifically, the dollar's share as an invoicing currency is 3.1 times its share in world exports and 4.7 times its share in world imports. To highlight how special the role of the dollar is it is useful to contrast this with the share of the other major global currency, the euro, in trade. The euro's share as an invoicing currency in world trade is around 1.2 times the share of euro-country exports and imports in world trade. In other words, while some non-euro countries invoice exports in euros, this is of a much smaller magnitude than the use of dollars. The bottom line is that most countries, including developed countries, rely heavily on dollar invoicing when they trade internationally.

As a consequence, the strength of the US dollar is a key predictor of rest-of-world aggregate trade volume and consumer/producer price inflation. For several countries, the value of the country's currency relative to the dollar has greater consequences for its trade with countries that are not the US, as compared to its bilateral exchange rate with its trading partner; for example, the rupee price and volume of India's imports from China depends more on the rupee-dollar exchange rate than the rupee-yuan exchange rate. These findings run counter to the standard assumptions made in the literature, where it is assumed that a country's exchange rate is as important as its role in global trade. What my coauthors and I show is that the dollar has a special role in global trade that far exceeds its share in world trade. Specifically, a 1 percent US dollar appreciation against all other currencies in the world predicts a 0.6 percent decline within a year in the volume of total trade between countries in the rest of the world, controlling for the global business cycle.

These findings significantly alter our understanding of interdependence across countries. It alters the answers to questions such as: How do exchange rate fluctuations impact inflation and trade? How does monetary policy in the US transmit to the rest of the world? As regards inflation, a good rule of thumb for a country's inflation sensitivity to exchange rate fluctuations is the fraction of its imports invoiced in a foreign currency. The greater the fraction of a country's imports invoiced in a foreign currency, the greater its inflation sensitivity to exchange rate fluctuations up to a horizon of two years. For the US, with 93 percent of its imports invoiced in dollars, the consequences of exchange rate fluctuations are far more muted than for a country like India that has 97 percent of its imports invoiced in foreign currency (mainly dollars). Dollar dominance in international trade implies that pass-through into inflation is relatively weak for the US and much stronger for the rest of the world, especially developing countries. As regards export competitiveness, when a country's currency depreciates the expectation is that it will stimulate demand for the country's products as it lowers the relative price of its goods in world markets. This is unlikely to be the case for many countries that rely on foreign currency invoicing for their exports. Lastly, there are asymmetries in monetary policy spillovers. A monetary policy tightening in the US that is associated with a dollar appreciation generates inflationary pressures in countries that import primarily in dollar-invoiced prices and this induces these countries to tighten monetary policy to address inflationary concerns. On the other hand, monetary tightening in the rest of the world has a small impact on US inflation and therefore triggers almost no response from the US central bank.

GITA GOPINATH is Chief Economist at the International Monetary Fund and Professor at Harvard University.

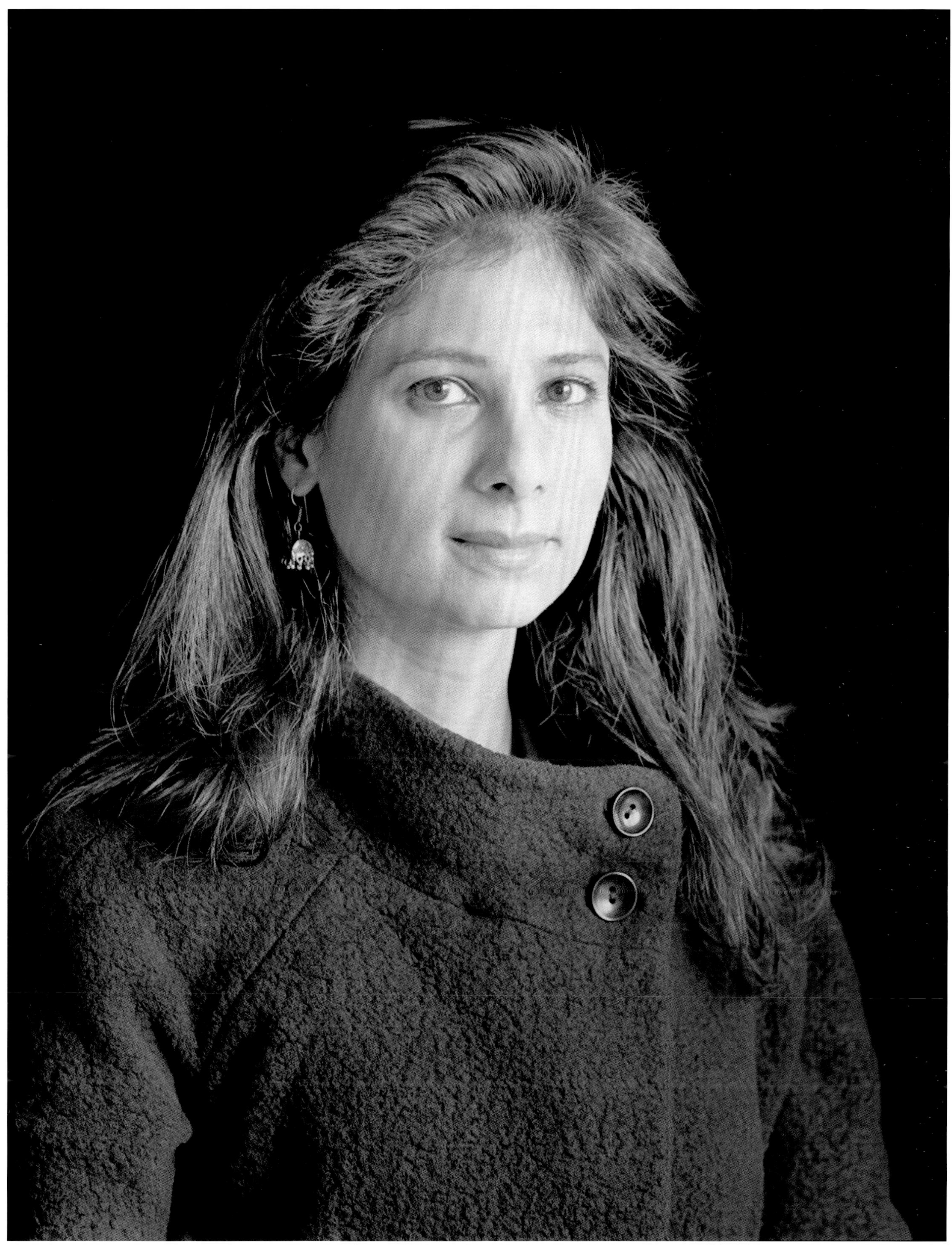

Robert Gordon

"Is the slowdown in productivity growth good news for employment?"

GROWTH ECONOMISTS WOULD scoff at the idea that there is a negative relationship between productivity and employment growth. After all, the long-run evolution of productivity growth depends on innovation, education, and capital deepening in the form of more machines per worker. In contrast, in the long run, employment growth depends on growth in the labor force, because in the long run the unemployment rate is roughly constant, about 4 percent in 1955 and again in 1968, 2000, and 2017. Long-run growth of the labor force has depended on demographic trends that have little or nothing to do with productivity growth, particularly the fertility of the baby-boom generation, the set of social changes that brought women into the labor force in the 1970s and 1980s, and the current reduction in labor-force participation caused by the retirement of the baby-boomers.

The question addressed here is whether there is a negative causal relationship between productivity growth and employment growth. History provides several examples of the opposite causation, namely of employment growth affecting productivity growth. A common explanation of slow productivity growth in the 1970s and 1980s was the inexperience of the teenage baby-boomers and the newly arrived female workforce. Another period when employment negatively affected productivity occurred during the global financial crisis of 2009, when the fact that employment dropped faster than output led to a temporary bubble in productivity growth. Christina Romer, chair of Obama's Council of Economic Advisers during that period, referred to this phenomenon as "excess layoffs" that by definition created "excess short-run productivity growth."

These episodes suggest that there can be a negative feedback from employment growth to productivity growth. What about the reverse? By definition output growth is equal to the growth of output per hour plus the growth of hours of work. From 2010 to 2017 output growth was weak and so was productivity growth, which grew at a meager rate of only 0.6 percent per year from 2010 to 2017. Assuming that the weak 2.2 percent annual growth of output during this interval was entirely caused by demand factors like the government spending sequester and weak investment, then, as an arithmetic fact, slow productivity growth must have made possible the robust growth in hours of work, which amounted to roughly 1.6 percent per year during this 2010–2017 interval.

A primary issue facing the US economy in 2019–2020 is how the demand stimuli of tax cuts, increased government spending, and rising stock market valuations will work themselves out on the supply side. The tightness of labor markets, with the lowest unemployment rate since the late 1960s, suggests that it will be difficult to raise hours of work sufficiently to meet the increased demand. Will productivity growth have another revival like that in the 1990s, when unemployment was also low? For the optimistic forecasts of demand growth to come true, productivity growth must rise above the meager 0.6 percent achieved in 2010–2017. Will higher investment, stimulated in part by the corporate tax reductions, join together with labor shortages to provide the productivity boost the economy needs to keep moving ahead?

ROBERT GORDON is Professor at Northwestern University.

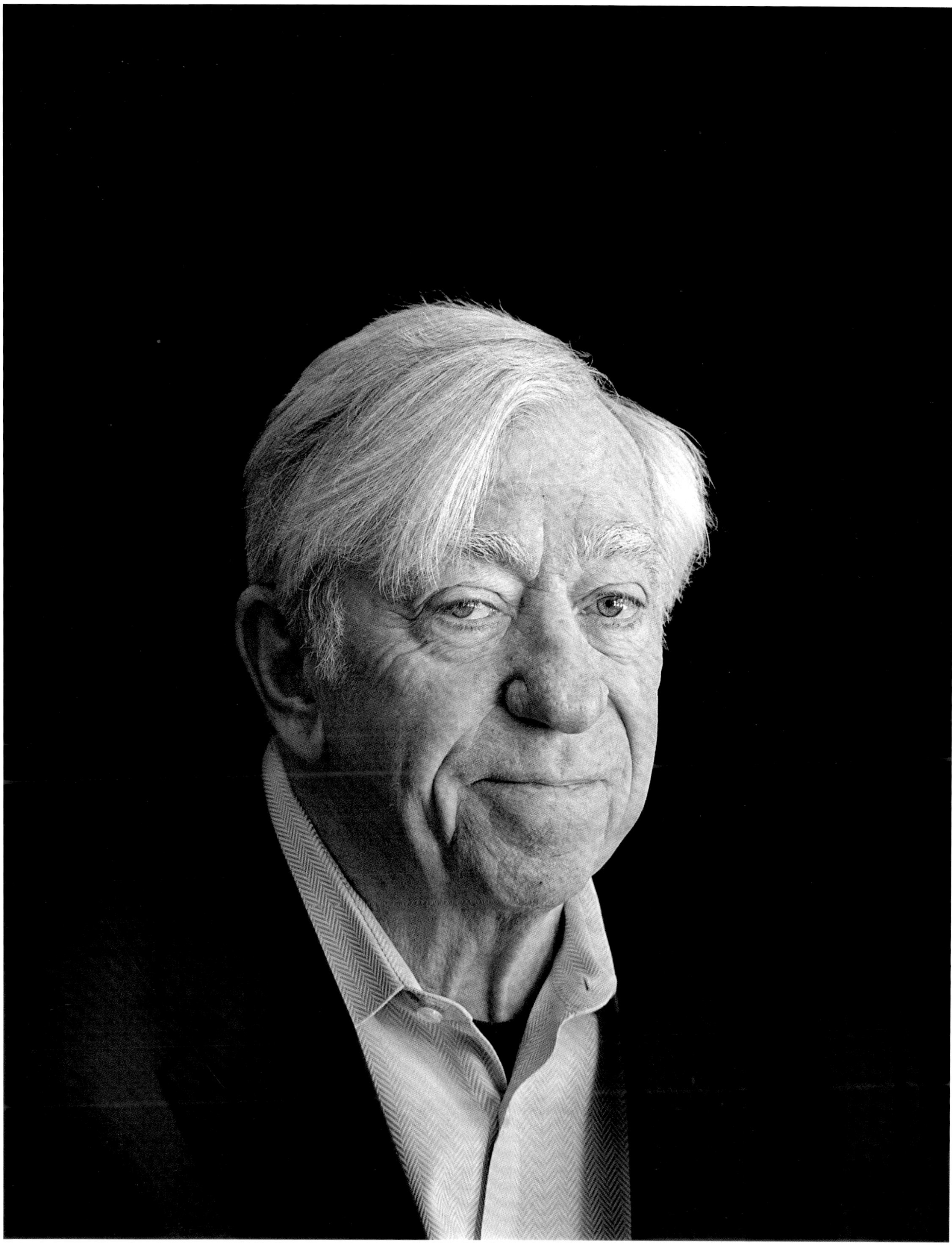

Alan Greenspan

"Many observers expect a fairly long period of historically low interest rates. How would you interpret that prospect?"

TIME PREFERENCE IS the self-evident propensity to value more highly a claim to an asset today than a claim to that same asset at some fixed time in the future. A promise delivered tomorrow is not as valuable as that promise conveyed today. That many buyers of Apple's immensely popular iPhone 5 (released in September 2012) would have paid for immediate delivery to bypass a waiting list is a clear reflection of time preference. We experience this phenomenon mainly through its most visible counterpart: interest rates and savings rates. The stability of time preference over the generations can be demonstrated; indeed in 5th-century-BC Greece, interest rates exhibited levels similar to what we see in today's markets. The Bank of England's official policy rate for the years 1694 to 1972 ranged between 2 percent and 10 percent. It surged to 17 percent during the inflationary late 1970s, but has since returned to its single-digit historical range. It is reasonable to conclude that time preference, too, has no evident long-term trend.

Such inferences of the stability of time preference are also consistent with behavioral economics. A famous experiment, conducted in 1972 and 1990 by Stanford psychologist Walter Mischel, concluded that the ability of children between the ages of four and six to forego immediate gratification was reflected years later by the high SAT scores of those who deferred gratification as children compared to those who could not. A follow-up study of the same individuals in 2011 confirmed the response, indicating a *lifelong* inbred propensity to a specific level of time preference, though not the same for each individual. To forgo short-term gratification for greater rewards in the future is generally consistent with higher intelligence.

Real (inflation expectation adjusted) market interest rates, I assume, are continually converging toward a stable time preference, though we cannot be sure because time preference is rarely directly visible.

ALAN GREENSPAN is President of Greenspan Associates, LLC. He was Chair of the Federal Reserve from 1987–2006 and Chair of the Council of Economic Advisers from 1974–1977.

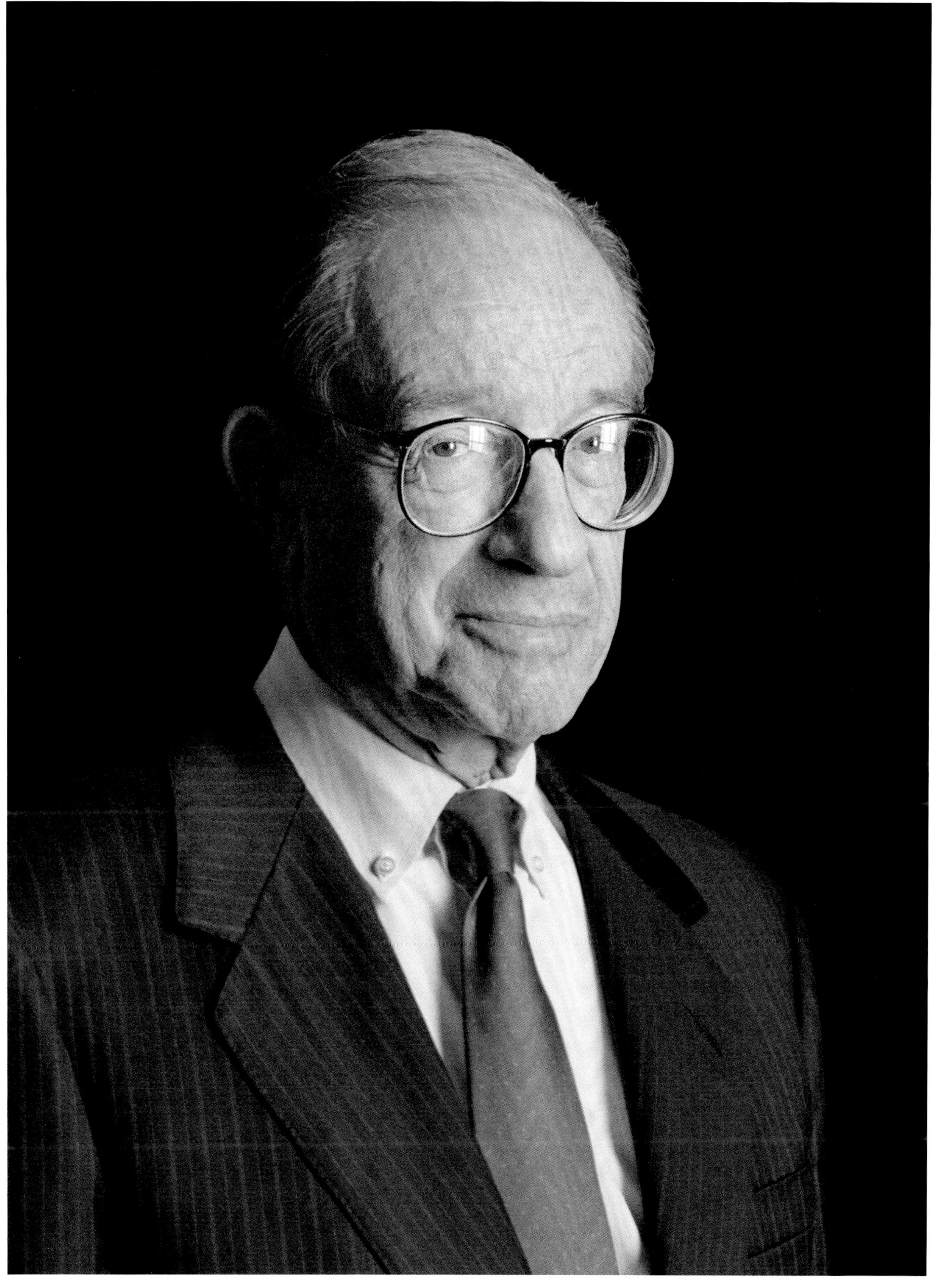

Robert Hall

"Why do you think real wages have fallen so far behind productivity in the past two decades?"

THE FIRST REASON that real earnings of American workers have failed to keep up with productivity is that the share of total income going to workers has declined. Opinion among economists on the subject is converging on declining competition as the main source—profit is rising relative to wages because some industries, such as internet search engines, are natural monopolies, and markets in general are becoming more concentrated. Small numbers of ever-larger firms account for growing fractions of sales in many US markets. Some economists believe that antitrust policy has permitted too many mergers. Another factor is that the cost structure of many industries has shifted toward fixed costs and away from variable costs. Fixed costs deplete earnings of workers in the same way as profits. The decline in the earnings share over the two decades amounts to 6.5 percent of earnings, or $4,000 for the average family, as of 2017.

The second reason for the shortfall of earnings growth relative to productivity growth is that a smaller fraction of the population is working. Unemployment is not a source of the declining fraction working—the unemployment rate was 5.4 percent in 1996 and 4.7 percent in 2016. The onset of retirement in the baby-boom generation is part of the story, but it appears that about 3 percentage points of the shrinkage is from other factors. The decline in the fraction employed is biggest among people under thirty, especially teenagers. The wages available to people who have not completed college have lagged well behind the fairly rapid growth of wages for college graduates. Accordingly, parents who are college graduates are increasingly able to support their offspring into early adulthood. Some research has found that inexpensive electronic entertainment has attracted young men who, in earlier decades, would have chosen work rather than staying at home, where there was little to interest them before video games became popular. The declining state of health of people aged over forty also appears to be a factor in lower employment rates among more senior generations. The past two decades have seen considerable increases in dependence on disability programs, both because of the aging of the population and because of worsening health within older age groups. These programs prohibit work. Some economists are concerned about increased dependency on other benefit programs, especially Medicaid and food stamps, which discourage work. Both of these programs have been expanded substantially over the past two decades, especially after the recession that began at the end of 2007. The decline in the fraction of the population working, over the two decades, amounts to 5.5 percent of earnings, or $3,300 for the average family, as of 2017.

The third, less important reason that earnings have not tracked productivity is that workweeks have become shorter. The typical worker put in 39.3 hours per week in 1996, which fell to 38.7 in 2016. The decline in weekly hours over the two decades amounts to 1.5 percent of earnings, or $900 per year, for the average family, as of 2017.

The combined effect over the twenty years from 1996 to 2017 from these sources was to reduce earnings relative to productivity by 13 percent, or $8,000 per year, for the average family.

ROBERT HALL is Professor at Stanford University.

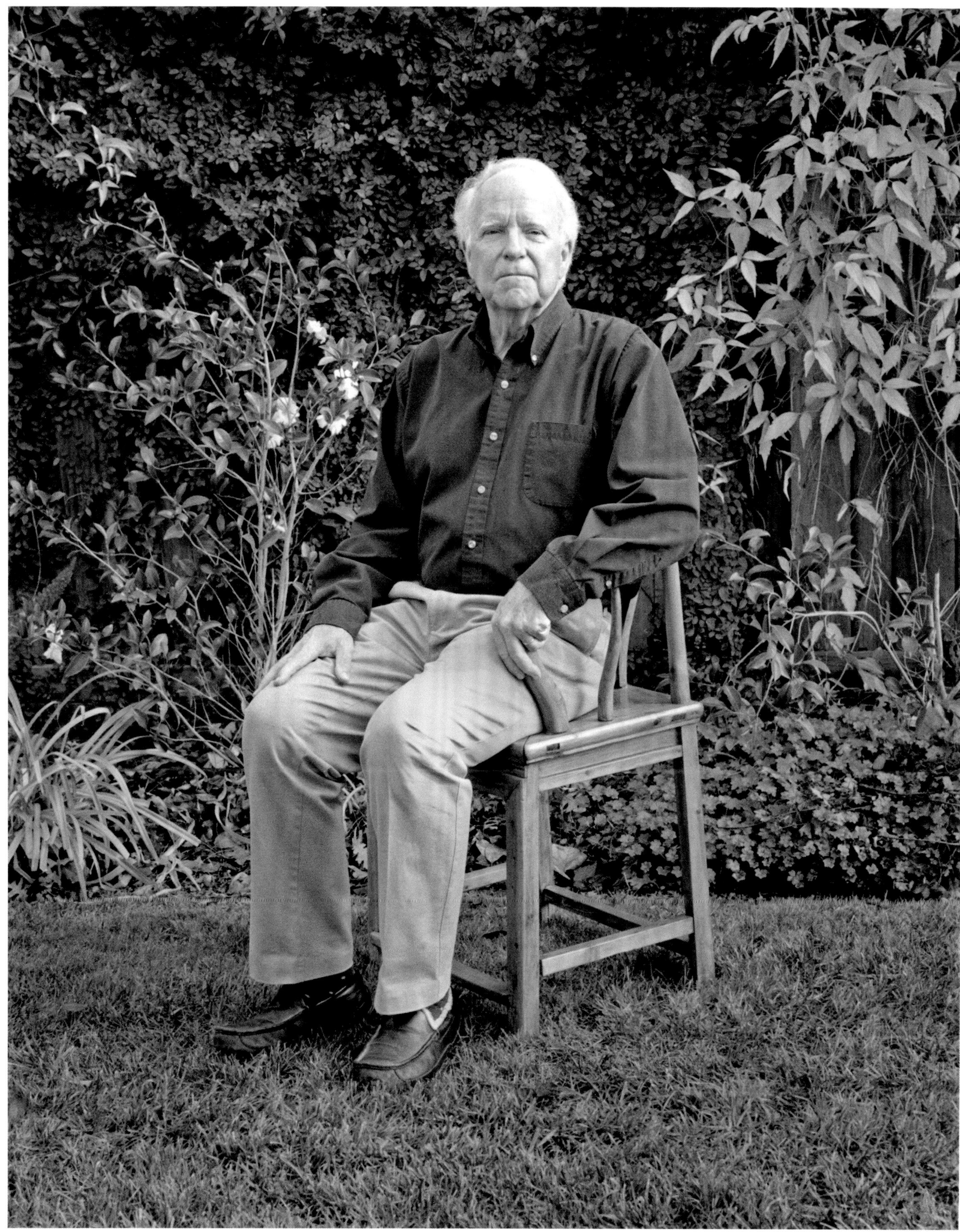

James Heckman

"What are the most productive strategies for helping disadvantaged children in the US today?"

SUBSTANTIAL GAPS BETWEEN the environments of advantaged children and those of disadvantaged children raise serious concerns about the state of social mobility in America. The effects of adverse early childhood environments persist over a lifetime.

High-quality early childhood education programs enrich the nurturing and learning environments of disadvantaged children. The evidence from a variety of high-quality early childhood programs, whose reported results can be replicated by objective analysts, tells a consistent story. They have substantial effects on life outcomes beyond just IQ or achievement test scores that are the focus of attention in popular discussions of public policy. They promote physical and mental health, reduce criminal activity, and boost earnings and social engagement. The economic and social rates of return are high—comparable to returns on equity investment. The evidence supports a public subsidy of high-quality programs targeted to disadvantaged populations. At current quality levels and costs, their social benefits greatly exceed their social costs. The economic and social case for universal early programs for promoting development is weak.

On average, the children of affluent families do not benefit from the public provision of early childhood education aimed at disadvantaged populations. Any benefit to affluent families comes from receipt of childcare, which subsidizes the employment of parents, sometimes at the cost of exposing children to low-quality environments with adverse lifetime outcomes.

Programs should be evaluated by their impacts on a multitude of outcomes over a lifetime and not just by their impacts on IQ or achievement test scores measured shortly after children complete the programs. Instead, analysts should measure a full range of skills that enable children to become more productive adults. Many analysts equate program effectiveness with performance on short-term measures of cognition that poorly predict life success. Socio-emotional skills—such as attentiveness, impulse control, sociability, and conscientiousness—are primary drivers of achievement, health, and increased social and economic productivity. Unfortunately, these skills often go unmeasured.

Demonstration programs such as the Perry Preschool Project and the Carolina Abecedarian Project provide valuable information on the effects of early education, because they measure socio-emotional skills in youth and collect data on education, employment, health, and criminal activity through adulthood. Evaluations of these programs show favorable effects on high school graduation, long-term employment, and reduced criminal activity. There are also beneficial effects on health and healthy behaviors. Both programs have high rates of return. The Perry Preschool Project measures life outcomes through age 40. It has a benefit-cost ratio of 6.6 and an annual rate of return per dollar invested of 7.7 percent. Analysis of adult outcomes at age 35 for the Abecedarian Project that consider a broader set of returns show substantial benefits on health and rates of return above those of the Perry Program in the range of 13–14 percent per annum.

These long-term impacts persist despite fadeout of childhood IQ and scores of cognition that receive so much attention in public policy debates. Enhancements in socio-emotional skills explain a substantial part of these impacts—much more so than cognitive skills. These enhanced socio-emotional skills have large payoffs in terms of health, earnings, educational attainment, and reductions in criminal prosecution. High-quality early childhood enrichment programs targeted to disadvantaged children are both socially fair and economically efficient.

Lessons from these older programs are still highly relevant today because current programs are based on the major components of these programs. The mechanisms producing success are the same for many of these programs.

JAMES HECKMAN is Professor at the University of Chicago. He received the John Bates Clark Medal in 1983 and the Nobel Prize for Economics in 2000.

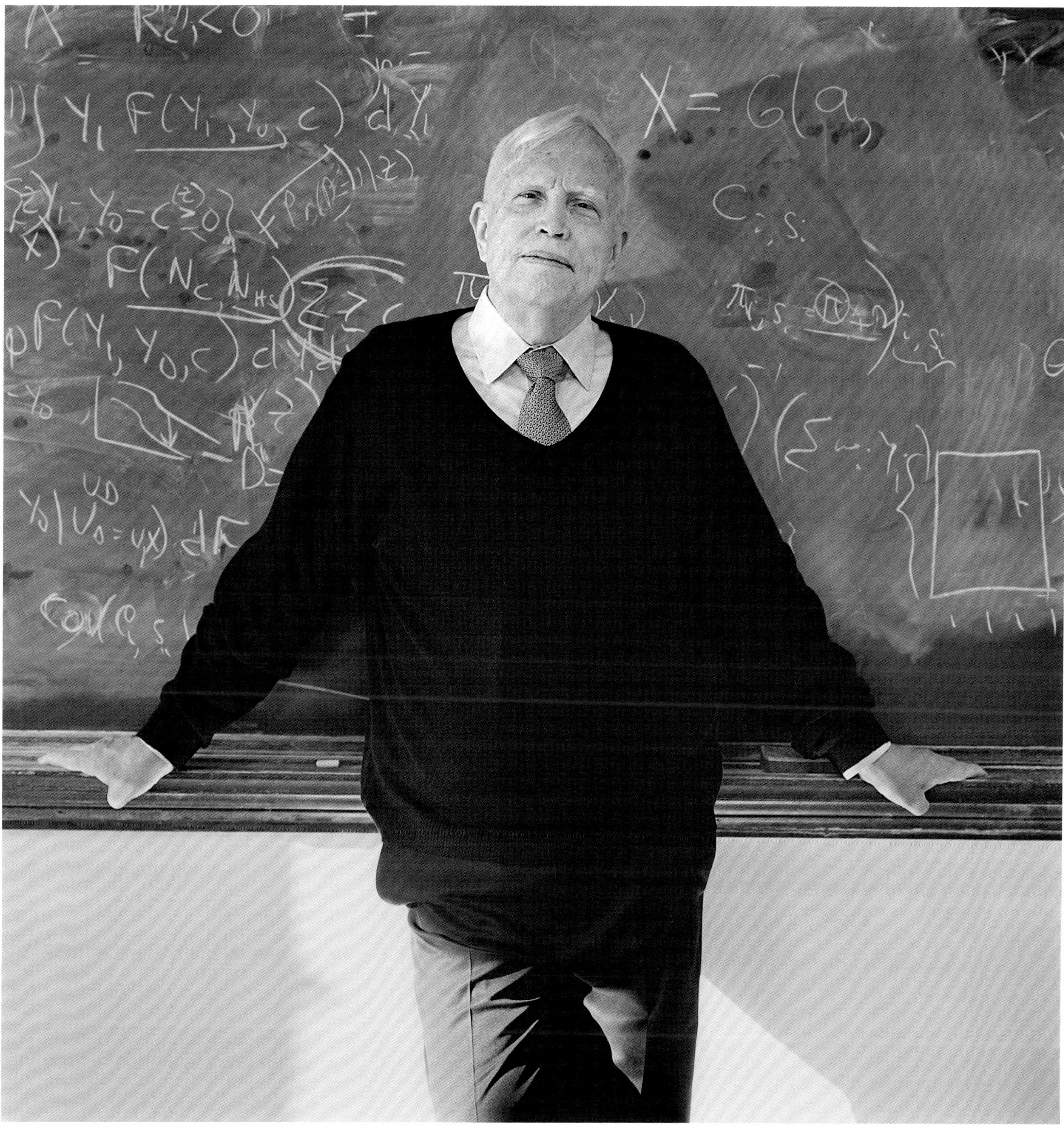

Peter Blair Henry

"Did the financial crisis bring about any change in the growth prospects of the emerging economies?"

THE 2008–2009 GLOBAL financial crisis damaged the growth prospects of emerging and developing countries. Since the crisis, the growth rate of the gross domestic product (GDP) of these economies has fallen by twice that of developed nations, and as the total production of goods and services in emerging economies now accounts for more than half of worldwide GDP, their slower growth is cause for significant concern.

At the heart of the slowdown, a prolonged decline in capital flows from advanced to emerging economies—which plummeted as the crisis began and remain at their lowest level since 1980—jeopardizes the virtuous cycle of increased prosperity that has driven global growth since 1945. While developed nations have struggled with the most anemic economic recovery in the post–World War II era, their anxiety has fueled nationalism and eviscerated public support for free trade, immigration, and the process of economic integration more generally. But understanding the importance of capital flows to developing nations, and the history of economic turnaround in these countries, provides the key to future growth and prosperity in advanced nations as well.

From 1994 to 2007, the period just prior to the financial crisis, emerging and developing countries grew by 5.4 percent per year—2 percentage points faster than they did from 1980 to 1993. The leaders of these countries engineered this turnaround by changing the economic policies that previously had characterized their history as independent nations. The most striking example involves policies that reduced inflation to single-digit price increases, down from levels that exceeded 3000 percent per year at times during the prior decade in places like Argentina. Economic change throughout much of the developing world also manifested through the adoption of a more modest role for government in the economy, a larger role for the market in allocating goods and services, increased respect for the rule of law, and increased openness to international trade. As countries created more business-friendly environments and welcomed the participation of nonresidents in the local economy, foreign savings and technology poured in, triggering an increase in investment, wages, productivity, and growth.

Importantly, the economic progress of developing countries did not come at the expense of advanced countries. The average annual growth rate of advanced nations was just as high between 1994 and 2007—2.9 percent—as it was from 1980 to 1993. Indeed, rising incomes in developing countries increased the purchasing power of their people, enabling them to buy more goods and services from the G7. Freer flows of goods, people, and capital across borders fueled a continued rise in the average standard of living in advanced countries, even as it lifted hundreds of millions of people in developing ones out of poverty.

Today, however, rather than dealing with their own realities of aging populations, weakening productivity, undisciplined economic policymaking, and low prospective returns on capital, many leaders in advanced nations falsely claim that rapid growth in emerging economies has caused slower growth in rich countries. In this deceptive version of the globalization narrative, economic success in emerging economies is a zero-sum proposition that exacerbates a tepid recovery, when in fact rich countries would be better off if emerging markets grew even more rapidly.

And more rapid growth in emerging markets is possible because of their demographics. While the working-age population in advanced economies is declining, during 2018 more than 1.1 million new workers will join the labor force each month in developing countries. That number will rise to 1.7 million per month by 2030. Policies that reinvigorate a sustained flow of capital from low-return rich countries to more productive investments in poor ones would bring employment benefits to emerging economies while also boosting global growth and the performance of retirement portfolios in the aging rich world. Opportunity abounds for developing and developed countries, but we need leaders in both places to step forward and seize it. Global growth is not a zero-sum game.

PETER BLAIR HENRY is Dean Emeritus and Professor at the New York University Stern School of Business.

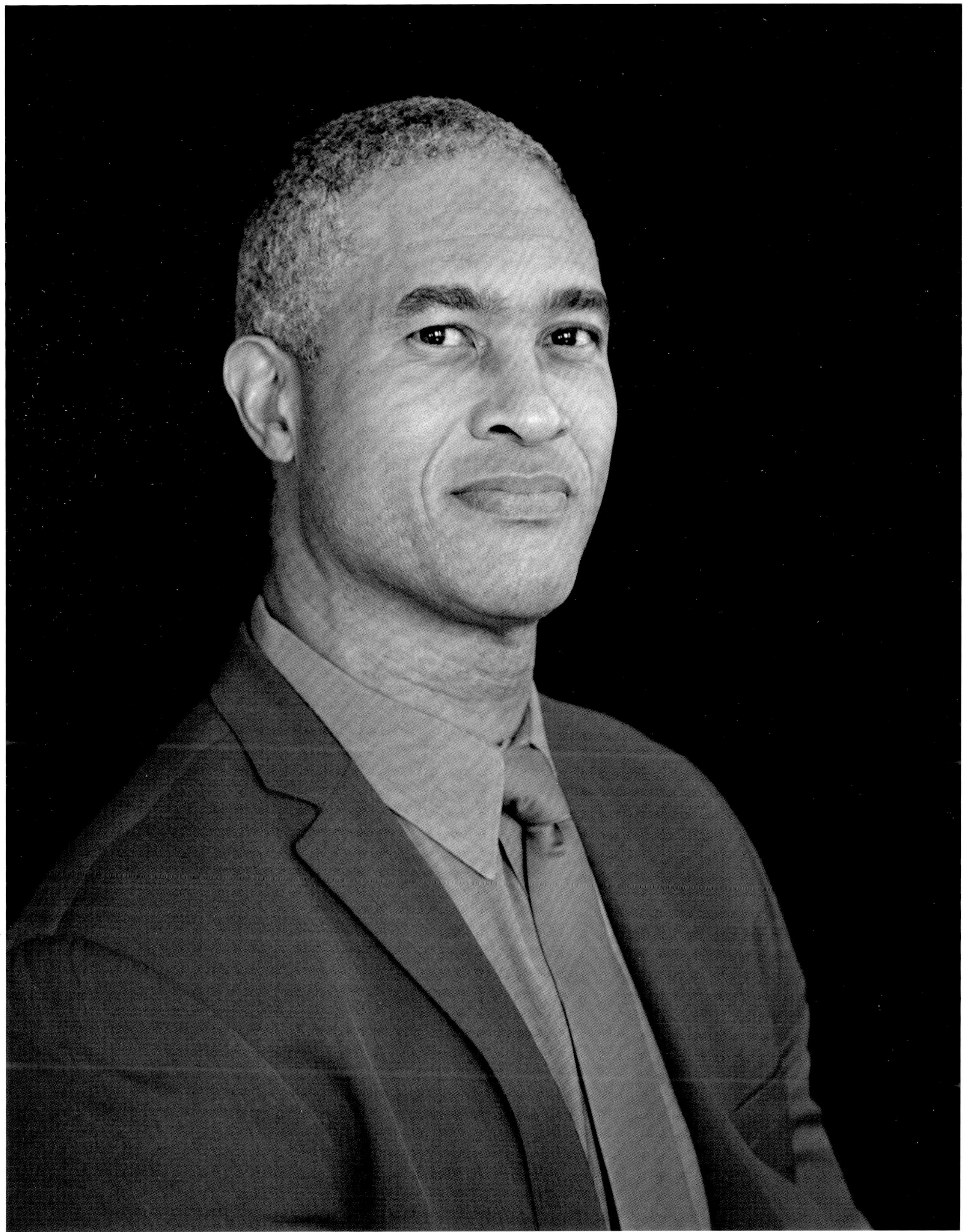

Bengt Holmström

"How do you interpret the surge of executive compensation over the past couple of decades?"

EXECUTIVE COMPENSATION LEVELS have indeed reached exorbitant levels. The median compensation of executives in the S&P 500 is $10 million. This is about 250 times more than the average American worker earns. In 1980, the inflation-adjusted compensation was $1.8 million, so the rise has been dramatic over the past three decades.

A popular explanation for this surge in compensation is that CEOs have too much power over their boards, which give in to executive demands. This theory does not explain the sudden rise after 1980, nor does it square well with the fact that private equity firms provide even more generous packages to their executives than publicly traded firms. A more plausible explanation is the increased competition for executives, driven by globalization. Another plausible driver is the fact that since the early 1980s major newspapers have published executive compensation figures. These figures can be used as benchmarks, and since few CEOs want to be paid less than the relevant average, the result is an upward drift. This story fits the timing of the onset of the surge. It gains added credence when one realizes how thin the CEO market is for any given job, resulting in a large bargaining wedge. A top CEO can add billions to the value of a big company. How much of the value added should the CEO receive, especially given that finding a good substitute is difficult and fraught with risk? It seems possible to me that the observed rise in compensation is consistent with a move within the bargaining wedge, driven by increased transparency.

As economists, we do not typically take a stand on where in the bargaining wedge an outcome should lie. For this reason, the structure of executive compensation has received much more attention in economic analyses than the level of pay. Corporate scandals and the financial crisis exposed weaknesses in the structure of compensation, leading to major changes. Some of them are welcome. Restricted shares have replaced options as the most common form of contingent pay for two reasons. Shares do not lose their incentive effect even when the stock price goes down, while options have to be reissued in order to maintain their incentive strength. Furthermore, restricted shares have longer vesting times (the time until shares can be sold) adding to the stability of incentives. Options could be designed to vest more slowly, too, but this increases the likelihood that they will end up worthless, adding to the frequency of reissues and making the pay system less robust and less transparent.

Unfortunately, in an effort to make executives more accountable and to curtail the growth of compensation levels, compensation consultants have developed a host of more complicated contingent pay instruments. So-called performance-based equity plans give executives a predetermined amount of shares, or options, as a function of how well the executive has performed by a set of metrics that typically include shareholder return as well as accounting measures of various kinds. These plans usually stretch over several years with varying triggers over time. They are bewilderingly complex to understand and to value, and they violate one of the most basic principles of incentive design, namely that the executive can see a connection between what he does and what he gets as a reward. How did we ever get into something this confusing? The answer is that executive pay, since the scandals and crises, has been driven by fairness and political considerations more than incentive considerations. I hope fairness concerns could be addressed more transparently and directly without compromising incentives. It is not an impossible task.

BENGT HOLMSTRÖM is Professor at the Massachusetts Institute of Technology. He received the Nobel Prize for Economics in 2016.

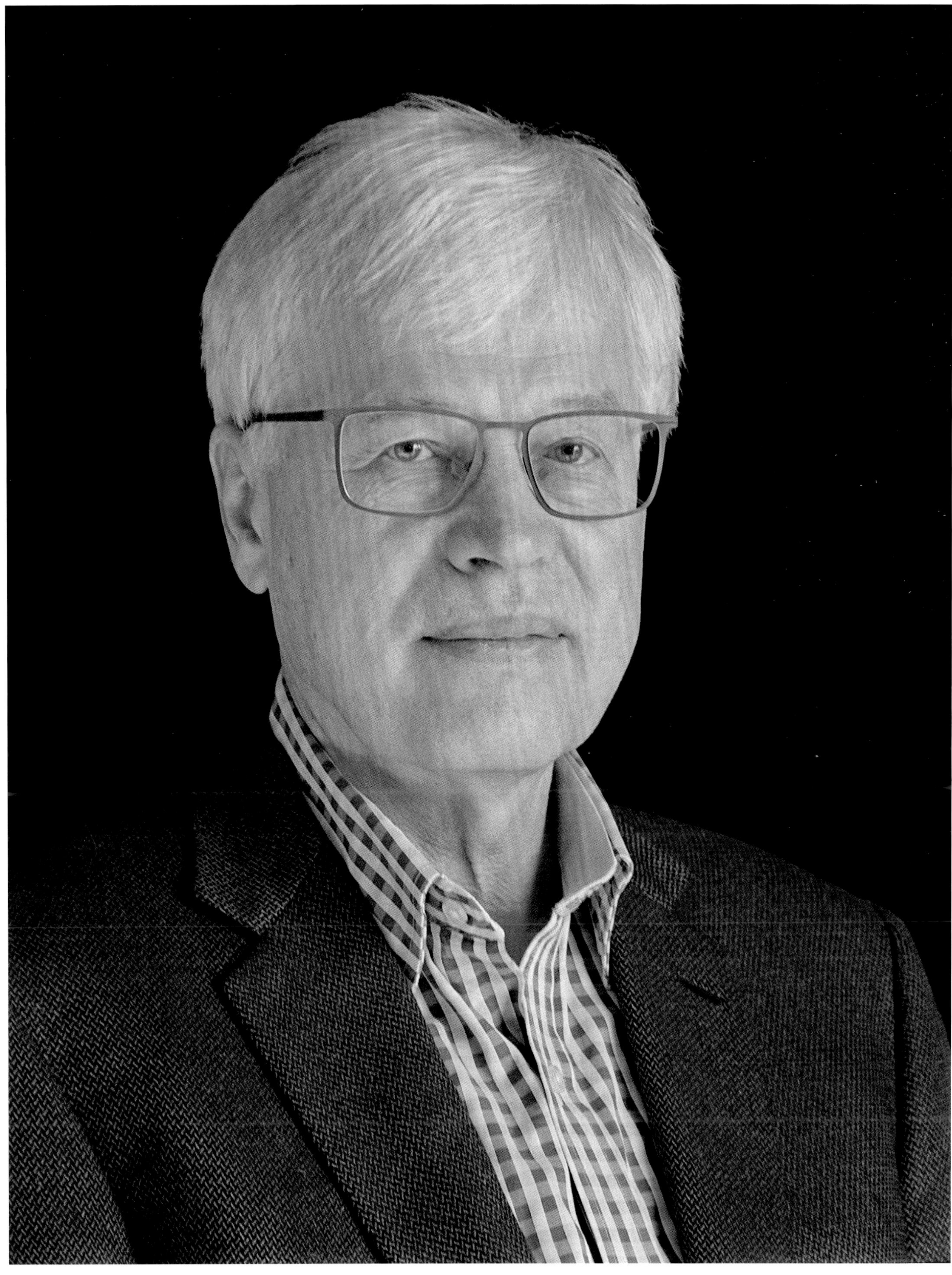

Caroline Hoxby

"Do you think online education is a good way to improve the access of bright low-income students to higher education?"

FROM 1970 TO 2014, per-pupil expenditure on public elementary and secondary education tripled in dollars adjusted for inflation. Over the same period, high school seniors' scores on the National Assessment of Educational Progress hardly changed. About 25 percent of high school seniors scored "proficient" in math in the early 1970s. About the same percentage score proficient now. Moreover, only about 20 percent are proficient if we account for high school drop-outs (who do not take the test).

The proficiency bar is meaningful because students who score below it struggle greatly in postsecondary school, usually dropping out without a degree. They rarely acquire the skills needed for employment in the growing sectors of our economy, all of which are intensive in advanced education. Not only is the share of our population that is capable of performing high-skilled jobs no greater than it was forty-four years ago, but the share of high-skilled people who reside *outside* the US has grown greatly over the same period and continues to grow. This matters because, in the future, high-skilled industries will locate where high-skilled people are. The situation constitutes a crisis.

We are unlikely to alleviate this crisis by doing "more of the same" since achievement stalled over decades in which real per-pupil spending rose greatly. Therefore, a question often asked of economists of education is whether technology and online schooling could be the solution. The answer is partially "yes" but mostly "no."

Key evidence can help us understand why technology may be useful but not the silver bullet for which many people hope. First, numerous rigorous studies indicate that instructors differ widely in the amount that they teach students: their "value-added." Value-added varies widely among instructors in the same school, who use the same curriculum, and have the same training. Thus, value-added is not a simple function of a college degree or good instructional materials. Rather, it appears to be a complex bundle of intelligence, knowledge, charisma, and management skills. Second, talented people tend to move out of teaching (or fail to enter it) because talent is rewarded outside of the teaching profession but rarely rewarded within it. Teachers are not paid on their value-added or other merits: they are paid on the basis of seniority. Third, most students need to be engaged if they are to learn: they are not autodidacts. Indeed, many students appear to learn less, probably owing to distraction, when given greater access to the internet. Fourth, students learn at different rates so that, as they move into higher grades, a given cohort contains students whose needs are further and further apart.

Does technology address any of these key issues? It addresses the last issue well. Technology can allow students to learn at more individualized paces, and this can help both high-achieving and low-achieving "outliers."

However, most of the other issues are not remedied by technology. Although online schools potentially allow great instructors and advanced curricula to reach wider audiences, these changes appear primarily to help highly self-motivated, intelligent students. Such students very disproportionately account for successful online learning at all levels (primary, secondary, postsecondary). Indeed, the student who likely benefits the most from technology is an unusually self-directed, able person living in circumstances where he would be deprived of curricular content in the absence of the internet. These people exist—especially in developing countries—but they are not the heart of the educational crisis in the US or other developed economies. (Indeed, by benefitting unusually smart autodidacts disproportionately, technology arguably increases the "learning gap" between the more and less able.) My recent research demonstrates that when our struggling students—those who fail to attain proficiency in traditional primary and secondary schools—enroll in online education, more than 90 percent fail to earn a positive return. They mostly drop out without attaining a credential, and they rarely move into jobs that require more advanced skills.

We *can* help our struggling students and address our educational crisis, but we should not expect technology or the internet to be a silver bullet. Rather, we need to wrestle with fundamental issues like the structure of teacher pay, which makes it extremely difficult to put a high value-added, highly engaging instructor in front of every student.

CAROLINE HOXBY is Professor at Stanford University.

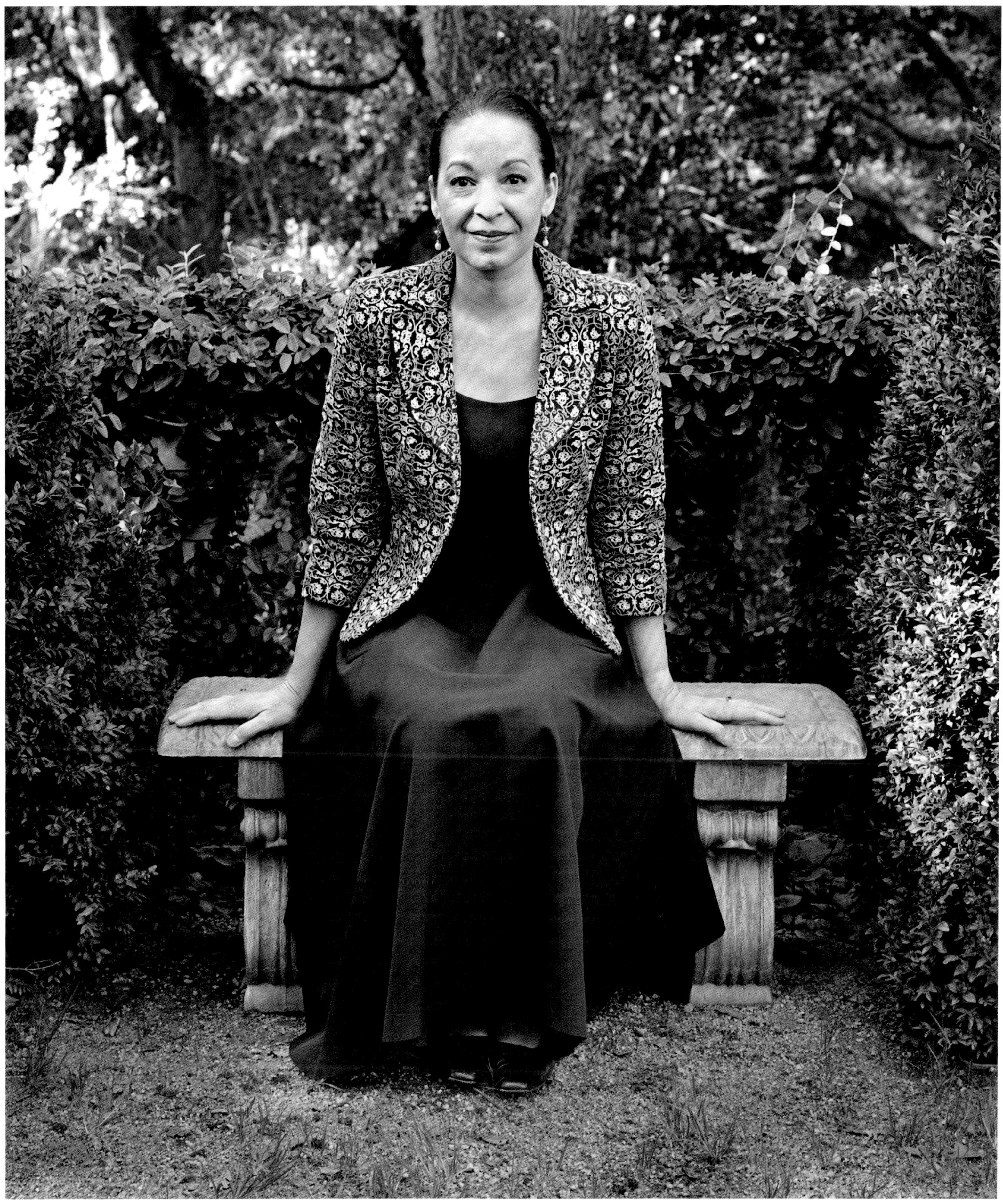

Daniel Kahneman

"What is a psychologist doing among economists?"

SOON AFTER AMOS TVERSKY and I set out to understand the Allais paradox around 1974, our attention was drawn to an odd assumption in applications of utility theory—then and now the dominant theory of decision-making under risk. The assumption we questioned was first made by Jacob Bernoulli in 1738. His famous theory proposed that people evaluate gambles by the expected utility of their possible consequences, and defined consequences as states of wealth. In his model, the choice between a 50 percent chance to win $100 or $40 with certainty is evaluated by the utilities of "my current wealth," "my wealth plus $100," "my wealth plus $40."

Bernoulli had in mind risky financial decisions with very large stakes, as in the famous example of the merchant who sends a ship loaded with spice from Amsterdam to St. Petersburg. There is a 5 percent chance that the ship will be lost and the merchant tries to work out how much insurance he should be willing to pay. It would be natural for the merchant to compare the utility of his remaining wealth if the ship sinks to the utility of his current wealth. The assumption that states of wealth are the consequences is plausible in that context, but it appears far-fetched when the stakes are a tiny fraction of wealth. Applications of utility theory, however, did not treat high stakes and low stakes differently. Amos and I quickly decided to develop a theory in which the objects of valuation are gains and losses and we tested that prospect theory in the context of small or moderate losses. Harry Markowitz had made a foray into the same terrain, but our exploration was more thorough.

Why was Bernoulli's implausible assumption retained for so long? One part of the answer is a phenomenon that I have called "theory-induced blindness": it is generally very difficult for scientists who are firmly attached to a productive theory to admit or even to consider serious flaws in that theory. The other answer is that the alternative to Bernoulli's assumption leads very quickly to choices that appear unreasonable. If people assign utilities to gains and losses, the utility of a particular state of wealth will depend on the reference state to which it is compared. Consider a choice between a gamble that could result in states of wealth of 3 or 4 million dollars with equal probabilities and a certain state of 3.5 million. The gamble's appeal is determined by a feature that is not represented in utility theory: the current state of wealth. The gamble is more attractive when current wealth is 4 million than 3 million: it appears that the value of a state of wealth differs, depending on whether it was reached by winning or by losing a gamble. Other observations show that losses loom larger than gains. But is this reasonable? The difference appears myopic: the financial decisions of a reasonable person should not be dominated by the emotional response to a recent change of wealth. The standard assumption that economic agents are rational requires consequences to be evaluated as states of wealth.

The assumption of rationality plays an important role in making economics mathematically tractable, and there are good reasons for its continued influence, even in behavioral economics. It is of course not uncommon for simplifying assumptions to be useful. However, behavioral economists led by Richard Thaler have demonstrated that the competing assumption of myopic utilities for changes of wealth also has implications that are both distinctive and interesting. And this is at least part of the reason that a psychologist is found in a crowd to which he does not really belong.

DANIEL KAHNEMAN is Professor Emeritus at the Princeton University Woodrow Wilson School of Public and International Affairs. He received the Nobel Prize for Economics in 2002.

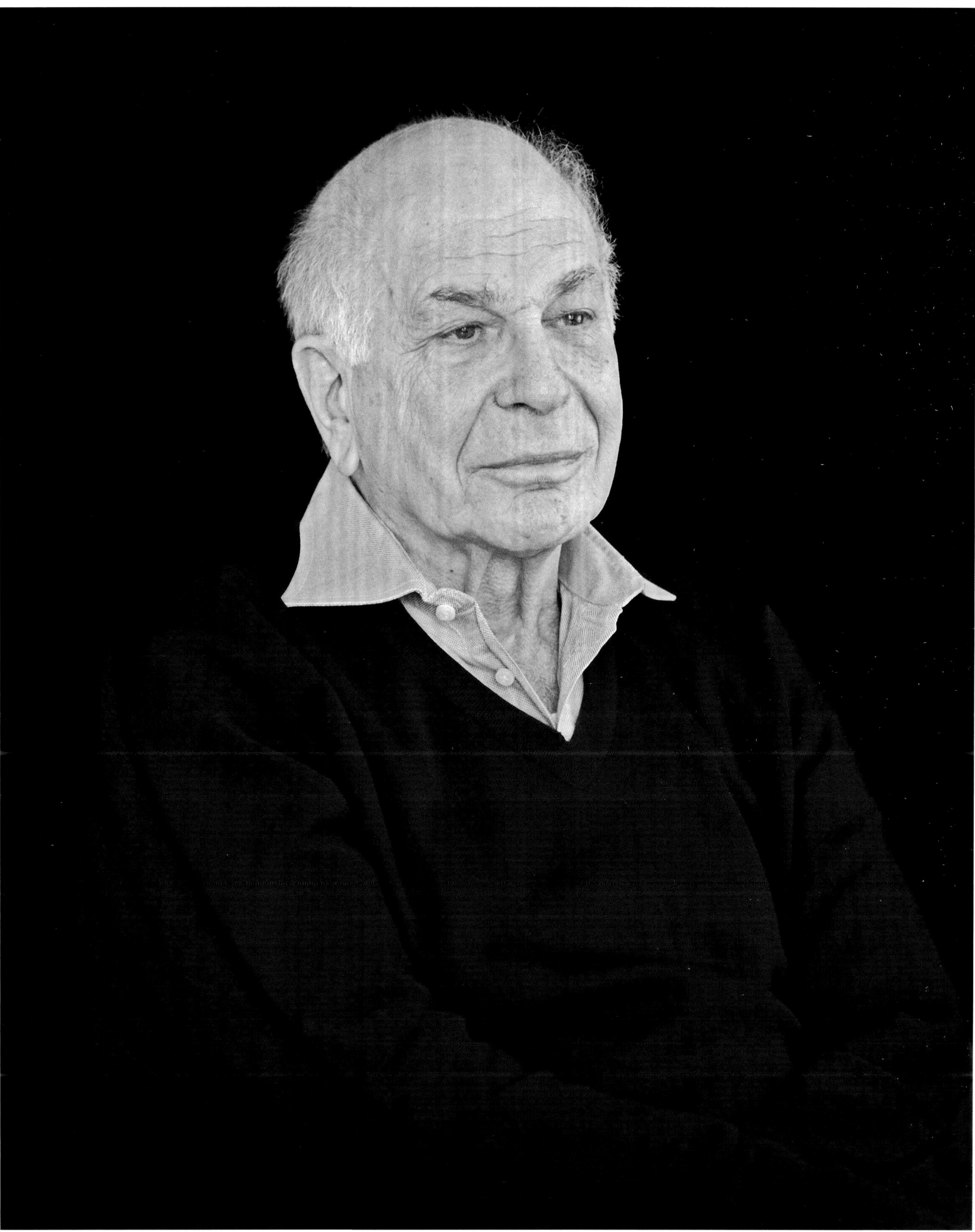

Lawrence F. Katz

"Do you think that better and better-located housing arrangements for poor families could measurably increase intergenerational income mobility in the United States?"

THE UNITED STATES has experienced substantial increases in residential segregation by income in recent decades, particularly for families with children. Poor children are increasingly living in areas of concentrated poverty. This is a greatly worrisome trend since (1) children who grow up in high-poverty neighborhoods fare worse as adults on a wide range of economic, health, and educational outcomes; and (2) metropolitan areas with greater residential racial and economic segregation have lower rates of upward intergenerational mobility than less segregated areas. A core research question in the social sciences has been the extent to which large differences in economic and social outcomes by neighborhood reflect the causal effects of place (neighborhood effects) as opposed to the difficult-to-measure differences of the individuals and families themselves (sorting or selection effects) in terms of their resources, motivations, and attitudes.

My research (along with many collaborators) using the large-scale Moving to Opportunity (MTO) housing mobility experiment operating in five major US cities starting in the mid-1990s sheds light on these issues. MTO offered randomly selected families with children housing vouchers and assistance to move from high-poverty housing projects to low-poverty neighborhoods. The participants in the MTO experiment have been tracked for almost twenty years. And we have found that MTO moves to lower-poverty areas substantially improved the health and well-being of the parents and led to large increases in the long-run adult outcomes (earnings, family incomes, and college attendance) of children who moved before they reached adolescence. Recent complementary quasi-experimental research by Raj Chetty and Nathaniel Hendren that studied millions of childhood moves across the US similarly found a correlation between longer childhood exposure to high-poverty and low-opportunity areas and adverse effects on adult economic outcomes.

Thus, I conclude from the emerging evidence from MTO and related research that enacting policies to reduce US residential economic segregation and to help more low-income families move to higher opportunity neighborhoods could substantially improve the prospect for upward intergenerational mobility of poor children. I am currently working on the Creating Moves to Opportunity project, which uses additional randomized field experiments to test more effective ways to use funding for low-income housing assistance and housing vouchers to help low-income families with children move to areas with better prospects for children's long-run outcomes. My ongoing research also examines the efficacy of place-based policies to invest in and improve chances for upward mobility of individuals living in distressed neighborhoods.

LAWRENCE KATZ is Professor at Harvard University.

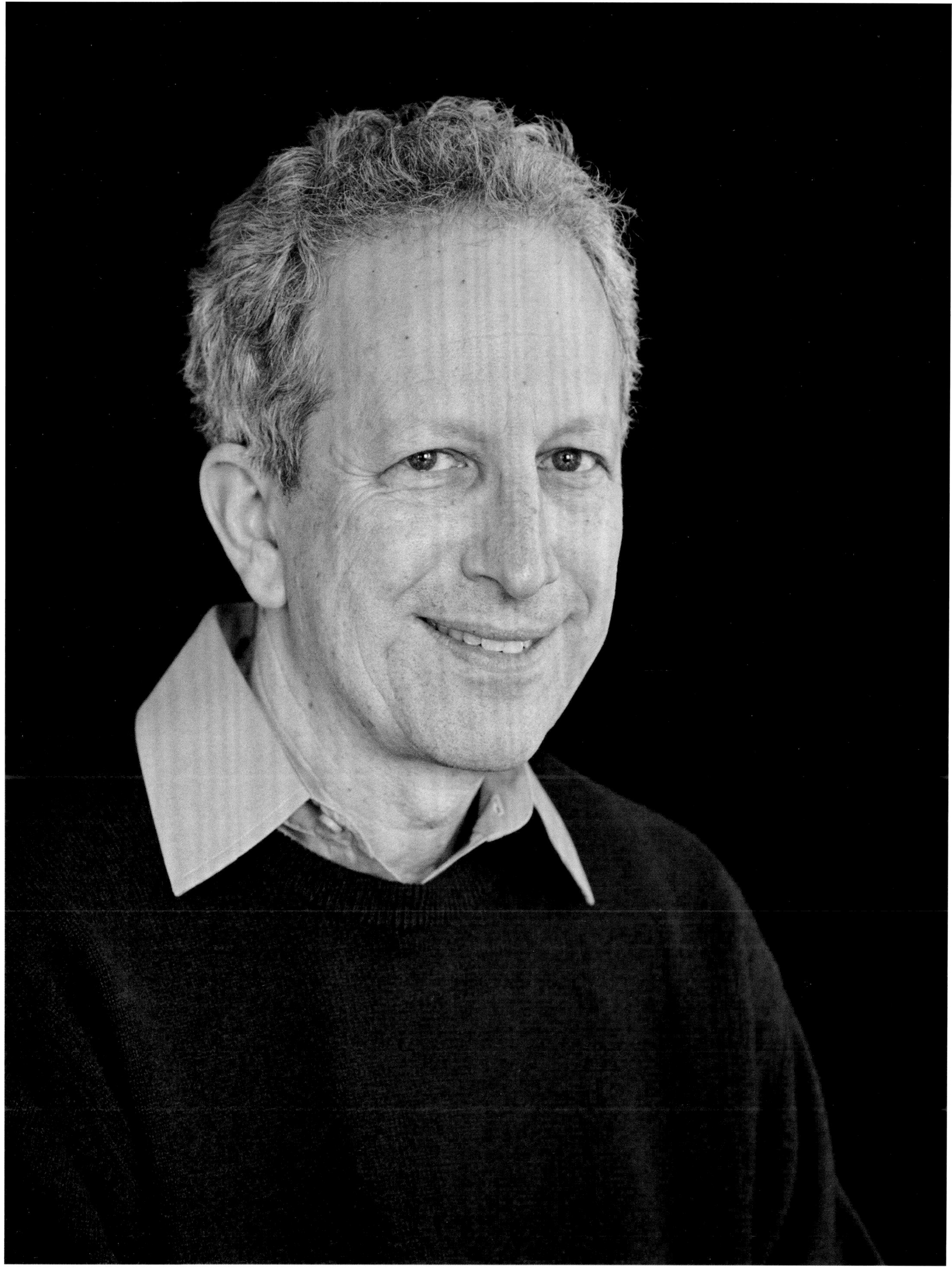

Mervyn King

"Has the world community done enough to reduce the chance of another financial crisis? What should the next step be?"

ONE OF THE strange features of financial crises is that countries seem to learn lessons only after they have experienced their own crisis. So perhaps the advantage of a global financial crisis is that we can all learn together!

Much has been done to reduce the vulnerability of the banking and financial system since its collapse in 2007–2008. But the system is not invulnerable. What we saw, especially in the fall of 2008, was a run on the banking system as confidence in the immediately realizable value of many of the assets on bank balance sheets evaporated; and those running the fastest were other financial institutions. History records many examples of bank runs by retail depositors; until 2008 there had been fewer examples of a run by professional institutions or "wholesale" investors in banks.

The fragility of the banking system stems from the fact that banks borrow short to lend long. When creditors decide to take their deposits away, or no longer to continue to provide short-term finance, banks are in no position to demand the return of their loans made to finance long-term mortgages or capital investment in factories and other illiquid assets. Over a long period, it seems that this maturity and risk transformation has some value to the economy. Yet it certainly constitutes what I call "alchemy" in my book *The End of Alchemy*.

Can we retain the advantages of traditional banking while eliminating the risk of bank runs? In my book, I proposed a scheme under which banks would, in effect, have to take out mandatory insurance in normal times in order to qualify for central bank lending in times of crisis. Just as motorists must take out third-party insurance before they are allowed on the roads, so banks should be forced to take out this insurance before they engage in alchemy. In effect, the central bank would become a pawnbroker, and banks would leave some of their assets with the central bank as a guarantee against which they could borrow in a crisis. I call this scheme the "pawnbroker for all seasons."

By making banks take out this insurance in normal times, the risk that we, as taxpayers, will be gamed in a crisis into providing massive loans against risky assets at low interest rates is eliminated. With the "pawnbroker for all seasons," a new era for banking beckons.

MERVYN KING is Professor at the New York University School of Law and Stern School of Business. He was Governor of the Bank of England from 2003–2013.

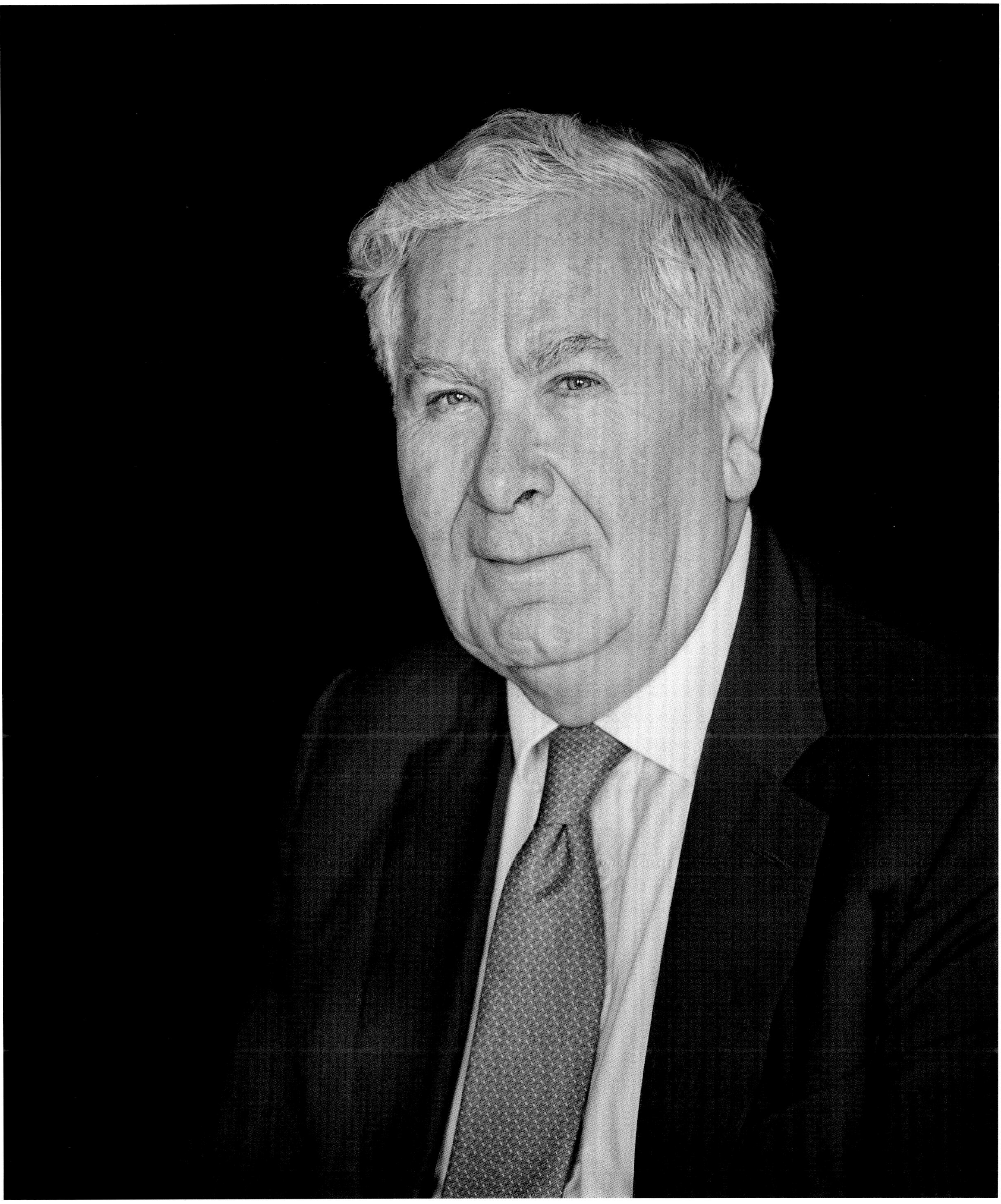

János Kornai

"Do you think democratic institutions can survive a long period of extreme inequality of income and wealth?"

A SUBSTANTIAL PART of the world's population is lucky, because they live in a democracy. However, the fact that a given country is governed by a democratic regime at a given point in history does not guarantee that it will stay that way. From the point of view of their fragility, we should distinguish between *weak* and *strong* democracies.

Weak democracies do not have a long history behind them. Democratic ideas have not had time to take root properly in people's mentality and in social norms; the institutional system that serves to defend democracy is not sufficiently stable. There have been many tragic examples in history, including the recent past: cases when, having demolished democracy, a tyranny has taken control. In all of these cases many factors contributed to trigger the change.

Following World War I, an exemplary democracy emerged in Germany during the Weimar Republic. The new order had not even had enough time to reveal its favorable features when Hitler and the National Socialist Party launched their attack on it. Hitler's populist demagogy appealed to the emotions of a significant proportion of the population: to their anger over the humiliation of a country defeated in war, the despair caused by unemployment, and the dire consequences of inflation. Indignation over inequality was an important factor here too—not in itself, but because it coincided with other factors which turned the people against the fragile democracy.

In Russia, when the communist system collapsed, certain important elements of a democratic state began to emerge: a multiparty system and parliamentarism. These, however, did not last long: Putin took over and within a few years the new autocratic system was established. Behind Putin there are great masses of people—and those numbers continue to increase. He achieved political success by using populist demagogy to blame the permissiveness of the democratic political order for the corruption that had emerged during privatization, and for the inevitable difficulties of the transitional period. Due to the presence of nationalism in populist rhetoric, millions of people, who feel that once-mighty Russia has been humiliated, now support the regime, as it demonstrates spectacularly that their country is a great power once again. For several years the standard of living rose, and most of the population has come to terms with the fact that this development has ceased. The unequal distribution of income, wealth, and power is outrageous. Oligarchs possess unbelievable wealth. Putin himself decides who is to remain an oligarch and who is to disappear; he raises from his own clique those who are to become wealthy at amazing speed. Great masses suffer from poverty, and many decent people are outraged by this inequality; however, this does not lead to the destabilization of the autocratic regime. The leader at the top of the pyramid of power cannot be removed by civilized, peaceful elections. In weak democracies the primary factor leading to the overthrow of democracy is not outrage over inequalities, though it does influence the course of events.

In *strong* democracies the order of events is different, and the interaction between inequality and democracy emerges differently. Deeper-rooted democracies with long histories are able to survive inequality, mainly because those who suffer from it are able to articulate their interests in the political arena, and sooner or later they force through reforms. The most farsighted among those who govern countries and economies realize that without change democracy could be endangered. Not only a few leaders understand this; enough parliamentary support is acquired by democratic means to bring about reforms. The 20th century offers clear examples from the US and Britain: when mass dissatisfaction threatened to break out, the government took important preventive measures. Consider Roosevelt's New Deal in the 1930s, the Beveridge Plan in the '40s, or Johnson's Great Society in the '60s.

Now with Trump we are witnessing the rise to power of a President who strives to become a real autocrat. The nationalistic slogan "America first" resonates with his supporters. Behind him stand, at least for the time being, the unemployed who have been deprived of their workplaces by globalization. It is not for me to make predictions about how American domestic affairs will develop over the next few years. I am, however, convinced that American democracy is strong enough to defend itself.

However outrageous inequality might be, in strong democracies it is not in itself a powerful enough factor to enable a tyranny to replace a well-established democratic state.

JÁNOS KORNAI is Professor Emeritus at Harvard University and Corvinus University of Budapest, Hungary.

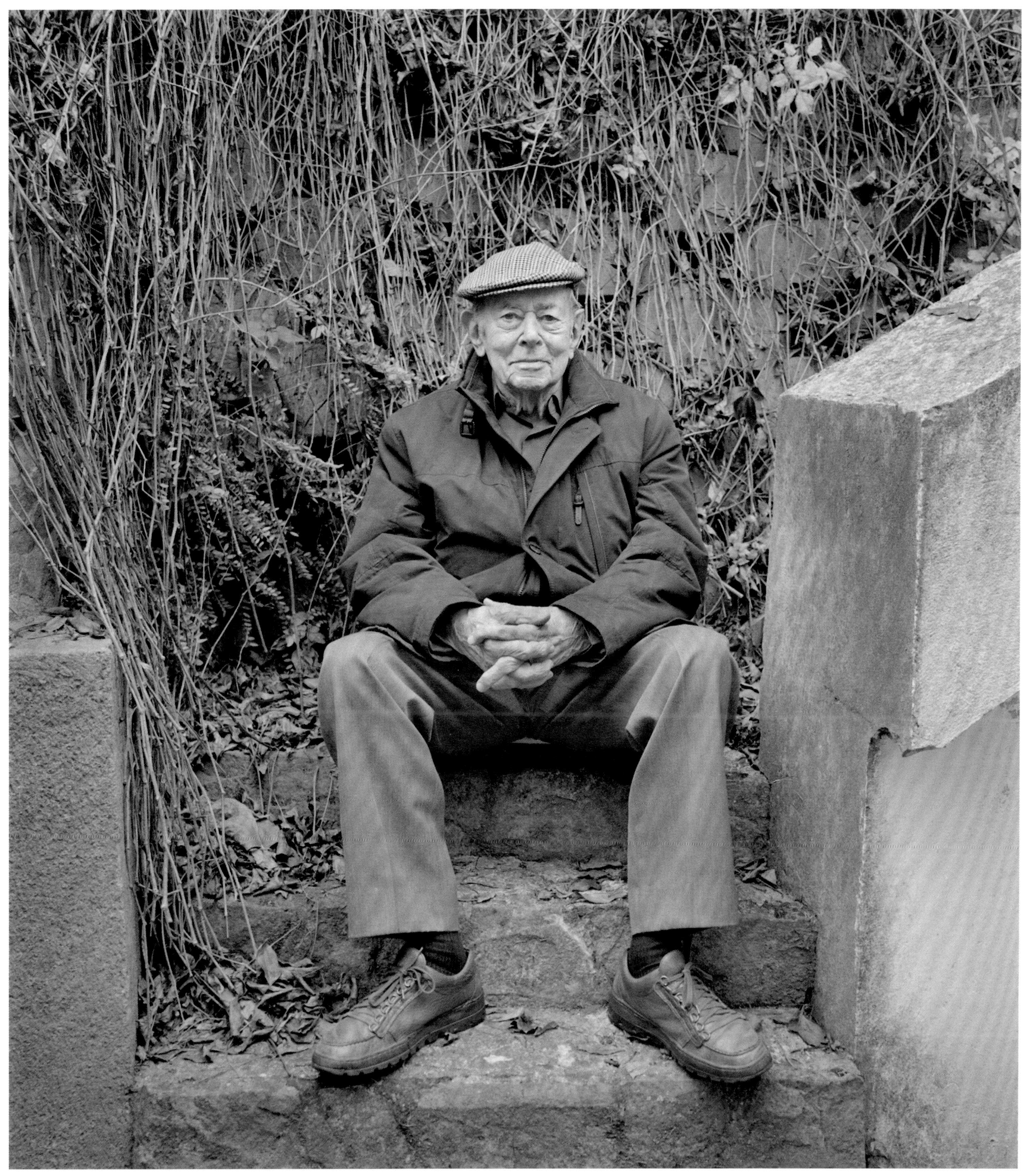

David Kreps

"Does your work on credible and non-credible threats in games inspire any thoughts on interactions between the United States and North Korea?"

IN "GAMES ECONOMISTS PLAY," Franklin Fisher distinguishes between generalizing theory and exemplifying theory. Generalizing theory aims to say what *must* happen if certain broad conditions are met; exemplifying theory describes what *might* happen, based on a more narrow and specific set of assumptions. Exemplifying theory provides possibilities that pass the baseline test of being deductively sound, but whose premises are . . . special.

My work (with various colleagues) on credible threats is exemplifying theory. The issue: How is one party's promise to a second party credible, when it is "known" that, when the time comes, it will not be in the first party's immediate interests to fulfill the promise?

The promise can be to treat the second party favorably, to induce the second party to take some action today in anticipation of the favor. Or it can be a threat to do something that the second party wishes to avoid, typically to induce the second party to forebear from some action.

Classically, credibility is fostered by changing conditions so that fulfilling the promise becomes the first party's best interests. For instance, the general of an army, confronting another and perhaps stronger force, burns his proverbial bridges, so a promise of no retreat becomes credible, both to convince the enemy that he must stand and fight and to give his own forces backbone borne of desperation.

My work has explored the role reputation might play. Suppose keeping the promise is costly for the first party in the short run, but failing to fulfill it will damage the first party's reputation in the longer run, a reputation that is valuable because it provides credibility. Then, despite the short-run costs, the promise may gain credibility. The logic is circular, but in a deductively sound way: Reputation is valuable because it provides credibility; and it provides credibility because it is valuable. In particular, reputation may result from uncertainty about the interests that actuate the first party's actions; in a phrase, the second party worries that the first party is a "crazy type" who—short-run interests be damned—will carry out any promise or threat he issues as a matter of "principle." The first party, even if not crazy, acts as if he were, to keep this possibility alive; the second party, understanding that the first party wants to act in this fashion, responds accordingly.

This theory inspires many thoughts about the confrontation between the United States and North Korea. How credible is Kim Jong-un's threat to engage in a nuclear conflict with the US, if the US doesn't back off, given that promised retaliation will be devastating? But then, is the threat of that retaliation credible? How credible is the US threat of a first strike, if North Korea doesn't roll back its program of nuclear development? If any of these threats are credible because a party's reputation is at stake, what is the reputation in question, and with whom? Do the reputation interests of each side make a vicious cycle of escalation likely? How do the interests of the US and North Korea in maintaining good relations with third parties affect the bilateral conflict? "Crazy type" models suggest that leadership in both countries, to enhance their credibility, should act just as the other side perceives a crazy type would act. (This is theoretical speculation and *not* a comment on the behavior of either Kim Jong-un or Trump.) What behavior is perceived as "crazy," exactly? And is being perceived as a crazy type a good idea, when third-party relationships also hang in the balance?

The economic theory of credibility inspires many thoughts. But the wealth of thoughts inspired makes predictions impossible. The most this theory can do is provide historians with more and better tools to explain, after the dust has settled, what happened and why.

DAVID KREPS is Professor Emeritus at the Stanford Graduate School of Business. He received the John Bates Clark Medal in 1989.

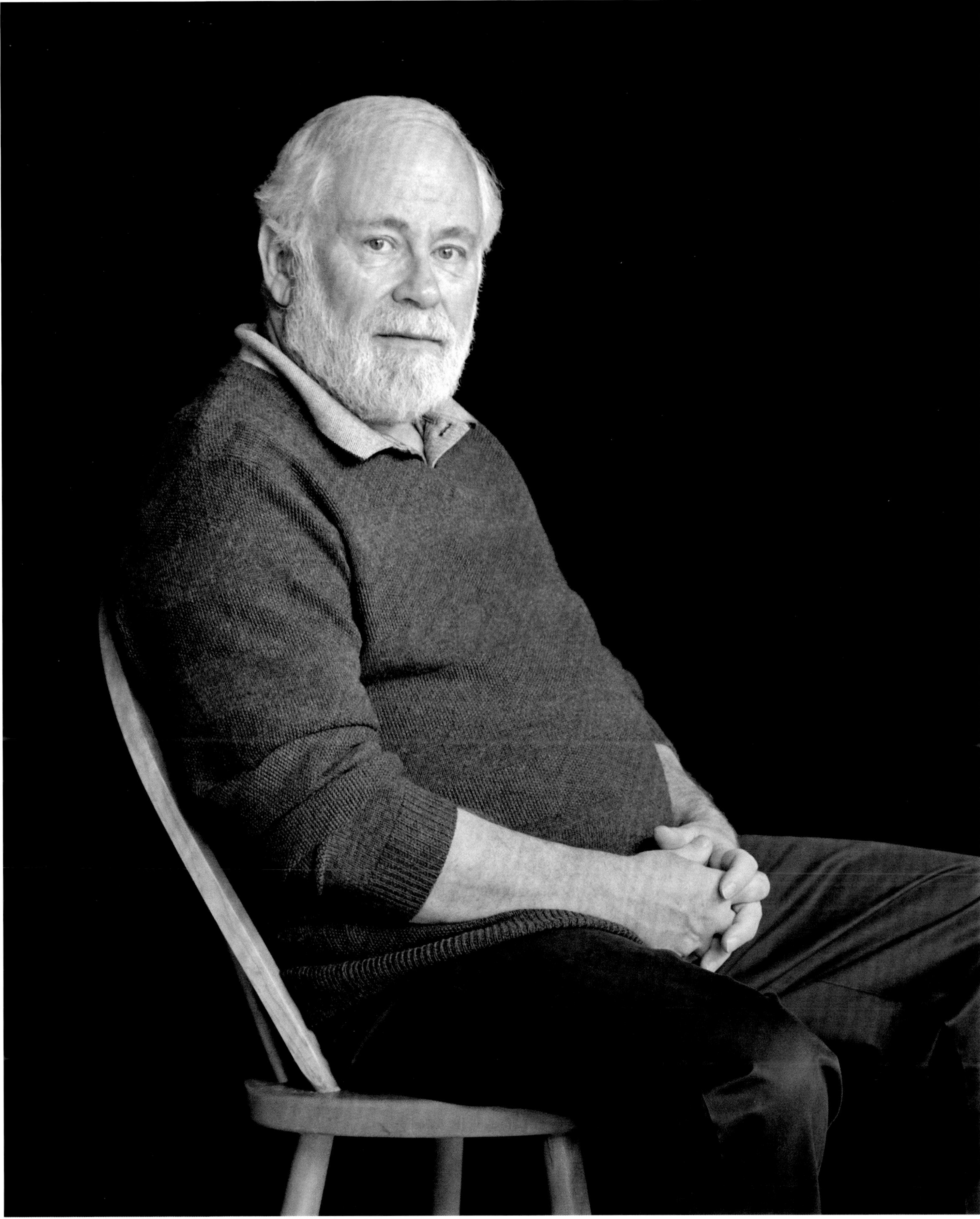

Alan B. Krueger

"How would you sum up the current evidence on the employment effects of a higher minimum wage?"

WHEN I BEGAN studying the minimum wage in the early 1990s, I did not expect to challenge the conventional wisdom that minimum wage increases inexorably lead to lower employment. In fact, when we first designed it, I thought that my 1994 *American Economic Review* study with David Card that compared job growth in New Jersey and Pennsylvania at fast food restaurants around the time that New Jersey increased its minimum wage would confirm the conventional wisdom. To my surprise, however, job growth was at least as strong in New Jersey after the state increased its minimum wage as it was in Pennsylvania. Instead of white knights rescuing the conventional wisdom, Card and I were considered pariahs in some circles that clung to the neoclassical model of the labor market.

But the finding from the New Jersey-Pennsylvania study was not an isolated anomaly. Card and I found similar results when we looked at other states, or the US as a whole. We also found lots of other behavior that was inconsistent with the economic orthodoxy of the minimum wage. For example, many employers chose to give workers, who were already earning more than the new minimum wage, a pay raise when the minimum wage increased. Such spillovers are not supposed to occur in the atomistic neoclassical model of the labor market; instead, they highlight the important role played by considerations of perceptions of fairness and worker morale in the labor market. David Card and I wrote up these and other findings in our 1995 book, *Myth and Measurement: The New Economics of the Minimum Wage*, arguing that they were consistent with a model of the labor market that emphasized dynamic frictions and market "imperfections" that create monopsony power—and then we basically stepped aside to let others evaluate our findings and produce new studies.

Although they are not unanimous, most subsequent studies have found that minimum wage increases have no discernable effect on employment. This was the conclusion reached, for example, by Paul Wolfson and Dale Belman in a comprehensive meta-analysis of over four hundred estimates of the employment effect of the minimum wage from twenty-three separate studies published between 2000 and 2013. Some of the best recent research has built on the New Jersey-Pennsylvania study, looking at the effects of statewide minimum wages using transparent comparisons between counties on opposite sides of a state border.

So how high can the minimum wage rise without jeopardizing employment? This is a difficult question to answer with currently available research because the political process typically constrains the minimum wage to lie within a narrow range. Additionally, most minimum wage hikes probably have offsetting effects on employers, causing some to reduce employment and others to be able to fill their vacancies and increase employment—with the net effect resulting in hardly any change in aggregate employment as long as the minimum wage remains in a moderate range. I am comfortable predicting that minimum wage increases in the range historically observed likely have inconsequential effects on employment, but I am reluctant to extrapolate to levels that are outside historical experience.

In light of the accumulation of evidence over the past quarter century, Paul Krugman recently wrote, "our understanding of wage determination has been transformed by an intellectual revolution—that's not too strong a word—brought by a series of remarkable studies of what happens when governments change the minimum wage." Equally importantly, there has been a revolution in the types of empirical methods that labor economists use to study wages, employment, and other job-related outcomes, and this shift started in large part with research on the minimum wage over the last quarter century. I am hopeful that in the next quarter century research will be able to pinpoint the turning point where further increases in the minimum wage lead to lower employment.

ALAN KRUEGER (1960–2019) was Professor at Princeton University and was Chair of the Council of Economic Advisers from 2011–2013.

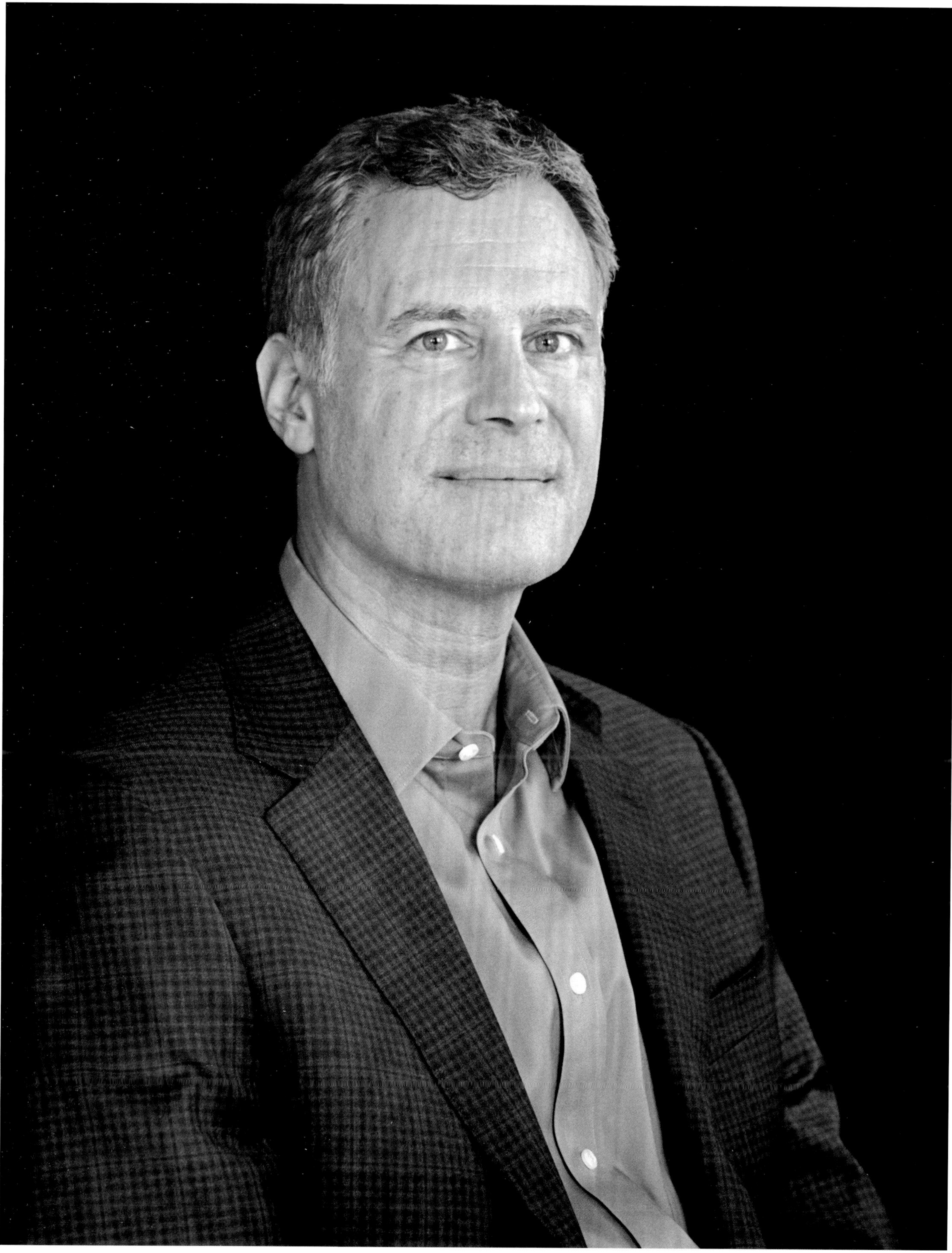

Anne Krueger

"Long ago you analyzed the political economy of 'rent-seeking.' Is it your impression that the share of rent in total income has been increasing? If so, why?"

THE TERM "RENT-SEEKING" describes activities that use resources (such as labor and capital) and produce no additional product. For example, in some fields students are forced to take exams or pay for years of training, when there are more than enough qualified people for these jobs. There is clearly a strong economic cost (the wasted years of applicants' time and effort), and no new wealth is created from it, but it is not illegal. When a company hires an expediter to secure an import license and provides the expediter with funds to bribe the license-granting official, it is not only illegal, but there are also economic costs associated with the expediter's efforts. Both activities involve rent-seeking.

A distinction is often made between "high" and "low" rent-seeking. The former refers to large expenditures and efforts seeking lucrative government contracts and other big-ticket deals. The latter refers to smaller things, such as having to pay a little extra to get the postal service to mail a package.

It is hard to say whether there is now more or less rent-seeking than in the past. There is probably less low-level rent-seeking, because some governments have effectively cracked down on it. But "high" level rent-seeking may be more prevalent because there are more government expenditures on infrastructure and because people have learned how to do it more easily.

There are obvious reasons why data on illegal activities related to rent-seeking are nonexistent and/or unreliable. The situation probably varies from country to country. In many countries, measures such as import licenses, subsidies, and rent controls were important sources of returns for rent seekers. But the lesson has been learned that in many cases quantitative restrictions and the allocation of import licenses are economically inefficient as well as costly, and countries have therefore elected to remove or significantly reduce import quotas, so there are probably less.

Procurement regulations and supervision have probably cut down on rent-seeking, even for big-ticket items in some cases. But in others, rent-seeking may have gone up. It remains unclear whether reports of corruption and other forms of rent-seeking have become more frequent or whether, in fact, the amount of big-ticket rent-seeking has gone down.

ANNE KRUEGER is Senior Research Professor at the Johns Hopkins School of Advanced International Studies, and Emeritus Professor at Stanford University. She was Chief Economist at the World Bank from 1982–1986 and First Deputy Managing Director of the International Monetary Fund from 2001–2006.

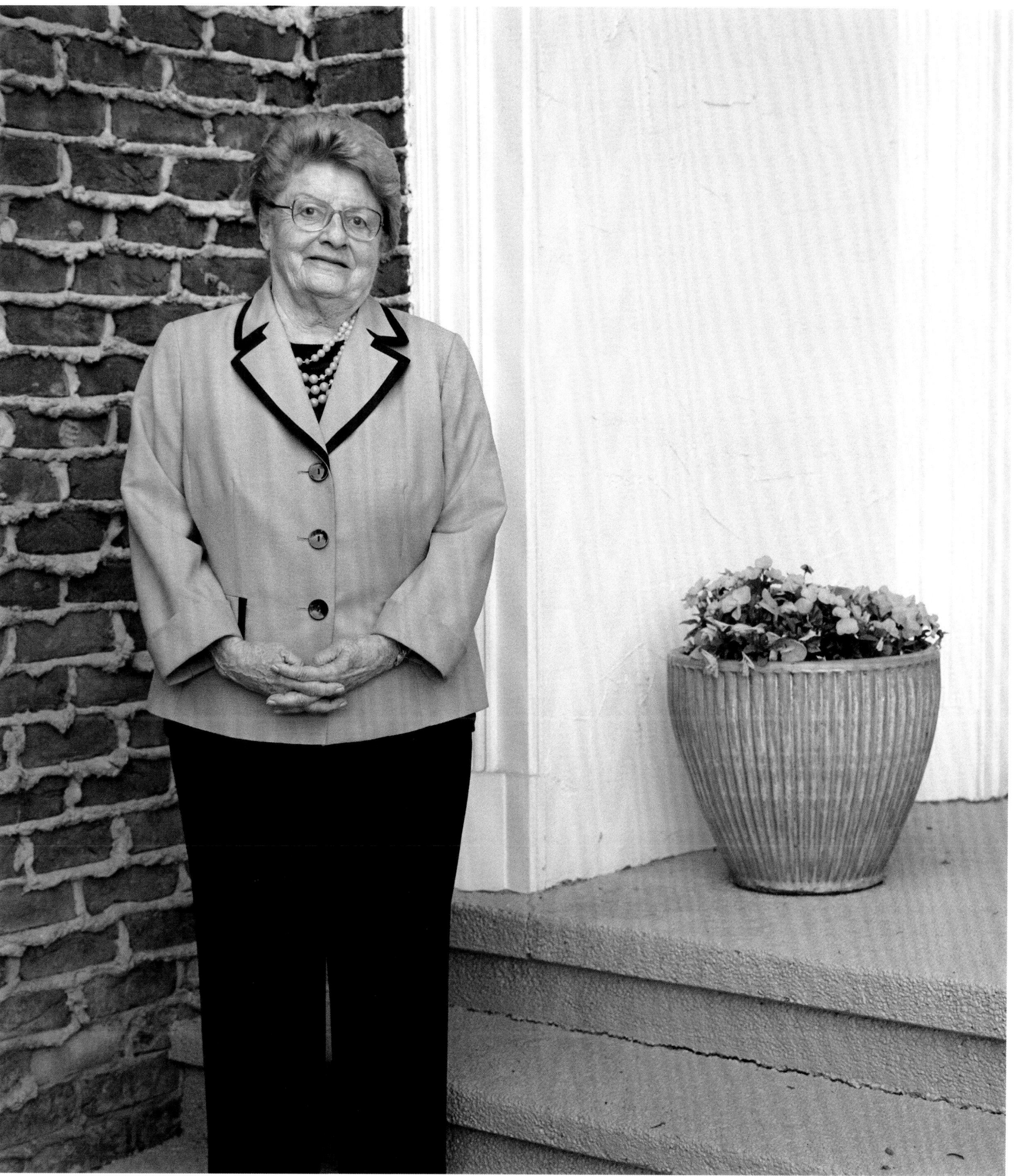

Paul Krugman

"Can we bring back good jobs?"

I GREW UP during the great postwar boom, a rising tide that really did lift all boats. Since around 1980, however, we have seen huge wealth gains at the top but stagnation or worse for many ordinary workers. Can this be turned around? Can we bring good jobs back?

Well, not the way many people think. Those high-paying manufacturing jobs we used to have aren't coming back, because manufacturing employment as a whole isn't coming back. The fact is that modern economies don't need many industrial workers to produce the physical goods they want, just as they only need a handful of farmers to feed themselves. Even if the US was to eliminate its trade deficit, manufacturing would employ only a small fraction of the working-age population.

But good jobs don't have to be in manufacturing. What we need are policies ensuring that ordinary work in service sectors, which make up the bulk of our economy, pays decently. What would it take to make that happen?

As I read it, the evidence says that it is easier than you might think, at least in terms of the economics. What we need is to enhance workers' bargaining power, and that is something both history and current international comparisons show is very doable.

What about supply and demand? Won't trying to raise workers' wages reduce employment? You might think so, and even progressive economists admit that, say, a $30 minimum wage would be a problem. But we have a lot of evidence on the effects of smaller minimum wage hikes, and this evidence overwhelmingly says that employment effects are small to nonexistent.

The reason, probably, is both that markets are imperfect—employers limit hiring to hold wages down—and that workers are people, not commodities, so things like employee morale matter a lot and can outweigh simple dollar-per-hour issues.

What goes for minimum-wage workers also goes for workers further up the scale. If we had strong unions again, they could negotiate much better deals with minimal effects on overall employment. The point is that wages are a much more malleable social construct than decrees from the Invisible Hand, which one defies at one's peril.

Where would the new good jobs be? Lots of places. Health care, which has overtaken manufacturing as our biggest employment sector, would be a key source of middle-class incomes. Retailing and wholesaling could also provide good jobs—probably fewer in retail stores, since that business is changing, but there's no reason workers in Amazon warehouses need to be at or near the poverty line.

Of course, none of this obviates the need for guaranteed health care and other social benefits.

The bottom line is that the economics of good wages do not look particularly daunting. All we need is the political will. And that, of course, is the problem.

PAUL KRUGMAN is Professor at the Graduate Center of the City University of New York. He received the John Bates Clark Medal in 1991 and the Nobel Prize for Economics in 2008.

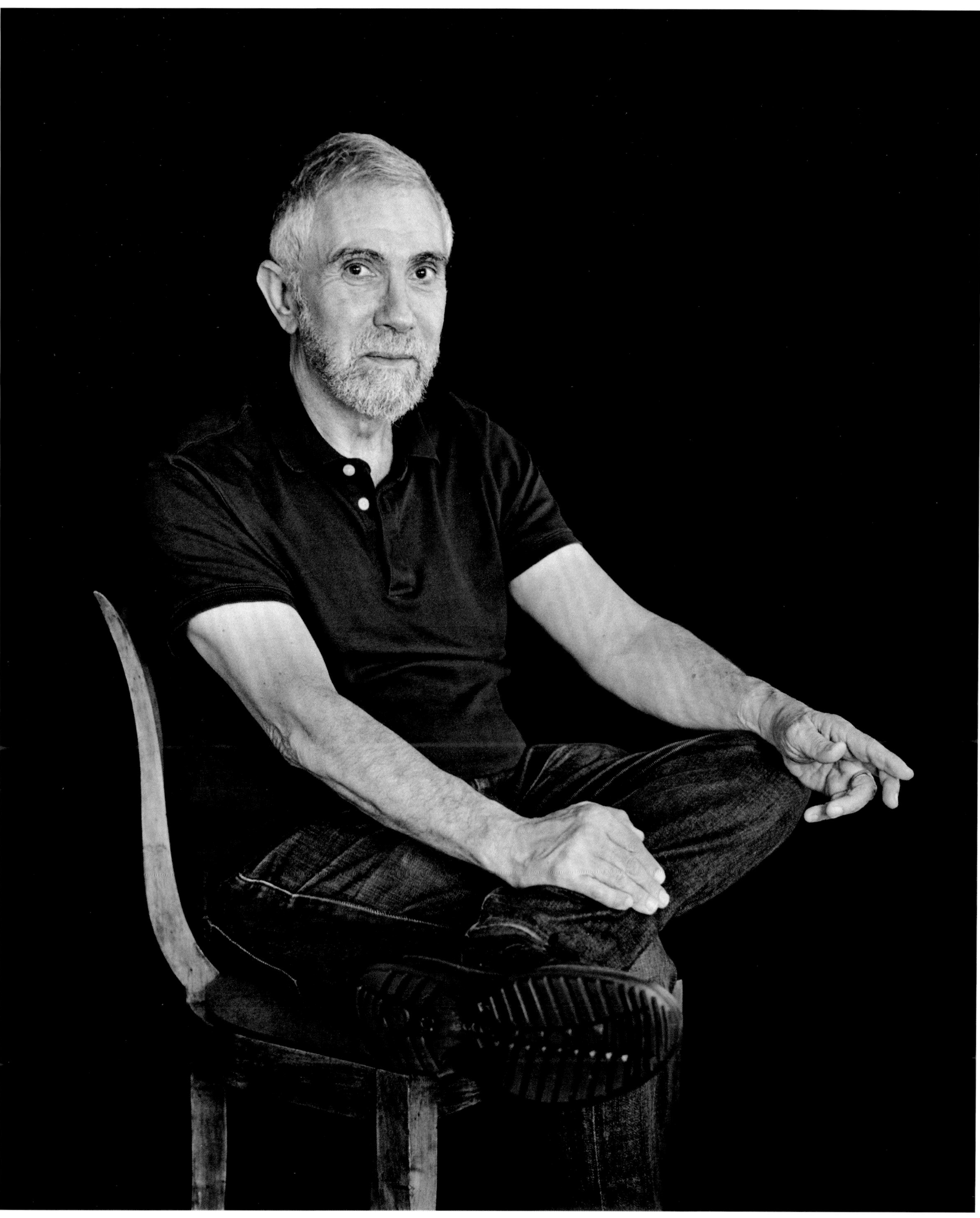

Steven Levitt

"As an economist whose career has focused on analyzing data, how do you think economics has been, and will be, affected by changes in technology?"

IF THERE IS one thing all economists agree on, it is that prices matter. Over the last fifty years, the price of doing computations has fallen to roughly *one-billionth* of what it used to cost. When prices of a good fall, people demand more of it. That is exactly what has happened in economics.

Academic economics can be roughly divided into two broad categories: theory and empirics. Theoretical economics uses logic and mathematics to derive conclusions from a set of assumptions. Every economist you've ever heard of born before 1950 was primarily a theorist. Empirical economics combines the predictions of economic theory with data to provide estimates of real-world phenomena. In the past, the computational cost of empirical research was simply too high, so economists mostly specialized in theory. As empirical work became "cheaper," economists moved away from theory towards data work (just as economic theory predicted!).

The impact of this transformation on the field of economics has been immense. Because there had been so little prior empirical work by economists, the last few decades have been bountiful ones for empirical economists. A generation of economists spent much of its time identifying "basic truths" in the data. The demand for empirical work fueled an explosion in the techniques and tools used to analyze data (what economists call "econometrics"). Data analysis in economics today, however, is at a crossroads. The "easy pickings" from data are largely gone; we've learned most of what we can learn from standard data sources. This has led researchers in different directions.

One powerful force today in economics is to build increasingly complete empirical models—essentially to more deeply intertwine economic theory and empirical analysis in what economists term "structural estimation." While this is the emerging norm in economics, I personally have my doubts. One of the enduring beauties of great economic analysis—whether theoretical or empirical—has been transparency. Almost any economist can read and understand a great theoretical paper or a great empirical paper. At least so far, however, economists have not found a way to do structural estimation in a transparent manner.

For my tastes, a much more promising future for economics involves economists moving from consumers of data (which is what we have been forever) to producers of data. Economists are increasingly designing and implementing experiments in partnerships with firms and governments that create just the right data for testing economic theories.

Another promising trend in economics is using computational advances to transform things we did not used to think of as data into data. New advances provide ways to turn words into data, allowing economists to empirically analyze transcripts of conversations between customers and call centers, or the words of politicians. There are tools to turn satellite images into data to study urbanization and environmental degradation.

The greatest limit to empirical research to date is the lack of imagination of the researcher. And yet, I have to say I'm not that optimistic about the insights that will be generated by academic economists in the foreseeable future. There is a basic problem with the incentives that are at work: the academic field rewards research that is "hard." By "hard," I mean only a few people are able to do it well, either because the math is very difficult, the programming is hard, or the ideas are extremely complex. The kind of empirical research that I think generates the greatest returns for humanity—simple, understandable, thoughtful analysis of problems that matter—has ironically gotten to be too easy! As a consequence, it is hard to build a good career as an academic economist doing that kind of research. Responding to these incentives, economists gravitate more and more to harder types of empirical work that other economists appreciate, but aren't very useful. What to do about this is a great question for economists to start working on.

STEVEN LEVITT is Professor at the University of Chicago. He received the John Bates Clark Medal in 2003.

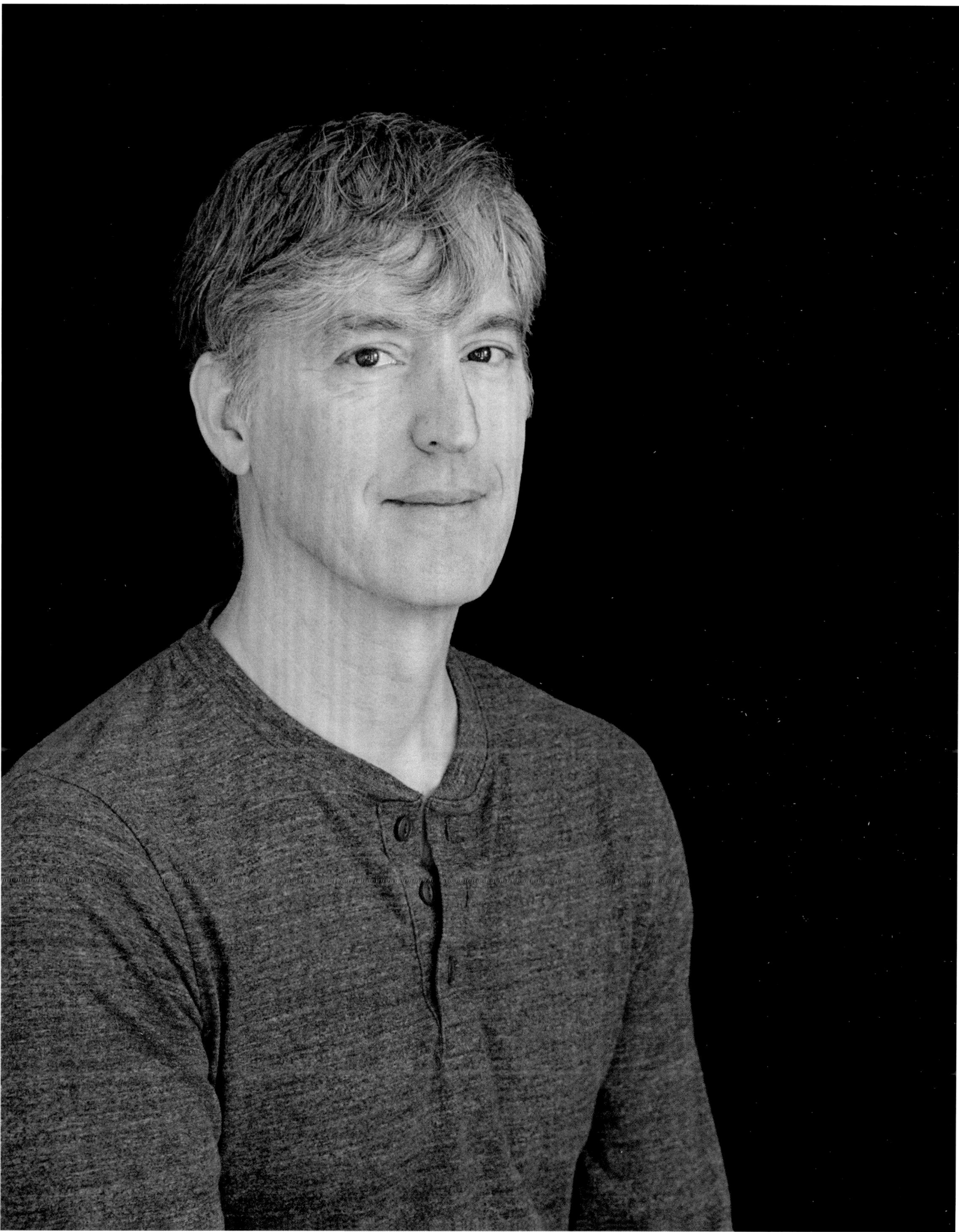

Glenn Loury

"What is your current view on affirmative action programs in college admissions, as they are now and as they might be improved?"

WHEN DISCUSSING RACIAL affirmative action programs in college admissions it is important to distinguish between moral questions of principle: Can such programs be made consistent with our values?; and pragmatic questions of efficacy: Do such programs achieve desirable goals at an acceptable cost? Having thought hard about this matter for many years now, my answer to the first question is "yes," but it is "no" to the second question.

The US Supreme Court has repeatedly affirmed that racial affirmative action programs (when narrowly tailored to meet the compelling public interest of establishing diversity in higher education) are consistent with the so-called "equal protection" requirements of the Constitution. Beyond that, I find the arguments of legal scholars and social philosophers convincing, which contend that racial preferences for applicants to selective institutions of higher education are consistent with, and sometimes even required by, defensible norms of social justice. I would even go further and say that the Court's justification of affirmative action as a legitimate tool to achieve racially diverse student bodies is too narrow a moral argument, in that it ignores the issue of social justice across generations. A major argument for using such preferences is that they may partly counter the ill-effects of historical racial discrimination that are propagated across generations due to racially segregated social structures. Indeed, I would argue that the opportunities available to black youngsters today depend, in substantial part, on the opportunities that were made available to their parents and grandparents. As a result, in the face of ongoing racial segregation in private affiliations, achieving racial equality of opportunity in the present may require programs like affirmative action.

However, the goal of achieving genuine equality between racial groups in the US is, over the longer run, *not* consistent with the special treatment of black applicants to selective institutions of higher education. If the long-run goal is racial equality, then I believe affirmative action must be a transitional policy. To the extent that it becomes enshrined as a conventional, ongoing practice, it becomes self-defeating. Only after many decades of struggling with these questions have I reluctantly come to believe that so long as black Americans are dependent on being admitted to the most elite sites of intellectual development in this country based on a lower objective standard of their own prior academic achievement, then we will not be truly equal participants, regardless of how loudly we cry out about the legacies of racial discrimination. We are now some fifty years past the dawn of racial affirmative action practices at elite universities. Much has changed in America since then. Over this period, I have watched other racial minorities take the lead at places like Cal Tech, MIT and in Silicon Valley based upon their skills, while black Americans are reduced to the position of competing by insisting that our presence is required in order to ensure "racial diversity and inclusion." Put plainly, there is "fake power"—deriving from one's ability to protest and issue demands if one is not included; and there is "real power"—deriving from one's having attained mastery over the technical material at hand. Personally, I prefer to root black Americans' standing over the longer haul in real power. I prefer to close racial gaps at the most selective institutions by elevating the ability of blacks to compete on their merits, and on a level playing field, rather than by applying different standards of evaluation to black applicants under the auspices of affirmative action programs.

Real power is the only solid ground from which genuine racial equality can emerge. It is rooted in the kind of deep human development that, in the case of black Americans, necessitates facing and overcoming the horrible effects of many generations of racial discrimination. It is worth working towards, and waiting for. Fake power hides from the sad reality of what history has wrought, while making excuses for a noncompetitiveness that history has bequeathed us—it is the easier path, but, ultimately, it is rooted in wishful thinking.

The folks who are running these institutions will accommodate demands for racial diversity so as to make the protesters go quietly to their corners. It turns out that racial affirmative action is the path of least resistance for them. But it is *not* the path to equality for black people in America. Developing the latent human talents of a disadvantaged and discriminated-against population is time-consuming, hard work, which, sadly, too many people seem eager to avoid.

GLENN LOURY is Professor at Brown University.

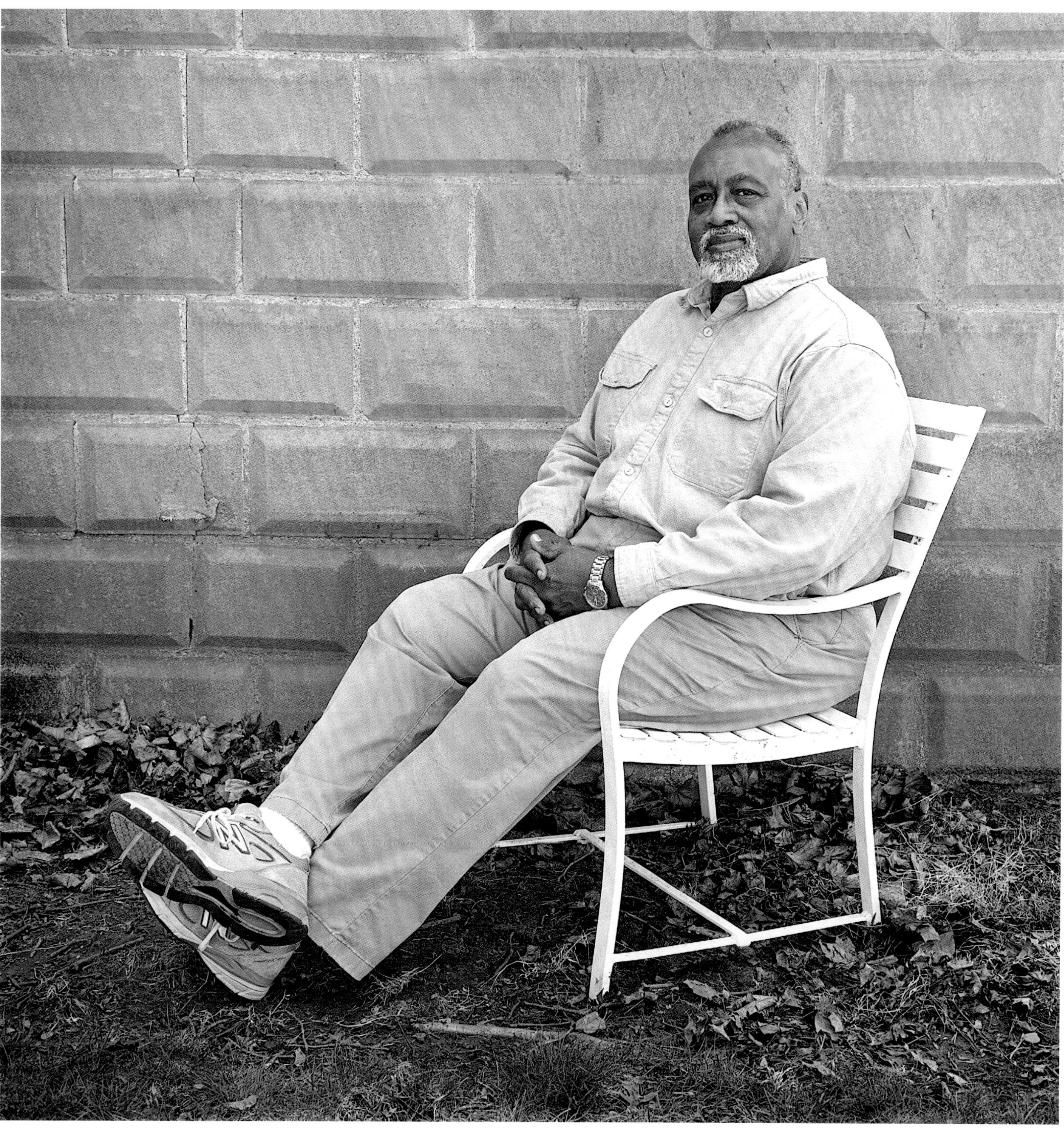

Robert Lucas

"You wrote that once you start thinking about economic growth it is hard to think of anything else. What are your current thoughts on that subject?"

AT SOME POINT in the first half of the 19th century average real incomes in the United Kingdom and the United States began to grow at something like 1 to 2 percent per year and have continued to do so up to the present. Two percent growth means real incomes that multiply sixfold every century. In the 18th century and earlier there were some very wealthy people, primarily the owners of land. But the mass of landless working people, along with their parents and their children—something like 90 percent of the population—lived at an unchanging subsistence level.

Over the decades since, many countries have attained the income levels of the UK and the US but others remain at or near the subsistence levels of their ancestors. An enormous difference in real incomes of working people, not just of a few landowners, has emerged.

What brought about these changes? Why didn't they develop in ancient Greece or the Ottoman Empire or the England of Shakespeare's day? Why have countries in Africa and South Asia developed so slowly? Those with green cards merge into American life in a generation, wherever they are from. Why not in their original country? These are questions that we might expect economists to answer, and indeed much progress has been made since we have come to understand that racial and cultural differences are not where the answer lies.

A good place to begin is with David Hume, Adam Smith, and David Ricardo—the creators of modern economics. They had worked out much of the logic of a supply-and-demand equilibrium of an entire economy by the early 1800s. Smith had identified and analyzed specific improvements that led to some societies producing more than others. But neither he nor any of his contemporaries had ever seen, or as far as I know ever imagined, an economy with sustained growth in productivity, decade after decade. Instead, Ricardo and Smith followed Thomas Malthus's successful theory that people without property would choose more children until a subsistence level was reached. The ongoing expansion of human populations combined with the constancy of incomes of working people fit the Malthusian model to a T.

Marx and Engels, in their 1848 *Communist Manifesto*, had more evidence than Ricardo had and they made good use of it. But, like Ricardo, they were Malthusians, convinced that any improvements for working people would soon be undone by population increases. We now know that this did not happen. Why not? I think the answer to this may also be in the *Manifesto*, in the inspiring passage: "The bourgeoisie has subjected the country to the rule of the towns. It has created enormous cities, has greatly increased the urban population as compared to the rural, and thus has rescued a considerable population from the idiocy of rural life." Migration from rural to urban could mean a variety of jobs besides farm labor, and possibly schooling—if not for yourself, then maybe for your children. Taking advantage of schooling options comes with a cost for each child. Gary Becker called this a choice between "quality" of children and "quantity."

In any case, most of the successful economies began with increases in production and population, followed by continued production and declining population. Is this a result of a turn from more children to "better" children as people migrate from farm to city? It may be a long shot, but that is what theoretical economists are paid for.

ROBERT LUCAS is Professor at the University of Chicago. He received the Nobel Prize for Economics in 1995.

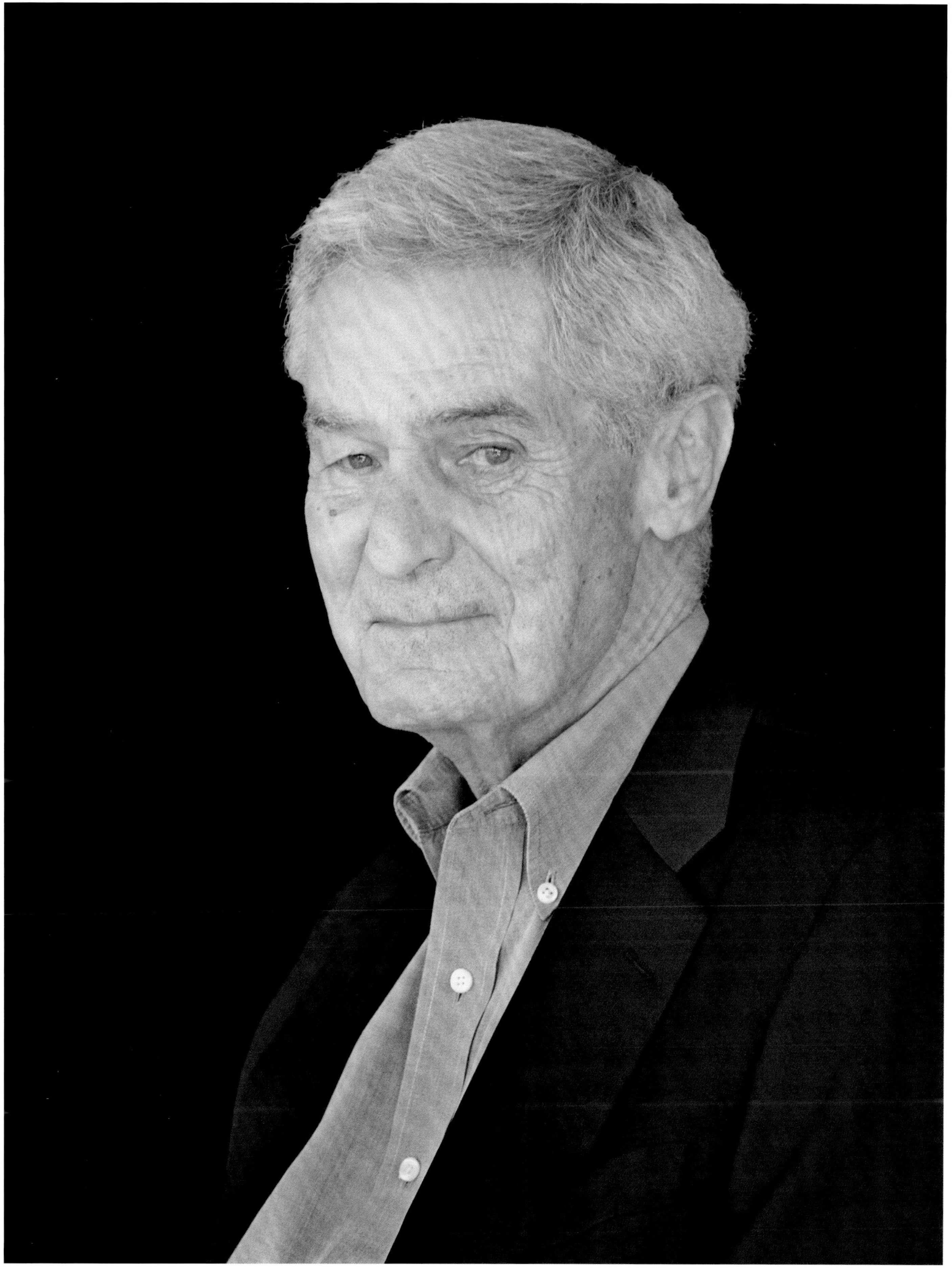

Gregory Mankiw

"Do you think it likely that, in your children's lifetime, robots will be able to outperform humans in so many tasks that human labor will be almost superfluous? And even if that is very unlikely, suppose it happened: What then?"

THROUGHOUT HISTORY, WORKERS have at times viewed technological progress as a threat to their standard of living. A famous example occurred in England in the early 19th century, when skilled knitters saw their jobs threatened by machines that could produce textiles using less-skilled workers at lower cost. The displaced workers organized violent revolts against the new technology. They smashed the weaving machines and set fire to the homes of the mill owners. Because the workers claimed to be led by General Ned Ludd (who may have been a legendary figure rather than a real person), they were called Luddites. The Luddites wanted the government to save their jobs by restricting the spread of the machines. Instead, the parliament sent in troops to suppress the Luddite riots. Today, the term "Luddite" refers to anyone who opposes technological progress.

Economic history teaches that, more often than not, technological progress is the worker's friend. Living standards are higher today than they were a century ago mainly because new technologies have increased labor productivity and thereby the wages we earn. To be sure, an advance in technology can destroy some jobs, but it usually reduces the cost of producing what we want, gives us a greater variety of goods and services, and frees up our time for other, more valuable tasks. The invention of the automobile reduced the need for the blacksmith's horseshoes, but it increased the need for the mechanic's car repair.

The rise of robots, I believe, will exhibit a similar pattern. Some routine tasks will be automated, some jobs will be destroyed, and modern Luddites will object; but overall, we will benefit from the higher quality of life. Your bank's ATM is a robot of sorts. Who would prefer to wait in line for a human teller to perform the simplest bank transactions? And there is no cause for alarm: the economy has found other jobs for all those would-be human tellers.

Two centuries ago, most Americans were farmers. Today, thanks to advances in agricultural technology, farmers are less than 2 percent of the population. If we traveled back in a time machine and told someone of the earlier era that we are now able to produce all the food we need with so few farmers, he would wonder how people spend their time. We could tell him about the new jobs that have been created—software engineers, website designers, CAT scan operators, and so on—but he would have trouble comprehending what these jobs are. Similarly, I expect advances in robotics to create new human jobs that today we cannot begin to describe.

But suppose I am wrong. Imagine a future in which robots, with little human input, can produce almost every good and service that we desire (including new robots). What then? In such a world, the distribution of capital's ownership, determined by past saving and inheritance, would be even more important for peoples' standards of living than it is today. We would need to think hard about how society distributes wealth. The problem of inequality could loom very large.

On the other hand, with robots so amazingly productive, we might have largely solved the fundamental economic problem—scarcity. Perhaps the economy would be capable of giving us almost everything we want without the toil of our labor. We would then face the ultimate first-world problem: how to occupy ourselves. We could spend our time reading great literature, taking walks on the beach, enjoying the company of friends, and mentoring our children and grandchildren. In essence, a comfortable retirement would begin at birth. This prospect may raise its own challenges, but there are worse problems to have.

GREGORY MANKIW is Professor at Harvard University. He was Chair of the Council of Economic Advisers from 2003–2005.

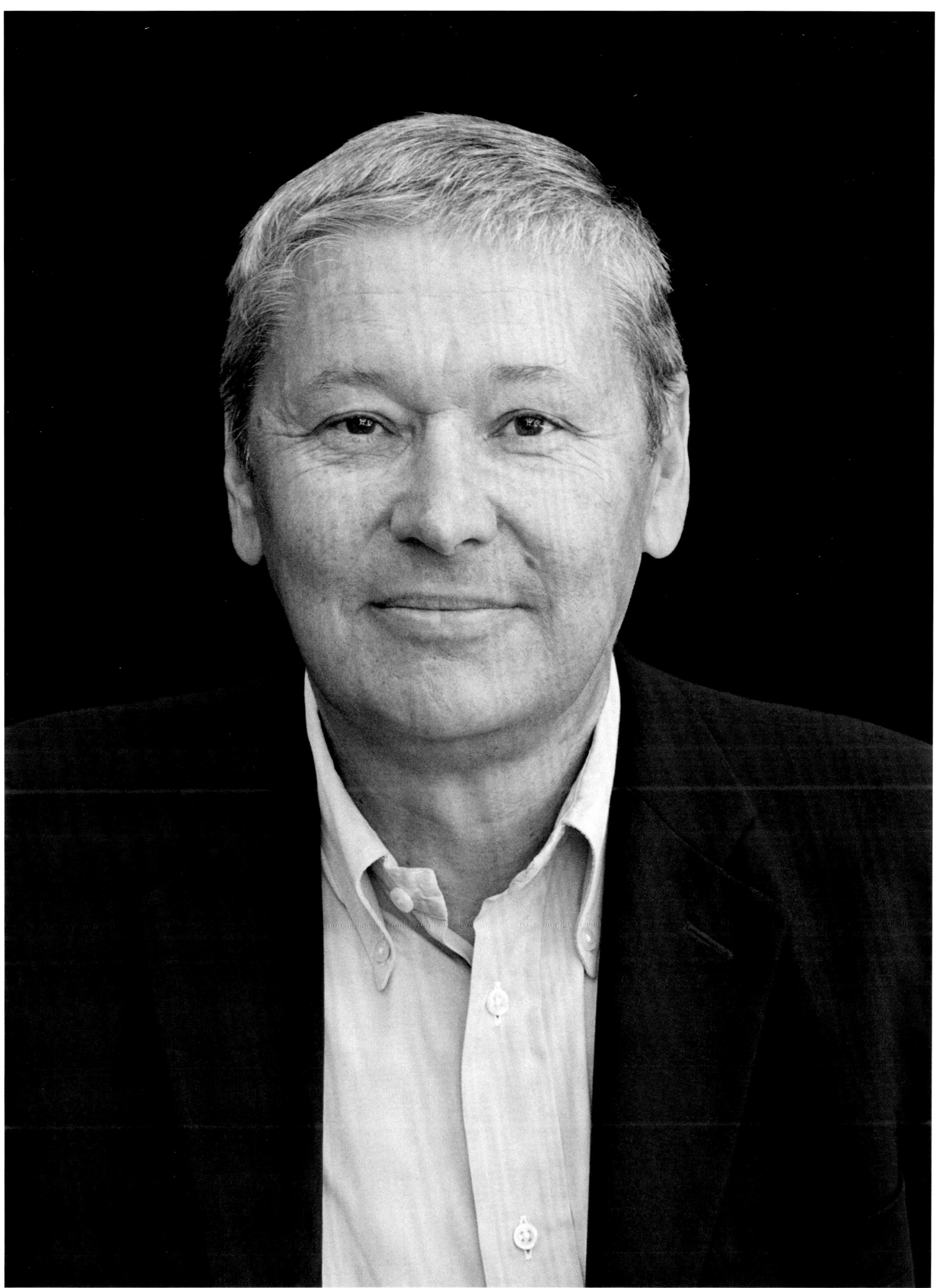

James G. March

"Does organization theory have anything to tell us about the current boom in executive compensation?"

MOST MODERN IDEAS (theories?) about deliberate decision-making by individual human beings emphasize the basic idea that action should be, and is, guided by utilitarian hopes for future consequences. The idea fills many parts of the literature at least since the Greeks, and much of contemporary economics is built around refined versions of such a *logic of consequences*. Similar ideas are central also to large parts of political science and psychology. Individuals are assumed to be "rational" in the sense that they seek to act in such a way that it maximizes the subjective value of the expected consequences of their behavior.

Many traditional theories of organizations are similar. They assume an organization's choices are made in order to maximize expected consequences. Decisions are assumed to be made by the highest-ranking executive, or through a system of shared values and information, and hierarchical obedience, so that an organization acts as though it were a single actor.

Modern theories of organizations, however, reflect empirical observations of processes of choice that reveal seven important elaborations that collectively paint a different picture. First, they show *uncertainty and ambiguity both about the world and about desires*. Both the beliefs about probable consequences and the preferences explicitly held are incomplete, inaccurate, inconsistent, and changing. Rationality is bounded by these limitations.

Second, organizational theory recognizes that organizations are not single actors but *involve multiple individuals and groups* with varying objectives and understandings. There is conflict. There is well-justified mutual distrust. There are problems of agency, coordination, and implementation. Resolution of the conflict involves various forms of bargaining, contracting, and the exercise of power that each have their own logics.

Third, theories of organizational action emphasize *the complications of attention*. Attention is scarce, and the scarcity of attention dictates that only some alternatives and consequences will be considered, that only some values will be evoked. As a result, some theories of organizational decision-making are more properly seen as theories of attention than as theories of choice.

Fourth, theories of organizations are likely to see the fundamental individual logic of choice as based not on consequences but on a *logic of appropriateness*. They portray organizational actors as acting to fulfill the obligations of an identity. The obligations are sometimes obscure or conflicting, so the logic of appropriateness, like the logic of consequences, is only a framework for action; but it is a different framework with different implications.

Fifth, students of organizational theory are likely to see the actions of various organizations as *linked through imitation within networks of diffusion*. Premises and courses of action spread among individual organizations. Decisions are made by imitating the actions of similar organizations. Emphasis is placed on an organization's ability to observe and to copy what another organization is doing.

Sixth, those who study organizations view *decision-making as symbolic*. Substantive outcomes are less important than the symbolic meanings given to them within and outside the organization. Decisions symbolize who and what are important, and concerns and conflict over those issues dictate the course and outcome of a decision process.

Seventh, modern organizational theory regards the major premises of decision—for example, the values held by actors and the map of consequences—not as completely imposed by some external process but as *partly endogenous to the process of decision-making itself*. What individuals and organizations want and what the world offers are not given entirely ex ante but develop within the experience of making choices.

These observations make theories of organizations generally more powerful as instruments for understanding or interpreting history than as predictors of it, a posture that does not always endear them to modern soldiers of logical positivism. For example, although the theories do not, in general, predict phenomena such as executive compensation with any precision, they identify seven factors that provide plausible partial explanations of what is actually observed.

JAMES MARCH (1928–2018) was Professor Emeritus at Stanford University.

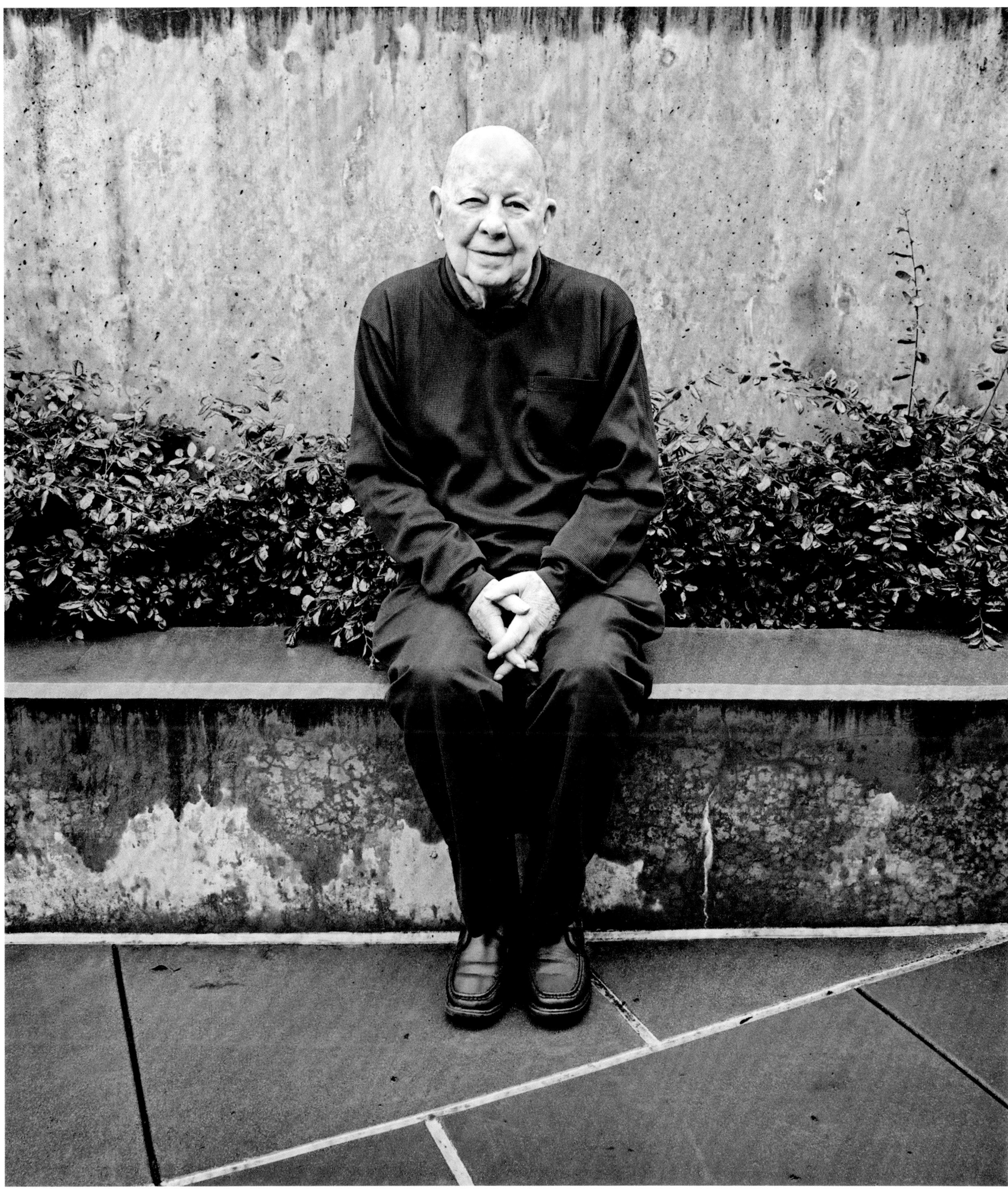

Eric Maskin

"What got you interested in studying alternative voting systems? Was it idle curiosity, a relation to mechanism design, or the hope of reforming current practice?"

I'VE SPENT MUCH of my career working on mechanism design, the theory of "reverse engineering" in collective decision-making. The theory tells us how a group of people, starting from some goal (say, reducing local air pollution by some percentage), can work backwards to figure out what institutions or "mechanisms" will best achieve the goal (e.g., which combination of taxes on polluters, subsidies on clean technology, and outright bans on certain factories will attain the reduction with the least disruption).

Constructing a good voting system—one that truly reflects citizens' preferences—is certainly connected to mechanism design. Indeed, it can be viewed as a particular application of the general theory. But that connection wasn't what got me thinking about voting in the first place. Rather, I agreed to contribute to a volume in honor of my friend Amartya Sen, and then had to find something to write about. So, I went back to Amartya's work on voting from the 1960s for inspiration.

Plurality rule is the voting system most often used in the US and it's very straightforward: each voter endorses one candidate and the candidate with the most endorsements wins. Unfortunately, it's also badly flawed. To see why, imagine that there are three candidates—A, B, and C—running for office and that the electorate breaks down into three groups: 40 percent of voters (the "A-supporters") like A best, B least, and C in between; 35 percent of voters (the "B-supporters") have the opposite preference; and the remaining 25 percent (the "C-supporters") rank C highest, then B, and then A. Under plurality rule, voters in each group will presumably vote for the candidate they support. That means that candidate A will win the election (with 40 percent of the vote). Notice, however, that all the B- and C-supporters—60 percent of the electorate—actually prefer C to A (and also prefer B to A)—so, electing A seems wrong and undemocratic. Candidate A wins because the anti-A vote (despite being in the majority) is *split* between B and C.

Can we necessarily avoid vote splitting—electing the wrong candidate because the opposition is divided—by replacing plurality rule with some other voting system? Unfortunately, the answer is no—Kenneth Arrow established in 1951 that *no* reasonable election system can always stop vote splitting. But that doesn't mean that plurality rule can't be improved on. Indeed, nearly two hundred years before Arrow, the Marquis de Condorcet proposed an alternative system—namely, *majority* rule—that constitutes a considerable improvement.

Under majority rule, a voter doesn't just endorse her favorite candidate; she submits her entire ranking. So, in the example above, an A-supporter would rank A first, then C, and then B. Given the submissions, the winner is then the candidate preferred by a majority to each opponent (hence, the term "majority rule"). In the example, candidate C is the majority winner: 60 percent of the electorate (the B- and C-supporters) prefer C to A, and 65 percent of voters (the A- and C-supporters) prefer C to B.

Condorcet himself was aware that majority rule doesn't get around vote splitting all the time, but not until 1969 was there a complete analysis. That year, Sen and Prasanta Pattanaik showed exactly when majority rule avoids the vote-splitting problem and when it doesn't. Their paper was the starting point for my own thinking. Specifically, in the Sen Festschrift and in a more general paper with Partha Dasgupta, I showed that there is a sense in which majority rule is actually the *best* voting system: it gets around vote splitting more often than any other.

In the meantime, plurality rule has repeatedly been electing the "wrong" candidates in practice: for example, George W. Bush in 2000 (when Ralph Nader split off votes from Al Gore) and Donald Trump in 2016 (when vote splitting prevented any mainstream Republican candidate from mounting a successful challenge).

Perhaps we can hope that majority rule is an idea whose time has come, not just theoretically but practically.

ERIC MASKIN is Professor at Harvard University. He received the Nobel Prize for Economics in 2007.

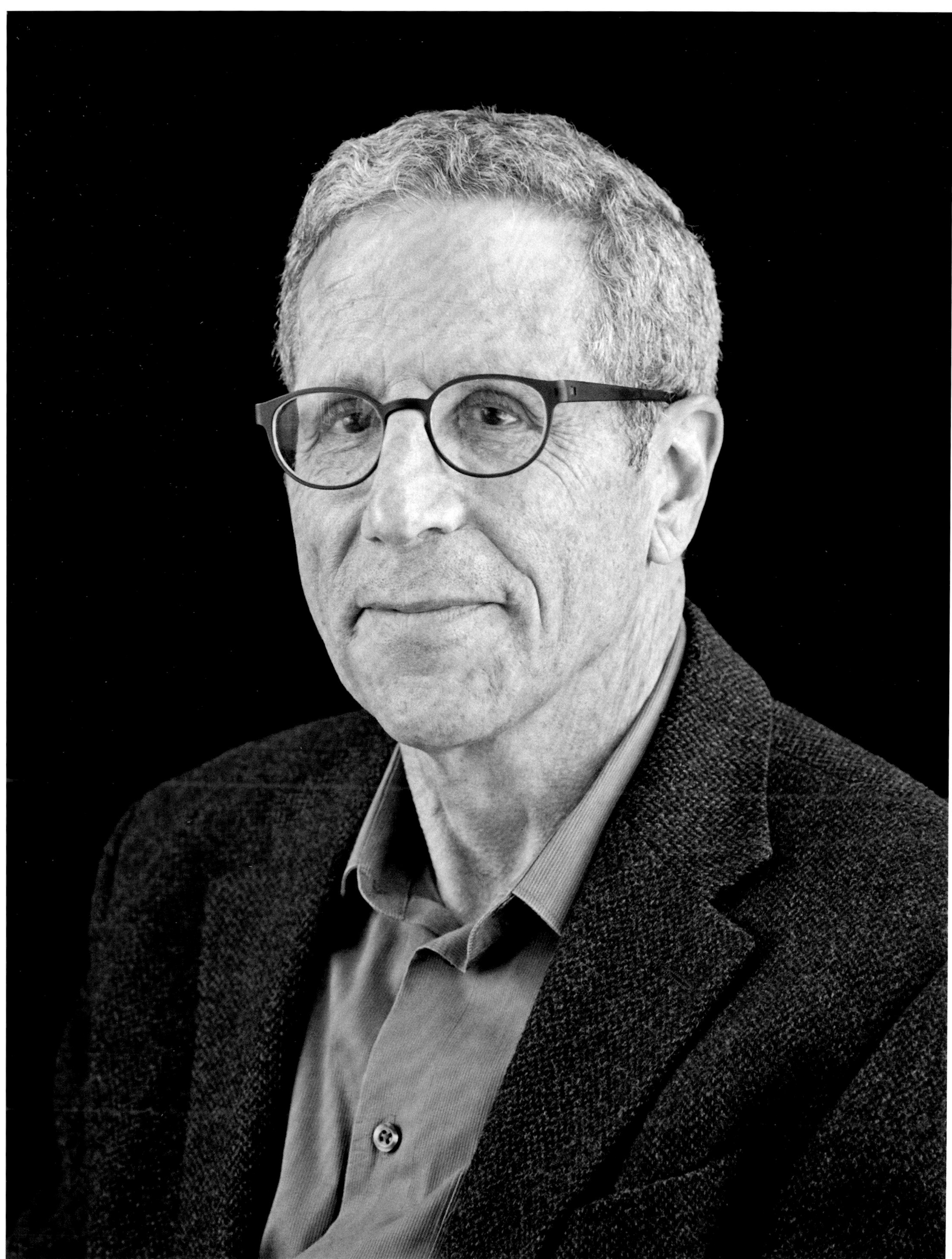

Daniel McFadden

"Does Medicare help much to narrow the health advantage of the high-status elderly?"

YES! OF COURSE, the question is, Medicare compared to what. I take the alternative to be America's largely private system for financing and delivering health care prior to the adoption of Medicare in 1965, or the mixed system in place today for non-elderly health care. Before Medicare, the well-off often had private insurance or the ability to pay out-of-pocket for any health costs, while the poor were often uninsured, and cost was a deterrent to seeking timely health care. Health catastrophes could immiserate patients and their families. By reducing financial risks, Medicare reduced stress and depression, which in turn benefited health, particularly among the elderly poor. The economic status of the Medicare population reveals the importance of this protection against financial risk: in 2016, 25 percent of recipients had incomes below the federal poverty level of $12,070, savings below $14,550, and home equity below $7,350. Obviously, these elderly individuals do not have the ability to pay major medical bills. In a world without Medicare, would these people have had a private insurance alternative? The answer is that such insurance was largely not offered before 1965, or offered at premiums that were out of reach for this socioeconomic class of people. Further, these elderly poor almost certainly share with their non-elderly contemporaries a reluctance to buy voluntary health insurance even when it is actuarially fair, a reflection of a general behavioral tendency to discount or neglect future risks, and an expectation that if something bad happens, someone or something will come to the rescue.

A more complicated question is how Medicare influences delivery of health services across the socioeconomic spectrum. Medicare is primarily an insurance program, not a directive for health-care delivery. However, its coverage rules and reimbursement rates for providers affect the availability and use of health-care services. Medicare revenue is critical for hospitals and practitioners in urban areas where the elderly poor are concentrated. Without it, many elderly would not have access to needed services. The American health-care system is poor at diagnosing, monitoring, and treating chronic and mental health conditions, particularly for the uninsured, but even-handed at treating acute health conditions, independent of insurance status. The well-off may get prompter treatment and more follow-ups for acute conditions; this is largely palliative.

The "wealth-health" gradient, with the wealthy having fewer health problems and living longer, is a phenomenon that spans eras and health delivery systems. The gradient is linked to childhood nutrition and illness, behavior, the environment, and the ability of healthy people to work and accumulate capital. In the US, this gradient increases with age, so that when people in America reach age 65, health problems are much more common among those with low socioeconomic status. Other developed countries also have a wealth-health gradient, but with nearly universal health coverage and stronger social safety nets, the poor are not as sick and the gradient is not as sharp. If one focuses just on the health of those aged 65 and older, the Medicare population has a life expectancy comparable to individuals in the same age bracket from other developed countries. Further, the incidence of new health conditions in those 65 and over and the outcomes from their treatment show no socioeconomic gradient for life-threatening illnesses (including cancer) and a modest gradient for non-life-threatening medical problems, but it does show a continued sharp gradient for mental health problems. This pattern coincides with levels of Medicare coverage, best for life-threatening conditions and worst for mental illness. Together, these comparisons provide clear evidence that Medicare results in better health outcomes for elderly individuals with low socioeconomic status than the alternative of a voluntary private health insurance system. Furthermore, the level of coverage matters, with Medicare having the least impact for health conditions for which it provides the least coverage. In conclusion, Medicare reduces the wealth-health gradient by improving health outcomes for low-status enrollees, while underwriting care for the well-off that is comparable to what they would buy in a private system.

DANIEL MCFADDEN is Professor at the University of Southern California and the University of California, Berkeley. He received the John Bates Clark Medal in 1975 and the Nobel Prize for Economics in 2000.

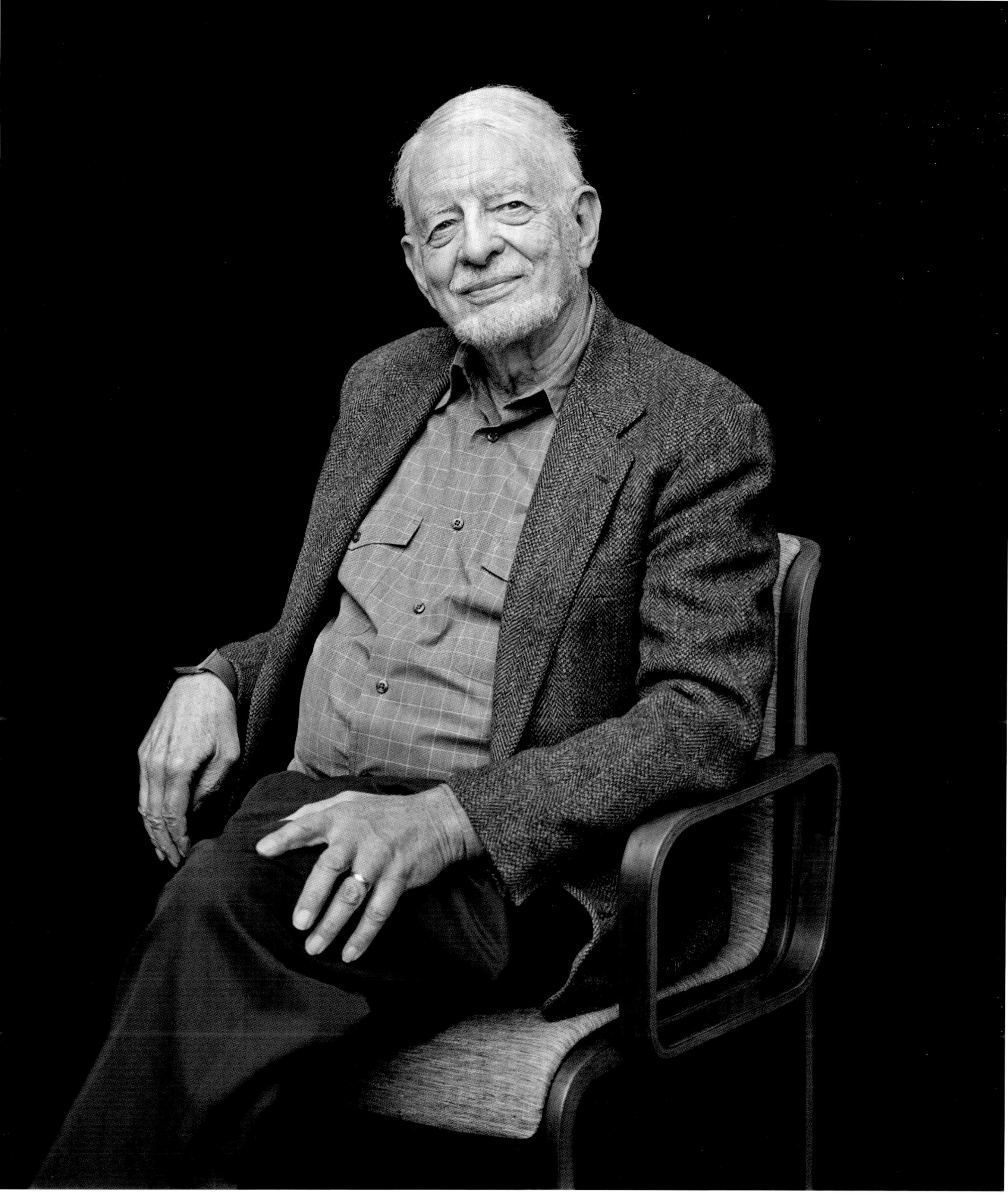

Robert C. Merton

"Is rapid financial innovation destabilizing?"

IN THE 1970s the US experienced multiple shocks that greatly increased uncertainty and volatility. These include the collapse of the Bretton Woods global currency system, two oil crises, a stock market decline of 50 percent, and double-digit inflation levels not seen in the US in more than one hundred years. Contrary to macroeconomic theory, this inflation was accompanied by high unemployment—a combination that stymied using traditional monetary and fiscal remedies. Both long- and short-term US Treasury interest rates were also double-digit, and as a consequence of a ceiling placed on the deposit rates that banks could pay, there was no money for home mortgages, regardless of credit rating or a willingness to pay high rates.

Following these shocks there was an explosion of financial innovation and reform. Derivative markets were created to efficiently manage the new and increased levels of risks: financial futures hedged currencies, interest rates, and equities; option exchanges provided financial value insurance; and negotiated commissions on stock trading were mandated, triggering the institutionalization of stock market investing. The first electronic stock exchange was created, while diversification capabilities for both institutions and individual investors were greatly increased by the advent of low-cost index funds. Money-market funds, floating-rate and high-yield bonds expanded fixed-income saving. The establishment of a national mortgage market and debt securitization created a global base of funding for residential housing, which, along with the elimination of destructive bank deposit rate ceiling regulations, assured the uninterrupted availability of mortgage money in the US ever since. The innovation of the interest rate swap permanently eliminated the need for banks to bear the risks of maturity-mismatch interest rates in order to service the preferences of both their depositor and borrower customers. Thus, the 1970s showed us the potential for a financial crisis to engender large social benefits through innovation. Derivative markets and other innovations that were developed in the US largely during periods of economic stress have subsequently been adopted around the world and have continued to provide substantial social dividends for the past four decades.

I do have considerable concerns about excessive expectations around the future of financial innovations driven by digital technologies, "FinTech," especially with respect to nongovernment digital currencies. In particular, so-called fiat currencies that are legal tender for a country actually have an intrinsic value because they can be used to settle tax payments and legal-tender-dominated private obligations. Fiat currencies that are not legal tender have no such intrinsic value. The viability of any currency depends on collective trust and the lack of any material intrinsic value is a prime source of instability, as in any Ponzi scheme. Because governments hold the ultimate responsibility for failures in their payment systems, it is difficult to imagine their accepting as legal tender a currency that was not essentially under their control. As the ban on ownership of gold by US citizens prior to 1971 demonstrates, governments have the power to effectively ban the holding of any currency surrogate. In sum, the only successful digital currencies will be government ones.

The potential benefits of FinTech in reducing financial transactions' costs and improving clearing and settling (including establishing clear titles to real estate) are enormous, especially for developing countries. It is likely to be most rapidly successful in activities involving calculations and data storage/access where performance can be readily verified and involves little judgment so that transparency can be substituted for opaqueness. FinTech will likely face greater resistance in financial services that are "inherently opaque," such as financial advisement and integrated product solutions. The only means of providing such services and products is through "trust"—a critical and valuable asset that encapsulates three essential elements: trustworthiness, competence, and reliability. Retail consumers of such opaque services lost trust in both providers and regulators in 2008–2009, and the impact is still being felt nearly a decade later. Technology by itself is not a substitute for trust. Indeed, FinTech increases time efficiency and lowers cost by substituting "black box" technology for human efforts, but in doing so it also increases opacity—what motives were behind the design of the advice? What is the quality of the advice model embedded in the technology and what data are used to feed that model? However it is achieved, FinTech will make trust an even more important and valuable asset in the future.

ROBERT MERTON is Professor at the Massachusetts Institute of Technology Sloan School of Management. He received the Nobel Prize for Economics in 1997.

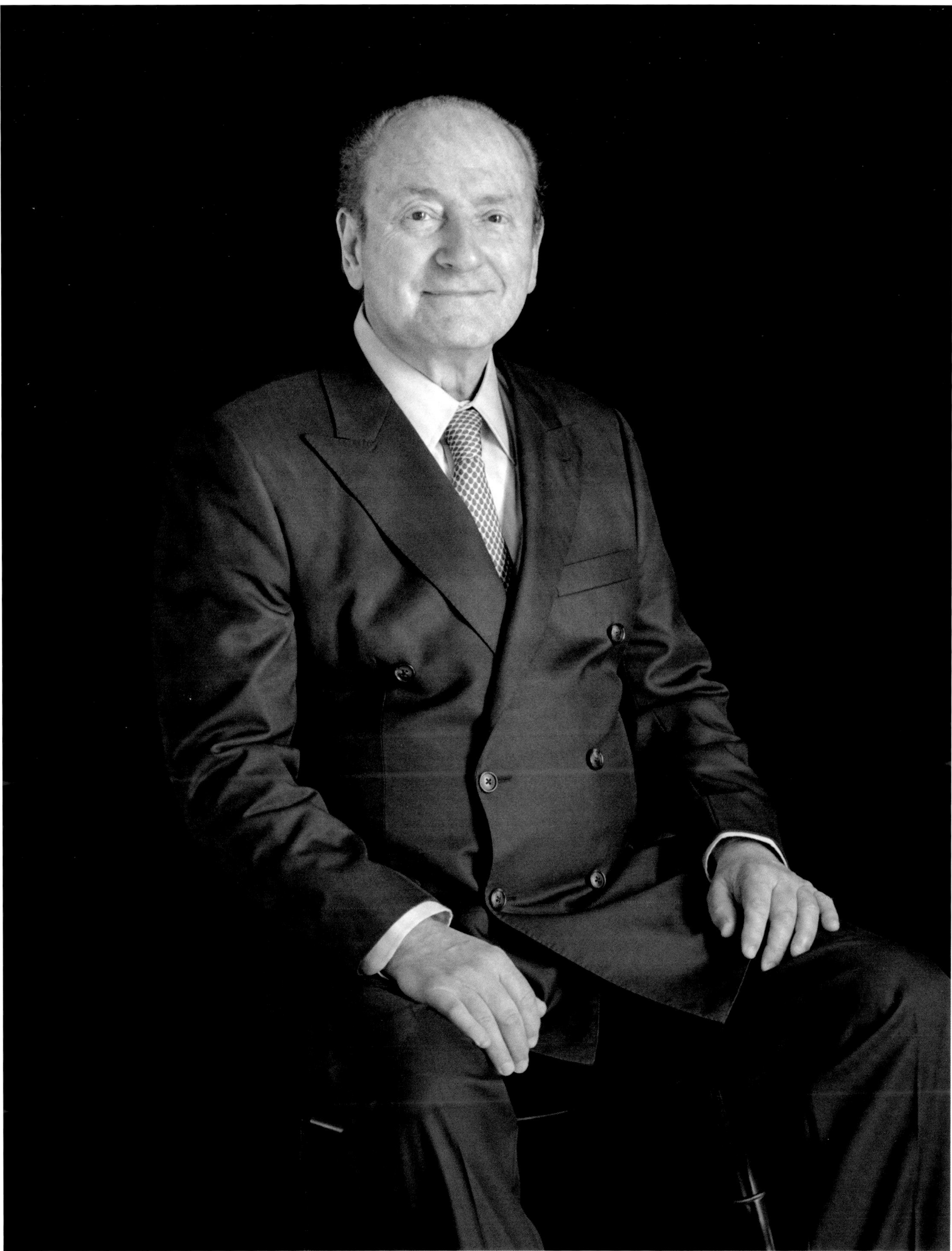

Paul Milgrom

"You were a designer of the method our government uses to auction off the radio spectrum. Can you explain the uses of auction theory to nontechnical readers?"

WHEN NONECONOMISTS THINK about auctions, they most often imagine the sale of individual rare items, like a piece of art or antique furniture. Most of modern auction design is *not* focused on these simple sales, but rather on the sale of multiple related items. As a simple example, suppose you're bidding to buy tickets for a sporting event and your group wants six seats in a row. Somebody else wants four seats in the same row. If the tickets were sold individually in separate auctions, this could be bad for both of you. You might buy two tickets before finding that you must bid very aggressively to win the other four, or you might be forced to accept seats spread over different rows. If such outcomes were common, the bidders might bid lower prices for the first few seats or might be discouraged from participating at all, which is bad for the sellers, too. Neither buyers nor sellers are well served by a too-simple auction process.

Auction theory is the branch of economics that solves problems like that: it studies how auctions can be designed to achieve desirable outcomes, even accounting for bidders' strategic behavior. The theory has important applications on the internet. Every time an internet user browses a new web page, the search engine or publisher runs an automated auction to determine which ads to show and how to arrange them on the page. In a close analogy to the ticket auctions, some advertisers may want to show only large ads, or may offer to pay more for such an ad. Well-designed auctions are vital to the profitability of this industry: in 2017, there was more than $200 billion of digital ad revenues received by publishers and search engines, mostly through auctions. With such high stakes, companies have struggled with how to design effective and profitable auctions for digital online advertising.

Although I have personally worked on auction design for a number of industries, my most exciting project was an auction to assign rights for using the radio spectrum in the US. Called the "incentive auction," it was completed in 2017, and it solved the most complicated auction problem in history. I led the team of economists and computer scientists which designed and implemented the incentive auction, in which the US government re-assigned TV broadcast rights to free up the spectrum for telephone and cable companies. Some special challenges made the incentive auction exceptionally complicated. First, the new channel assignments needed to avoid broadcast interference among stations, which involved checking more than one million noninterference constraints. Due to these constraints, determining whether a given assignment is feasible is a computationally hard problem and implementing the auction required that my team innovate new computational algorithms. Second, the revenues from the sale of the mobile broadband licenses needed to cover the cost of acquiring TV stations. So, the number of channels that could be reassigned from TV broadcast to mobile broadband would depend on the bids in the auction. There was no fixed set of licenses to sell, and no fixed set of channels to be cleared by purchasing broadcast rights. Finally, despite all this complexity, the auction needed to be easy for bidders to understand, to keep costs relatively low, and to discourage strategic behavior.

In spite of these challenges, the incentive auction was a resounding success. The US government bought rights from TV station owners for about $10 billion, assigned the TV stations that did not sell to continue broadcasting in a smaller set of channels, and sold the freed spectrum rights for about $20 billion of gross revenues. The incentive auction illustrates the need to develop new economic theory, and new science in related fields, in order to cope with the complex problems that arise in practical applications. This is what makes auction theory such an exciting and active area of research.

PAUL MILGROM is Professor at Stanford University.

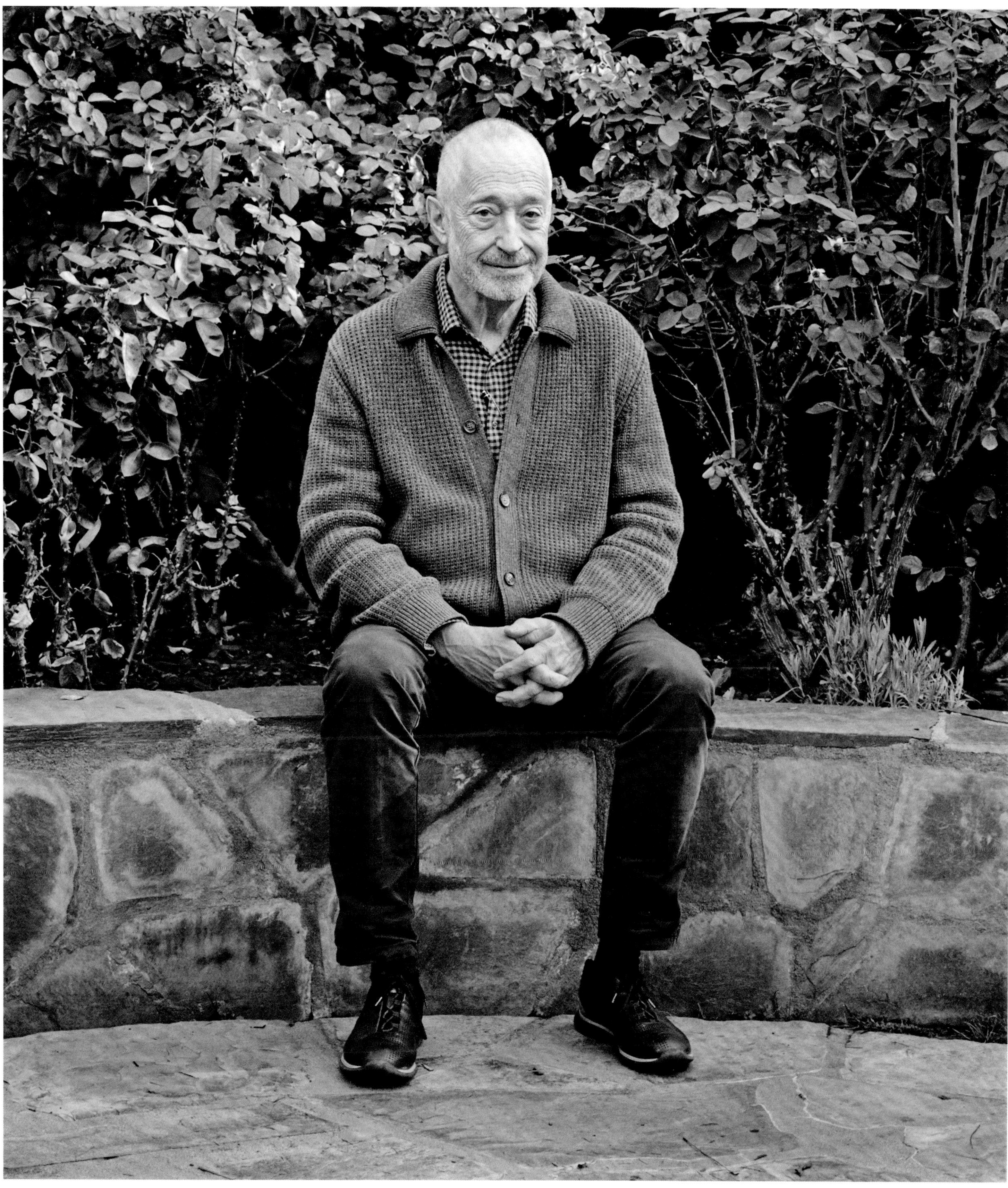

Maurice Obstfeld

"Does trade cooperation have a future?"

INTERNATIONAL TRADE IS an unloved child. Historian Thomas Babington Macaulay wrote in 1824 that "Free trade, one of the greatest blessings which a government can confer on a people, is in almost every country unpopular." That unpopularity gives politicians an opening to mobilize nationalism for their own purposes, and gives vested interests an excuse to pursue gain at the country's expense.

International surveys by the Pew Research Center show that the United States is exceptional in the extent of people's skepticism about the merits of trade. In 2016, both major US presidential candidates ran against trade in some way. Not only NAFTA and the planned Trans-Pacific Partnership, but the World Trade Organization and other US trade commitments became major punching bags for Republican Donald J. Trump. He tagged them all as ways that foreigners profit at US expense. As President, he has withdrawn from TPP; renegotiated NAFTA (achieving minimal changes at the cost of major disruption); levied tariffs on "national security" grounds against a variety of trade partners including Canada; bullied Korea into adopting a US steel export quota; delayed naming judges to the WTO appellate body; and initiated a large-scale trade conflict with China. Further actions loom.

In the background, a clear and consistent objective is absent. Sometimes the goal is "fair reciprocal trade"—you treat us as we treat you. But that will not bring manufacturing back. Moreover, Trump also regards US trade deficits with specific trade partners as *prima facie* evidence of unfair, nonreciprocal trade—the deficit partner is losing, the surplus partner winning, in a zero-sum vision of trade.

In reality, the pattern of bilateral surpluses and deficits reflects the international division of labor, from which all countries gain through higher global productivity. Clumsy attempts to manipulate bilateral trade are therefore likely to bring unintended negative consequences. Moreover, they will have little impact on the United States' *overall* foreign trade deficit (its deficit with all trade partners). That deficit is expanding under the pressure of the US tax cuts and government spending increases that Trump happily signed into law. Trade policy and macroeconomic policy are on a collision course, which will likely lead to more blame and pressure on US trade partners.

In truth, some US bilateral trade balances are distorted away from efficient levels by foreign policies designed to tilt the playing field. China has certainly been an offender here—through import restrictions, inward investment restrictions, lax enforcement of intellectual property rights, and support to state-owned enterprises, for example. Rather than unilateral confrontation, a more effective approach would be for the US to team up with one or more of China's rightly aggrieved trade partners and exert multilateral pressure—for change that could simultaneously make the WTO more effective and bind China more closely to a rules-based trading system. Trump's preference for bilateral deals, his suspicion of international cooperation, and his continuing threats to all US trade partners have foreclosed long-term gains for the entire global community.

Worst of all, perhaps, the dramatics around trade (and immigration) distract the United States from urgently needed measures to ease American workers' adjustment not only to globalization, but also to a range of other foreseeable structural changes, such as the impact of new technologies incorporating artificial intelligence. These developments call for a big upgrade in the under-developed US social safety net, including substantial educational and training investments. But they are not happening: Trump's biggest spending priority is a wall. It is no surprise that in continental Europe, with more developed welfare states, support for trade is stronger than in America.

Other countries are moving to protect themselves. The eleven former TPP countries, the European Union, and Japan have struck major trade agreements. Expect trade blocs to proliferate—without the United States. And expect more trade conflict down the road. With both major US political parties now largely aligned against free trade, prospects for a return to trade cooperation—until now a major American goal of the postwar era—are bleak. We will all be poorer.

MAURICE OBSTFELD is Professor at the University of California, Berkeley. He was Chief Economist at the International Monetary Fund from 2015–2018, and a member of the US Council of Economic Advisers from 2014–2015.

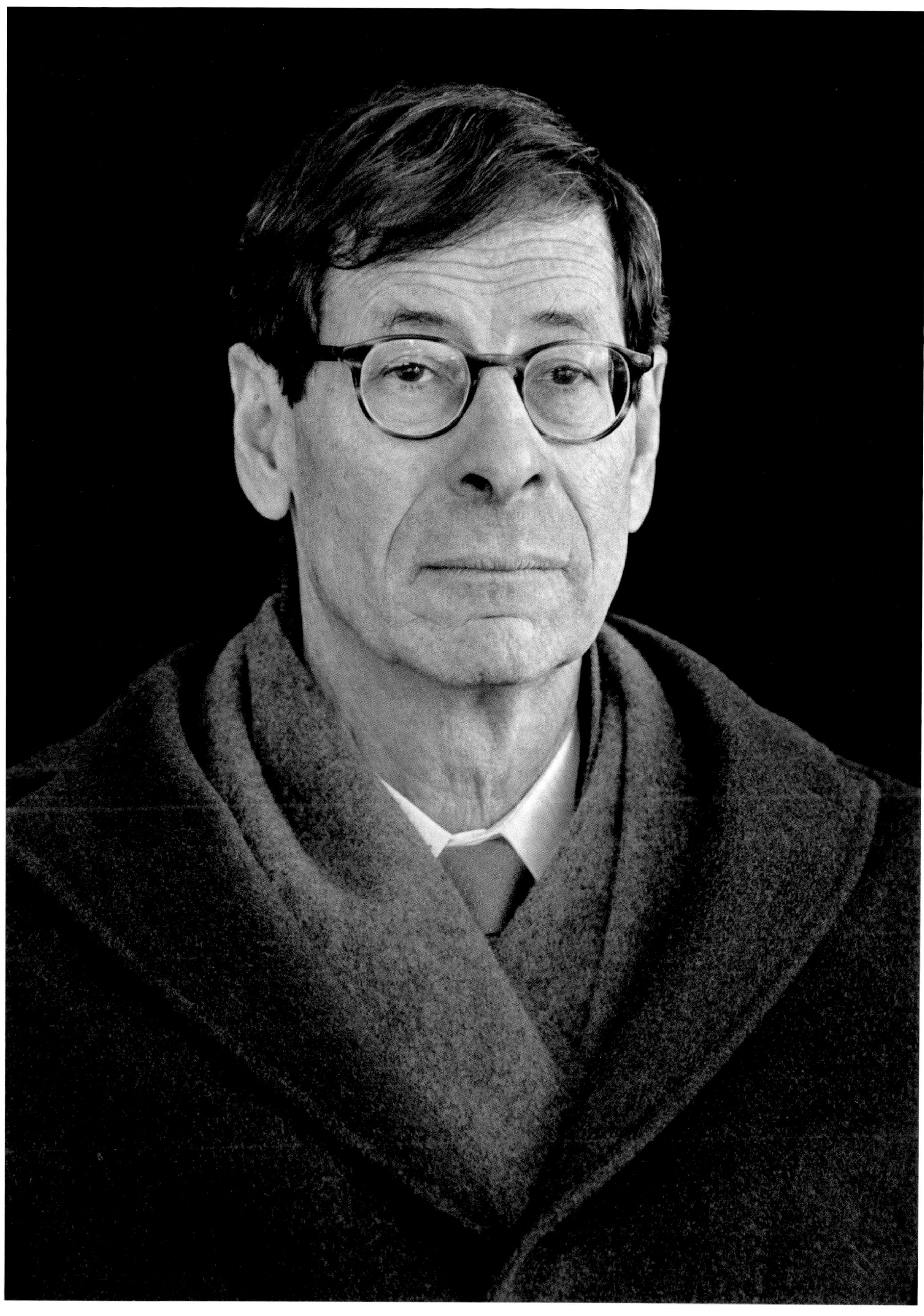

Lucas Papademos

"Was it a good idea for Greece to join the eurozone in the first place?"

OVERALL, GREECE HAS benefited significantly by joining the eurozone. The goal of euro membership acted as a motivating force and a catalyst for stabilizing the economy and achieving high rates of uninterrupted growth for more than a decade following a prolonged period of high inflation, excessive deficits, rising debt, and mediocre growth. In the seven years after euro adoption Greece experienced strong and steady growth in an environment of relative price stability, and per capita income rose considerably. Moreover, important reforms were implemented in several areas, albeit rather slowly and to a lesser extent than planned and required.

The debt crisis that erupted in 2010 was mainly a result of inappropriate policies that were incompatible with the fiscal discipline and prudent labor market policies required by Greece's participation in the eurozone. Another important contributing factor was that necessary reforms were delayed or only partly implemented. Persistently excessive and partly concealed budget deficits and wage increases greater than productivity growth led to the accumulation of high debt and a significant erosion of competitiveness, which led to a sharp rise in external public debt that eventually could not be financed at reasonable cost and be sustainable. Warnings and recommendations by European institutions and the ECB, as well as by the Greek central bank, proved insufficient to influence domestic policy and prevent the crisis.

The severity and persistence of the Greek crisis were not really due to constraints imposed by Greece's membership in the eurozone. The unprecedented decline of output and employment was the result of several factors. Fiscal and external imbalances in Greece were greater than in other crisis-stricken eurozone countries. Since government debt and deficits as well as future pension liabilities were exceptionally high, achieving debt sustainability required substantial fiscal adjustment. Importantly, the policy-mix was not sufficiently well balanced to support growth, laying more emphasis than warranted on fiscal consolidation than on structural reform. Some growth-enhancing reforms, which would also have facilitated fiscal adjustment, were only partly implemented or postponed for various reasons. Although labor cost and price competitiveness have substantially improved, structural competitiveness has not been sufficiently enhanced, thereby preventing a stronger growth performance.

Crucially, intense political antagonism, rising populism and extremism made it impossible to reach a consensus among political parties on the economic policies being implemented. The toxic atmosphere that prevailed undermined public confidence and increased uncertainty about the economic outlook, thus impairing policy effectiveness and dampening aggregate demand and economic activity.

A "Grexit" would neither have helped to resolve the crisis faster nor would it have improved the economy's export performance and growth prospects. On the contrary, in all likelihood it would have had devastating effects on the country's stability and prosperity for years to come. As almost all debt is denominated in euros, the adoption of a national currency would lead to a default against both external and domestic creditors. External public debt is mostly held by European governments, and the cost of the default would have to be borne by the taxpayers of Greece's European partners. The economic and political repercussions of such an event would be extremely serious and long lasting. Domestically, the banking system would effectively collapse and would have to be recapitalized by the government increasing the budget deficit and public debt. The implications for economic activity and financial stability would be detrimental.

The competitiveness gains and expected beneficial effects on growth, if any at all, would be temporary, as Greece's own experience in the 1980s has shown. A substantially devalued currency would create inflationary pressures and strong demand for wage increases, especially following the sharp decline in real incomes during the crisis. Moreover, the country's default and the strain on its banking system would adversely affect exports. Most likely, inflation would rise sharply, while the envisaged positive impact on economic activity would be small.

In view of the above, it is not surprising that the Greek people have overwhelmingly been in favor of Greece's membership in the eurozone, even during the darkest days of the crisis. That support reflects the desire for stability that the euro entails, the memory of the mediocre performance of the Greek economy in the 1980s, and the concern that economic policy would be less effective, while necessary reforms would be less likely to be implemented outside the eurozone. More generally, it reflects the understanding that participation in the eurozone is an essential component of the large and ambitious project of European integration—a project that most Greek people believe offers economic, social, and security advantages in the long run.

LUCAS PAPADEMOS was Prime Minister of Greece from 2011–2012, Vice President of the European Central Bank from 2002–2010, and Governor of the Bank of Greece from 1994–2002.

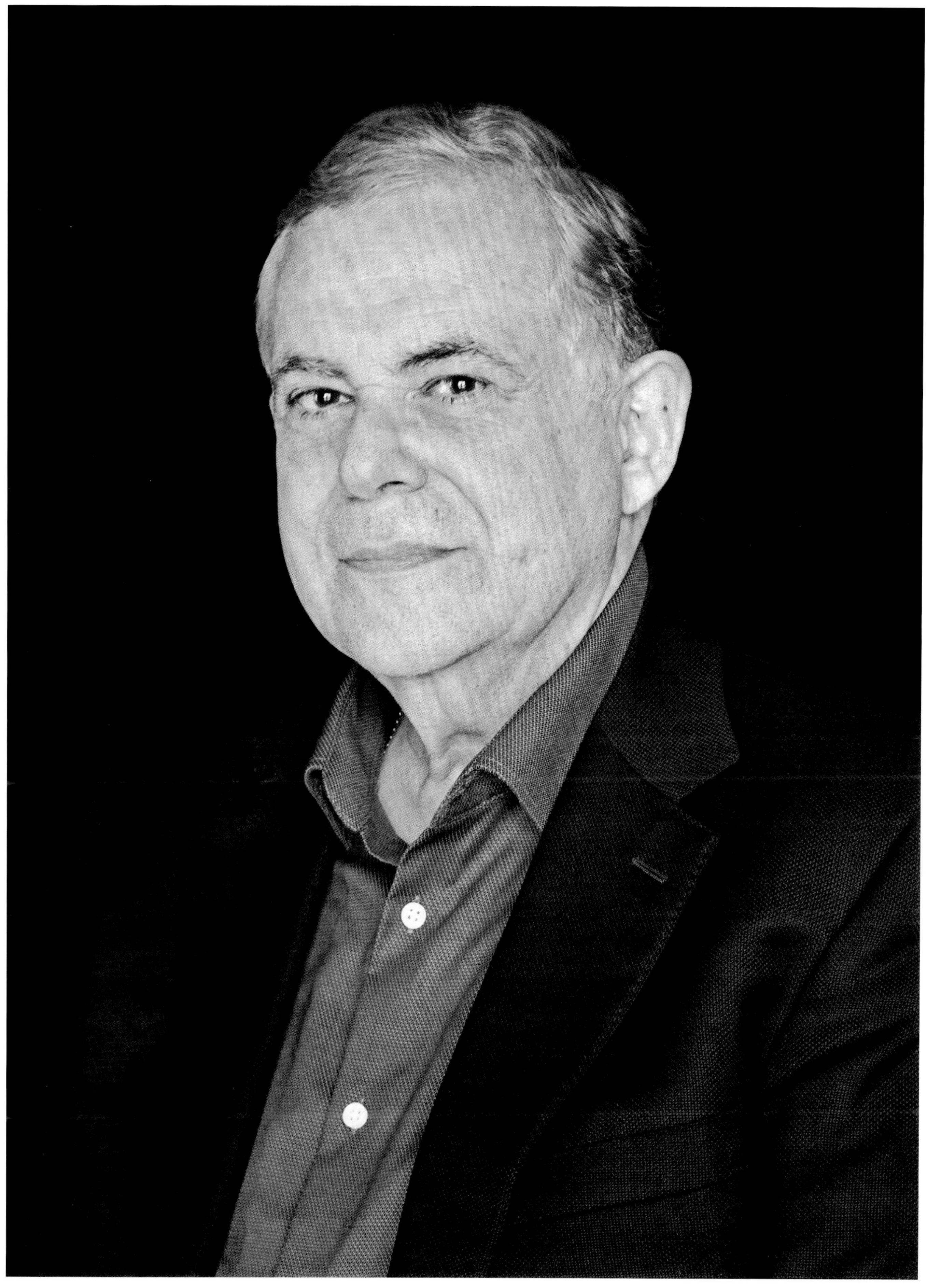

George Perry

"Can low unemployment be sustained?"

LOW UNEMPLOYMENT AND low inflation have long been the goals of US fiscal and monetary policy. But success in meeting these goals has varied widely over time. For nearly a half century after WWII, US economic performance was characterized by frequent bouts of recession and high unemployment along with episodes of excessive inflation. More recent years have seen longer expansions, lower unemployment, and low inflation rates. What have we learned from all this, and where does it leave the future prospects for stabilization policy and the economy?

In the initial postwar years, the main concerns of US stabilization policy were the frequent recessions—four between 1949 and 1960—that characterized the 1950s. The Kennedy-Johnson years met that challenge, producing a decade of uninterrupted expansion and declining unemployment. But as Vietnam War spending continued to grow, labor and product markets eventually overheated and inflation picked up. The prominence of union contracts indexed to inflation created wage-price spirals that further added to overall inflation when the OPEC cartel quadrupled world oil prices in 1973. When Paul Volcker's Fed committed to ending inflation in 1979, it raised short-term interest rates to 20 percent and caused the massive double-dip recession of 1980–1982. For policymakers, the abiding message from the 1970s was that inflation, once established, is stubborn and costly to get rid of.

These developments also informed academic modeling of stabilization. The Phillips curve—a strong cyclical relationship between inflation and unemployment—was first described in the 1950s, but the strong empirical regularity had no formal model behind it. After the late 1960s, with unemployment rates reaching very low levels and inflation quickening, a model describing a natural unemployment rate became prominent in academic thinking. Absent shocks or policy interventions, unemployment would gravitate to the natural rate. Inflation would accelerate if policy kept unemployment below the natural rate and decelerate if policy kept unemployment above it. Such a natural rate had messages for policymakers. Any pickup in inflation warns of the need to tighten policy. And because the natural rate can be sustained at any steady inflation rate, the optimal goal is price stability. By the 1990s, empirical estimates of the natural rate ranged between 5½ and 6 percent. And these were part of Fed policy discussions about what unemployment rate to aim for.

Fortunately, the Fed governors were cautious about relying too much on such estimates of a natural rate and tightening policy prematurely. And in early 1996, George Akerlof, Bill Dickens, and I published new research that rejected the natural-rate model altogether. We established the empirical importance of downward wage rigidity in the labor market and showed that incorporating observed rigidity produced a model in which, over a range of moderate inflation rates, higher inflation sustains lower rates of unemployment. The message for policymakers is that inflation can be too low as well as too high.

Subsequent events have supported this model. The Fed allowed modest increases in inflation in the last half of the 1990s and unemployment continued to decline to around 4 percent. In the next expansion, unemployment again got below 5 percent before the financial crisis brought on the Great Recession. In the long expansion that followed, the unemployment rate fell from 10 percent to 3.8 percent by the last half of 2018. This is the lowest rate in many decades, and reflects a labor market that has brought jobs to many workers who had become too discouraged even to look for work.

Throughout this expansion, policy discussions have centered on whether inflation is high enough to justify monetary tightening. Unlike the inflation-prone 1970s, today's economy is open to strong foreign competition and is not dominated by institutions that threaten a wage-price spiral, which could escalate moderate inflation into dangerous inflation. Policymakers should continue to pursue moderate inflation and the more efficient labor markets that it enables. Recessions will continue to happen from shocks, cyclical excesses, and financial surprises, but hopefully not from misguided attempts to fight modest rates of inflation. Low levels of unemployment like today's should remain an achievable goal for the foreseeable future.

GEORGE PERRY is Senior Fellow at the Brookings Institution.

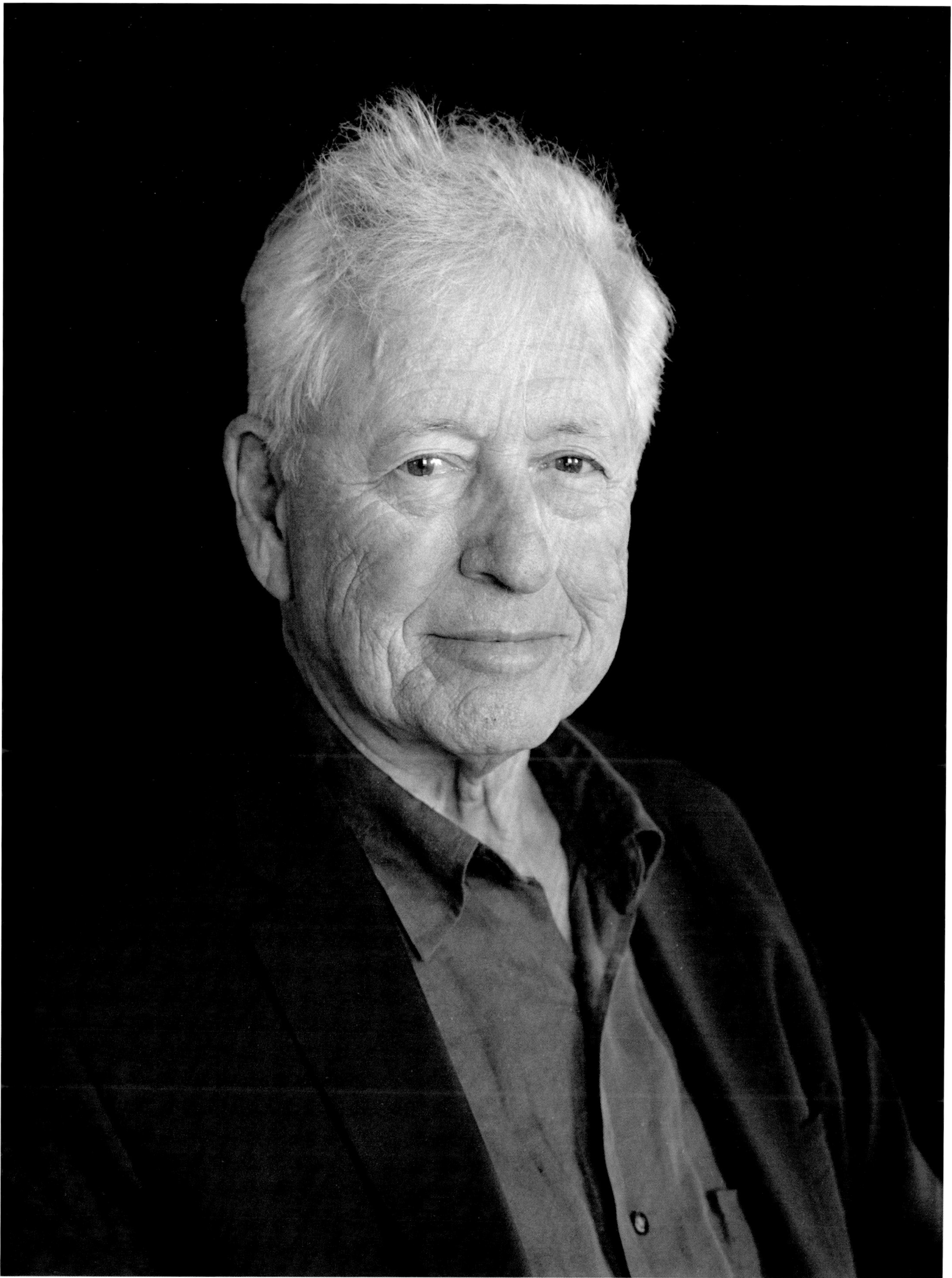

Edmund Phelps

"Why are real interest rates so low during this long expansion?"

IN THE FIRST half of the 1960s the Depression had long since lifted, the war was over, and postwar growth was pretty good. Real rates of interest on long-term Treasury bonds were in familiar territory. Ten-year real rates were about 3 percent per annum—ranging from 2½ percent to 3½ percent. Since then, real rates have fallen enormously. In the relatively tranquil period from 2003 to 2006, real rates on ten-year bonds were about 1¾ percent—ranging roughly from 1½ percent to 2¼ percent. Now, in the period from 2014 to the present, those rates have been around ½ percent, and in recent months, near 1 percent. What may account for the sickly rates?

Before proceeding, we ought to recognize that US real rates could be below European real rates only if, in real terms, the dollar is appreciating relative to European currencies (and vice-versa), and this real exchange rate cannot drift up or down without bound. So it may be desirable to view the question in terms of real interest rates in the entire West.

I think part of the explanation lies in the substantial slowdown of productivity—more precisely, "total factor productivity" in the West, which in my book *Mass Flourishing* I attributed to a *net* decline of *aggregate* innovation in the American economy at the end of the 1960s and later in France and Britain. This near-global decline in the "rate of technical progress," as Robert Solow dubbed it in his growth model, put the incomes from work and wealth on a less-steep trajectory, with the result that people could expect their consumption to take a less-steep path as well, so households no longer required the high interest rates of previous decades to induce them to lend what they were saving. In the beloved model of Frank Ramsey, the path of the interest rate would descend to a lower level corresponding to a flatter steady-growth path than the one the economy was headed to before the slowdown of total factor productivity.

The question asked, however, is why real interest rates have been "so low during this long expansion," meaning, I suppose, the period from early 2014 to the recovery's completion in mid–2017 and subsequent boom. We would have expected by 2014, had we thought about it, that real rates would begin to recover—even though those rates may still have a very slow descent remaining as they approach their new steady-growth levels.

A development that may account for the super-low rates in the last few years is that the public, having observed a further decline of innovation in the past dozen years or more, has lost some of the remaining hope it had held out that innovation would soon return to a level closer to the heydays of innovation. That development would pull downward the real interest rates of recent years.

Another development that may explain the still very low rates is that actors in the bond market have stopped giving appreciable weight to the possibility that the Federal Reserve Bank will soon unwind a substantial part of its mountainous stockpile of long-term Treasurys that the bank purchased on the belief that such further monetary easing was necessary to push up the economy to a full economic recovery.

Now a correction has been in progress and no one can know how far that will go. For the record, real ten-year rates have risen from around ½ percent at the start of 2018 to around 1 percent at the end of 2018. So the long-term decline of real interest rates from the '60s to now—2019—is striking and indicates a similar decline of the growth rate.

It is surprising that there has not been more of a reversal. Why is the decline since 2006 so strong? The answer, perhaps, is that the Fed, after purchasing massive amounts of long-term Treasurys, did not sell enough of them as the recovery proceeded and, ultimately, a boom emerged.

EDMUND PHELPS is Director of the Center on Capitalism and Society at Columbia University. He received the Nobel Prize for Economics in 2006.

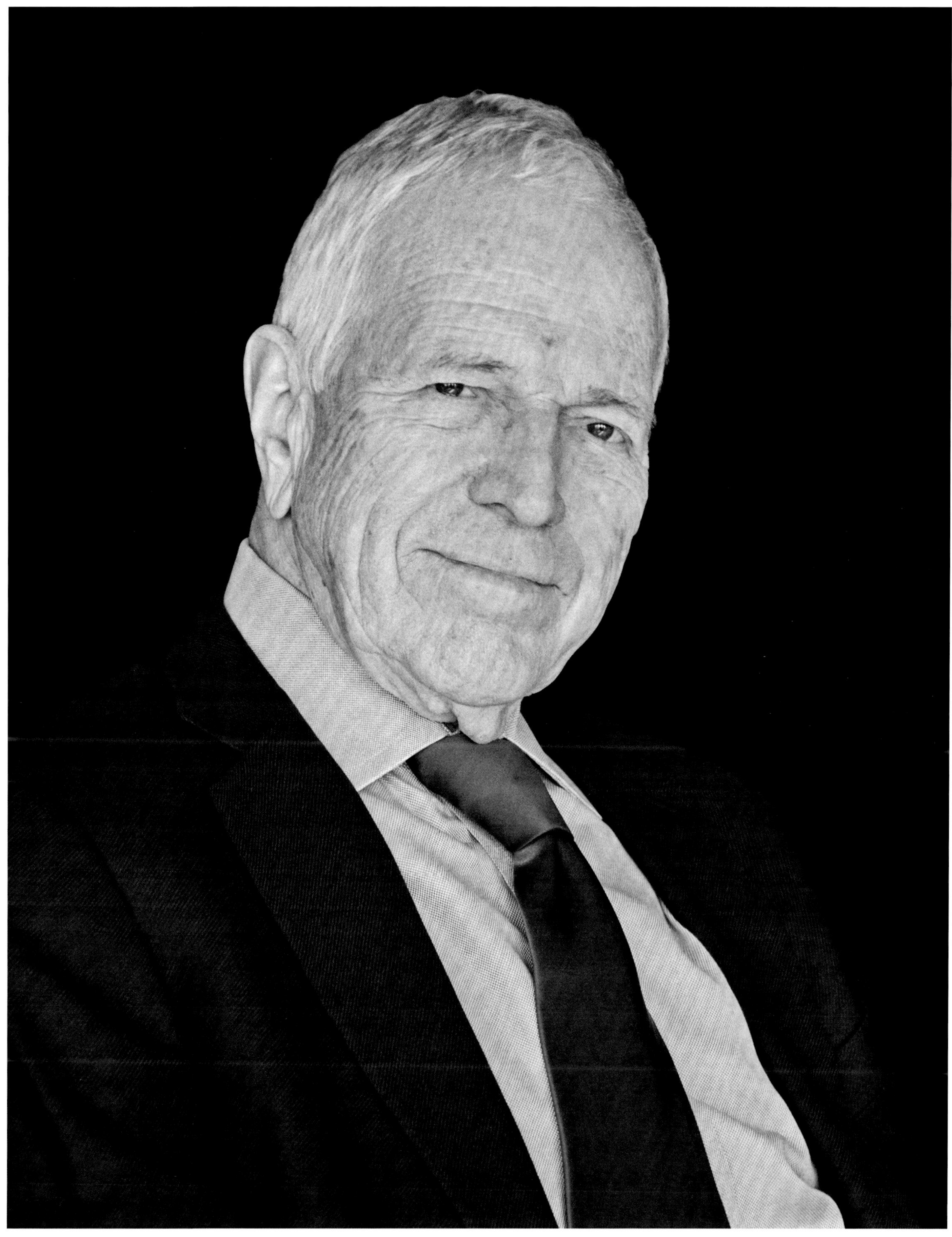

Alice Rivlin

"Do you see a way out of the current impasse over the financing of health care?"

THE AMERICAN HEALTH-CARE system is extremely expensive. We spend 18 percent of our GDP on health care and that fraction will grow as the population ages and new treatments emerge. We pay for health care with a patchwork of public and private programs that leave some people without coverage. Fixing the financing system means filling in the coverage gaps, preferably in ways that contribute to delivering good quality care more efficiently.

We are no longer arguing about the goal. Almost everyone believes that all Americans should have access to good quality, affordable health care. However, our wariness of centralizing power in Washington kept us from setting up a national health-care financing system as many other countries did. Instead, we gradually patched together public and private programs that provide health insurance coverage to most people. The heavily tax-favored employer-based system covers most working Americans and their families. Medicare covers older and disabled Americans. Medicaid and the Children's Health Program cover very low-income households.

This patchwork of public and private financing provided at least 80 percent of Americans with health insurance that they found reasonably satisfactory. However, for decades a small but growing number of people were not covered by any of these programs. They had to fend for themselves in the market for individual health insurance, in which insurers competed for healthy customers who were less expensive to insure. Sicker people (those with preexisting conditions) were offered high premiums, often for inadequate coverage, or rejected altogether.

The Affordable Care Act (ACA), enacted in 2009, reformed the individual market to eliminate discrimination based on health status and require that all insurance products cover a minimum set of essential benefits. It set up electronic marketplaces in which consumers, armed with income-related subsidies, could chose among competing health plans. It also encouraged states to expand their Medicaid programs and required everyone to have health insurance, so the healthy could not opt out and leave only the unhealthy in the insurance pool.

The ACA was a creative solution to the coverage gap problem that combined market competition with regulation, but it did not operate perfectly. Competition among health plans proved difficult in sparsely populated areas and the newly insured needed more care than insurers anticipated. Mandating insurance purchases proved unpopular. However, the biggest problem for the ACA was that the Democrats were unable to attract any Republican collaborators, so they enacted it alone. If Republicans and Democrats had worked together on designing it, they could have produced a bill with broader support and they could have cooperated in fixing the glitches that emerged in implementation. Instead, Republicans felt free to exaggerate the ACA's flaws, sabotage its implementation, and call for its repeal without offering a workable solution of their own.

What to do now? Conservative Republicans talk about market solutions, in which insurance plays a smaller role and consumers buy health care directly from competing providers. Progressives talk about moving to a single-payer system in which everyone is covered by government insurance like Medicare. But "free markets" and "single payer" are political slogans rather than realistic solutions. Most Americans like the security of health insurance and known providers. They fear having to shop for health care when they need it. Most Americans with employer-based coverage want to keep it. They don't trust the government to run a single-payer system well and they don't want to pay the higher taxes it would require.

I believe the only way out of the current impasse is for the sensible moderates in both parties to work together to make the major elements of the existing patchwork function better so that everyone has affordable coverage and providers have strong incentives to produce good care efficiently. The first step is to stabilize the private insurance market and make sure that people with no other alternative can afford adequate coverage. There are plenty of viable ideas for using both market competition and the regulation of payments to improve efficiency, but bipartisan participation and buy-in is imperative. The sensible moderates must craft incremental solutions and remove health-care finances from the partisan line of fire.

ALICE RIVLIN (1931–2019) was Senior Fellow at the Brookings Institution. She was Vice Chair of the Federal Reserve from 1996–1999, and Founding Director of the Congressional Budget Office from 1975–1983.

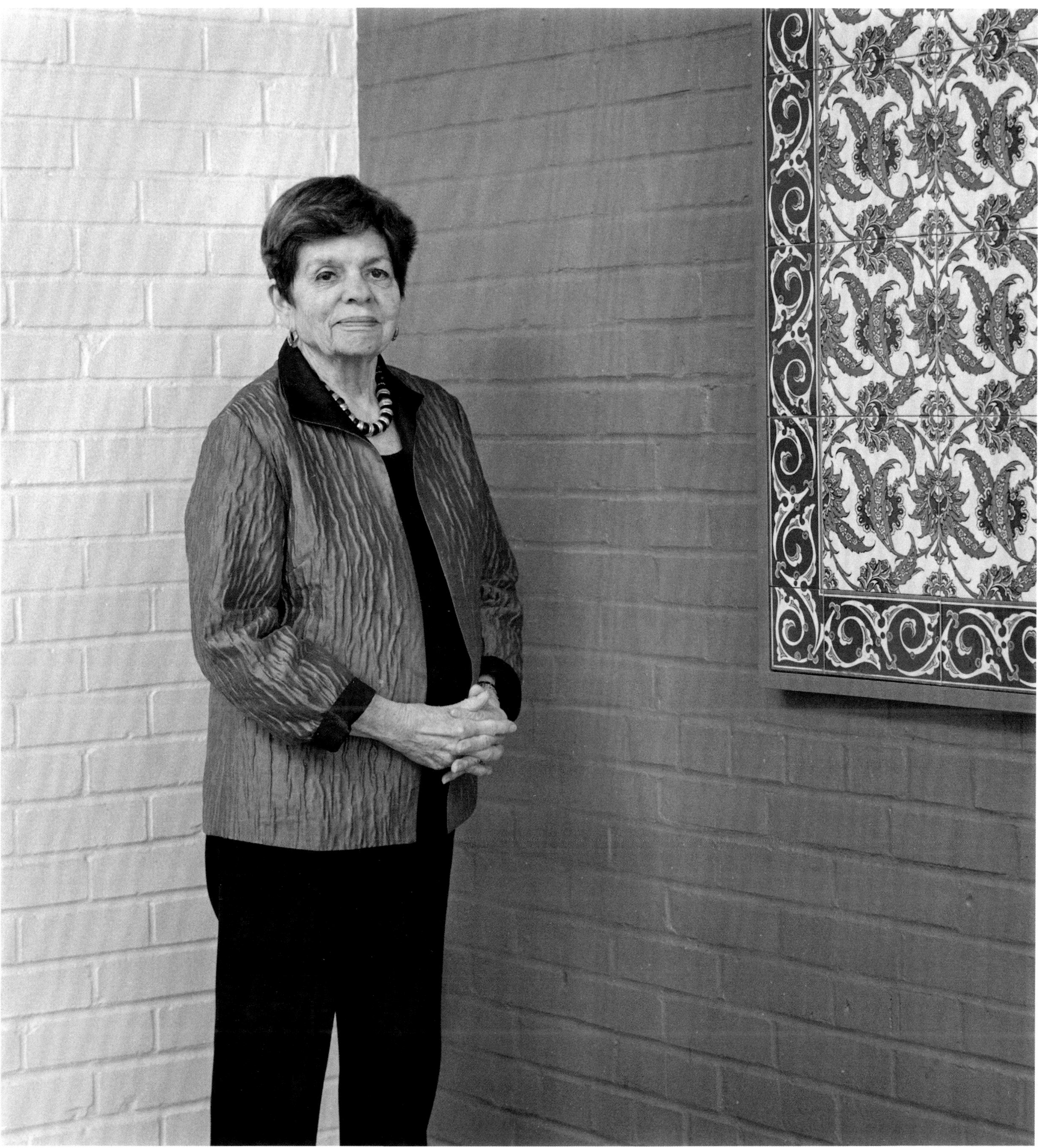

Dani Rodrik

"Who gains and who loses from globalization?"

THE POPULIST BACKLASH against globalization in the United States and Europe seems to have caught people by surprise. But globalization, particularly of the type practiced since the 1990s, should never have been expected to benefit everyone. The redistributive implications of opening up to trade and finance are, in fact, understood quite well by economists. The surprise, if there is one, is that economists were not more cautious in their support for globalization.

There is little question that multiple rounds of multilateral trade negotiations after the end of the Second World War did the world economy a lot of good. Import tariffs and quotas on trade in manufactures were extremely restrictive and they needed to come down to reap the gains from trade. At first, this liberalization affected trade mostly among relatively advanced economies. But as developing countries began to join the world economy, their low wages began to create more severe distributional tensions in the importing countries.

Even in the best of circumstances, freeing up trade causes some pain in addition to the gain. But from the late 1980s on, the balance between pain and gain began to look worse and worse. Take NAFTA, for example, which entered into force in 1994. A recent study of NAFTA's labor-market impact finds substantial negative effects for blue-collar workers in the US and the communities in which they live. Meanwhile the overall economic gain to the US was well below 0.1 percentage points of GDP—that is, less than one-tenth of 1 percent of GDP.

It is just as economics teaches. According to the celebrated Stolper-Samuelson theorem of trade theory, in countries that are well endowed with skilled workers—such as North American and Western European nations—unskilled workers see their living standards decline under freer trade. The theorem is built on special assumptions, but it has a version that is quite general: openness to trade always hurts some people in society, unless the economy is completely specialized (that is, produces none of the imported goods at home).

Moreover, after the 1990s, actual trade agreements were increasingly no longer about free trade. They began to focus on regulations beyond the border—agricultural subsidies, food and product safety rules, investment regulations, intellectual property rights, banking and financial measures. Institutional arrangements, often the results of domestic political bargains, came to be seen as trade barriers and were subject to renegotiation through trade agreements.

Perhaps the hyper-globalizers' most egregious mistake after the 1990s was to promote financial globalization. Free flow of finance across the world was supposed to channel savings to countries where returns are higher, enable smoothing of consumption for nations through international borrowing and lending, and allow global portfolio diversification. But these gains were offset by painful financial crises and the damaging austerity policies that followed them. Countries that opened themselves to free capital flows saw inequality rise, the labor share of income fall, and the tax burden on workers increase.

In retrospect, the gainers and losers were clear-cut. The greatest beneficiaries of globalization were the corporations and professional elites that benefited from the new rules, and nations like China that eschewed the rules of hyper-globalization and danced to their own drummer (by managing capital flows and their economy). The losers were large segments of the working class in advanced economies and those countries (like Mexico) that simply opened up their economy and waited for globalization to work its magic.

DANI RODRIK is Professor at the Harvard University Kennedy School of Government.

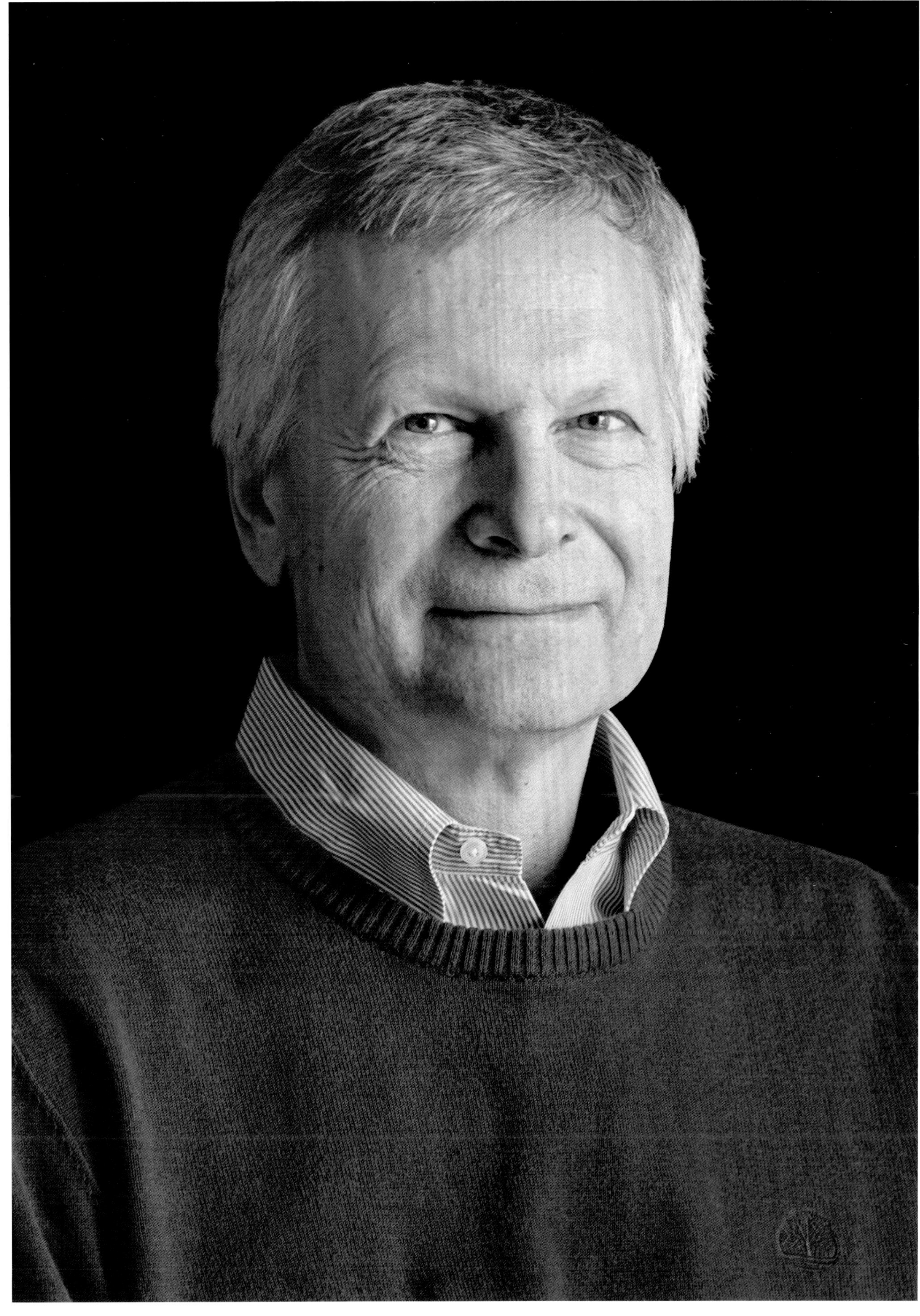

Kenneth Rogoff

"What made you decide to start a campaign against the use of cash?"

OVER THE PAST two decades I have argued that properly calibrating and regulating the currency system is a far more important problem than most economists and policymakers realize. It affects public finance, crime, and even the monetary authorities' ability to fight financial crises.

I have nothing against the small bills most of us use in day-to-day transactions. Rather, my focus has been on large denomination notes such as the $100 bill, the Swiss 1000-franc note (worth about US$1000), and the €500 note (about US$600). These constitute the overwhelming share of paper currency in most advanced economies, yet are used mainly for the purposes of crime and tax evasion. Believe it or not, there are more than thirty-five $100 bills in circulation for every man, woman, and child in the United States. Yet in surveys by the US Federal Reserve, less than 5 percent of adults admit to ever using them, and those that do claim to only carry a few occasionally.

Sure, perhaps half of the US's hundreds are held abroad in places like Russia, the Middle East, and Mexico, but the rest do enormous damage at home. The same issue holds across all advanced economies, and it is by no means the worst in the United States. Curiously, the demand for big bills continues to grow vigorously even as the use of cash in legal transactions continues to fade rapidly for all but relatively small payments. For example, for purchases over $100, cash is now a distant fifth behind credit cards, debit cards, electronic transfers, checks, with smartphone payments coming on strong.

Central banks like the big notes because printing them is enormously profitable. A $100 bill costs perhaps twelve cents to print, and yet allows the government to buy a $100 worth of goods. By standard accounting measures, the US Federal Reserve, the European Central Bank, and the Bank of Japan are vastly more profitable than any of the world's largest companies. So, what could possibly be wrong with that? The problem is that the likely collateral damage to these countries in terms of crime and tax evasion are both approximately ten times as large as the profits they get from printing big bills. Ending big bills is not going to end crime; crime existed long before King Croesus issued standardized coinage in ancient Lydia. But if crime and tax evasion can be reduced even a few percentage points each by eliminating large bills, society will come out ahead.

I would not advocate getting rid of all physical currency; indeed most people would not know if hundred dollar bills were phased out unless they heard about it in the media. My issue is not a moral one. Of course there should be some means of doing entirely private transactions on a modest scale. But we should make it more difficult for individuals engaged in recurrent wholesale tax evasion and crime to hide, port, and spend their ill-gotten gains. And please don't tell me about people who hide massive sums of cash in their walls because they don't trust banks. Someone buying a $10 million apartment with a suitcase of cash in New York, Los Angeles, or Miami isn't doing so because they are worried their bank might issue a bad check.

My recent book, *The Curse of Cash*, looks at the past, present, and future of currency, from the invention of standardized coinage in 7 BC to what might come after Bitcoin. There has been some shift since I began my work: for example, the eurozone is finally starting to phase out its 500-euro note, and many other countries, such as Australia, are looking into the problem. The recent advent of the cryptocurrencies such as Bitcoin (another way of doing nearly anonymous payments) will be worth little over the long run; as governments will eventually have to ban their use in retail transactions as well as in banks. The fact that this hasn't happened yet is more a result of governments temporarily holding back from regulatory action and allowing the technology to evolve. But a central lesson from the long history of currency is that the private sector innovates, whereas the government eventually regulates and appropriates.

KENNETH ROGOFF is Professor at Harvard University. He was Chief Economist at the International Monetary Fund from 2001–2003.

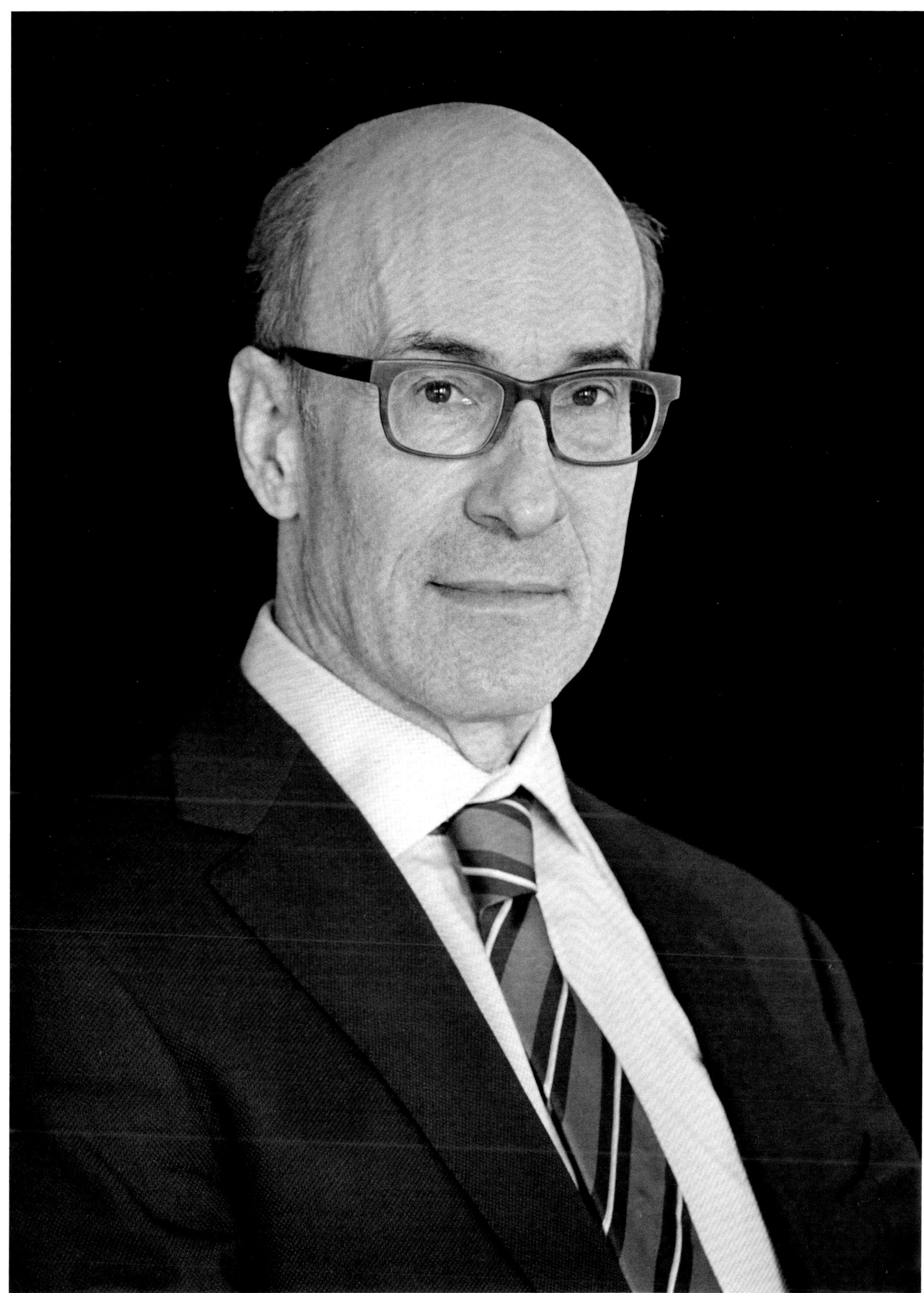

Christina Romer

"Does the experience of the financial crisis suggest major changes in the way we do fiscal and monetary policy?"

THERE ARE MANY lessons from the crisis for fiscal and monetary policy, but two stand out. First, before the crisis most economists thought short-run stabilization—that is, keeping inflation and unemployment fairly stable in the face of various kinds of disturbances hitting the economy—could be left to monetary policy. But monetary policymakers ran out of room to cut interest rates early in the crisis, and so fiscal policy had to play a central role in stemming the economic collapse. As a result, one lesson of the crisis is that fiscal policy can play a major role in economic stabilization. As a research economist, one question I am especially interested in is how fiscal policy could be used more effectively to aid recovery. For example, would it be possible to set up fiscal programs that kicked in more quickly and automatically, so that the economy gets the needed help in a timely manner (and so that fiscal stimulus ends appropriately as well)? Similarly, is it possible to devise a public employment program that could put many unemployed workers back to work quickly and doing jobs that would be useful to society?

The second lesson involves the value of having the ability to use monetary and fiscal policy to respond to a huge shock, such as a financial crisis. Recent research that David Romer and I have been doing finds that the ability to use monetary and fiscal policy is crucial to how bad the aftermath of a financial crisis is. If a country enters a crisis with very low government debt and lots of room to cut interest rates, a financial crisis typically has only small effects on the economy; but if it starts with high debt and very low interest rates, the effects are often disastrous. In the recent crisis, this pattern was very evident. Countries like China, South Korea, and Australia, which had ample fiscal space, took very aggressive fiscal measures and the aftermath of the crisis was very mild. On the other hand, countries like Greece and Italy, which started the crisis with high levels of government debt, were forced to take fiscal contraction at exactly the time their economies needed fiscal stimulus. The result has been years of high unemployment and economic hardship.

One implication is that while conducting policy in normal times, policymakers should think about putting themselves in a position where they will be able to respond if a crisis hits. In the case of fiscal policy, this is an argument for very responsible fiscal policy in good times to keep government debt low relative to the size of the economy. But perhaps counterintuitively, in the case of monetary policy the findings may actually be an argument for being somewhat less responsible in good times. If central banks let inflation get a little higher, normal interest rates will be somewhat higher, giving them more room to cut if they are faced with a crisis.

CHRISTINA ROMER is Professor at the University of California, Berkeley. She was Chair of the Council of Economic Advisers from 2009–2010.

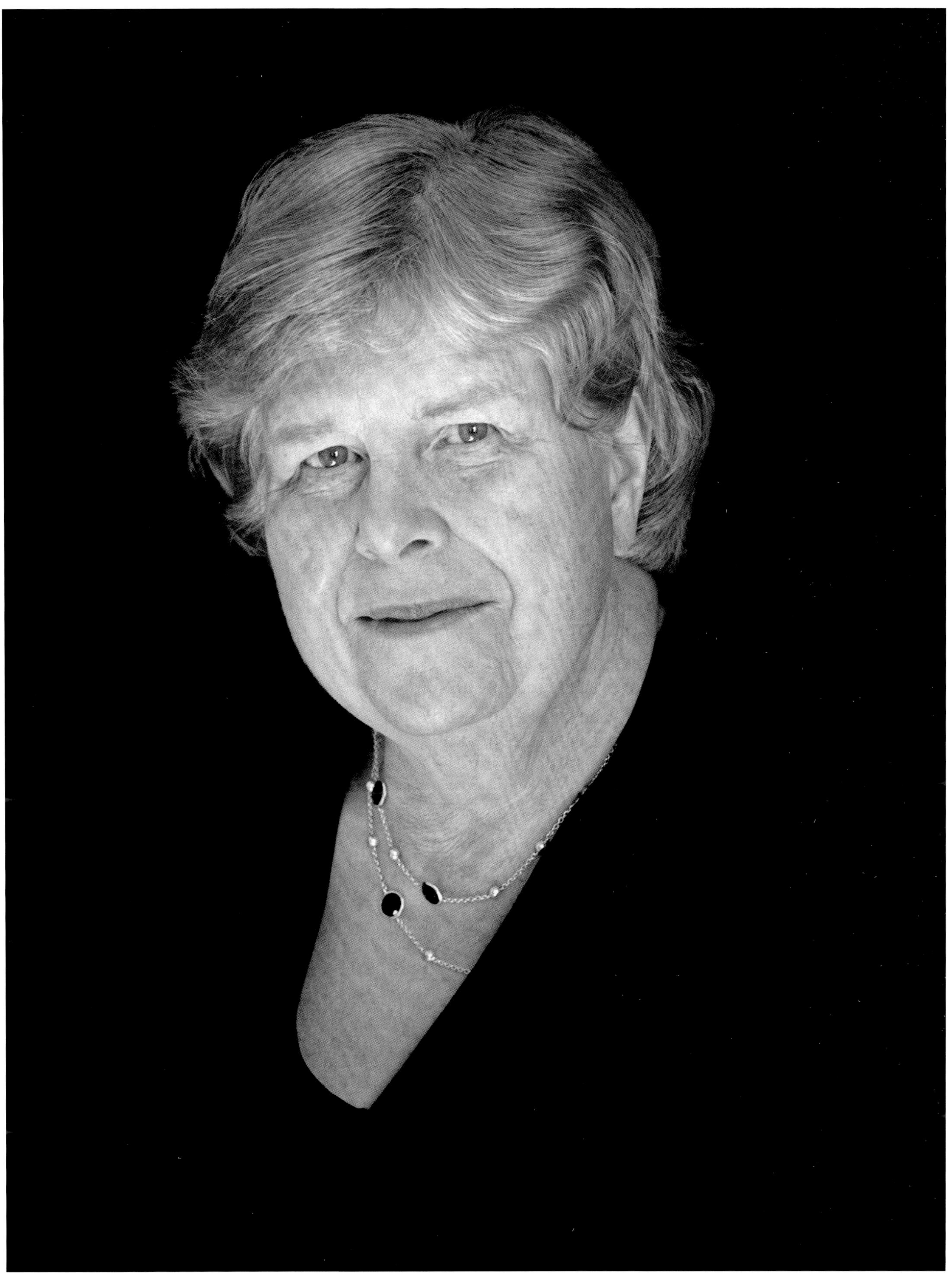

David Romer

"What do we actually know about the short-run effects of increases in government spending and cuts in taxes on the economy?"

ONE OF THE very few silver linings of the recent crisis is that it has led to an explosion of work on the effects of fiscal policy on the economy. One thing that I like about this work is how broad and creative it is. Some people are finding clever ways to get new insights from looking at data on the overall performance of the economy and the behavior of government spending and taxes. But the area that has really come into its own is using microeconomic data—that is, data at the level of individuals, firms, and households, or of regions within a country—to learn about the macroeconomic effects of policy—that is, its effects on the economy as a whole.

The message that pretty consistently comes out of these studies is that fiscal stimulus works. At the macroeconomic level, researchers find that when the government raises spending or cuts taxes for reasons unrelated to other factors affecting the economy in the short run, the economy tends to boom over the next few years. At the microeconomic level, researchers find that when individuals get tax cuts or payments from the government, they increase their spending by a lot, and do so very quickly; and when the government spends more in one region of the country than another for reasons that are more or less random, overall employment and output go up substantially in the first region relative to the second. And when researchers think through what these microeconomic results are likely to mean for the effects of fiscal policy on the economy as a whole, they conclude that these results imply that the effects of national fiscal policy in situations where we are likely to want to use it—for example, an economy that is depressed rather than booming, and where monetary policy is limited by the fact that interest rates cannot go below zero—are likely to be quite large.

Unfortunately, this message has not gotten through to policymakers. Despite the accumulating evidence that increases in government spending and cuts in taxes can help a weak economy a great deal and that the fiscal actions that were taken in the recent crisis were extremely important in turning things around, "stimulus" is almost a dirty word in policy circles at the moment. I very much hope that changes before the next crisis hits.

DAVID ROMER is Professor at the University of California, Berkeley.

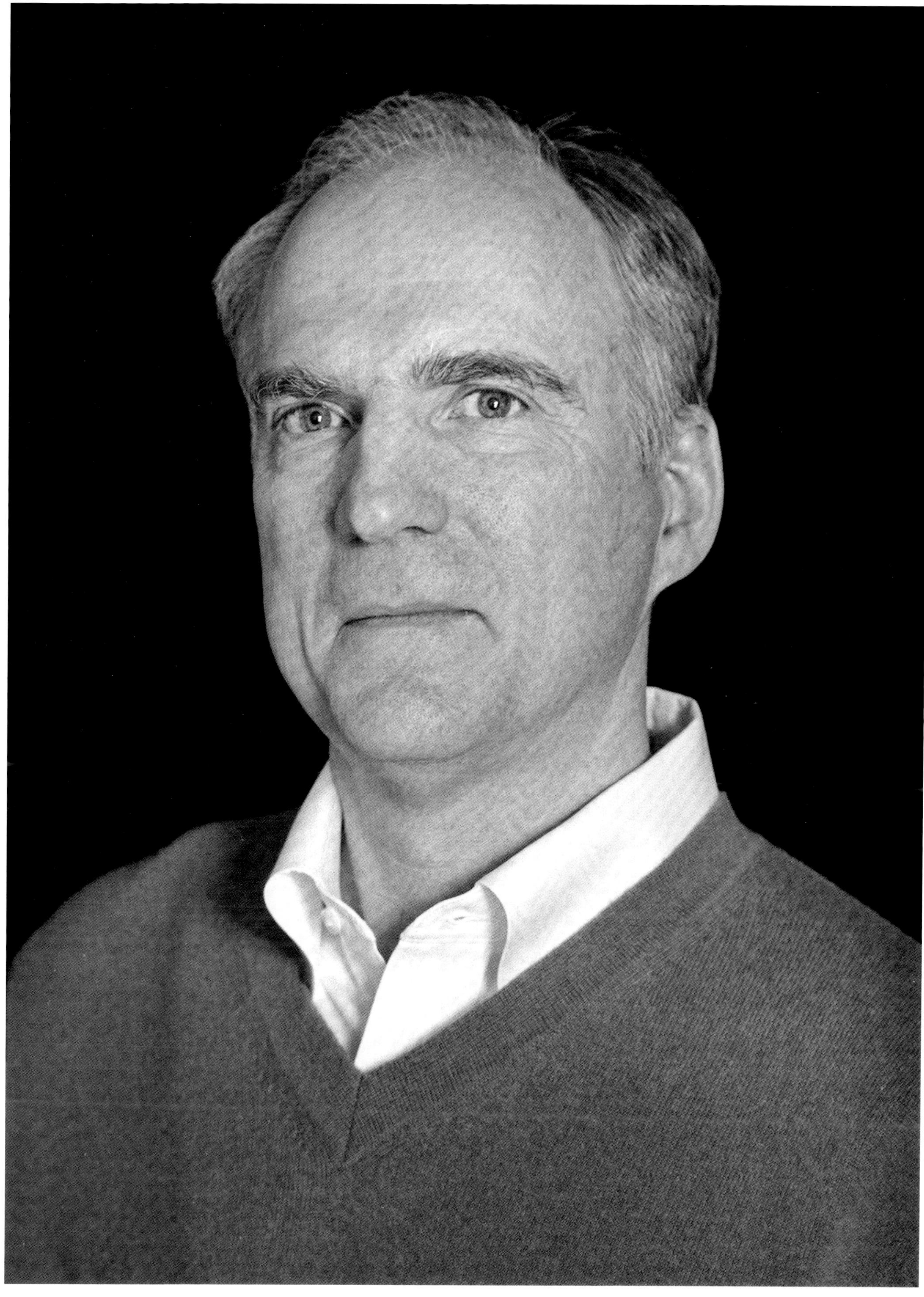

Paul Romer

"What do you think people who make practical decisions can learn from the abstract models of economic growth?"

THE QUESTION THAT has always interested me is why the rate of progress has increased from century to century. I will get to a justification for considering it, but I should admit up front that it is self-serving. I work on the theory of growth because I love the chance it offers to switch between two extremes—abstract analysis of fundamentals and careful attention to the specifics of practical decisions.

The essential abstractions for thinking about progress are technology and two types of knowledge—codified knowledge in books and tacit knowledge in brains. The connection between technology and codified knowledge is straightforward. Better steam engines encouraged a deeper understanding of thermodynamics, and vice versa. The connection between technology and tacit knowledge is more complicated. New technology increases the value of many new things to learn. However, as the Luddites warned, it can destroy the value of things people already know; the codified knowledge of the design for a mechanical loom made the tacit knowledge of skilled weavers obsolete.

In the abstract, adjustments to an educational system can help students acquire new knowledge that complements new technologies. The best illustration comes from the first half of the 20th century, when the high school movement in the United States replaced the "Latin schools" tailored for elites with mandatory high schools that followed a new curriculum and prepared students for work in large organizations.

It takes attention to specific details to turn the abstract insight that school systems must evolve into practical steps people can take today. How will we know if a way to teach gives students knowledge that the market will value? To answer this question, economists have started using scores on achievement tests to measure what students know. Nations with better test scores seem to enjoy better economic outcomes. But as they compare test results across more countries and over longer spans of time, they struggle with vexing details about which tests to use and how to link their heterogeneous scores.

These details raise questions about the abstract fundamentals of what it means to measure. Usually, measuring means counting. When children grow taller, we measure height by adding like to like, centimeters to centimeters, and counting how many. But when children learn, they add apples to oranges; then on top, they add quadratic equations, punctuation marks, topic sentences, an assortment of historical facts, etc. Because learning always piles unlikes on top of unlikes, we cannot measure what a person knows by counting up the number of likes.

Economists have progress to make at the abstract level of understanding what it means to measure using the plethora of incomparable numbers that tests generate. Together with statisticians, they will need to work through the specific details of practical suggestions about how to include new measures of knowledge in our system of national statistics. Educators will have to decide what to teach. Should Python replace Latin? (You have to root for a computer language named after a comedy troupe.)

The lesson from the long run is that sustained progress is possible; perhaps even progress at a faster rate. But it requires work that is never finished. To avoid the negative outcomes that the Luddites flagged, each generation has to find its own version of the high school movement. Economists can help by showing how to measure the actual effects of the different ways that societies use to teach new skills.

So what then is the justification (or excuse) for asking questions about our long-run prospects? It helps sustain a spirit of realistic optimism that encourages action. The biggest risk now is that unthinking pessimism will spawn denial, confusion, apathy, and then passive acquiescence in the face of change that is not progress.

Progress is not something that happens. Progress is something that a society has to make.

PAUL ROMER is Professor at the New York University Stern School of Business, and was Chief Economist at the World Bank from 2016–2018. He received the Nobel Prize for Economics in 2018.

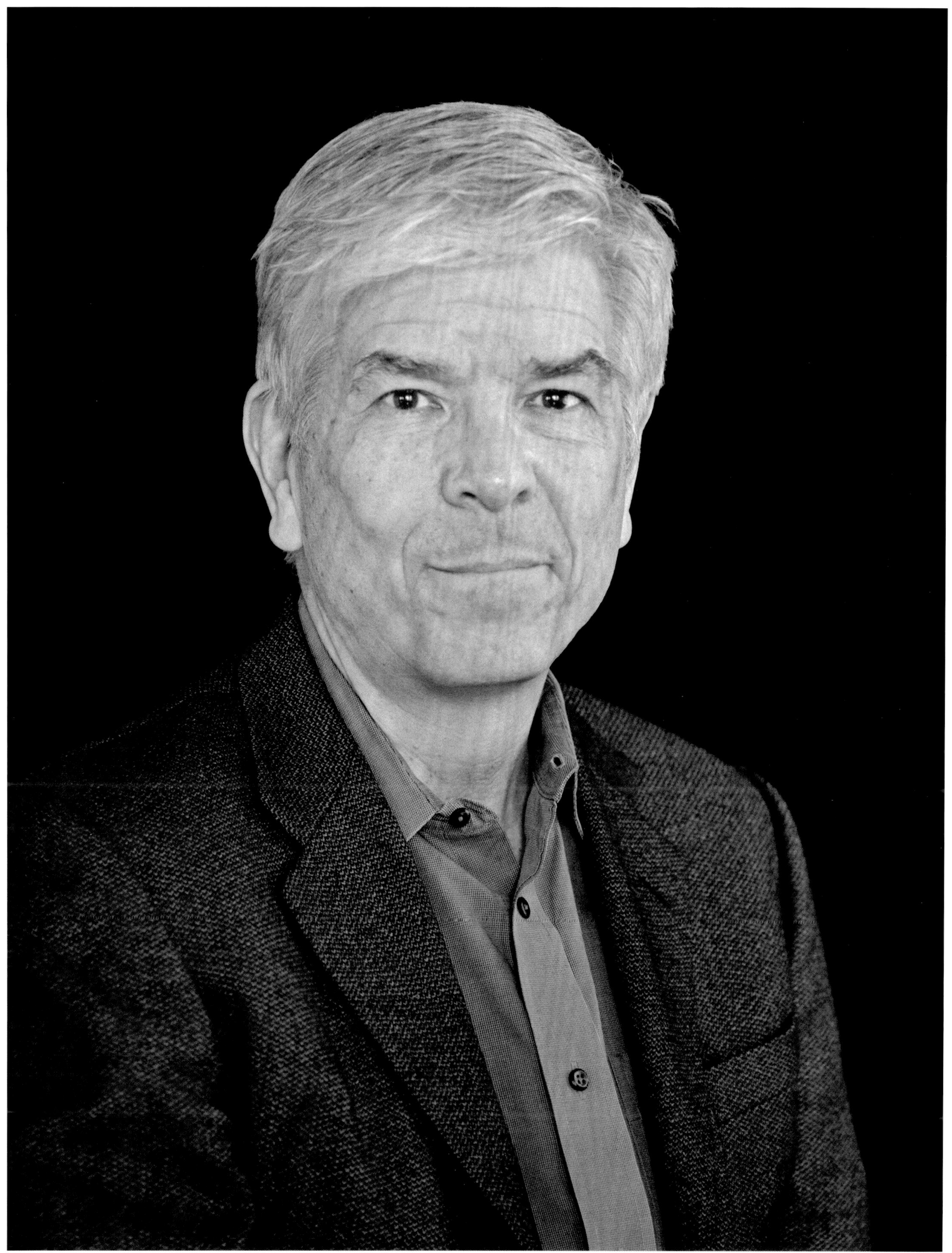

Alvin Roth

"How are markets like languages?"

MARKETS AND LANGUAGES are both ancient human artifacts, tools that we humans build to help us cooperate, coordinate, compete, and generally organize our activities. And just as there are many languages, there are many kinds of markets and marketplaces.

Often when we think of markets we think of commodity markets, in which the objects being sold have been made so standardized—into commodities—that you don't have to care who you are dealing with. (God made wheat, and every field of wheat is different, but the Chicago Board of Trade [CBOT] sells contracts for Number 2 Hard Red Winter Wheat, which is a commodity that can be bought and sold without further examination.) So in commodity markets, prices do all the work. The job of the CBOT is to find the prices at which supply equals demand, throughout the day, for each of the commodities that it sells.

But not every market is a commodity market. In some markets you care who you are dealing with. In matching markets you can't just choose what you want (even if you can afford it), because you also have to be chosen. Stanford University doesn't choose its freshman class by setting the tuition just high enough so that the number of students who want to attend equals the number of classroom spaces. Similarly, Google doesn't lower the wage of software engineers until just enough of them want to work at Google. You can't study at Stanford unless you are *admitted*, and you can't work at Google unless you have been *hired*, so college admissions and labor markets are matching markets. We encounter matching markets at some of the most important junctures in our lives. (You can't just choose your spouse; you also have to be chosen . . .)

I imagine that if a Martian scientist came to observe the goings-on of Earthlings (and if that scientist focused on humans) the first report sent back to the Martian Science Foundation (MSF) would say that humans were always talking, and always transacting, coordinating, cooperating, and competing. That is, the MSF would learn that language and markets were basic human tools.

Once we think of markets as tools, we can start to think about understanding them well enough so that we can fix them when they're broken, and build new and better ones. Those are the tasks of market design.

ALVIN ROTH is Professor at Stanford University and Emeritus Professor at Harvard University. He received the Nobel Prize for Economics in 2012.

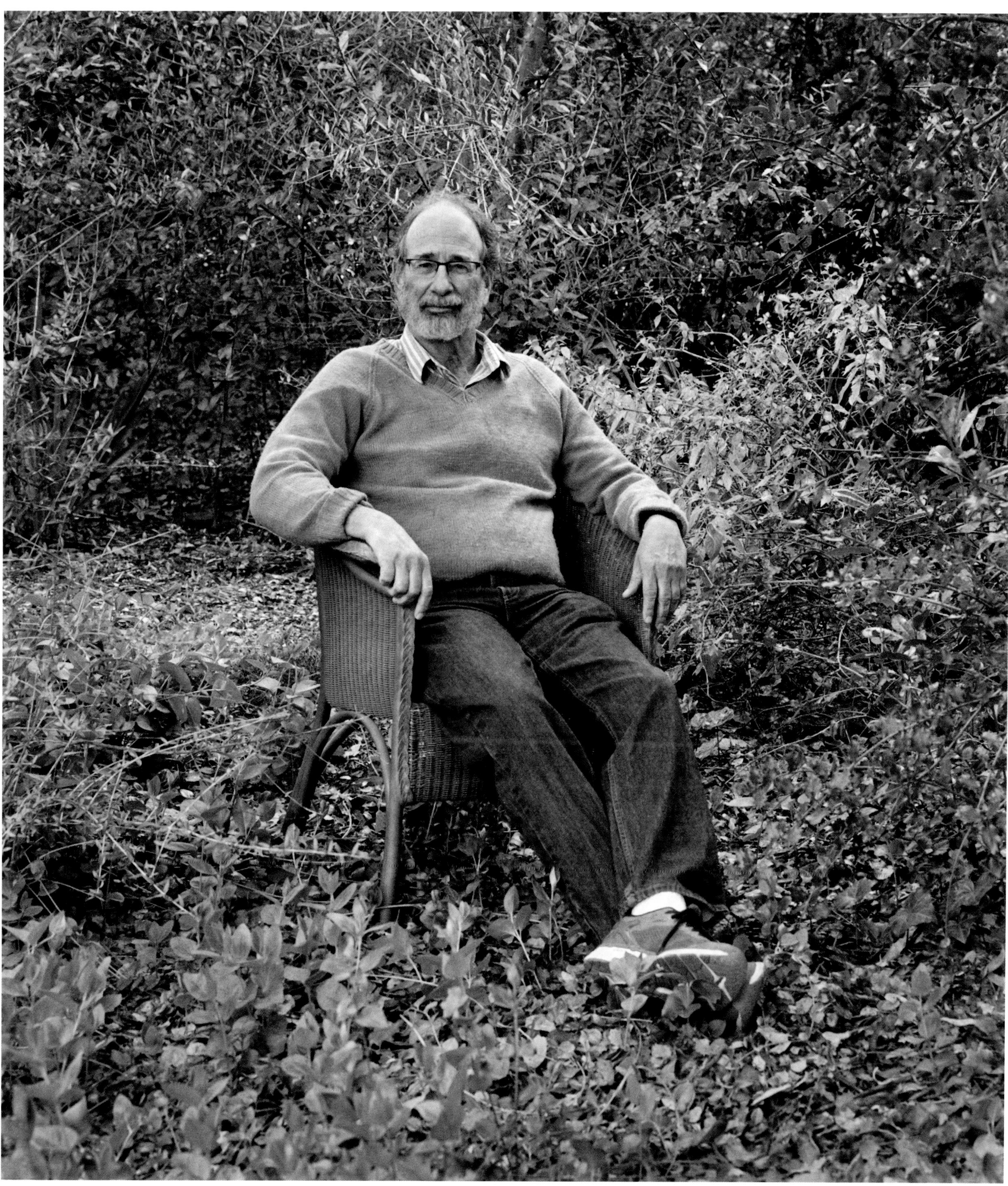

Cecilia Rouse

"Is our system of mainly local finance for K–12 education a good idea? Could it be improved?"

IN THE US we spend approximately $700 billion (in 2018 dollars) on elementary and secondary education annually (or about $14,000 per student) of which about 92 percent is financed at the state and local levels. About 45 percent is raised at the local level, which represents nearly 14,000 school districts and over 98,000 public schools. The US has historically had such decentralized financing when it comes to elementary and secondary education. While there are many benefits that come from decentralization, there are also costs and the outcomes of our students may well be improved with a bit more centralization, or coordination, in strategic areas.

Advantages of local financing (and hence, control) are that schools can be designed and managed to suit the needs and desires of the local population and labor market. Important decisions about budgeting, teacher hiring, extracurricular and other supplemental activities, which surely vary by locale, are devolved to those closest to the action. In fact, it has been well documented that households with the means to choose place significant value on the perceived quality of the local school district in their decisions about where to live, which helps to generate healthy competition among school districts eager to attract students, and to better align the offerings of the local schools with the interests of the families that live within that district.

And yet there is another side to such decentralization. Thirty-six percent of elementary and secondary school revenues in the US are generated by property taxes, which means there are districts that have much greater capacity to generate revenue than others. As an example, the wealthiest school district in the US in 2015 was Scarsdale, New York with a per capita income (a close correlate to the value of property) of $238,478. In comparison, the poorest district in the US at that time was San Perlita, Texas, which had a per capita income of $16,384. Recognizing that this gross inequality in school resources contributes to inequality in student outcomes, most states attempt to equalize spending to some extent, often by supplementing revenues in property-poor districts. Similarly, the contribution from the federal government largely comes through the Elementary and Secondary Education Act of 1965, whose intent is to equalize educational opportunities. This is to say, a large part of the contribution by states and the federal government is to compensate for the inequality in "ability to pay" that exists at the local level.

To my mind, there are two big negative consequences of our largely local system of education finance. The first is that income inequality across our country perpetuates educational inequality. While more money does not guarantee better student outcomes, it is difficult to implement proven educational reforms such as lowering class sizes and hiring more qualified teachers without leaving students in property-poor districts at a distinct disadvantage. The second is that with local control can come costs to student mobility, which can be large in some districts. A 2010 National Academy of Sciences report estimated that in some high-poverty urban schools, more than 50 percent of the students turn over within an academic year. And yet, with local control can come large differences in curricula across schools and districts; when children move mid-year, they can find that what they had been studying in their last school bears little resemblance to what they are learning in their new school. If the setting of curricula were even a bit more centralized, these kinds of moves, while disruptive to the student in many ways, would at least guarantee some level of educational continuity.

While decentralized education has many virtues that are well suited to American society, there may be gains from some greater centralization. Specifically, increased attempts to ensure that districts and schools serving the neediest students (who often need greater services at school to compensate for a lack of resources at home) have the necessary resources to generate strong outcomes, along with attempts to minimize the impact of student mobility, such as ensuring that curricula have some common standards, would likely improve our system of education.

CECILIA ROUSE is Dean of the Princeton University Woodrow Wilson School of Public and International Affairs.

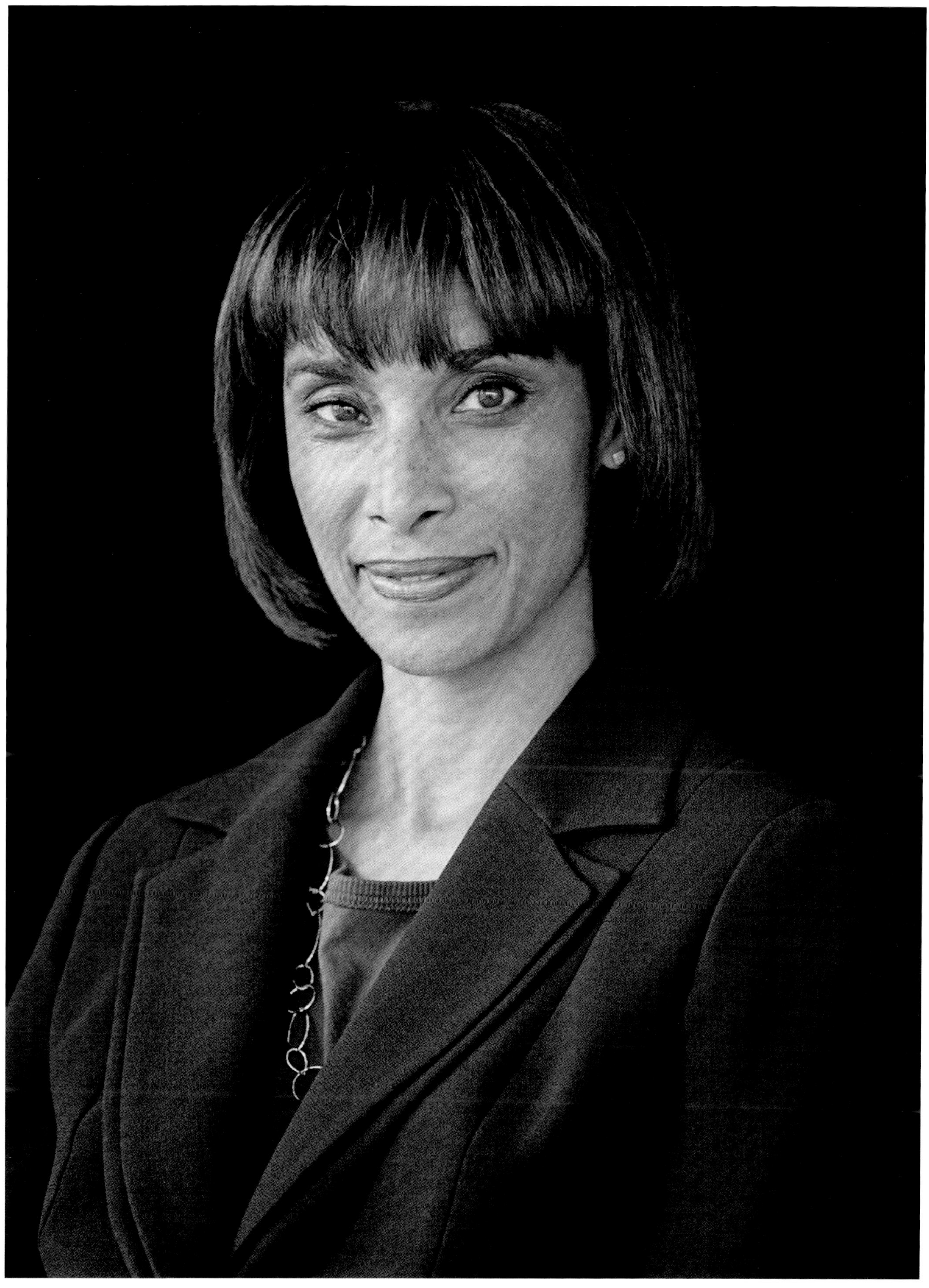

Emmanuel Saez

"Do you think there is anything like an optimal degree of income or wealth inequality in a modern society? Is it achievable?"

IN ALL SOCIETIES, people care deeply about inequality. Economic production is based on a complex web of work and ownership relationships. Nobody can produce in isolation and everybody depends on the rest of society. We also evaluate our own economic success relative to how others do in our society. Hence it is not surprising that people have strong feelings and views on how the fruits of economic growth should be distributed. Some believe that the market economy is generally fair and that people earn what they deserve. Others believe that markets can be unfair and that society should provide opportunity and protection from economic misfortune for all.

Is there anything like an optimal degree of economic disparity in a modern society and is it achievable? Ultimately, this is up to public debate and to the democratic political process: people express their views, debate, vote, and policies are enacted. The work of economists can neither answer this question for the public nor make everybody agree about ideal inequality, but it can help enlighten these debates. The deep question that has motivated my work is this: Can good public policy make society more equal while maintaining its economic vitality? Jointly with many colleagues, we have built data that document the level and evolution of income and wealth inequality across many countries and long time periods. We have strived to make our data accessible and understandable to the broader public and have attempted to understand the drivers of inequality and the role of government and public policy. What are the key findings?

First, virtually all modern societies have large governments that collect typically between one third and one half of all national income in taxes to fund public education and health, retirement and income support programs, and many other public goods. Therefore, through our governments, we have universally made the choice to pool a large fraction of our economic resources. Even in America, total taxes are almost one third of national income. This is the most powerful illustration that people care about inequality, and support pooling a large fraction of their individual market incomes for more equality, opportunity, and the common good of society.

Second, inequality has increased substantially in many advanced economies in recent decades, particularly so in the United States. The share of US national income going to the top 1 percent of adults has doubled from 10 percent in 1980 to about 20 percent today. Conversely, the share of national income going to the bottom half of American adults has declined from 20 percent in 1980 to about 12 percent today. As a result, the bottom half of adults have essentially experienced no growth at all in their incomes since 1980. An economy where half of the population is shut out of economic growth for over a generation is bound to generate discontent.

Third, other countries—particularly in continental Europe—have experienced much less increase in inequality and hence have been able to distribute the fruits of economic growth much more equitably. This implies that inequality is not the ineluctable consequence of technological progress and globalization but that societies can actually choose the level of inequality they want through public policy. Growth in America was once both strong and equitable from the New Deal up to the post-World War II decades thanks to progressive taxation, strong financial and anti-trust regulations, and an empowered work force. Unequal growth in America since 1980 is primarily a consequence of the unraveling of these policies. While inequality will always exist and generate heated debates, we can as a society change institutions and policies to ensure that economic growth is broadly shared. If the political will exists, economists can help shape the right tools to achieve more equality while preserving economic growth.

EMMANUEL SAEZ is Professor at the University of California, Berkeley. He received the John Bates Clark Medal in 2009.

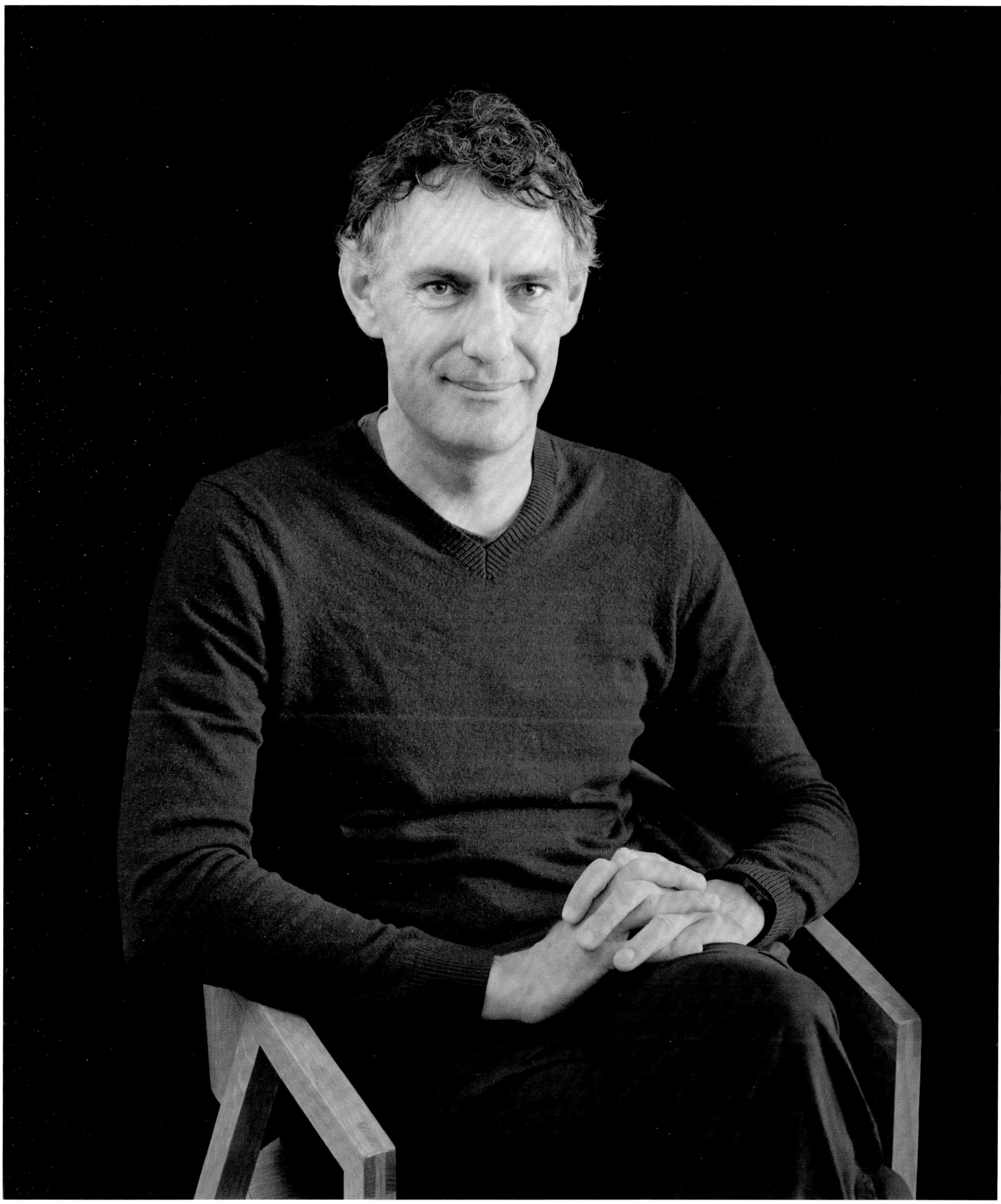

Thomas Sargent

"Does your work on inflation dynamics offer any hints as to why the rate of inflation in the United States has been so low during the last ten years? Any other ideas?"

MY WORK ABOUT the causes and cures for high and moderate inflations contains few, if any, insights about US and eurozone inflation outcomes during the last decade. A key relationship driving outcomes during the high inflation episodes that I have studied is a stable and smooth inverse dependence of the demand for real balances on positive levels of expected inflation. In other words, when inflation is substantial and interest rates are pretty high, people and firms don't like to hold cash or bank accounts because inflation erodes their "real" values, and they get no compensation in the form of interest. So they would rather own bonds or other assets that do pay interest; so the higher the interest rate, the less cash they are willing to hold. This behavior is a foundational element of my work on inflation.

In the last decade, whether it can be attributed to "regime change" or "nonlinearities" (which are probably concepts meant to describe the same things), nominal interest rates have dropped so close to zero and made the demand function for real balances so very elastic with respect to nominal interest rates that we have fallen in to what Keynes called the "liquidity trap." When interest rates are persistently very low, as they have been recently, people and firms see no point in bothering with bonds and other assets; instead they hold cash and bank accounts and are insensitive to the minor fluctuations in interest rates and inflation that may occur. So the inverse relationship (a high interest rate leading to a low willingness to hold cash, and vice versa), as discussed above, disappears. Monetary policy thus becomes less effective than in "normal" times.

Essentially, my work about high inflations uses the very same "classical" economics that Keynes used when he wrote *The Tract on Monetary Reform* in 1923. To understand inflation outcomes in the last ten years, that book is less useful than the parts of Keynes's 1936 *The General Theory of Employment, Interest and Money* in which he analyzes consequences of the liquidity trap.

How to get a coherent story that merges these two economic behaviors has been a problem at the frontier of macroeconomics ever since Paul Samuelson sharply posed the problem when he discussed policies designed to bring a "neoclassical synthesis" between the two regimes. Using new tools that allow them to model various "frictions" in realistic ways, young scholars today are making headway on this problem in ways that I wish I had but did not.

THOMAS SARGENT is Professor at New York University. He received the Nobel Prize for Economics in 2011.

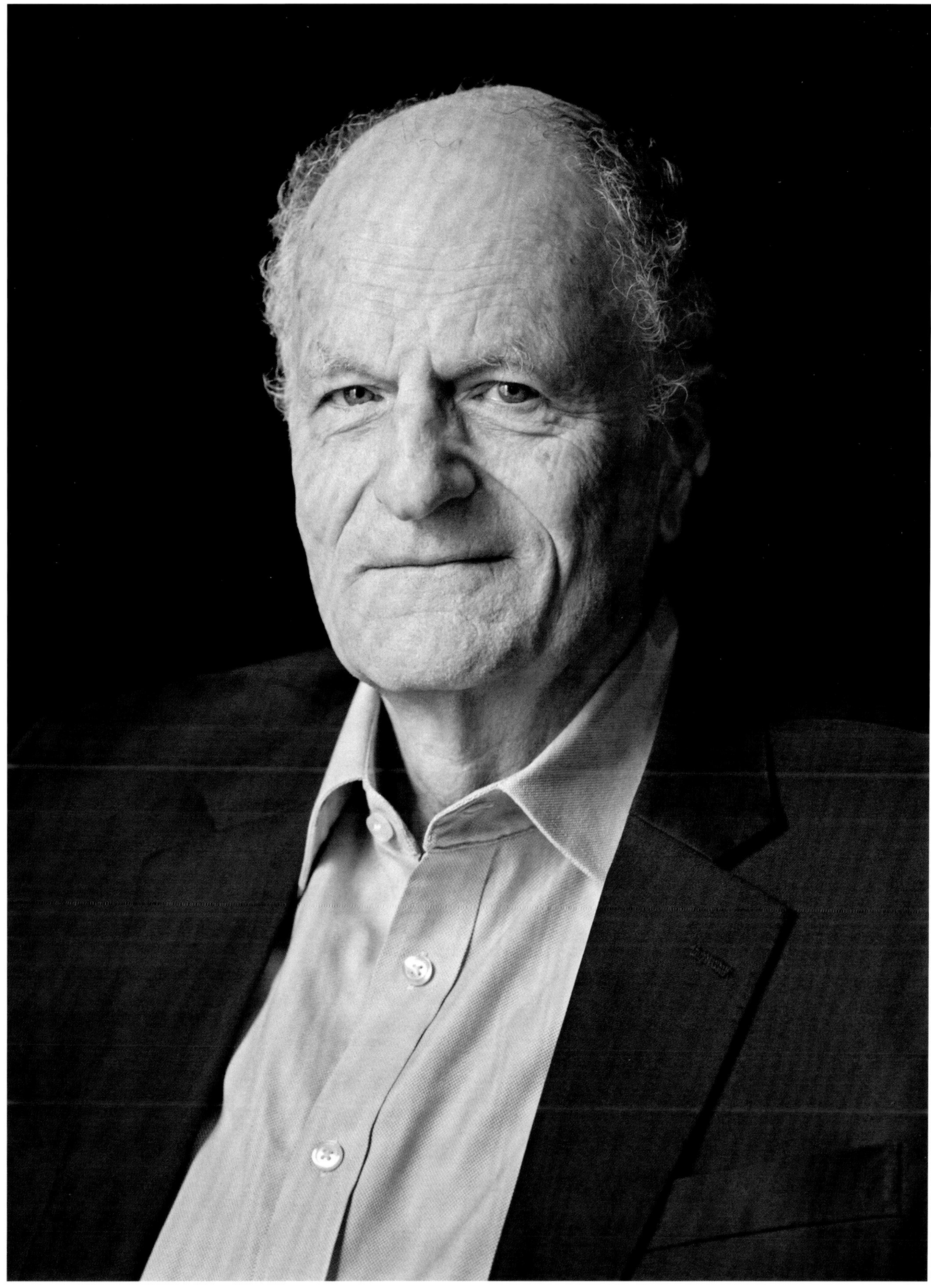

Amartya Sen

"Do you think that giving women control of their own fertility would be an adequate population policy for the world? What else would you suggest?"

THE LIVES THAT are most strained by over-frequent bearing and rearing of children are those of young women, and it is not surprising that anything that increases the influence of young women on fertility decisions tends to moderate birth rates. This connection is seen in statistical studies across the world. For example, the observation that women's education and remunerated employment have a very strong influence in cutting down birth rates reflects this relationship, since both increase the voice of women within the family. In comparisons over the hundreds of districts that make up India, these are the only two influences on fertility rates that have consistently emerged as being statistically significant.

It is necessary to understand the role of giving women influence and control over their own fertility, since that important connection is often missed. For example, in popular understanding, the rapid fall of birth rates in China is often attributed to its coercive "one-child" policy. However, the big decline in Chinese fertility rates occurred *before* that draconian policy was introduced in 1978, and it can be linked particularly to the expansion of women's schooling and employment. In the decade *preceding* the introduction of the one-child policy, the Chinese fertility rate fell from 5.87—in 1968—to 2.98 in 1978. That was the biggest drop-off in the story of China's falling fertility rate, which is 1.67 now—four decades later (following the introduction of the one-child policy, along with further improvements in girls' schooling and women's employment).

Women having control over their own fertility cannot, however, be the only plank in devising an adequate population policy. Some countries are beginning to face the problem of declining population, with extraordinarily low fertility rates. There may be a need for taking note of social concerns that go beyond the interests of young women themselves. It is, however, implausible that decisions on so private a subject as fertility can be sensibly taken away from the parents themselves, and particularly from the mothers. What is not beyond legitimate social discourse is the way a society may reform itself to reduce the burden of family work, including the rearing of children, that tends, in most societies, to fall unequally on the mothers. The importance of making sure that young women have control over their own fertility may need supplementation by fairer sharing of household and familial work. In addition, parental leaves, good preschool facilities, and other social arrangements can all play a part in influencing the way women's control over fertility decisions is exercised.

Finally, population policy must also take note of pervasive "boy preference" in the use of sex-selective abortions in many parts of world, including China, North and West India, West Asia, and to varying degrees in much of South and East Asia. Various studies have shown that the mothers in those places often make the decisions on selective abortion of female fetuses, so that relying on the control of young women in relation to these decisions may not be an adequate solution. There is an opportunity for critical and better-informed discussions about the roles of boys and girls in the society at large, and also about the possibility of social arrangements (like pensions) that obviate the perceived necessity in certain countries—where that perception is consequential—of having boys, rather than girls, for the sake of the parents' economic security in their old age. While appropriate control is important, it cannot remove the need for social reform and of enlightening public reasoning.

AMARTYA SEN is Professor at Harvard University. He received the Nobel Prize for Economics in 1998.

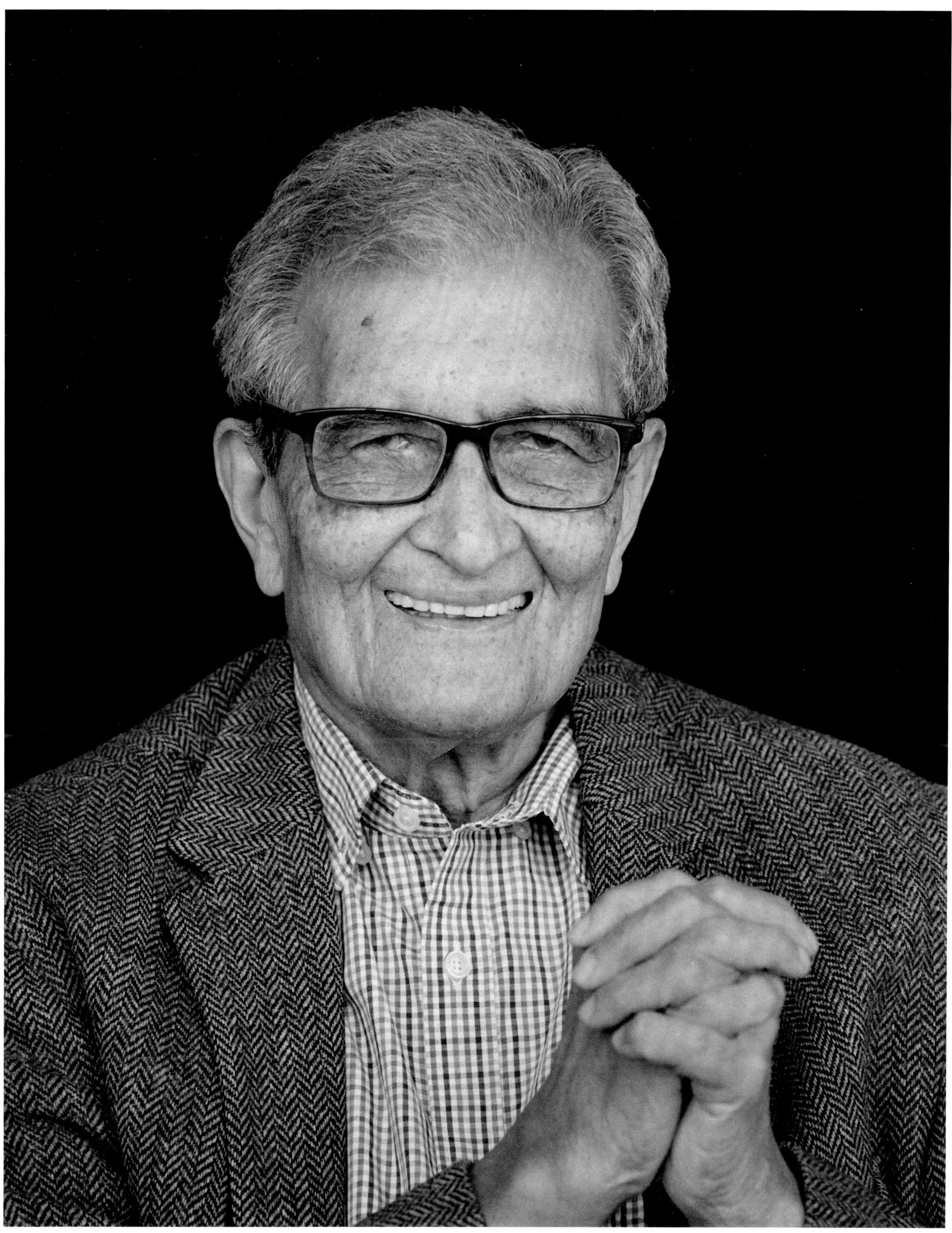

Eytan Sheshinski

"How should we allocate property rights and tax income from natural resources, like mineral deposits of natural gas?"

THE TAXATION OF nonrenewable natural resources such as gas, oil, and minerals is an important source of government revenue in many countries. Over 80 percent of government revenue comes from petroleum in several Middle Eastern countries, about 50 percent in some African countries, a quarter in Russia, and a significant fraction in several Organization for Economic Cooperation and Development (OECD) countries. The design of natural resource revenue is thus of considerable importance.

The state as sovereign owns a country's natural resources. The US is an exception in that private owners are entitled to economic resources discovered on their property. Governments can extract income from natural resources either "in-house" by publicly owned firms or by outsourcing the right to extract income to privately owned firms in return for a contractual obligation to pay taxes that reflect the government's ownership. Inefficiencies of state-owned enterprises lead almost all governments to grant franchises to private firms.

The most common fiscal instruments used by governments are *royalties,* whose tax base are revenues. This tax, as other indirect taxes, is distortive, having negative effects on explorations, development, and production. Governments favor this tax as it provides a relatively stable and fast stream of income. The alternative to royalties is a *rent tax*, based on excess profits and therefore nondistortive. Rent taxes require information on costs and have to compensate for risks. Asymmetric information and potential manipulations, inflating and the timing of costs, make the existence of a credible regulatory governmental agency necessary for the use of a rent tax. This is the reason why most developing countries rely exclusively on royalties instead of a rent tax. Government auctions, if properly conducted (with open access and full information), can be another efficient method to extract rents. In the US, offshore auctions for oil tracts specify that the winner pays the government the highest "signature bonus" up front.

There are economic and normative arguments for smoothing expenditures from income obtained from exhaustible natural resources. When resources are depletable it is a moral principle to enable future generations to share in the benefits by separating expenditures from income, and stretching the former over a long horizon.

While far-sighted governments can invest (say, in infrastructure) to provide for future generations, realism and political economy require the imposition of spending constraints on governments. These are the arguments behind the establishment of Natural Resource Funds (NRFs), or sovereign funds, by resource-rich countries. In addition to the moral argument there were also macroeconomic goals. In the 1960s, after the discoveries of North Sea oil deposits, the inflow of large amounts of foreign exchange associated with the sale of oil led to the revaluation of exchange rates in countries such as Norway and the Netherlands. This hurt traditional export industries and led to economic slowdown. This phenomenon is termed the "Dutch disease." NRFs, by investing their proceeds in world markets and spreading the inflow, can mitigate these negative effects. Today, there are close to forty NRFs worldwide, the largest being the Norwegian and Qatari funds, each worth close to a trillion US dollars. The empirical case, though, for NRFs is surprisingly weak. Some NRFs perform well while others fare poorly. Norway is often mentioned as an example of the former, while the governments of some African countries have raided their NRFs.

These observations are related to another phenomenon, the "resource curse." There is a negative empirical relation between the rate of growth of countries and the level of their natural resources. This paradox, or puzzle, is explained in political economy terms: governments that rely largely on an extraneous source of income, independent of the performance of the economy, tend to be negligent on economic policy and susceptible to corruption. Strict rules for the disbursement of revenues for NRFs are recommended though not sufficient. In Norway the NRF disbursement rules are lax yet the "political culture" makes management adhere to long-term goals (e.g., pension support).

Given the need for more balanced and durable contracts between large, extractive private firms and governments in developing countries, the OECD is in the process of formulating guiding principles for extraction contracts—a welcome initiative.

EYTAN SHESHINSKI is Professor Emeritus at the Hebrew University of Jerusalem.

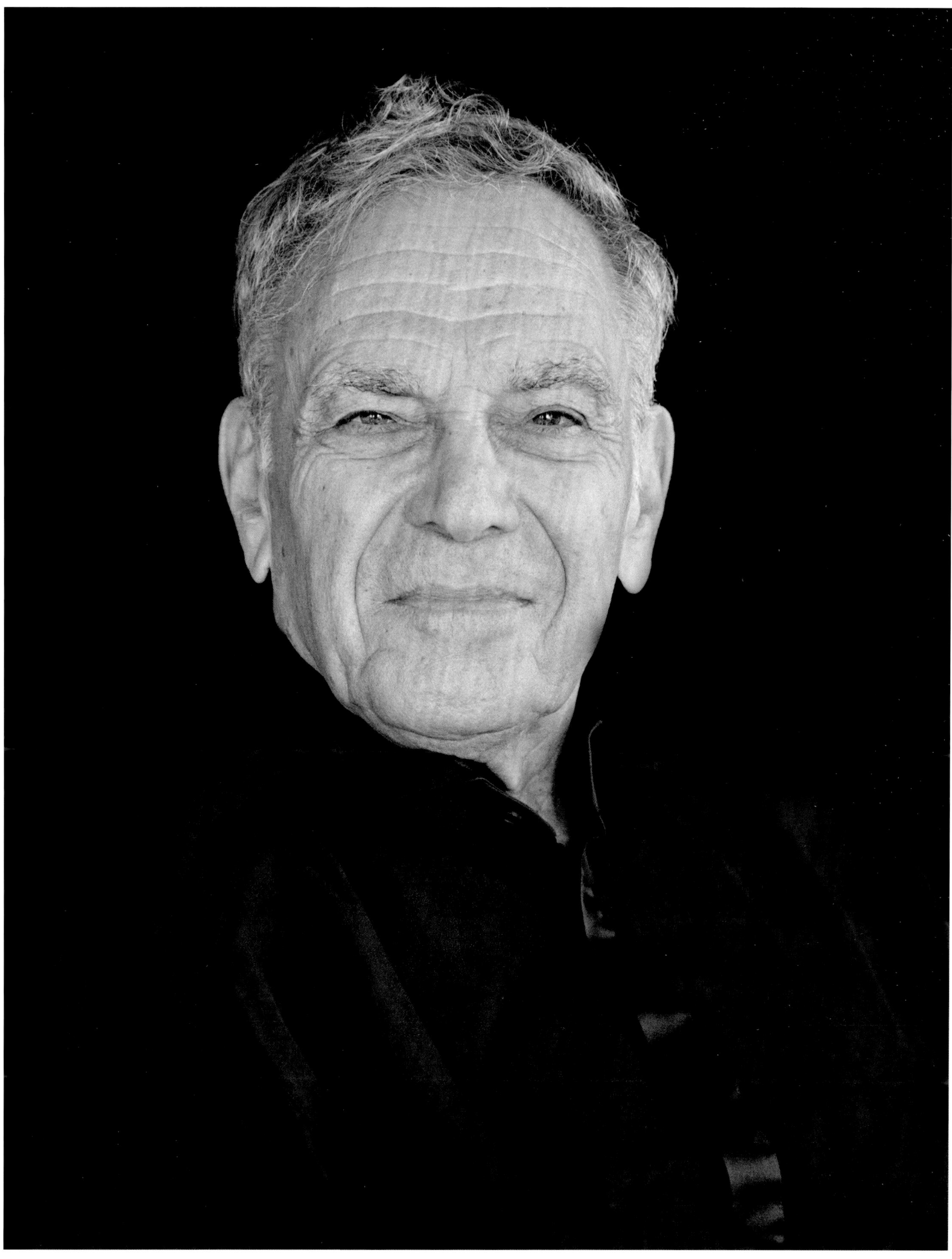

Robert Shiller

"What is narrative economics?"

IN THE PALGRAVE *Dictionary of Political Economy*, 1896, there is an entry on "Narrative Economics." But the definition given there is not up-to-date. It reads: "In narrative or historical economics are included not only accounts of past events in chronological order, but also comparisons between different societies, whether contemporaneous or not." This definition makes narrative economics largely the same as chronology or geography of economic events.

I suggested a different definition of narrative economics in my 2017 presidential address "Narrative Economics" before the American Economic Association. Narrative economics should be the study of *popular narratives*, as economic forces themselves. That is, narrative economics does not construct narratives but studies the narratives that focus public attention, which have actually been active in the making of historical events. Narrative economics should focus on the narratives that are contagious, that travel from person to person by word of mouth or social media and that motivate the kinds of economic decisions that millions of people make. Narratives of past major economic events can be viewed in digitized historical newspapers, books, sermons, diaries, social media communications, and other sources.

We should remember that the word "narrative" is not the same as "story." Narrative is the *telling* of a story from the narrator's view of the world, conveying a sort of theory or motivation. A single objective story, like the story, for example, of the stock market crash of 1929, could be told from a million different perspectives. Certain perspectives won out just after 1929, namely, a story that the crash was the harbinger of bad times to come. Indeed, people became fearful of their future and stopped spending. Sales of new Ford cars dropped almost 80 percent from 1929 to 1932. Most people thought they could perfectly well do without a new car for some more years, until the fear passed, but in postponing their purchases they caused auto plants to shut down and lay off workers, and they created a depression.

Even now, that narrative is remembered. Today, television news broadcasts dutifully report the change in the Dow Jones Industrial Average every market day, and the *Wall Street Journal* includes this just below its banner on every front page. The Dow did not have such resonance before 1929: 1929 made the Dow famous. People today still think of the Dow as a harbinger of possibly another Great Depression. That is a narrative that will not go away—it is so strongly entrenched in public thinking. The Great Depression narrative resurfaced in the 2007–2009 world financial crisis, and arguably made it much more severe than it would have been had it not rekindled public fears.

Economists have been much less interested in narratives than have practitioners of other social sciences. Anthropologists and sociologists are much more interested in narratives. Part of the reason that economists show so little interest is that it is hard to establish the direction of causality between narratives and economic events. They wonder how they can prove whether some popular narrative is actually actively affecting economic behavior. They want to see quantitative evidence on any determinants of economic activity, so that statistical significance can be established.

The problem with quantifying the impact of narratives is that they are complex and amorphous. The impact of a given narrative may depend on just a few critical words contained in it. The meaning—and significance to people of the time—of the nuances of a narrative seem to require human judgment in interpreting them.

But we have to try to systematically study changing popular narratives if we are ever to understand and forecast economic events.

ROBERT SHILLER is Professor at Yale University. He received the Nobel Prize for Economics in 2013.

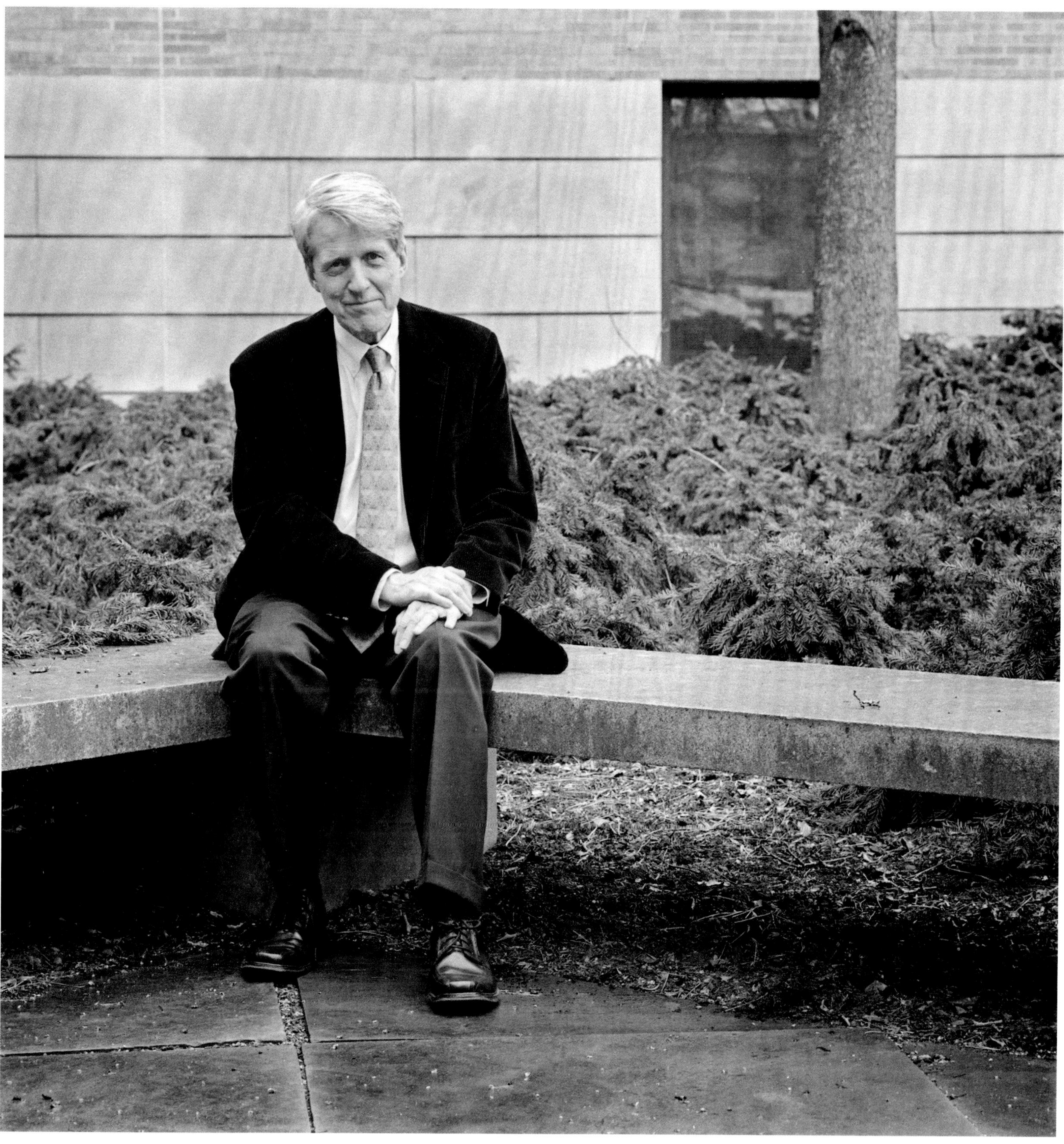

George P. Shultz

"Why do you think private sector unions and collective bargaining have practically disappeared? Is that a good thing?"

IN THE LATE 1920s and '30s, private sector unions grew. They had a dramatic and positive impact on the workplace. They were not just beneficial to the economics of wages and working conditions, but created a system of private jurisprudence that brought justice to the workplace; unions were positive things. But in many cases the businesses that had unionized had also monopolized their industry, for example the automobile industry. Because of this monopolization, industries went to sleep and diminished quality, and for a while consumers were worried about their cars. This opened the market up to Japanese and German imports, which people saw were much better than the cars the US was producing. These US businesses lost market share and broke down. As automobile makers from Japan and Germany began to establish plants in the US, in states other than Michigan, there began to be a lot of well-paid autoworkers who were not unionized. People in other states thought that one reason this was happening was perhaps not just because of wages, but to escape union conditions which had begun to be more and more restrictive. This shift brought the proportion of the labor force organized by unions down a great deal.

It is probably a good thing that this happened for natural reasons. I think that the union movement established a kind of standard of how the workplace should treat people, and while that varies, on the whole I think it has been a permanent rearrangement. In the US now, non-union employers by and large treat people reasonably well, and in part that's because the labor market is fairly tight. It is worth noting that there are over 7 million jobs in the United States right now that aren't filled, which is indicative of how tight the labor market is. If unions want to regain, then they're going to have to find out more about the grievances and problems of today's workers, and address those in a constructive way.

"Can you see a route to clean energy for the United States? For the world?"

WE BETTER FIND our way to clean energy, and avoid having the climate warm further than it has already. We are now feeling the effects of it. I was exposed recently to a paper by a wonderful biologist named Lucy Shapiro, in which she talks about the diseases that are now here because of global warming. As the climate warms, tropical diseases move north, and we're not ready for them, neither in terms of our diagnostics nor our treatment. So we better pay attention and take action.

I think it is dawning on almost everybody that climate change is not a hoax. It is a reality; it is not something that's coming, it is here. There are things we can and must do to address it. As an economist I tend to think in terms of incentives, so I have been advocating a revenue neutral carbon tax. If you want to have people use less of something, tax it, and then let the market sort out how best to produce less carbon.

We want the tax to be revenue neutral so there will be no fiscal drag. Carbon dividends would be paid in an equal number of dollars to, say, everyone with a Social Security number. That would make the tax progressive.

I think it will work. Around the world measures are beginning to be made. Pretty soon, China is going to restrict gasoline cars. Electric cars are basically here. I have solar panels on the roof of my home on the Stanford campus. I have long since paid for them by what I've saved on my electric bill. I drive an electric car. The electric car doesn't use as much electricity as my solar panels are producing. So what is my cost of fuel? Zero. What's not to like?

GEORGE SHULTZ is Distinguished Fellow at the Hoover Institution. He was the US Secretary of State from 1982–1989, Secretary of the Treasury from 1972–1974, and Secretary of Labor from 1969–1970.

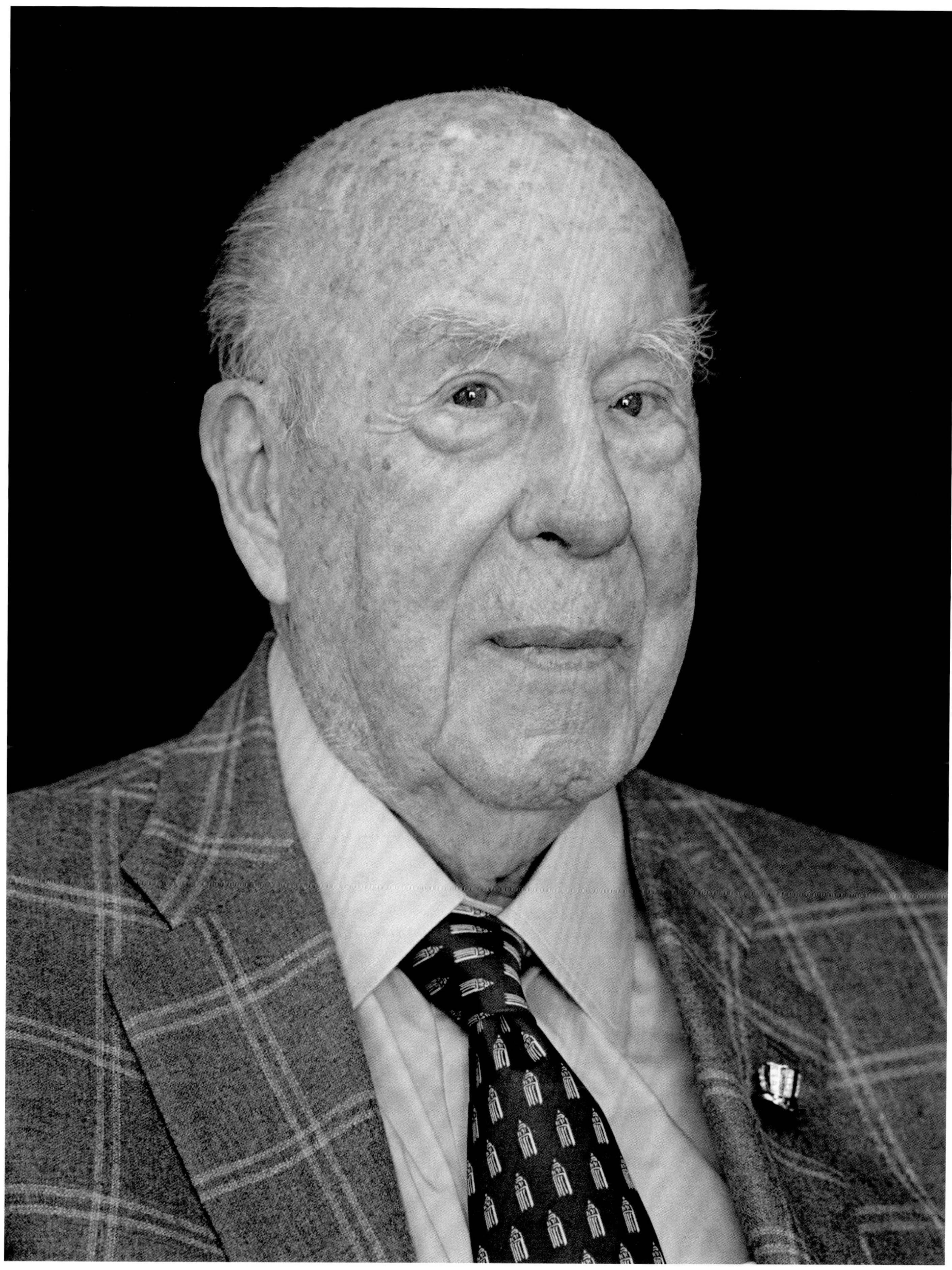

Christopher Sims

"Would our economy benefit from better coordination of fiscal and monetary policy? How could that be arranged?"

MOST RICH COUNTRIES, for the last half of the 20th century, tried a simple regime to coordinate monetary and fiscal policy: monetary policy was to be "independent," run by a depoliticized central bank with the responsibility of controlling long-run inflation, while possibly also supplying countercyclical stimulus, and fiscal policy was to maintain long-term budget balance, while also perhaps supplying countercyclical stimulus. Such a system can work, so long as interest rates don't hit zero. When they do, usually at a time of high unemployment and low inflation, monetary policy cannot control the price level with its main tool, the interest rate. Then expansionary fiscal policy is required. If this were widely understood, it would be easy to implement. It is not widely understood. For some reason, governments tend to make fiscal policy more restrictive even while zero interest rates and low inflation prevail.

A possible way out of this, short of policymakers understanding the situation, is for voter frustration to lead to the election of a government that thinks fiscal deficits are unimportant and runs large deficits with no plan for financing the resulting debt. This would end the period of low inflation and low interest rates, but might well lead to an encounter with a different kind of pathology of fiscal/monetary noncooperation. If inflation accelerates and interest rates rise, some increased fiscal austerity is required in response. Otherwise the interest rate rises will fail to restrain the inflation.

CHRISTOPHER SIMS is Professor at Princeton University. He received the Nobel Prize for Economics in 2011.

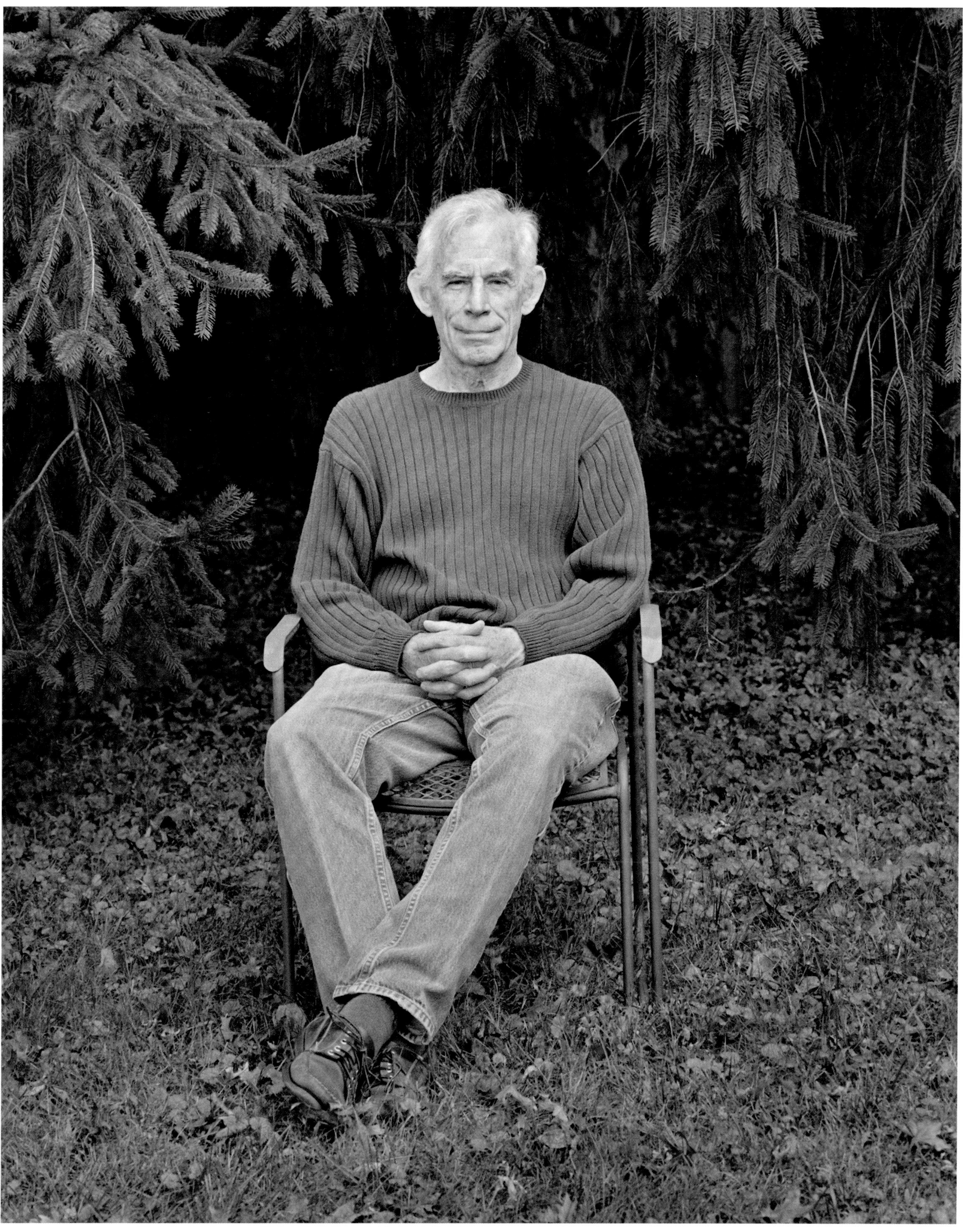

Robert M. Solow

"Does a modern capitalist economy have to grow to be healthy?"

THERE SEEMS TO be no reason of economic principle why an economy like ours could not function happily in a stationary state, just more or less reproducing itself over time. I inserted that "more or less" not as weasel words, but to allow for the possibility (not the necessity) that new goods and services could appear and old ones fade away, as long as overall trends remain flat. Creativity and novelty could remain. This is not to say that maintaining this balance would be easy. There would be difficult adjustments to be made, as much sociological and political as narrowly economic, but they do not violate economic principles.

In most advanced economies, the natural increase in population has already stopped, so it is easy to contemplate a stationary population. For this purpose it is fair to ignore net immigration. Net immigration into rich countries is not an intrinsic property of modern capitalism; it reflects the enormous gap in well-being between rich and poor countries, and the violent political instability that seems to go with poverty. So we can imagine that we are thinking about a modern economy with an unchanging population. Everyone goes through the normal life cycle: dependency, working life, retirement.

If productivity were constant, the constant working population would produce a constant supply of goods and services, and a constant potential income. To maintain equilibrium this supply of goods and services would have to be matched by demand. There would have to be a willing buyer for what is produced. All that potential income would have to be spent. Not by every family in every year: through the normal life cycle a family may first go into debt to acquire and furnish a home, for example, and then save enough to pay off that debt and build up a stock of assets that will be spent down in retirement. Added up over everyone, however, national saving must be zero.

In a growing capitalist economy, aggregate net saving will be positive: not all income is consumed. The overall supply-demand balance is maintained if net saving is offset by net investment. Businesses borrow the savings and use them to buy new productive assets like factories, office buildings, dentists' offices, power plants, drones. In our hypothetical happy stationary state there is no net investment so aggregate net saving has to be approximately zero. If the inhabitants keep wanting to save more than that, public policy will have to find ways to induce them not to: say by taxing away part of their income and spending the revenue on fireworks displays, chamber music performances, or child care. (There will of course be occasional imbalances. Neither a stationary nor a growing economy works like a well-oiled machine. Capitalism is neither well-oiled nor a machine.)

Most measurements of economic growth are defective. Even the ubiquitous Gross Domestic Product takes no account of the depreciation of buildings and machinery. Even more important, the irreversible depletion of nonrenewable natural resources and the reversible or irreversible damage to potentially renewable resources go unmeasured and ignored. This omission may be more important for poor countries that tend to depend more on the exploitation of natural resources. Even so, a rich country aiming at a stationary equilibrium should be careful that it is not really going downhill when resource depletion and environmental damage are included. This will require both active measurement and deliberate policy.

It is plausible that a growing economy offers more opportunities for social and income mobility than a stationary one. It is hard to know for sure because the data are not available. But the expansion of old industries and the appearance of new ones probably generate movements up and down the distribution of income and status. A stationary economy runs some risk of hardening into a hereditary hierarchy. That would be both hateful in itself and dangerous for democracy. Avoiding this outcome will require active policy to promote mobility.

ROBERT SOLOW is Emeritus Institute Professor at the Massachusetts Institute of Technology. He received the John Bates Clark Medal in 1961 and the Nobel Prize for Economics in 1987.

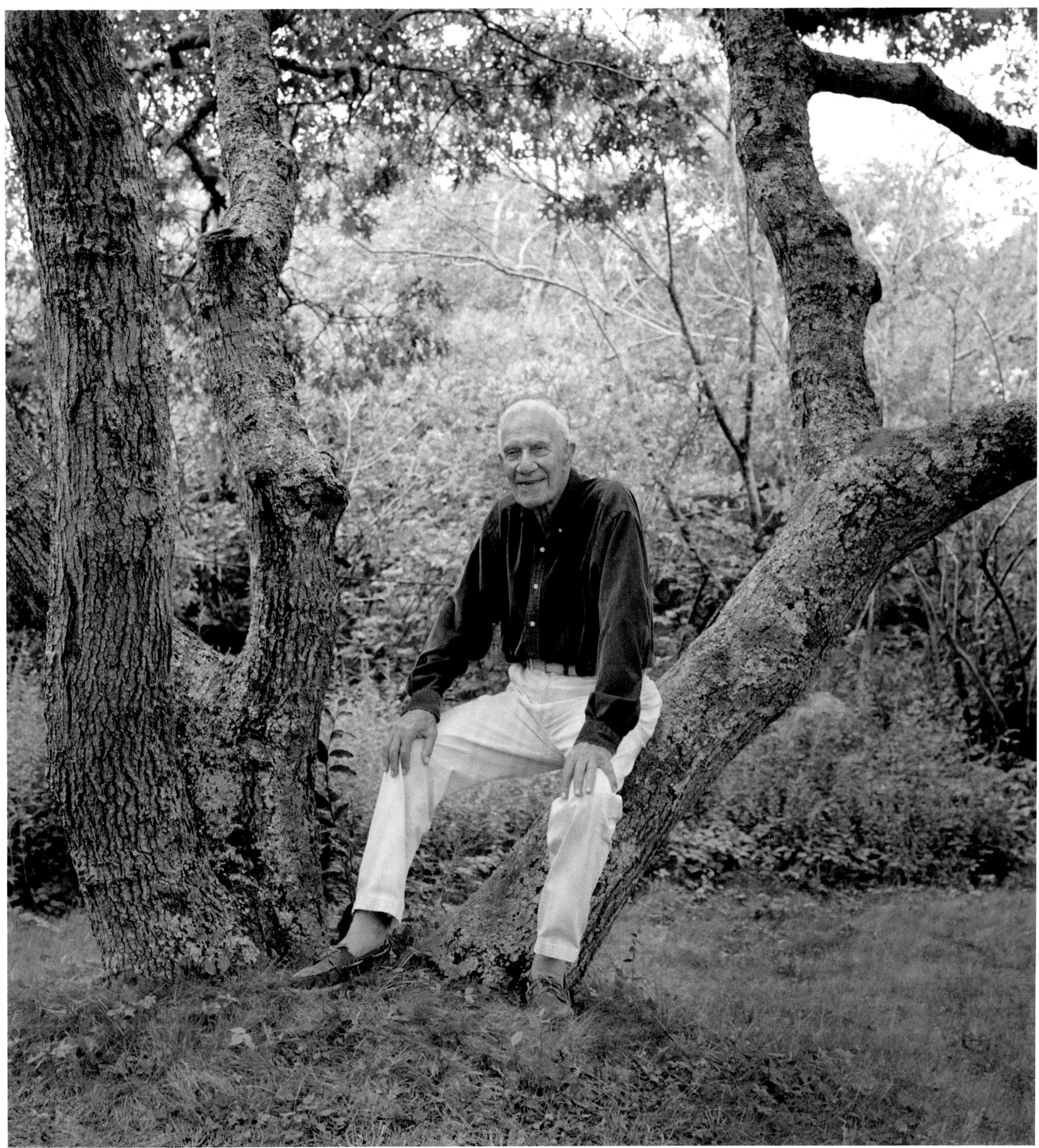

Michael Spence

"Why is jump-starting growth in poor countries difficult?"

THE POSTWAR PERIOD has seen real sustained growth in a number of developing countries for the first time. Through bitter experience, the principal ingredients have become reasonably well known. One might then have expected that the sustained growth patterns should have spread to the majority of poorer developing countries. That has not happened, at least not yet. One might elaborate and ask, why are there still many countries stuck in low or no growth patterns when the ingredients that support high growth patterns and poverty reduction are much better understood now than they were fifty years ago?

There are a number of real challenges for poor countries that help explain this variability across developing countries. But the simplest general answer is that knowing what should happen does not mean that it is easy to get all the pieces in place. Quite the opposite; the challenges are formidable.

One of the ingredients in sustained high growth is a high investment rate, on the order of 25-30 percent of GDP, with important complimentary components on the public and private investment sides. Investment means deferral of consumption and savings to finance the investment. Generally, funding investment substantially with foreign savings has not turned out well for many reasons. Domestically funded investment comes at the cost of reducing current spending on daily necessities. This is a hard choice to make when people are very poor.

There is a high correlation between countries that have struggled with growth and measures of income and wealth inequality. This concentration of economic power often translates to policy agendas oriented less to growth and poverty reduction and more to preserving the status quo and the interests of the owners of wealth. In other words the growth agenda is secondary and inclusiveness, a key ingredient in sustained high growth cases, is missing. In some cases, noninclusive and subdued growth patterns lead to a populist backlash, which may shift the policy agenda in beneficial ways, but all too often it instead leads to another set of growth suppressing policies: radical redistribution that suppresses investment, and the accumulation of unsustainable debt levels.

Good governance is a critical ingredient in successful growth recipes and has broadly two components: competence and good intentions. Both matter. Governments that are pursuing some agenda other than the longer-term inclusive growth of the economy do not invest enough in infrastructure and education to support powerful growth and employment engines. Typically they do not connect sufficiently with the global economy, its markets and technology, which, by experience, are major growth catalysts in the early stages of growth.

But even well-intentioned governments can struggle with getting the requisite ingredients in place. It is one thing to know that infrastructure is important, and quite another to select wisely and implement effectively with limited resources. Similarly, managing the sequencing and pacing of opening up the current and capital accounts takes considerable technical skill. Even successful developing countries have struggled with these issues and made progress through learning by doing, correcting mistakes promptly, and sometimes by taking advantage of external expertise in the development banks.

Natural resources are, in principal, assets that can be used to elevate investment and accelerate growth. But too often natural resource wealth distorts political incentives and results in corruption, battles over the ownership of the wealth, and policy agendas that have little to do with generating and sustaining growth. This is known as the natural resource curse. Africa is abnormally high in natural resource wealth relative to, say, Asia. Distinguished scholars like Paul Collier at Oxford, an expert on Africa's growth and development, believe that this has been a major contributing headwind to growth in a number of African countries. It is striking that the correlation between sustained high growth and natural resource wealth is significantly negative, lending credence to this view.

Finally, there is a widespread but mistaken belief that the form of governance is decisive when it comes to growth. There are numerous successful cases among developing countries that include both democratic and autocratic examples. Many citizens may prefer democracy for its own sake, and that is to be respected. But experience tells us that democracies, like autocracies, can be corrupted. The message from the postwar period is that the form of governance is neither necessary nor sufficient for growth. What is needed is a governance structure that is persistent and determined in pursuing the long-term public interest, and that learns, adapts, and becomes more effective over time.

MICHAEL SPENCE is Professor at the New York University Stern School of Business. He received the John Bates Clark Medal in 1981 and the Nobel Prize for Economics in 2001.

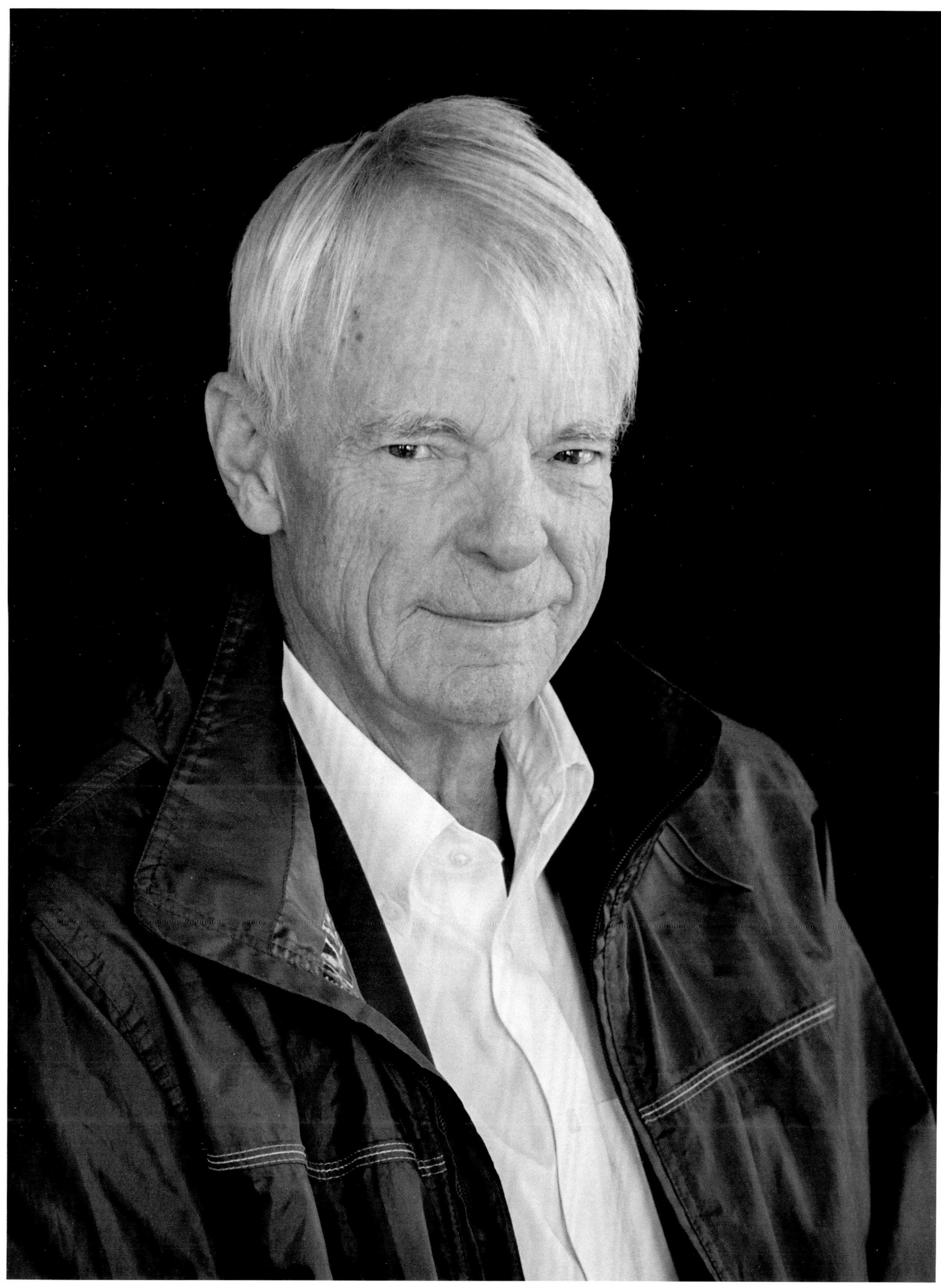

Nicholas Stern

"Is there a way for the developing and emerging economies to increase income and consumption per person without endangering the planet?"

THE SHORT ANSWER is *yes*. Managing climate change and overcoming world poverty are the two defining challenges of this century. If we fail on one, we fail on the other. It was the realization that we can and must put the two together that led to the extraordinary construction of a new global agenda in 2015: the Sustainable Development Goals (SDGs) for 2030 were agreed to at the United Nations in September; and in December of that year the United Nations Framework Convention on Climate Change came to its historic agreement in Paris to hold global temperature increases well below 2°C (relative to the late 19th century, the standard benchmark).

As a world, we currently emit each year around 50 billion tonnes of greenhouse gases. We have to get these annual flows down to net zero in fifty years or so if we are to hold to "well below 2°C." Business as usual might involve an increase of more than 4°C in a century or so, and the plans put forward by countries in Paris for emissions for 2030, when added across all countries, would likely lead to an increase of around 3°C in a century or so. The world has not seen a 3°C increase in temperatures for around 3 million years. *Three, four, or five degrees would redefine where and how we could live*, with radical changes in sea levels, flooding, storms and hurricanes, deserts, and so on. Hundreds of millions, probably billions, of people would have to move, resulting in severe, widespread and sustained conflict. The stakes are immense.

If we are to reach the Paris targets, we would have to cut annual greenhouse gas emissions by 30 percent or more in the next two decades. Furthermore, that reduction would have to be implemented during a period when concurrently, at a growth rate of 3 percent, we would roughly *double the world economy* and more than double the world's infrastructure. Such emissions reductions require rapid and radical change. The good news is that it is not only feasible but is also attractive.

At the heart of the story of change will be *sustainable infrastructure*. One way or another, infrastructure and its use are responsible for around two-thirds of our emissions. And around two-thirds of the growth in infrastructure will be outside the rich world, although, of course, the rich world has a great deal to do in rebuilding its own infrastructure. For this new infrastructure to be sustainable, we must manage the severe problems of pollution and congestion in our cities. It will require much greater efficiency in the way we use resources, particularly energy. And it will involve a rapid switch to new, zero-carbon sources of energy.

We can already see rapid change in the power sector where renewables like solar and wind are *already outcompeting fossil-fueled electricity generation* in many parts of the world. We can see the beginning of change in city design, that will accelerate with modern public transport, self-driving cars, the exclusion of fossil-fueled vehicles, and much smarter and more efficient buildings. We can see the beginnings of change in sectors such as steel and cement. Of course, we must do much better in the management of our forests, soils, and oceans. They are crucial in getting to net-zero emissions and provide us with hugely valuable resources through their natural ecosystems and water management, as well as food.

All this will require *good economic policy*. We understand what we have to do in tackling key market failures, namely, the intense damages from greenhouse gas emissions; but also the underrewarding of research and development; malfunctioning capital markets; the workings of networks such as electricity grids, public transport, and recycling; particulate air pollution; and so on. In all of these cases, we can see the economic policies that are necessary. Further, it is vital that these policies are clear and credible over the medium term, if the right investment is to be incentivized on a sufficient scale. This will require strategies and targets that can chart a sense of direction and commitment, and institutions that can give confidence in policy.

We will need *financial systems* that can bring the right kind of finance to realize investment and manage risk. The private sector will finance most of the investment, but the multilateral and national development banks must play a key role in not only financing investment, but also setting examples, giving confidence and helping build policy and capacity.

I am optimistic and confident about *what we can do as a world*. The future could be very attractive for us all, whether in the developed countries or in emerging markets and developing countries. In this century we can rise to the twin challenges of managing climate change and overcoming poverty. What we will do is now a matter of political will. And that is up to all of us.

NICHOLAS STERN is Professor at the London School of Economics and was Chief Economist at the World Bank from 2000–2003.

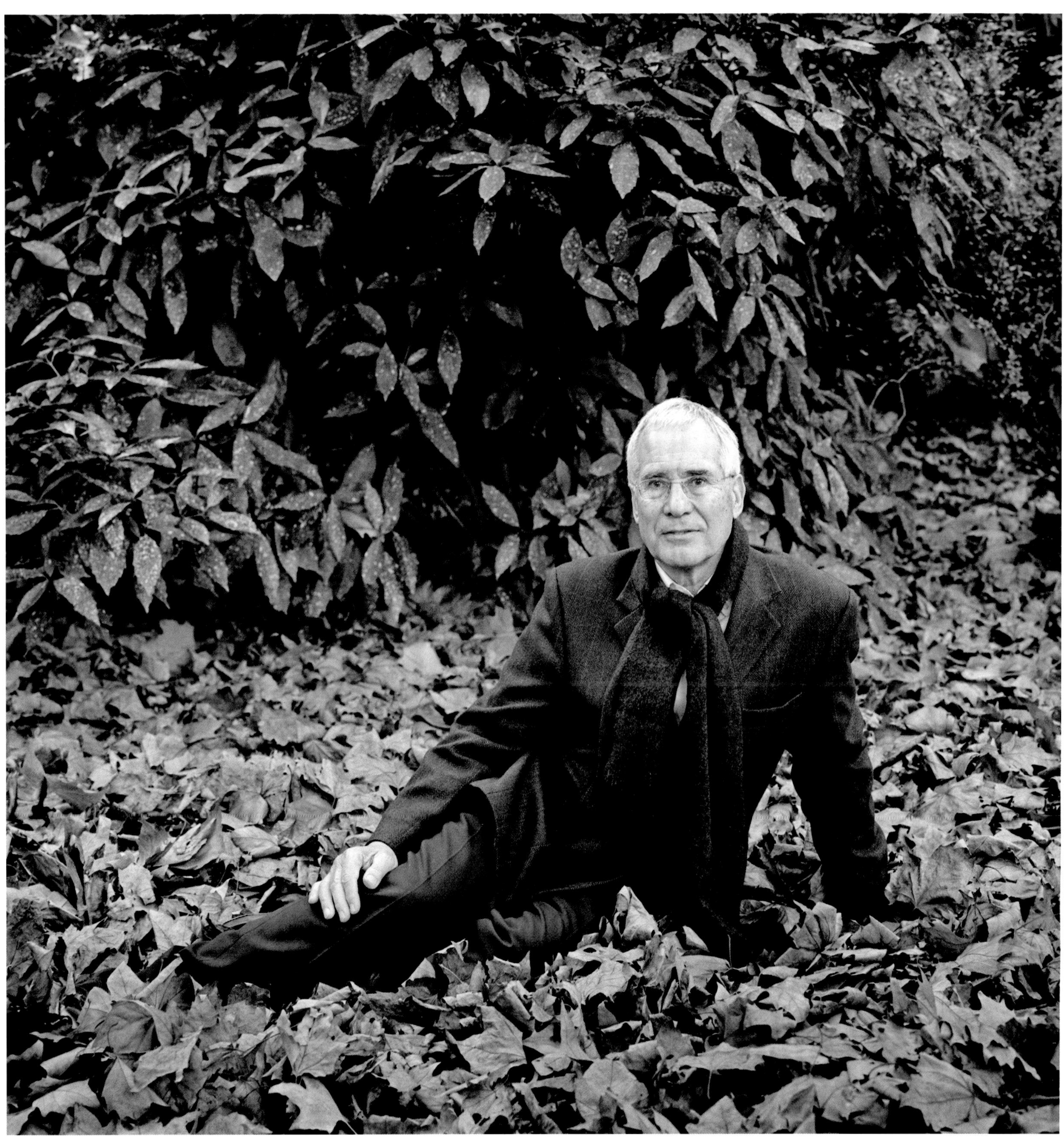

Joseph Stiglitz

"Can the trend toward greater inequality be reversed?"

THERE HAS BEEN an enormous increase in inequality in the US over the past third of a century, especially since Ronald Reagan became president. Those at the top have grabbed a large fraction of the entire increase in national income, while those at the bottom have seen incomes decline. Real wages (adjusted for inflation) are roughly at the level that they were sixty years ago. The typical full-time male worker—and those with full-time jobs are the lucky ones—receives a wage, adjusted for inflation, that is the same as it was more than four decades ago.

A look across countries shows that the level of inequality in the US (after taxes and transfers) is greater than in any other advanced country. Some countries have been able to keep inequality from increasing; a few have even managed to reduce it. The laws of nature are global. So too are the forces of globalization and the impacts of technology. The difference in the observed levels of inequality thus lies in the policies pursued by different countries. In short, inequality and its rise are not the result of the laws of nature, immutable and unchanging, but of human laws. These can easily be altered. In this sense, then, inequality is a matter of choice.

Laws in the US are biased towards helping the rich rather than those in the middle, let alone at the bottom. Those at the top pay taxes that are less than proportionate to their income, because of the favorable treatment of capital income—in particular, capital gains and dividends. They have access to tax shelters and make use of tax paradises and secrecy havens—islands and other jurisdictions that facilitate tax evasion and avoidance. The entire regime for taxing multinational corporations provides easy ways for them to shift both their money and financial activity to low-tax jurisdictions to avoid paying their fair share of taxes.

In fact, our entire legal framework has been changed to give the advantage to the rich. Workers find it more difficult to get together and engage in effective collective bargaining. So too, the rules of globalization have been written to weaken workers' bargaining power, contributing to the difficulties that they would, in any case, have had to face as new technologies increasingly replace unskilled labor.

Meanwhile, monopoly power has grown, not only because of changes in technology—which have provided more scope for monopoly power, for instance, in the high tech sector—but also because competition authorities have been lax and have not kept up with changes in technology and the innovative ways that firms have devised for creating, amplifying, using, and extending market power. CEOs and others in the boardroom have taken advantage of deficiencies in our system of corporate governance to enhance their incomes at the expense of workers and investments in the future of the firm. Bankruptcy laws have been changed to give first claim on a firm's available resources when it defaults to risky derivatives issued by financial institutions rather than to workers, as was traditionally the case. These same laws have also made it almost impossible for those who seek to get ahead through higher education to discharge their student loans in bankruptcy.

Our economic system has made it easier to pass on advantages from one generation to another. So too, those at the bottom have a high chance of remaining there. A weak and ineffective inheritance tax system does an insufficient amount to prevent the creation of a plutocracy, the members of which have inherited their position.

The inequality that has developed in the US and in some other countries, particularly inequality in its extreme forms, is bad for overall economic performance.

Politics aside, it would be easy to reduce inequality from the extremes it has reached. Because inequality is largely the result of man-made laws, all we need to do is to rewrite those laws, for instance, to make our tax system more progressive; modernize and enforce our competition laws; and rewrite the laws governing labor, globalization, and corporate governance. Doing so would not only create a more equal society; it would result in a more productive economy.

JOSEPH STIGLITZ is Professor at Columbia University, and was Chief Economist at the World Bank from 1997–2000 and Chair of the Council of Economic Advisers from 1995–1997. He received the John Bates Clark Medal in 1979 and the Nobel Prize for Economics in 2001.

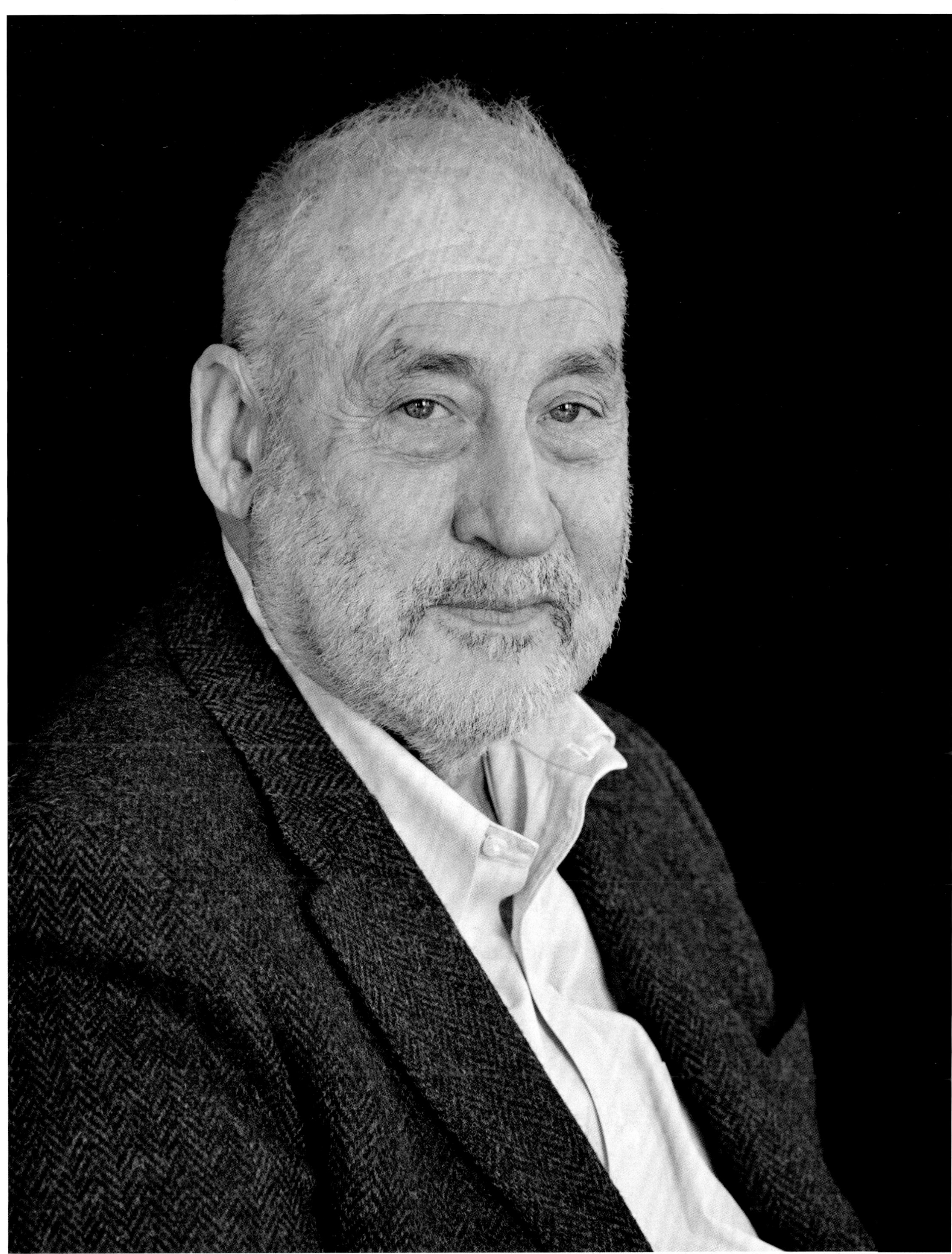

Nancy Stokey

"What is your understanding of the apparent tendency for the proportion of low-wage and high-wage jobs to increase while jobs in the middle of the scale become scarce?"

EMPLOYMENT AND WAGE differentials across skill or occupational categories change over time, as do the occupational categories themselves: "hostler" disappears and "auto mechanic" enters. Technology is one major cause of such changes. Another is the shift in patterns of consumer demand as incomes rise, women enter the labor force in greater numbers, and the distribution of income changes. As society becomes richer, we spend smaller shares of income on necessities like food and larger shares on travel and entertainment. With more women working outside the home, the demand for child care, cleaning, and food preparation services grows. And as income inequality increases, the demand for housekeepers, gardeners, and other services also grows.

Over the last quarter century, employment and wages in many middle-scale occupations have either declined or grown very slowly relative to occupations at the top and the bottom of the distribution. Many of the "missing" jobs are skilled blue-collar manufacturing jobs and clerical jobs. At the same time, employment and wages in occupations at the top and bottom have grown quite rapidly. At the top, those occupations include managers, health-care and other professionals, and technicians. At the bottom, they consist of service occupations, including hotel and restaurant workers.

What has caused the shift? Many of the "missing" jobs have been automated: robots have replaced assembly-line workers and computers have replaced billing clerks. In addition, manufacturing has been in a slow, overall decline for a century, as rising incomes have shifted demand gradually but inexorably from goods to services. And on top of all that, some of the remaining manufacturing jobs have moved abroad.

Will those jobs come back? It seems unlikely: robots and computers are not going away, and indeed we can expect them to gain ground. In my own industry, online instruction will surely give traditional colleges and universities increasing competition in the future.

For centuries there was almost no change in the occupational or wage structure of societies: the vast majority of employment was in agriculture and the vast majority of the population was dirt poor. Since the Industrial Revolution started changing employment patterns and raising incomes, change in the occupational and wage structure has been the norm. The steam engine, the internal combustion engine, and the electric motor all led to major changes in methods of production.

The useful response for a society in the face of technical change is, first, to realize that we cannot turn back the clock. We can then proceed with assisting displaced workers in retooling for new jobs and ensuring that new entrants to the labor force are equipped for the jobs of the future. And we can hope that, as in the past, enterprising innovators will discover new products and services that will refill the missing segment of the job distribution.

NANCY STOKEY is Professor at the University of Chicago.

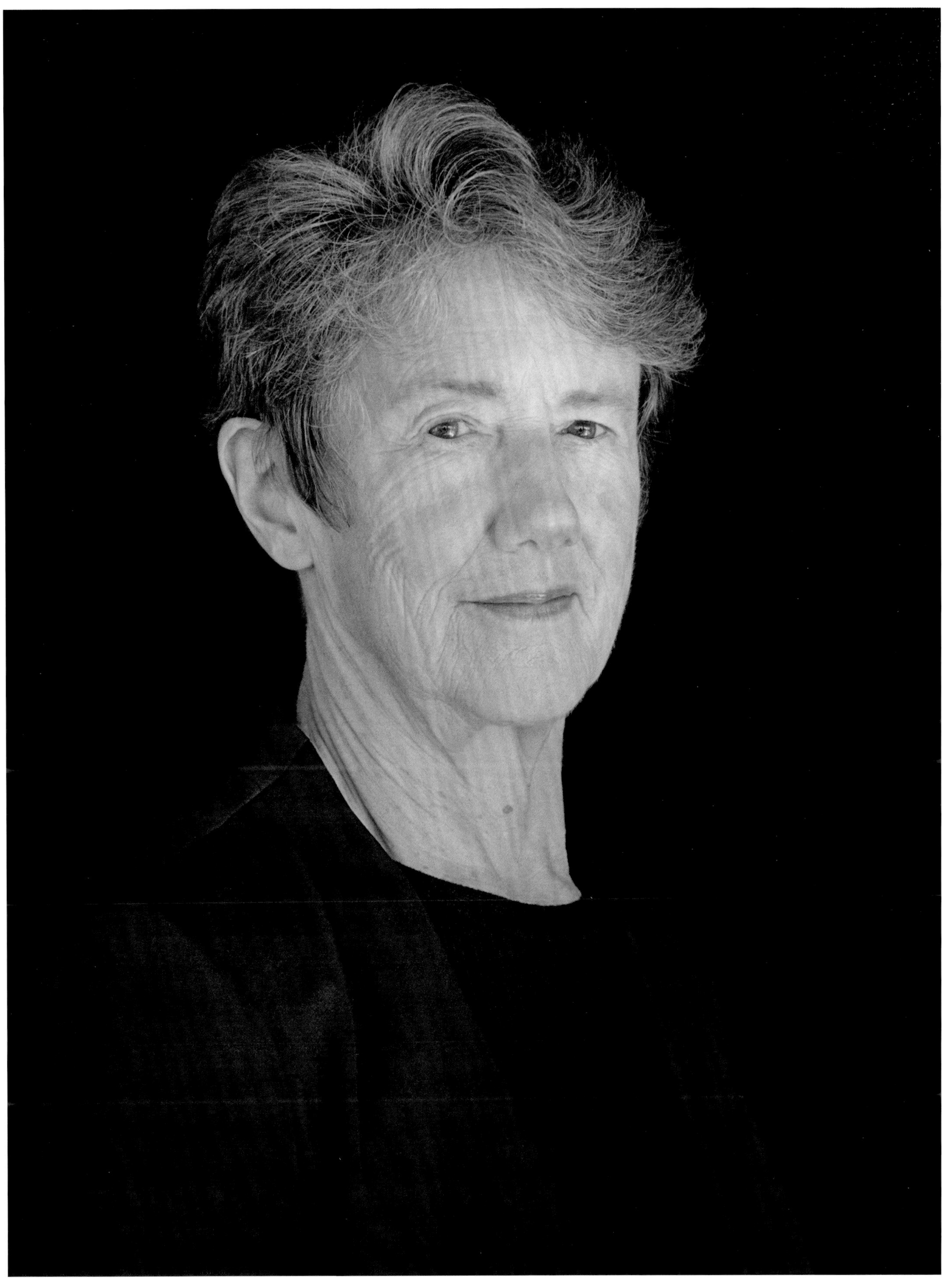

Lawrence H. Summers

"The US economy has been experiencing an extraordinarily long, if rather slow, upswing, since the Great Recession. What do you think is the underlying explanation for this?"

JUST AS WITH people, longevity should not be automatically equated with accomplishment. The economic expansion since the Great Recession is set to be the third-longest business cycle of the thirty-three on record and possibly the longest expansion on record. But by most objective measures this has been a very disappointing recovery, especially after factoring in the depressed starting point. Even now, labor and other markets show few signs of being tight. If this makes today's economy unusually "healthy" given the length of the expansion, it is in some sense a perverse consequence of prior weakness.

I think that, despite its length, this recovery's lack of vigor and chronically low interest rates are evidence in favor of the "secular stagnation" hypothesis originally put forward by Alvin Hansen in 1939. The idea was that there was a shortage of impetus to invest, and because of that shortage there would not be adequate demand to absorb all of the saving.

Secular stagnation ultimately did not occur at the time of Hansen's writing, as the impulse from war spending ended the Great Depression. However, it was a plausible hypothesis both then and particularly now. Today's chronically low real interest rates point towards a fundamental change in the supply-demand balance of savings and investment as the secular stagnation theory predicts.

Many current trends are likely contributing to low rates and the danger of secular stagnation. Population growth has slowed dramatically, particularly for those of working age. The decades-long trend of increasing female labor force participation has likely run its course. Technology has diminished the need for many types of physical investment. Increased inequality has increased the supply of savings relative to what it otherwise would have been, even if overall savings and undistributed profits numbers do not look high relative to historical averages. Many leading companies have much more cash than investment opportunities.

Whether it is next month, next year, or sometime later in the 2020s, this recovery will end. When it does, the chronic low growth and low nominal interest rates characteristic of the recovery will likely make managing the ensuing recession much more difficult.

LAWRENCE SUMMERS is Professor at Harvard University. He was President of Harvard University from 2001–2006, US Secretary of the Treasury from 1999–2001, and Chief Economist at the World Bank from 1991–1993.

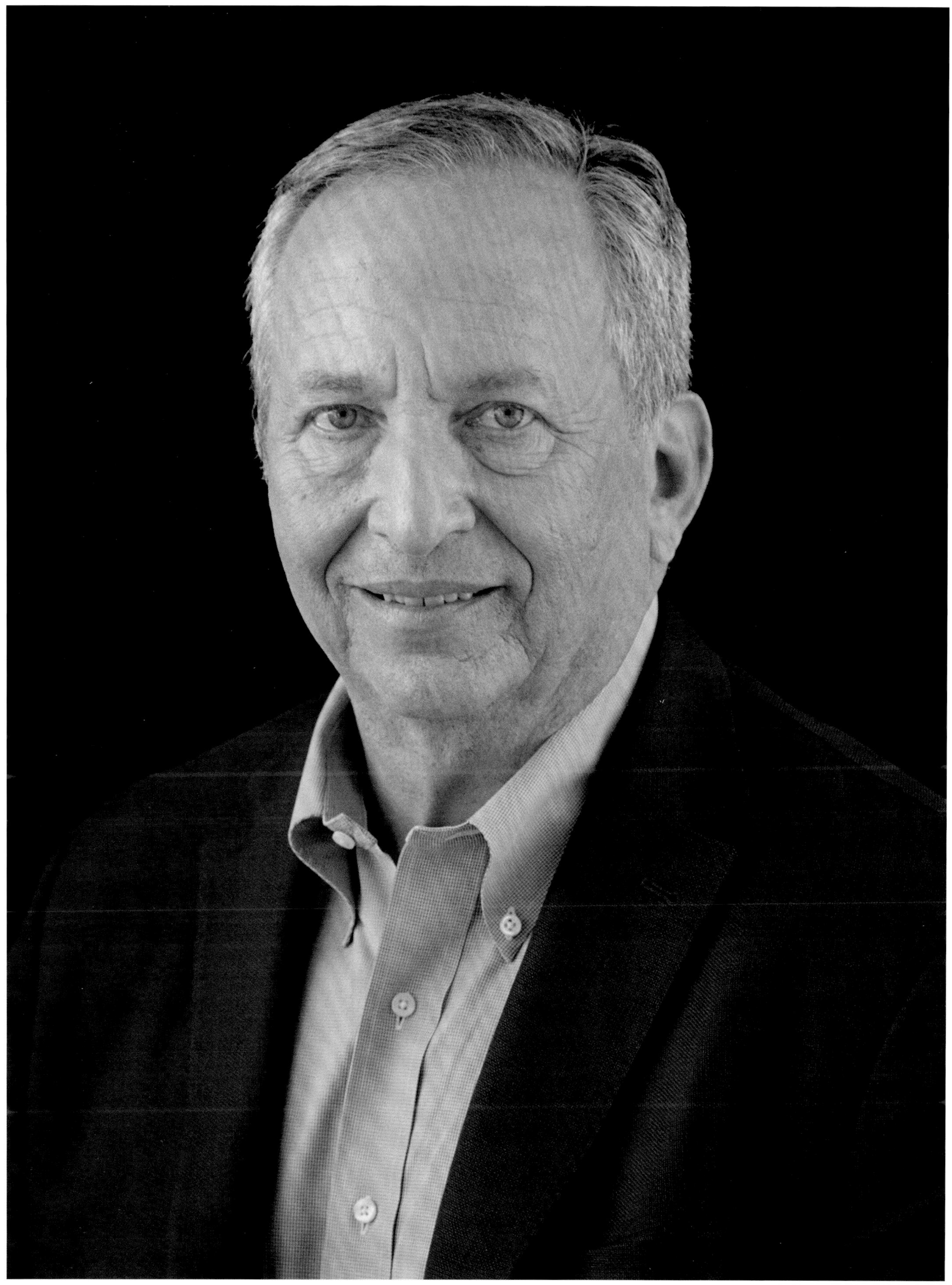

Richard Thaler

"If you could make one change to the way economists do economics, what would it be?"

THE MOST FUNDAMENTAL feature of standard economic theory is that people choose by optimizing. Which is to say that of all the bundles of goods and services consumers can afford, they choose the "best" one. Firms are also said to optimize; they choose the most efficient production process and then set prices to maximize profits. Along with a focus on markets, it is this assumption of optimization that distinguishes economics from other social sciences. But this feature also lies at the heart of a critical problem: economists use the optimization hypothesis for two distinct tasks, and it is only well suited to one of them. The two tasks are (1) characterizing the best solution to a problem, and (2) predicting how most people will solve that problem.

To provide a concrete example consider the problem of searching for a job. Suppose that Charlie loses his job and starts looking for a new one. Occasionally he gets offered a job and has to say yes or no quickly. If Charlie says yes and takes the job, then he will stop searching (at least for a while). By making some additional simplifying assumptions to make the problem tractable, economists can and do create models to determine Charlie's best strategy. A solution will take into consideration an accurate assessment of Charlie's market value in the existing economic climate. One approach that Charlie could take would be to choose an appropriate minimum salary (in addition to selecting other job criteria) and search until such an offer is found, or until he realizes that he had better lower his expectations. Finding good solutions to these kinds of problems is a highly productive activity. Both individuals and organizations face similar dilemmas all the time; for example, searching for a new employee or supplier.

Predicting what Charlie will *actually* do in this situation is an entirely different exercise. For example, Charlie might put too much emphasis on the salary he had at his previous job, even though the company he worked for closed down, and similar jobs are scarce. He might have an inflated (or deflated) opinion of his job prospects. He may narrow his search excessively, failing to consider jobs that he mistakenly thinks are too dissimilar to his previous one, and so forth. The ways in which Charlie's search might diverge from optimality are too numerous to name. But all these factors will be ignored in a model that is based solely on choosing optimally.

So my one wish for the economics profession is that we explicitly recognize that one theory cannot serve both purposes. The reason we have both hammers and screwdrivers is that different tasks require different tools. Those who work on descriptive theories will still have to master the art of optimizing, but they will then also have to branch out and learn about the many ways that people choose suboptimally. Findings from other branches of social science may prove useful in this task, as will new approaches using big data, such as machine learning. But it will also be useful to spend some time looking out the window and observing what people do.

RICHARD THALER is Professor at the University of Chicago Booth School of Business. He received the Nobel Prize for Economics in 2017.

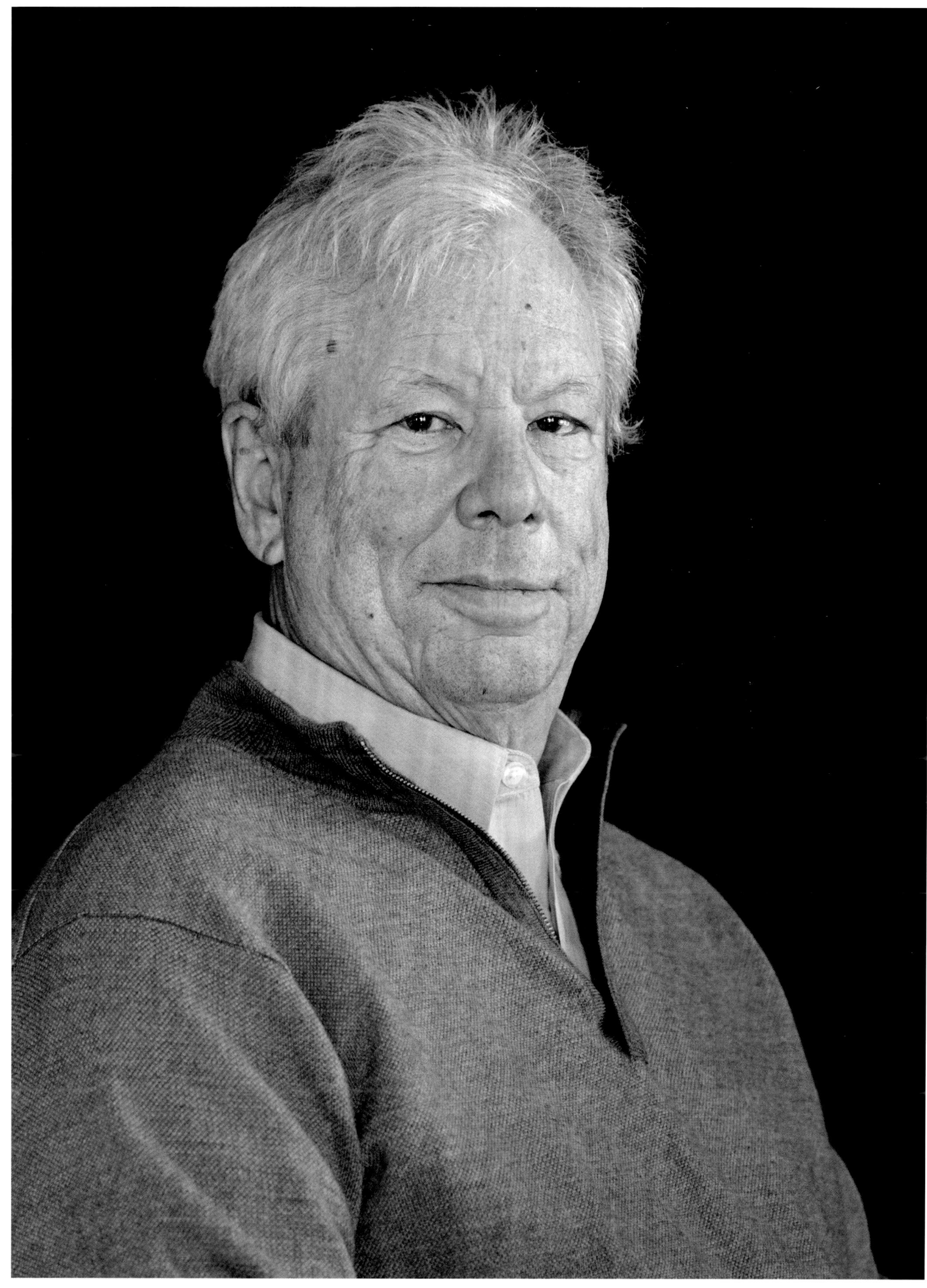

Jean Tirole

"Would it be a good idea if the tech giants had more viable competitors? Could that happen?"

THE INDUSTRIAL REVOLUTION of the 21st century is led by "multisided platforms." The seven largest firms in the world (Apple, Alphabet, Microsoft, Amazon, Facebook, Tencent, and Alibaba) and many of the successful startups (Airbnb, Uber, etc.) are all such platforms that bring together different communities of users (sellers and buyers, users and developers or advertisers, passengers and drivers) seeking to interact with each other. These platforms, which levy fees and collect data through this intermediation process, offer wonderful new services, but benefit from large network externalities. We go on Facebook because our friends and acquaintances are there. We use the Google search engine or Waze navigation app because many others do too, feeding more data into their algorithms and improving the service. We use Booking.com or Amazon because they have everything we need in one place. Such network externalities tend to create monopolies or tight oligopolies. This evolution comes with threats: superstar firms capture much of the surplus; they may erect barriers to entry; wage inequality may increase further. Are we up to the challenge?

Some propose to tame platform market power by breaking them up. Yet, unlike for AT&T or power companies, which were dismantled in the past, platform technology changes very fast and many of the services are built on data that are common to all services. But to keep the markets contestable, we must prevent the tech giants from swallowing up their future competitors. This is, of course, easier said than done, as the data necessary to ascertain that the start-up is indeed a competitor are often missing.

The bundling practices of the tech giants are also of concern. A start-up that may become an efficient competitor to such firms generally enters within a market niche; it's hard to enter all segments at the same time. Bundling may prevent efficient entrants from entering market segments to collectively challenge the incumbent on the overall technology. Again, this is not a straightforward policy to implement: antitrust can be slow and those industries are moving very fast.

Another antitrust issue is that most platforms offer best-price guarantees, also called "most favored nation" or "price parity" clauses, which dictate that the user is guaranteed to get the lowest price via the platform in question, as the latter has secured this "best price" from the merchants. This sounds like a good deal for the consumer, except that if all or most merchants are listed on the platform and the consumer is guaranteed to be offered the lowest price on it, there is no incentive for the consumer to look anywhere else; he has become a "unique" customer, and so the platform can set large fees to the merchants to get access to him. Interestingly, due to price uniformity, these fees are paid by both platform and non-platform users—so each platform succeeds in taxing its rivals! That can be quite problematic for competition. But there are solutions, provided that there is a will to act.

Finally, there is the tricky issue of data ownership, which will be a barrier to entry in AI-driven innovation. There is currently a debate between platform ownership (the status quo) and the prospect of a user-centric approach. Academics should take an interest in trying to make progress on this surprisingly neglected subject.

Almost one hundred and thirty years after the Sherman Act, economists need to reinvent antitrust. They must provide authorities with policies that will tame market power without stifling innovation.

Economists must also more broadly confront the vast challenges that the new economy is presenting to our social compact. Let there be no mistake: while technological change will keep bringing us more wealth and better healthcare, we cannot cut corners on regulatory oversight—whether it be by preventing health insurers from using data and algorithms to select risks, or protecting investors who are tempted to invest in cryptocurrency bubbles, or crowdlending platforms that intermediate without equity of their own. Nor can we fail to design new forms of worker protection; there is no silver bullet, but education, retraining, redistribution, and international cooperation will all be key ingredients in trying to prevent a deep societal malaise.

JEAN TIROLE is Professor at the Toulouse School of Economics and President of the Institute for Advanced Study in Toulouse. He received the Nobel Prize for Economics in 2014.

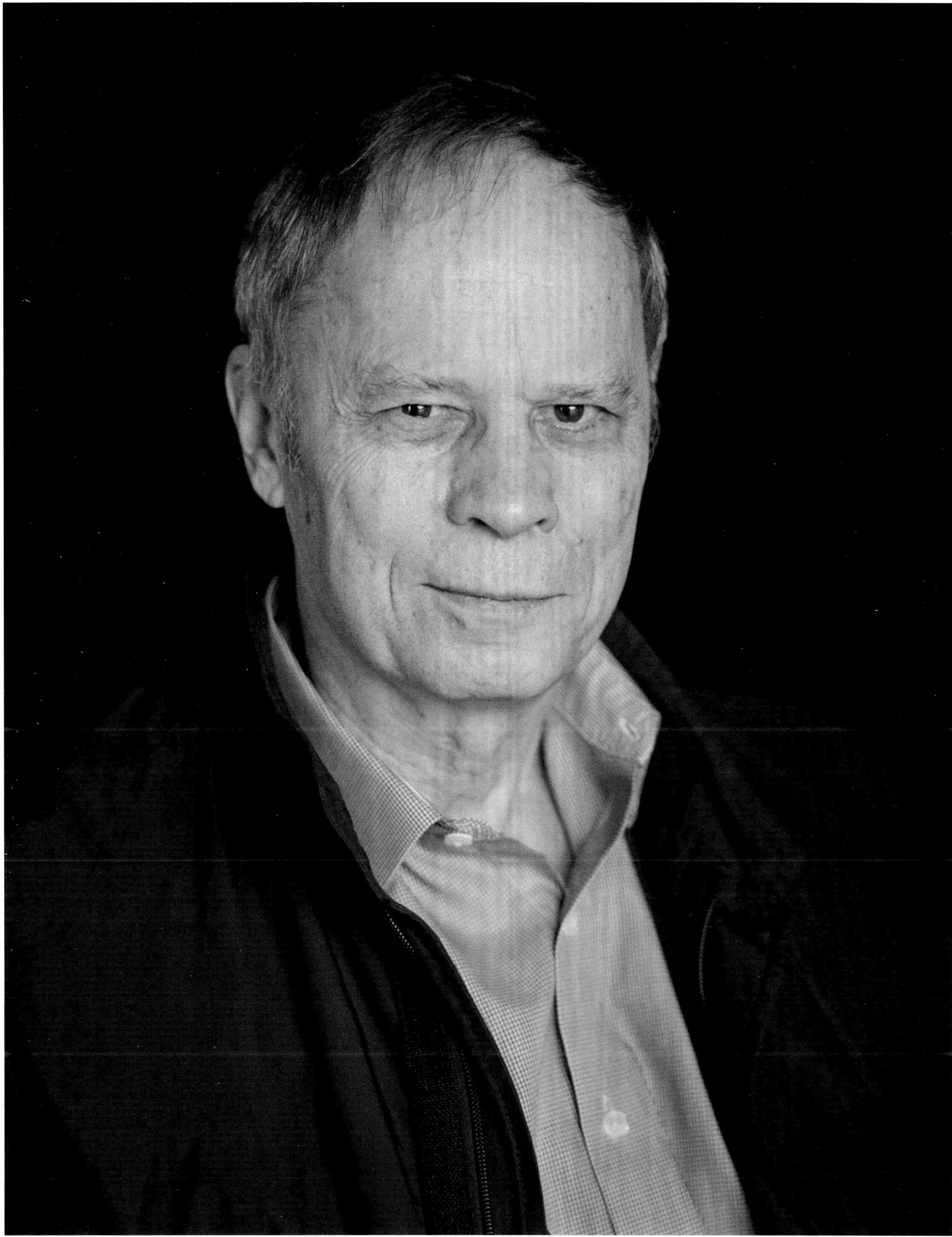

Hal Varian

"Thirty years ago you wrote a very successful microeconomics textbook. If you were to start over today, after your experience with Google, would you do it very differently?"

THIRTY YEARS AGO I wrote an undergraduate textbook on microeconomics that is now in its ninth edition. A colleague once explained to me that by the time the tenth edition comes around "having a successful textbook is like being married to a wealthy person you don't like much any more."

It's true. The publishers want you to publish an updated edition every three or four years and it's sometimes hard to come up with something new and fresh. This problem is much like Russell Baker's experience in writing a newspaper column: "Notified that I was now free to write three columns a week about almost any subject on earth, I was exultant. After fifteen years of living under the reporters' constraints, I was at last free to disgorge the entire contents of my brain. Somewhere between the third and fourth weeks, having written fewer than a dozen columns, I made a terrifying discovery: I had now disgorged the entire contents of my brain, yet another column was due at once."

Lucky for me I had two big breaks. The first was bumping into Eric Schmidt in 2001, shortly after he joined "this cute little company called Google." He invited me to come spend some time there. I thought I would spend a year there and write a book about yet another Silicon Valley start-up. Well, here I am fifteen years later and I still haven't gotten around to writing that book.

But I sure have learned a lot.

Quite a bit of what I learned at Google got folded into my textbook: I wrote a couple of new chapters devoted to network effects, auction design, matching mechanisms, and switching costs. The old chapters got updated to illustrate novel applications of workhorse concepts like marginal cost and marginal value.

But even a rich stream of ideas like this eventually plays out, so after two or three editions I was again struggling to find some new things to talk about.

Then I got lucky again: the Great Recession hit. My book is about microeconomics, not macroeconomics, but even so there were a lot of issues that suddenly showed up in the economy that somehow weren't discussed in the text. How could I have missed talking about "counterparty risk" or "financial bubbles"? These are rarely mentioned in quiet times, but when a financial crisis hits, they are on everyone's lips. So I added some discussion about these topics to the text.

It also became apparent that I needed to devote more space to behavioral economics. Not only had the field become mainstream, the concepts were clearly relevant in understanding what was going on in the economy.

People often ask me whether "textbook economics" is relevant to a business like Google. My answer is an unequivocal "yes." Very simple tools like demand and supply can be critically important to understanding the economic forces at work in an industry. When a new technology shakes things up, it is even more important to have a coherent theory since there are no commonly accepted rules to apply in such times.

Along with theory, businesses need measurement. Today, with all the sensors and systems available, collecting data has become more inexpensive than ever before. Once you have measurement in place, it is possible to do analysis and experimentation. Google does about ten thousand experiments a year; the knowledge gained from these experiments feeds back into design, allowing continual improvement in product offerings.

William Gibson has said, "The future is here, it's just not evenly distributed." It's true that at the moment only a relatively small fraction of firms can effectively apply the tools of modeling, measurement, analysis, and experimentation using new technology. But these skills are diffusing through the economy and as they do, more and more people will have access to the future. Bring it on!

HAL VARIAN is Chief Economist at Google and Professor Emeritus at the University of California, Berkeley.

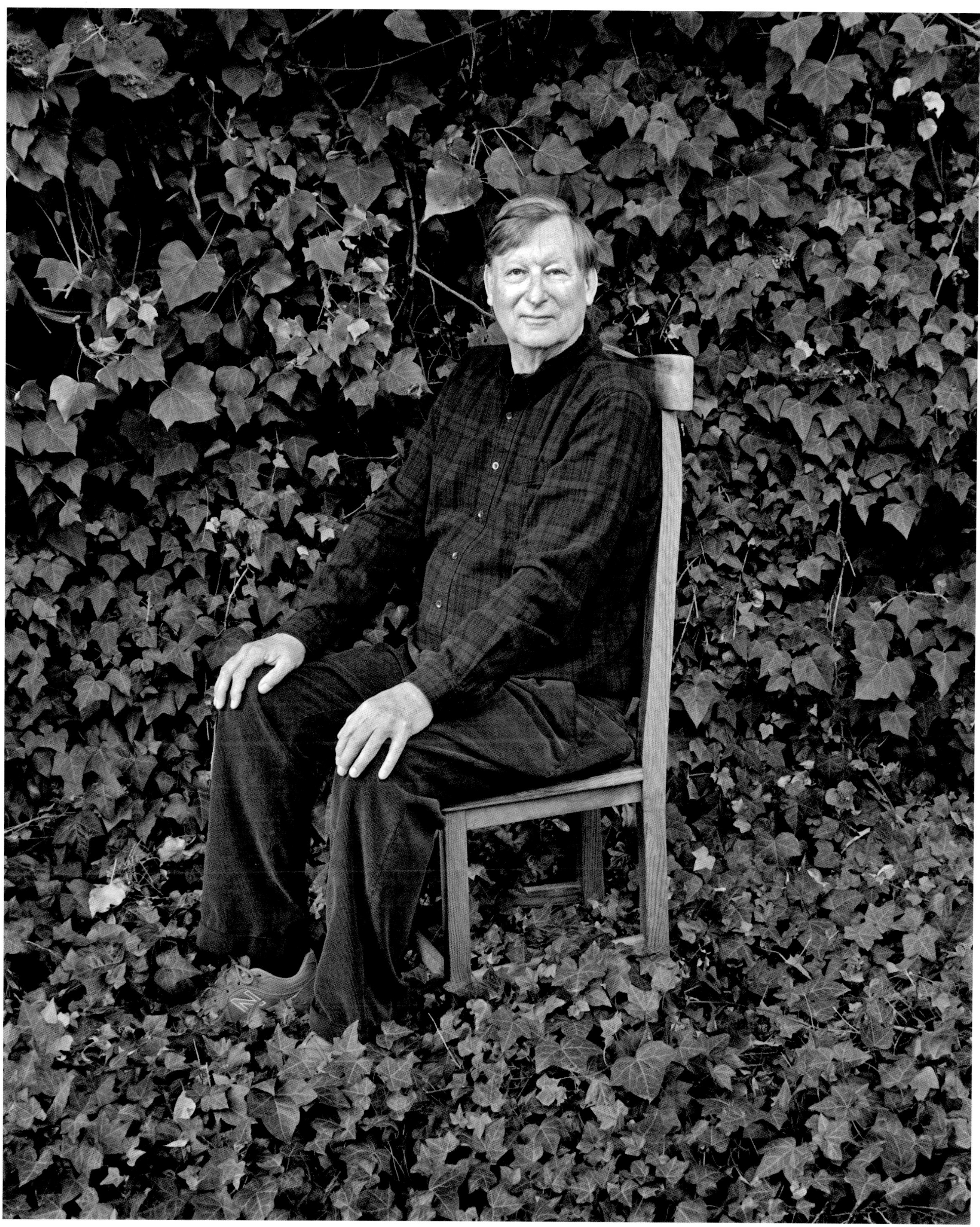

Paul Volcker

"Do you think we have done enough to deal with the 'too big to fail' problem in the United States? What should the next step be?"

WELL, HERE WE have a portrait of an elderly gentleman, in from the cold.

As it happens, he has spent a good part of his life concerned about the stability of financial markets and the recurrent breakdowns that have threatened economic growth.

Too often, the government has had to step in to restore order, adding new regulations and providing new capital, in the process "saving" some big banks from "failure." Understandably, taxpayers—ordinary citizens—have concerns about that pattern! Some institutions simply have been deemed "too big to fail," and that seems unfair.

Well, the "old man," along with the taxpayers, has seen enough of that. New laws are in effect. They can signal the end of taxpayer support for banks "too big to fail." We need to make sure those laws will be maintained. That's why the "old man" looks so determined.

PAUL VOLCKER is Founder and Chairman of the Volcker Alliance and was Chair of the Federal Reserve from 1979–1987.

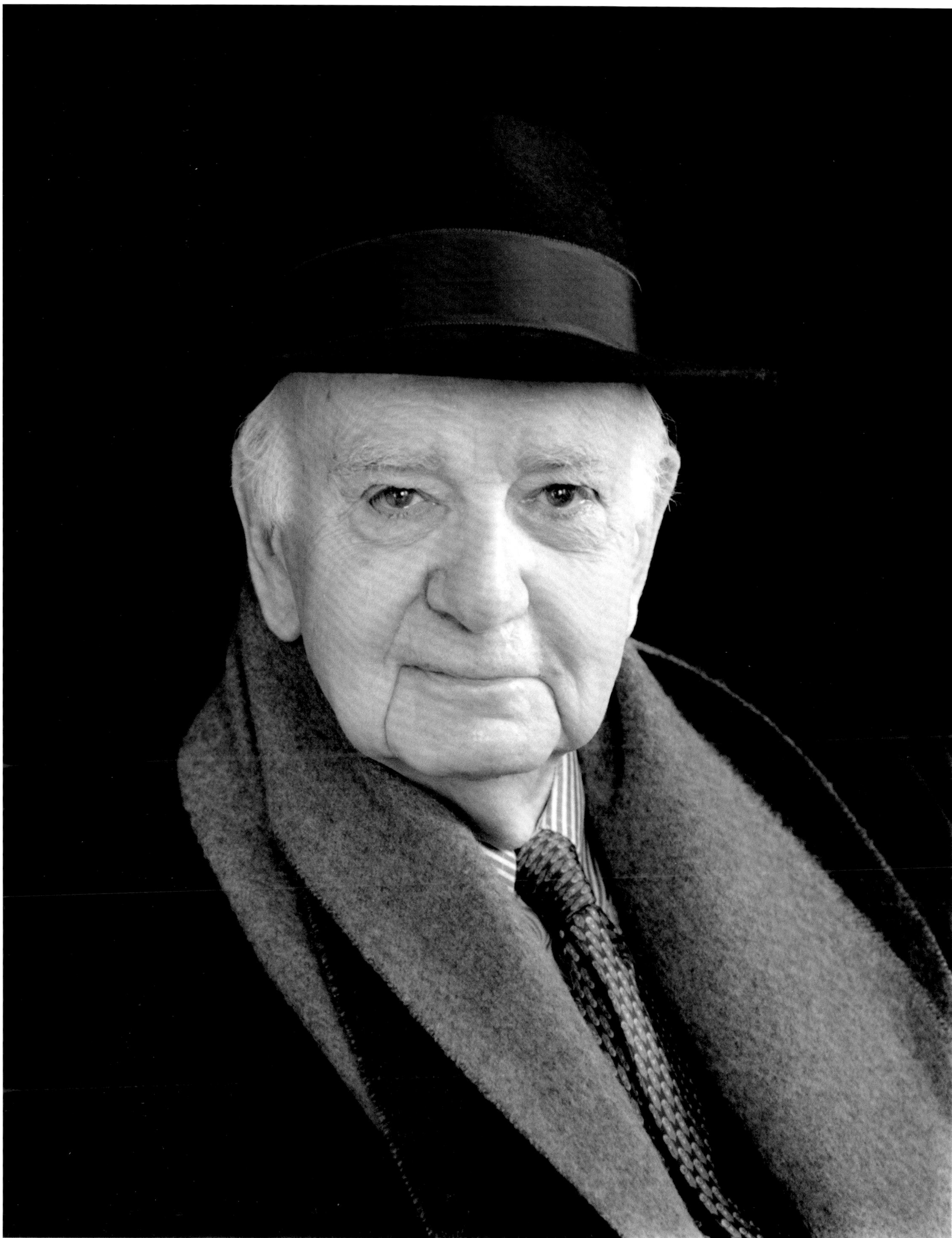

Heidi L. Williams

"Why is infant mortality in the US so high, and what should we do about it?"

IN 2010, AROUND 6 in 1,000 infants born in the US died before their first birthday. This infant mortality rate is much higher than in nearly all other countries with similar levels of economic development—comparable numbers for the UK, Czech Republic, and Finland are around 4, 3, and 2 in 1,000, respectively. Why is infant mortality in the US so high?

One theory is that this "fact" is not a fact at all, but rather is an artifact of cross-country reporting differences. The concern is that extremely preterm births in the US may be recorded as live births, whereas other countries may report these as miscarriages or stillbirths. To the extent that this type of differential reporting happens, the US infant mortality rate could look artificially high relative to other countries. But this theory can't fully explain the data. Cross-country reporting differences are real and are quantitatively important, but even after accounting for such reporting differences, it is clear that infant mortality in the US is higher than in similar countries.

The US infant mortality disadvantage is all the more puzzling when paired with the fact that the US spends a great deal of money on medical technologies designed to save the lives of at-risk newborns. As an academic economist interested in understanding technological change, much of my research has focused on medical technologies. For example, I have analyzed how providing additional medical care to very low birth weight newborns impacts their mortality outcomes. For these babies, even very expensive medical interventions appear to be "worth it" relative to the value of the lives they save. However, even though I think this type of evidence suggests that high-cost medical technologies can save lives, I would conjecture that cross-country differences in medical technologies likely do very little to explain cross-country differences in infant mortality. As economist Victor Fuchs famously wrote, "The most important thing to realize about . . . differences in health levels is that they are usually not related in any important degree to differences in medical care."

But this then still leaves the question: Why is infant mortality in the US so high? I have undertaken some efforts to understand this question using data on births in the US and four European countries (Austria, Belgium, Finland, and the UK). Infants of similar birth weight, one commonly used measure of health at birth, have much worse mortality outcomes in the US relative to these countries. But there is little difference in neonatal mortality—that is, deaths during the first month of life—across these countries. Instead, the most striking differences between the US and these countries arise in *post-neonatal* mortality—that is, deaths during months one to twelve of life. Put simply, infants of a given birth weight look similar during their first month of life, but their mortality outcomes then diverge over their first year of life.

I think the key question then is: Why is *post-neonatal* mortality so high in the US? I do not know for sure. But a clue—and an important fact in its own right—is that this excess post-neonatal mortality is distributed quite unequally. Infants born to higher socioeconomic status mothers in the US (for example, more educated mothers) have mortality outcomes similar to infants born to higher socioeconomic status mothers in Europe. In contrast, infants born to lower socioeconomic status mothers in the US have much worse outcomes than do infants born to similar mothers in Europe. That is, health inequality (or the so-called "health gradient") is much higher in the US.

These facts suggest that from a policy perspective, a sole focus on improving health at birth—for example, through expanding access to prenatal care—will be incomplete. Instead, policies that target lower socioeconomic status groups during the post-neonatal period, such as home nurse visiting programs, may be a productive avenue for reducing infant mortality in the US.

HEIDI WILLIAMS is Professor at Stanford University.

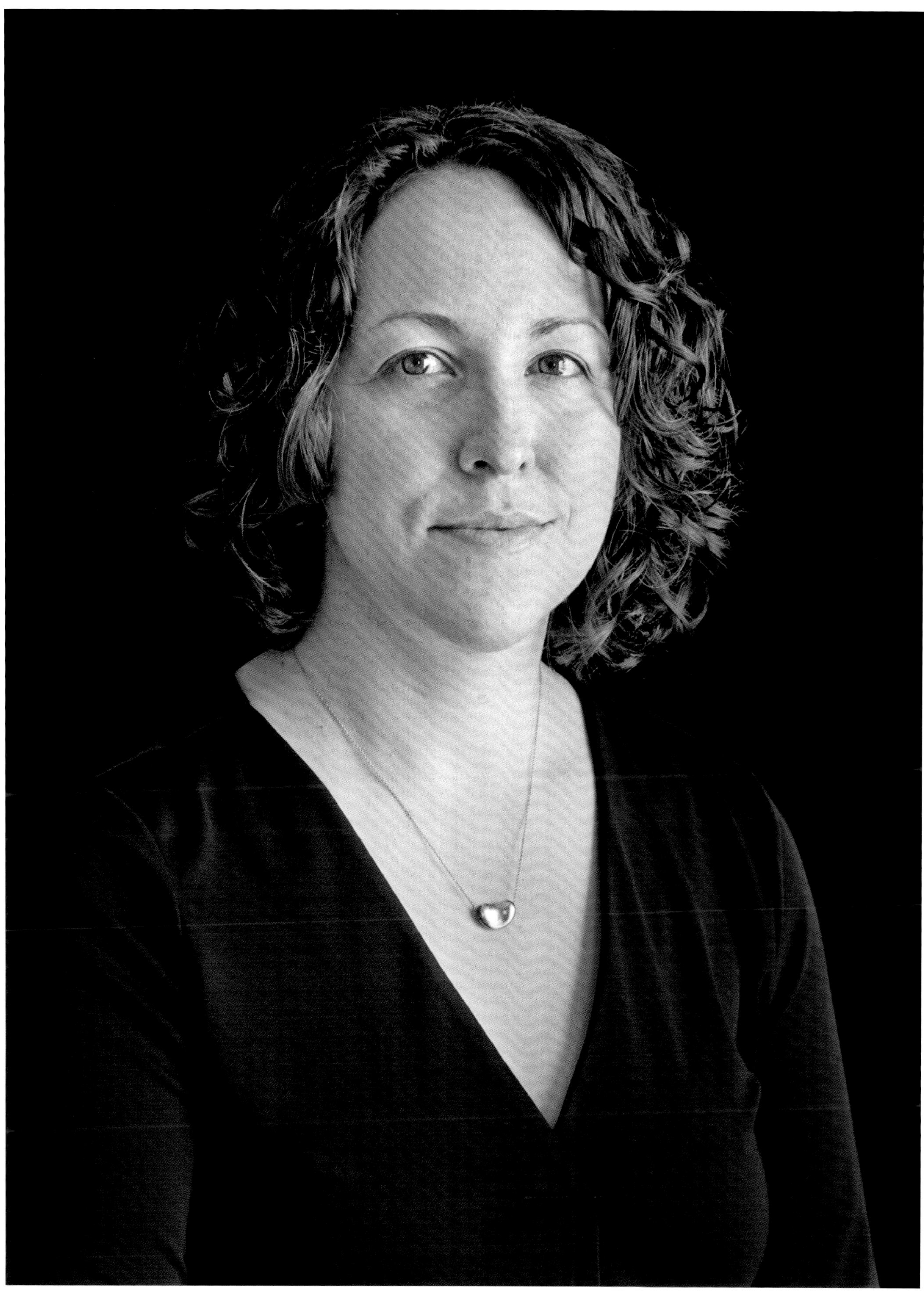

Robert Wilson

"How do the methods of game theory improve economic analysis?"

ECONOMIC STUDIES OF the allocation of scarce resources often focus on market prices and quantities. Game theory studies a microscopic view of how markets function. Its method is a precise description of agents' interactions, namely the timing of their decisions, and the information and observations available when an agent chooses among feasible actions; i.e., who knows what when. For example, a fine-grained analysis of bilateral bargaining depends on procedures for offers and counteroffers, and how one party's actions signal his motives and information to the other party. Bidding in a dynamic auction is similarly affected by procedural rules, and each bidder cares about what others' bids reveal about their information regarding the item's value. Similarly, the spread between bid and ask prices offered by a market specialist takes account of adverse selection, i.e., risks that some traders with superior information can trade profitably at his expense. Insurance markets are prominent examples of selection effects, as well as so-called "moral hazards," situations in which the customers' efforts to avert hazards are not observed by the agents working on their behalf. These features pervade labor and product markets too, such as when a salesman has superior information about his ability or market conditions and his effort is not observable, or a seller has superior information about quality attributes like durability, which is not evident to buyers. Rather than simple spot market transactions, participants rely on employment contracts and product warranties. Government policies, such as tax codes, address these features too, since results depend on how agents' incentives are affected by privately known abilities and opportunities.

Economic analyses that rely on prices equating demand and supply can be refined further by criteria used by game theory, namely that each participant's strategy is an optimal response to others' strategies. This more stringent equilibrium enables theories of price formation that elaborate the effects of market design and the roles of intermediaries and traders. It can also be invoked to analyze information revealed by prices, and in a normative vein, how trading procedures or contracts might be altered to improve efficiency of market outcomes. Models of strategic behavior capture familiar phenomena often missed by aggregate demand-supply analysis; e.g., besides signaling, as mentioned above, some dynamic games exhibit reputation effects, as when an agent's actions sustain others' beliefs that his ultimate motives might differ from those otherwise presumed. Such models are useful for analyses of strategic behaviors that affect market structure and contestability, such as limit pricing and predation by incumbents to deter entry.

In sum, methods of game theory provide opportunities for detailed analyses of economic activity. They focus on incentives affecting strategic behavior, and how they are influenced by procedures and contract provisions, and by information and observability. They are more complicated to employ, and rarely amenable to aggregate measures of market activity. In some cases, though, they are necessary to understand how a market's microstructure affects outcomes and thereby efficiency and welfare.

But game theory is imperfect. Such models rely on shared knowledge of the "rules of the game," especially how each agent's belief about how others' beliefs depend on their information. Predictions of equilibrium outcomes are very sensitive to assumptions that agents are rational, even hyperrational, to cope with complexities of elaborately detailed models. Because empirical evidence rarely justifies such strong assumptions, some alternative theories invoke behavioral anomalies, such as framing effects observed in experiments, while others examine scenarios less sensitive to shared knowledge and thoroughly rational behavior, and some assume agents guard against worst-case possibilities when they lack good predictions of others' behaviors. And, like economic theory generally, it remains to invoke further criteria to select among multiple equilibria.

ROBERT WILSON is Professor Emeritus at the Stanford Graduate School of Business.

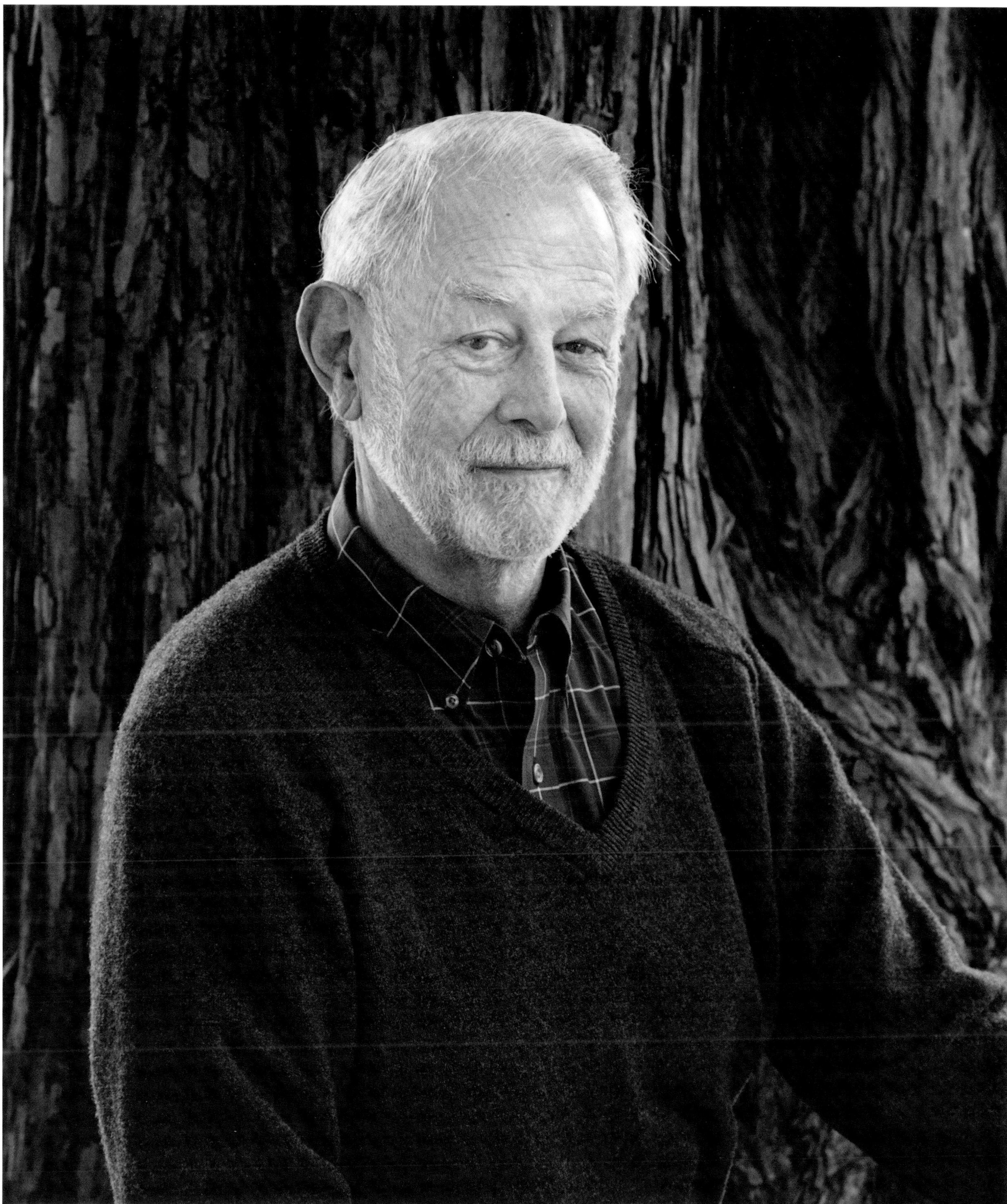

Michael Woodford

"Why do you think the rate of inflation has been so persistently below the Federal Reserve's 2 percent target?"

WHILE INFLATION IS a variable that Fed officials care a great deal about, and monitor closely, the Fed's ability to affect the inflation rate through its policies is relatively indirect, even under the best of circumstances. Moreover, it is asymmetric: while the Fed has a reasonably clear idea of how to force inflation lower when it is running too high—by sharply raising interest rates, and possibly taking other actions to restrict credit, as it did in the early 1980s—its ability to raise inflation when it is judged to be too low can be limited by the fact that interest rates cannot be reduced below zero. This became an important constraint on the Fed's ability to achieve its objectives in the years following the financial crisis of 2008.

Paradoxically, the Fed's ability to achieve its target rate of inflation may have been hampered by its official announcement of a 2 percent target in 2012. Announcement of an explicit target was the culmination of three decades of effort by the Fed to increase public confidence in the institution's commitment to keep inflation from ever getting too high. Arguably, the wage-price spiral that led to high inflation by the end of the 1970s would have been less likely to occur had there been fewer doubts in those days about the Fed's willingness to act decisively to contain inflation if necessary. After decades of calls for a firmer commitment in order to preclude a repeat of this scenario, the Fed finally committed itself to a numerical target for inflation in 2012—but in very different circumstances.

During the long aftermath of the financial crisis, the immediate problem for the US economy was no longer excessive nominal spending, but rather insufficient demand, and a risk that the US might slide, like Japan, into a sustained period of low inflation and low economic growth. Recognizing this risk, the Fed undertook a variety of extraordinary measures to try to increase aggregate demand, the unconventional nature of which created alarm in some circles. Critics charged that the Fed was recklessly risking the creation of out-of-control inflation. In order to deflect this criticism, while continuing its expansionary efforts, the Fed issued a public statement of its inflation target, assuring the public that were inflation to return at some later point, it would act promptly to bring it under control.

But while the commitment offered useful political cover for some of the Fed's efforts to stimulate the economy, it also boxed policymakers in on another front. In the absence of better tools with which to directly affect current financial conditions, it would have been especially useful to try to shape current decisions by influencing people's expectations about economic and financial conditions farther in the future. In the 1970s, the expectation that wage and price increases would be accommodated by the Fed made it easier for people to demand those wage and price increases. Similarly, in the current decade, an expectation that the Fed would act decisively to prevent any notable acceleration of inflation, while it might not be able to prevent further sustained under-shooting of its inflation target, was itself likely a factor that led to greater caution about agreeing to wage or price increases—as well as caution about hiring, or spending on investments that would only pay off in the case of robust future demand. But it was difficult for Fed officials to counter such expectations, given their newly stated commitment to a fixed target for the inflation rate.

The mistake, in my view, was not the idea that articulating the principles that would guide future policy could help to shape expectations in a way that might facilitate current stabilization policy. Rather, it was the Fed's failure to realize that the kind of fears that need to be calmed through policy commitments are not always the same.

MICHAEL WOODFORD is Professor at Columbia University.

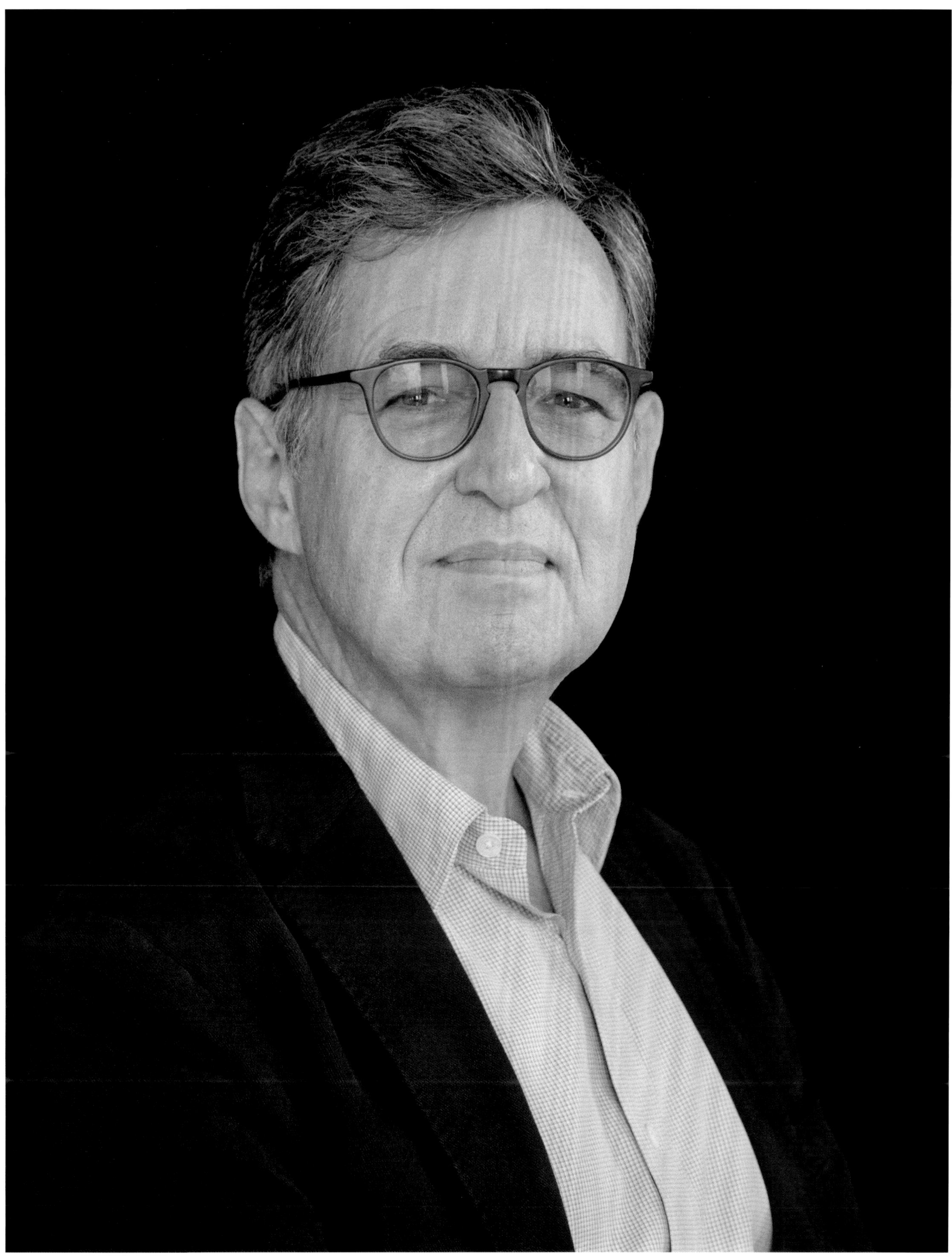

Janet Yellen

"Is there any way to improve the coordination of monetary and fiscal policy without endangering the independence of the Federal Reserve?"

EXPLICIT COORDINATION OF monetary and fiscal policy in the United States would almost surely endanger the independence of the Federal Reserve. Fortunately, such coordination is often unnecessary to achieve good economic outcomes although there are important exceptions.

Central bank independence is important to good macroeconomic performance because it shields monetary policy from political pressures. One source of such pressure may be a government's desire to finance unsustainable government budget deficits by printing money, which, historically, has resulted in chronic high or hyperinflation in many countries around the globe. Governments facing reelection may also pressure the central bank to pursue an excessively expansionary monetary policy to boost growth and lower unemployment—short-run gains that may come at the expense of higher inflation and unemployment in the longer run. For the Federal Reserve, independence enables it to take the long view—adjusting its policy settings based on professional and nonpartisan assessments of what is needed to promote objectives established by Congress with broad public support: price stability and maximum or "full" employment. It is now widely recognized and empirically documented that macroeconomic performance is better in countries with independent central banks.

Fortunately, explicit coordination of monetary policy and fiscal policy is often not required to achieve good macroeconomic performance. With the Federal Reserve assuming responsibility for stabilization objectives, fiscal policy can be directed at other objectives, such as incentives to promote long-run economic growth and the composition of output between competing uses. The Federal Reserve must take the stance of fiscal policy into account in deciding on its policy path as one of many factors affecting aggregate demand and the path of potential output. Fiscal policymakers need to understand that the Federal Reserve will respond to fiscal policy shifts in whatever manner is necessary to achieve its price stability and maximum employment objectives—a response that is possible if the fiscal shift is phased in slowly and if the Federal Reserve has adequate tools to control aggregate demand—an important proviso. With confidence in the Fed's commitment to price stability and full employment, Congress need not worry that, for example, a shift to tighter fiscal policy, when that's needed to bring down deficits, will undesirably raise unemployment. As an example, in response to Clinton-era initiatives to balance the budget, Fed Chair Alan Greenspan often stated that tighter fiscal policy would bring down interest rates, offsetting the contractionary impact of reduced government spending or higher taxes.

Although coordination of monetary and fiscal policy is generally unnecessary, an important exception arises if monetary policy tools are insufficient on their own to achieve the Fed's mandated employment and inflation objectives. In that case, an assist from fiscal policy may be desirable and appropriate. For example, in the aftermath of the severe financial crisis in 2008, unemployment soared. The Federal Reserve quickly cut its policy rate to zero, and later used unconventional tools, such as forward guidance and longer-term asset purchases, to address the economic weakness. But unemployment remained very high for many years and the Fed's tools were limited. Fiscal policy provided a meaningful boost in the first few years following the crisis. But in 2011, fiscal policy turned restrictive, creating headwinds that made it yet harder for the Federal Reserve to promote recovery. Unfortunately, monetary policy may well be constrained by the zero lower bound on interest rates more frequently in the future than in the past. Weak productivity growth and aging populations in the US and abroad look likely to lower the general level of interest rates compatible with maximum employment and price stability on a persistent basis. This creates a more frequent need for active fiscal policy, well coordinated with monetary policy. Unfortunately, with significant fiscal deficits and a high and rising debt-to-GDP ratio, the scope for such coordination in the United States appears to be limited.

JANET YELLEN is Distinguished Fellow at the Brookings Institution. She was Chair of the Federal Reserve from 2014–2018 and Chair of the Council of Economic Advisers from 1997–1999.

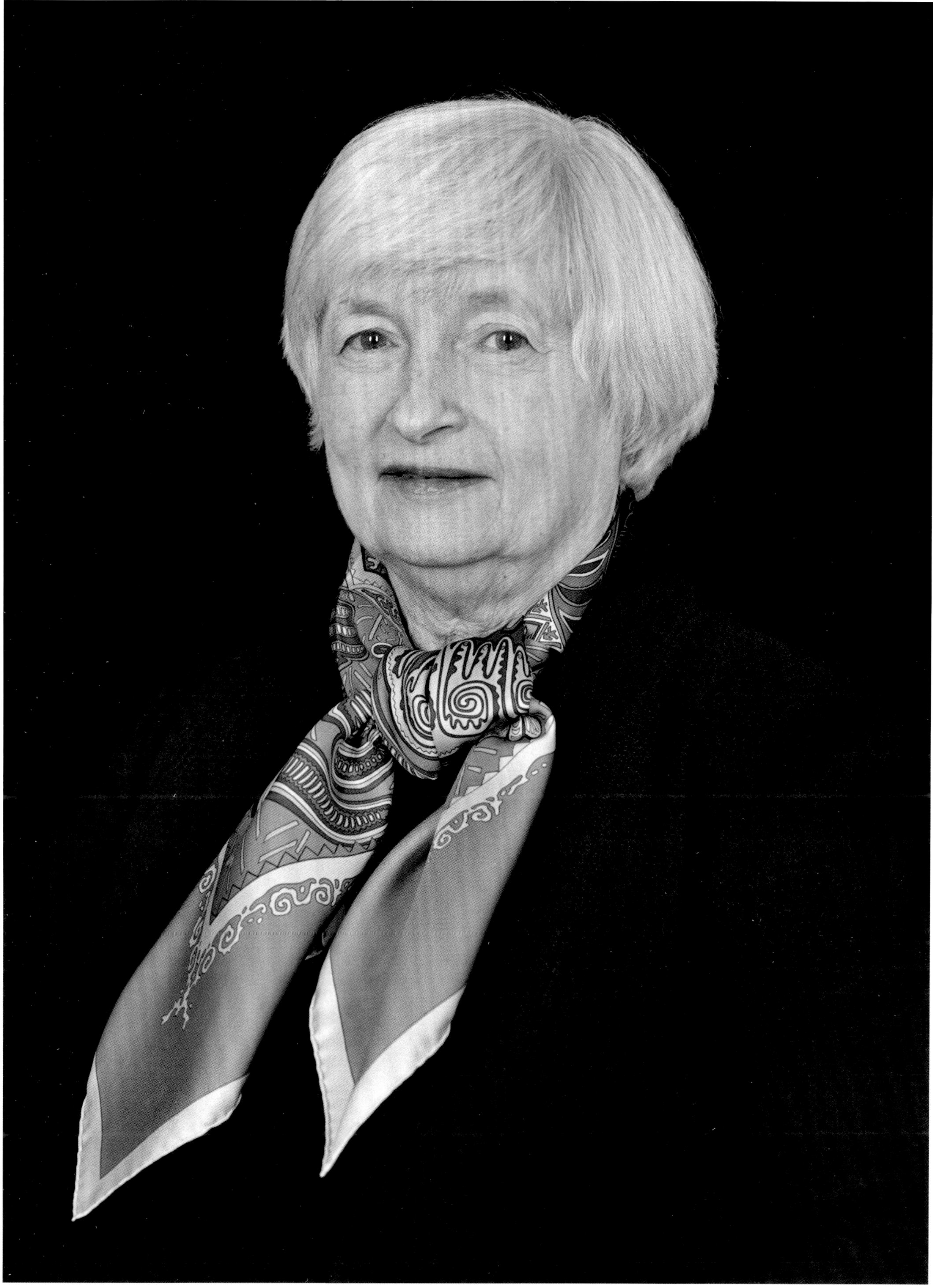

INDEX

ACKNOWLEDGMENTS

We would like to thank Sheldon Danziger for his interest in our project and the Russell Sage Foundation for its financial assistance in making this publication possible. Our gratitude goes to Peter Blair Henry for his enthusiasm and his enormous help in bringing the book to completion. At Cook Studio, Ruth Mirsky edited each text thoughtfully and meticulously; Richard Fegelman offered informed and constructive suggestions; and Trellan Smith kept us afloat. We are indebted to Seth Ditchik, the editor-in-chief at Yale University Press, for his guidance and vision.